*W*riting

Brief Third Edition

*W*riting
Brief Third Edition

**ELIZABETH
COWAN NEELD**

KATE KIEFER
Colorado State University

SCOTT, FORESMAN/LITTLE, BROWN HIGHER EDUCATION

A Division of Scott, Foresman and Company

Glenview, Illinois   London, England

For Jennie—May she someday know how motherhood and writing complement each other.

Credit lines for the photos and literary material appearing in this work are placed in the acknowledgments section on page 354 of this book. The acknowledgments section is considered an extension of the copyright page.

Library of Congress Cataloging-in-Publication Data

Neeld, Elizabeth Cowan, 1940–
    Writing / Elizabeth Cowan Neeld, Kate Kiefer. — Brief 3rd ed.
        p.   cm.
    Includes index.
    ISBN 0-673-38383-0
    1. English language—Rhetoric.   I. Kiefer, Kate.   II. Title.
PE1408.N416   1990
808′.042—dc20   89-10552

Preface

As a beginning teacher of freshman composition some dozen years ago, I first dipped into *Writing,* then in its first edition. I was especially grateful for its careful explanations of the writing process and its thorough descriptions of creating techniques. Not many texts were "process oriented" then. Over the years, I have returned to the text repeatedly and when training new teachers of writing, have praised it as one of the single best resources for prewriting. I have discovered in the past two years just how much of its advice has seeped into my everyday teaching, and I am now aware of its pervasive effect in shaping my own teaching and writing.

New Features

Working on *Writing: Brief Third Edition* has given me an opportunity to add some new ideas about the writing process to those presented so effectively by Gregory and Elizabeth Cowan in 1979.

In this edition, I have added material on the way reading and writing work together. Chapter 2 guides students through a brief overview of reading and asks them to consider what they know as readers, then applies their knowledge of the reading process to improving their skills as writers. Throughout *Writing: Brief Third Edition,* I have highlighted the text's attention to audience in order to reinforce the significance of what readers bring to writing.

The traditional research paper is also presented in the light of reading/writing connections. Chapter 15, Writing from Sources, describes what students do when presented with the opportunity to supplement their immediate knowledge with information from outside sources. The chapter moves students deliberately through a sequence of reading and writing activities that will give them the confidence to approach such writing tasks in any discipline or any non-academic setting.

Throughout the text, I have also tried to remind students that writing is a recursive process. While this brief version of *Writing* has always assumed recursion in its model of the writing process, explanations and writing tasks now remind students to create during revising, to revise during drafting, to revise during creating—in short, the text shows writing is not a straightforward movement from beginning to end.

Perhaps the most significant change in *Writing: Brief Third Edition,* however, is that I have reworked the implicit structure of the book into a more explicit and more manageable structure. The text still divides into the broad sections of the first and second editions, but now the large sections are more clearly parsed into readable chapters. As a trainer of teachers of writing, as well as a teacher of composition, I am reminded each year by those new teachers that just as writing is a skill that develops over time, so is teaching writing. Beginning to learn to write with smaller, more manageable steps builds students' confidence; so does beginning to teach with a text, such as this edition of *Writing: Brief Third Edition,* that provides more overt structure. The sequence of material in the third edition is much the same as in earlier ones, but the units are easier to incorporate in a syllabus taught by less experienced teachers. The veteran will still find that the text allows for flexibility in teaching, especially in assigning papers in a traditional sequence or for portfolio grading.

Acknowledgments

I want to thank especially the editors at Scott, Foresman who first suggested this project. Anne Smith and Constance Rajala have been exceptionally supportive and clear-headed about the project and have kept me on track more than they know. Constance, quite simply, is the best reader of reviews and the best editor I have worked with on three textbooks. Linda Bieze and Jenny Kamm have helped shape the revision significantly as well. In short, I have worked with professionals of the highest order on this project, and I have appreciated all of their hard work.

I would like to thank as well the reviewers and readers who have helped to shape this revision, particularly: Freddie Anttila, Paradise Valley Community College; Monica Barron, University of Cincinnati; and Ed Luter, Richland College. Their comments and criticisms have resulted in a text that still maintains the spirit of *Writing* but that students and teachers in the 1990s will find readable and helpful as they tackle the challenges of writing.

Kathleen Kiefer

Contents

PART 5   *Special Problems in Editing*

___

Writing

Brief Third Edition

PART *1*   *Getting Started*

As you start to write, this section will help you to

- think about what writing is and isn't
- keep a journal to record your writing
- think about whom you write to and why
- compare reading and writing to draw on your skills as both a reader and a writer
- practice creating techniques that will help you think of and organize ideas to write about

CHAPTER 1

Preliminaries

When you think of writing as making meaningful squiggles on a page, it sounds so simple. Writing, however, can be complex, frustrating, time-consuming—and satisfying. When you get a piece of writing to say exactly what you want it to, then all of your hard work and struggle pay off. Are there ways to make writing less of a struggle and more satisfying? Let's look briefly at what we know about the process of writing to help understand how you can improve what you write.

WRITING–JUST WHAT IS IT?

As a writer, you know more about how you write than anyone else can possibly know. You know the best time of day for you to write, the best pen, pencil, or word processor to use, and the best location to write in. You also know whether taking long walks or scribbling notes helps you get ideas for your writing. Remember that each writer applies different processes and may use a variety of them in different writing situations. Whatever process you use is the best—as long as it works. Trust your instincts as a writer as we explore the writing process.

What we don't know about writing processes is exactly how writers get from idea to finished piece every time they write. We know that writers generally begin writing with *creating* or *prewriting,* a phase when they collect and generate ideas. The ideas may be broad, general statements such as "war is evil," or they may be specific details to build on, such as "the irregular cobalt blue specks on my wallpaper." Most writers, however, begin writing by gathering materials to use in later phases of the writing process.

Often, writers then plan a basic arrangement for the parts of the essay or article they want to write and may spend time focusing ideas so that they concentrate on the exact points they plan to make. Writers may also specify the audience in great detail to be sure they make a point their readers care about. When planning, writers may quickly draft their pieces to get a sense of what to include where.

Then, having drafted the major chunks of the text, writers begin re-writing—reconsidering the audience and purpose of the piece; changing the order of parts; dropping sentences, paragraphs, or sections; adding new material; and reworking introductions and conclusions.

Only after reworking the larger elements of the text do most writers get to the picky details of editing. Not until the end of the process do they worry about using commas or semicolons, spelling correctly, making pronouns clear, and attending to other aspects of proofreading.

Most writers create, then draft, revise, and finally proofread or edit. Their path from stage to stage, however, is not necessarily a straight one. We know that even while writers create, they automatically discard ideas that don't seem workable; in effect, they revise *as* they create. Nor is drafting ever as straightforward as it sounds—creating and revising both occur while writers draft even a tentative first version of a paper. Even revising includes other stages such as prewriting to think of new ideas to supplement what's already on paper—and re-drafting to incorporate those ideas. Writing, then, is composed of many processes that occur simultaneously. We call writing a *recursive* process because it loops back upon itself repeatedly—even though writers ultimately move forward toward a final product. In textbooks, though, we simplify the writing process in order to explain each stage thoroughly.

We'll look first at techniques to help with the creating phase of writing. Then we'll take up the concerns of drafting, revising, and editing. Try the techniques presented here, but don't assume that there are any rules for making writing perfect. Choose the techniques that work for you to make your writing easier.

LEARN YOUR WRITING HABITS

Inexperienced writers are often surprised to find that they have already established habits that make writing easier. Many discover that they prefer to write on a certain kind of paper with a certain pen or pencil while others who have used word processors may have discovered that they prefer to write with a computer. Some students work best at certain times of day, usually in the late evening because of the quiet. There are writers who prefer music in the background when they write; some even go so far as to write only with a particular album playing. Take a few moments to analyze what makes you feel at ease about writing. You'll do a lot of writing in this course, and you should be as comfortable as you can while you do it.

But don't let your preferences get in the way of writing. Rarely do writers get perfect conditions for writing. Most professionals writing on the job do not get to take their writing home to a quiet table with the perfect lighting and background music. Many writers find that they must be able to concentrate despite background noise, inadequate lighting, uncomfortable chairs, and deadlines. Know your preferences but try writing in different places with different tools so that you're prepared for the big essay test or, later, the memo that has to be finished NOW.

One important writing habit that we often forget to take into account is procrastination. Almost all writers put off writing as long as they can. Some procrastination is useful because it gives you "brain time" to simmer ideas and remember details. Too much procrastination, however, simply leaves you with no time to finish the writing, and what often gets left out is the revising and editing that occurs late in the process. Writers who skip these crucial phases of writing will rarely be successful with readers who expect—and deserve—polished, finished writing.

If you simply cannot begin writing while you have dirty dishes in the sink or laundry to do, then do the dishes or laundry. But be sure to plan enough time for both the laundry *and* your writing so that your procrastination doesn't shortchange your reader.

WRITING *Getting Started*

1. Write a letter of introduction to a classmate in which you describe your writing habits. This is a reader who will be working with you on your papers throughout the term.
2. Carefully observe the way people write in public places—a library, a cafeteria, a computer lab, an examination room. Begin collecting notes for a sociology report on what writing habits these people reveal through their use of writing instruments, notes, printed resources, and horizontal space.
3. Begin making two lists—one of your writing habits when you are at home and one of your habits when you are writing in public. Add to the list as you have more experiences writing in public and in private during this term.
4. Many students discover, when they begin to think about their writing habits and processes, that they can best explain how they write by comparing writing to some other process. Read the following light-hearted essay in which Beth compares writing to eating liver. Think about how your experiences in writing compare with some other task you have to do.

LIVER AND ESSAYS

As I sit down to write this essay, one specific part of my childhood comes to mind. Growing up included rules and regulations requiring me to obey my parents. One rule I detested the most required me to eat liver. Comparing the writing of essays to eating liver may seem questionable, even impossible, yet the comparison directly relates to my experiences as a writer.

When I woke up in the morning and saw the raw, limp meat thawing for dinner, knowing I must consume it, I moped the rest of the day. Liver had a way of spoiling my day because I dwelled on the thought of eating the horrible, brown substance. Despite my protesting and raving temper tantrums, complete with breath-holding and floor-pounding, my parents ruthlessly forced me to eat the iron-filled meat. Their rationale for this insane cruelty never appealed to me; they always said, "Eat it, it's good for you. It will make you strong and healthy." I always thought I would rather die from drinking milkshakes than live and eat the unsightly organs of some animal. The mere sight of it made my stomach churn and my heart drop into the pit of my stomach.

Writing essays brings back the memory of eating liver because I have the same skeptical attitude about it. The assignment sits heavily in the back of my mind throughout the week, and a knot forms in the pit of my stomach when I think about writing. First, I complain about the assignment to others or to myself to vent frustration and make me feel better. These fits of frustration, however, do me no good because I still must write the paper. Although I know writing is "good for me" because it builds, develops, and strengthens writing skills, the necessary steps I must suffer through do not seem worth the trouble. Anxiety attacks and sleepless nights invade my life each time the professor assigns another essay.

Often I remained alone at the dinner table after the rest of the family finished eating. Most of the time I would put off eating the liver until the last possible moment, hoping my parents would either forget about it or decide to have mercy on me and give me dessert instead. The more I stared at the brown, lifeless, and somewhat shriveled portion on my plate, the more the idea of eating it repulsed me. Delaying only made me hate the liver more and love my life less. My sisters kept telling me to just eat it and get it over with. But that first step seemed impossible and I wanted to keep it that way.

Every time I think of writing an essay, I cringe and decide to put it off for a few more days. However, when I hesitate too long to begin writing, the assignment haunts me and I feel tortured until I finally produce it. For some unknown reason, I feel the teacher may show compassion for me and change or even cancel the assignment if I wait long enough to start it. Unfortunately, the professor never cancels the essay, and I am left staring at a blank piece of paper. Putting off writing only intensifies my anxiety, especially when the due date becomes nearer and my mind more blank. Sentence structure, word choice, creativity, and punctuation take so much concentration: I hate the thought of suffering through it, so I prolong taking the first step as long as possible.

Sitting alone at the dinner table, I thought of ways to escape my ill-fated circumstances. Perhaps I should run away, or join the army. But with those last moments and increasing threats from Mom and Dad, I held my nose, closed my eyes, and consumed the dreaded meat, secretly hoping I would die to show my parents that their cruelty had killed me. The first bite validated all my deepest fears—it tasted even worse than I imagined. The remaining bites did not get any easier, and I felt sicker with each one.

When I begin to compose an essay, ideas to avoid it wrack my brain. My thoughts include dropping out of composition class, dropping out of school, and dropping dead. As the pressure increases and fears of failing to receive a degree because of one paper surround me, I sit down to write. Solitarily secured in my room, I take pen in hand, a deep breath, and write the entire paper all at once to get it over with. With every sentence written, I doubt my writing skills even more but hope I satisfy my professor with the final product.

After the nightmare ended and I could enjoy a sweet dessert to wash away the repugnant taste of the meat, I wondered when the next time would come to undergo the terrible task of devouring liver. I fantasized liver would become nonexistent or inessential in my mother's diet plan for our family. But somehow I knew this could not happen and I would probably get the leftovers for lunch the next day.

I feel a great sense of relief after I complete a paper and can rest in peace for awhile. Again, I wish the impossible—that universities will ban essay writing from their requirements. However, I know I must enjoy my time off while I can, for soon I must begin the endless process of writing all over again.

Now answer these questions on a piece of looseleaf paper:

a. How has Beth compared elements of eating liver and writing papers?
b. Where do you see Beth's sense of humor coming through in the paper?
c. Can you think of a task that reminds you of your writing process? Jot down several possibilities for a similar humorous essay on your writing process or a specific writing habit. Now choose one comparison that will entertain your classmates and jot down two lists—one with details of your writing processes/habits and one list with details of the comparable task. From these lists and your reading, draft the essay.

WRITING–WHAT IT ISN'T

Just as many writers are surprised to find that they have deeply ingrained writing habits, many are also amazed to find that writing does *not* have rules. We cannot say, for example, that successful writers always prewrite or create for 20 percent of the total time they spend on a piece of writing. We cannot say that "good" essays always have five paragraphs and that "good" paragraphs always have at least seven sentences. We cannot even say that "good" sentences never begin with *and*.

Yet, you have surely heard certain "rules" applied to writing. Some principles apply in almost all successful or effective writing. Generally, effective writing takes specific readers and their reading goals into account. Effective writing also tends to use far more specific detail than generalization and usually begins with a clear focus to orient readers to the writer's intention in the piece.

If you know of other "rules for good writing," however, you might want to reconsider them now. Even punctuation changes over time, so we have contemporary *conventions* rather than rules. We follow guidelines that writers and readers currently agree upon for many aspects of punctuation, spelling, word choice, sentence length, paragraph length, and sometimes even sentence structure. For example, 150 years ago, skilled writers, following conventions of their time, used semicolons and commas in ways that we would not accept now. Likewise, although our conventions guide us to use apostrophes to show that an object belongs to someone, the apostrophe may not be used in the same way by our grandchildren.

Writing is not formulaic either. No writer can guarantee success by always starting a paper with an introduction, following the introduction with three paragraphs, each composed of seven (or nine or eleven) sentences, and closing with a summary conclusion. Nor can a writer depend on writing sentences of a specified length or using a certain percentage of transitional words and phrases to ensure success. We simply cannot reduce the complexity of writing to any simple formula.

If you can forget the notion of rules or formulas when writing and concentrate on communicating ideas to a real person reading your work, you will be far more successful.

WRITING   *The Writing Process*

1. Jot down all the "rules" you can remember being given for writing. Plan to discuss in class or in groups why these rules will or will not work to help you prepare essays.
2. You are undoubtedly an expert in completing some process. It might be baking bread from scratch, preparing a laboratory slide, drawing a three-dimensional object from different views, tuning an engine, making furniture, or designing and sewing a dress. You know, as an expert, that when you began learning the process you were given simple rules to follow. Jot down those rules and then explain how an expert sometimes follows and sometimes breaks the rules in completing the same process.
3. Write an essay detailing, as carefully as possible, the steps you follow as an expert in the process identified in item 2. Write to readers who have some knowledge of your process but who are not yet experts.

KEEPING A JOURNAL

Most writing comes in response to a specific assignment or requirement—thank-you notes as well as term papers, business memos, and essay tests. When teachers assign a piece of writing, they often specify the purpose and audience for the paper (as well as length and due date). Business and "maintenance" writing tasks, such as grocery lists, also come with fairly limited reasons for writing to a specific reader.

Not all writing need be done to fulfill specific requirements or obligations. Many people find that they enjoy keeping a diary in which they record daily activities. Some people even keep diaries over many years; published diaries and other autobiographical writing abound. For the people who keep diaries, simply wanting to write is the purpose. They want to record their impressions and descriptions of everyday events.

A *journal* is like a diary—it is kept for the writer alone. Writers usually don't share their diaries because the audience they write for includes only themselves, no one else. Journals, however, differ from diaries in that they are not simply daily records of activities. Instead, journals are more focused records of ideas and insights. For instance, Charles Darwin kept a detailed journal of his observations as he traveled in and around South America in the 1830s, and from his journal writings he later derived his hypotheses about natural selection and evolution. Scientists often keep journals recording the data they observe over weeks or even months in an experiment. The collected descriptions and other details often help them see the importance of an experimental result. Social scientists keep journals to record observations of people in certain settings or doing certain jobs; from the collected details, scientists can sometimes identify patterns of behavior.

Many professional writers keep journals as well. One noted journalist and English professor keeps his journal to capture ideas that he might develop in later essays. He jots down ideas to help him improve his teaching and notes snatches of conversation that highlight the arguments students often have over issues at his school. He also clips or jots down headlines and even complete newspaper articles that capture his attention. From time to time, when he needs a fresh idea to write about, he rereads his journal to see what material he has collected over the last few months.

Because the writer makes entries in a journal three or four times a week (and sometimes even more often), the journal becomes a wonderful repository for ideas to write full essays about. That's the value of a journal for most writers. Sometimes a recorded conversation becomes the opening dialogue to get readers' attention in a full essay. A description of a scene or crowd may fit right into the body of an essay. Old headlines occasionally spark ideas for titles. Even the readings that a writer might clip and save in the journal can become starting points for additional research on a topic.

A journal, in short, is a special place to record your observations about thinking, reading, writing. It can become your individualized place to practice a particular skill in writing.

The Double-Entry Journal

The *double-entry journal* format is especially useful for recording your ideas about your reading, writing, and thinking. You can either divide each page of your journal with a line running down the center or you can use the facing pages of your notebook for the two sections. In the left section, you record your observations—notes from your readings, passages you want to analyze in more detail, striking ideas you want to think about more. Then in the right-hand section, you record your questions, analysis, and reactions—both objective and subjective.

Students in all majors find this journal format useful for note taking while reading textbooks or other assigned reading. The left-hand section includes specific notes and page references. The right-hand section allows room for questions to ask later in class, for notes about classroom discussion on the same points, for connections that might be helpful when studying for tests.

The same format can also help you analyze readings, not for their content, but for their effectiveness as pieces of writing. In the left-hand section, you might, for instance, note the subject, the thesis, the major examples or supporting details, the form, and even striking word choices. In the right-hand section, you might analyze the audience the writer addressed, the effectiveness of the arrangement, and the quality of the introduction and conclusion. Some writing students even comment on each other's papers through the double-entry journal as they complete peer reviews of papers in progress.

Even if you are not planning a detailed analysis in your journal, try using the double-entry format. Often as you record a conversation or describe a special place, you will recall specific emotions. You might jot those emotional reactions in the right-hand column of your journal and free associate on your reaction. You might just generate a new list of questions or details that might help you write about this idea later.

Guidelines for Keeping a Journal

1. Write regularly in the journal. Set a goal for at least three entries a week. Many writers find that setting a particular time of day works best.

2. If you have trouble finding ideas to write about in your journal, link one or two entries a week to some other activities you commonly

do. For instance, if you always watch a particular TV show, write a weekly analysis of that show. If you always read a particular newspaper or news-magazine column, write about that. Or pick an editorial in the local paper and write a response once a week. Soon you'll find that you'll have plenty of ideas to write about in your journal because you'll be observing more and thinking of it as grist for your writing mill.

3. Don't simply record the activities of the day. Instead, pick the most memorable moment of the day and analyze why it sticks in your mind. Pick the most boring moment and think about how you could have changed it; or pick the most embarrassing or frustrating moment. Focus your description and analysis to keep from simply listing your daily routine.

4. Use your journal as a place to practice writing skills. Sometimes you may simply want to list possible topics to write about, but some-times you should actually try to write. You might write three different opening paragraphs modeled on reading you've done, imitate the style of a favorite author, or try a parody.

5. Occasionally use your journal to sharpen your ability to describe accurately. Focus on different senses as you make notes of a place you are in or as you recall a scene.

6. Share with others only those parts of your journal that you want to share. If you are assigned a journal as part of a class, be sure to use a loose-leaf binder so that you can remove pages you don't want your teacher or classmates to read.

7. Don't censor yourself. Put everything in the journal. Sometime in the future, that seemingly silly idea may be just what you need to spark an idea for an essay or to remind you of something you witnessed or felt strongly about.

WRITING *Starting a Journal*

To start your journal, collect all the writing you've done for exercises in this chapter.

Through the next chapters, you'll also have chances to include in your journal prewriting on possible assignments. You can collect lots of details to use in your first essays in this course.

Here are some specific tasks you might complete in your journal. Each one will help you to practice some observational or writing skill to get you started in keeping a journal.

Sharpening your senses

1. Go to a shopping mall, department store, grocery store, laundromat, or some other place where you can observe other people working on a task. Describe the place and one particular person who stands out.
2. Prepare one of your favorite foods. As you do, record what you smell, taste, and feel. Then do the same with one of your least favorite foods.
3. Record everything you can hear in your house, dorm, or apartment at midnight.

Practicing writing skills

1. Select an editorial that you disagree with. Write your rebuttal.
2. React to a controversial television show or movie you've seen.
3. Select another editorial. Write your rebuttal in the same form as the original article. For instance, where the original writer used an example, you use one. Where the original piece has a comparison, you also compare.
4. Write three headlines for one of your rebuttals.
5. Parody the style of a sports column by describing a fictitious game.
6. Write your epitaph.

Using your journal as a storage place

1. Record at least one conversation you overheard today.
2. Go to a place where you like to spend time. Now describe one person who exemplifies the mood of the place.
3. Write a letter to someone you don't know—maybe someone famous or dead or both. What would you say to Eddie Murphy? to Winston Churchill? to Katharine Hepburn? to Attila the Hun? Joan of Arc? Shakespeare? Billy Graham? Margaret Thatcher? Tell the person whatever you want. Admire, sympathize, scold—whatever.
4. Write about something you've changed your mind about. Why did you change your mind?
5. Collect at least one newspaper or magazine article you would enjoy reading again in five years.

Having fun with writing

Use your journal to trying some writing you wouldn't usually attempt. Be creative. Be wild.

1. Write about something you used to love as a child: marbles? cars? doing tricks with a yo-yo? skipping rope? riding a trike? playing dolls? splashing in rain puddles? eating popsicles in the summer? building a snowman? Tell how good that activity used to be.
2. Write a limerick.

3. Write funny lyrics for a favorite tune.
4. Describe the alien creature you will include in your first science fiction novel.
5. Describe the "monster in your closet" that you most vividly remember from your childhood.

SOME THOUGHTS ON WORD PROCESSING

Personal computers first began appearing in large numbers on college campuses in the late '70s, and soon after that, writers and writing teachers started to explore their use in composition classes. As you take your writing course, you may be asked to complete all of your writing assignments on a word processor. You might have your own personal computer you work on in your dorm or home; or you might use a personal computer in one of several labs and "mail" your papers to a special printer or directly to your teacher through a network. Teachers and students on campuses across the country are experimenting with the best ways to use computers to "process" writing.

Word processors have several distinct advantages over pencil and paper for writing. First, if you do all your writing from the earliest creating on a word processor, all of it is available for the final paper. Writers using paper often discover that a great sentence turns up early in creating, only to get lost in the paper shuffling between creating and polishing. If you keep all your creating and drafting in separate files, you will be able to recall every word and sentence you wrote during all the phases of writing a paper.

Second, if you revise a paper and decide later that an earlier version was better, the earlier version still exists. You might even take bits and pieces from several versions to patch together the most effective final draft.

Third, many students report that they are more willing to revise because they don't have to retype an entire page or several pages to make changes. In short, the least rewarding part of preparing a paper—the typing—becomes an automatic and relatively effortless part of writing a paper. As a consequence, the revisions that can make a paper more effective are easier to incorporate into a draft.

Fourth, closely related to the third point, some students feel that they can take more risks with a paper on a word processor. If an example doesn't work, it's easy to replace. If the comparison doesn't seem effective in block arrangement, moving blocks of texts is easy enough that they can try a draft in point-by-point arrangement. Thus, some students feel liberated and creative with word processing.

Any writing tool has its limitations. Although using pen and paper may be slower for some, those writers who use word processing must depend on access to a computer and stable electrical current. Although most writers using word processors are careful, most also can report that they have "lost" parts of papers. Some even complain that printer problems account for missing paper deadlines.

If, however, you've never tried writing on a word processor, do so. You may find that you like it and that ideas flow smoothly for you. If you aren't a particularly proficient typist or the computer makes you nervous, don't feel compelled to use a word processor for all your writing. Consult your teacher about his or her preferences, and be sure to check out the resources on your campus.

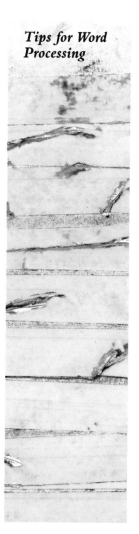

Tips for Word Processing

If you decide to use a word processor for writing, here are some tips that might help you use the tool most effectively.

1. Try to do as much of your writing as possible, not just the final version, on the computer. Label all your prewriting clearly, perhaps with a topic and date. Then you'll be able to find materials from your early work as you complete later drafts.

2. Instead of writing over a draft, keep each draft in a separate computer file. In other words, copy the most recent draft into a new file and then make more revisions. Label each draft with a date so that you can see the sequence of versions.

3. Use printouts liberally. It is harder to read text on a screen than on paper and easier to make many pencil revisions on a printed draft before you transcribe them into a computer file. Don't hesitate to make changes as you read your paper on the screen, but don't plan to do all your revising that way.

4. When you plan to revise extensively, print your text in a half column to leave half of the sheet for your written comments.

5. Take advantage of other readers—classmates, teachers, writing center tutors—to comment on your papers in progress. See how real readers react to your paper. Then return to your computer to make changes in the text.

6. Check with your teacher about special programs you might use with your word processor. Some prewriting or creating programs are widely available, and your teacher might have other special programs he or she has created for your class and your writing assignments. Some teachers recommend that students use style analysis programs or spelling checkers to help with proofreading.

WRITING *Using A Word Processor*

1. Find out where you can use a word processor on your campus. If you've never used a word processor before, ask for instructions from an experienced user or for an instruction manual. Complete at least one of the initial journal tasks on p. 11 to get some experience with the word processor.

2. Use the word processor simply as a transcription machine to learn its editing features. Take a handwritten draft or journal entry to the computer and transcribe the written material into a computer file. Be sure to make all corrections possible so that the printout of your piece will be perfectly typed.

3. Use the word processor as a composing tool. Turn the brightness down so that the screen appears black and type for at least three minutes, writing whatever comes into your mind on the topic you've been working on most recently. Then turn the brightness back up and reread what you've written. Did you turn up any ideas you would like to continue writing about? Print out this "invisible writing" to include in your journal.

CHAPTER 2

Reading and Writing

Although we don't know all the exact connections between reading and writing, we do know that, as mental processes, reading and writing depend on similar parts of the brain and that they share common ways of handling information. Furthermore, it's almost impossible to write without reading. Unconsciously, the eye glances back at what's been written, reminding writers where they still want to go. Consciously, writers reread to evaluate what they've written as well as to determine how much more they need to write to communicate the message.

In many other ways, reading influences your writing. You first learn many of the conventions of writing through reading. You discover formal language, tone, complicated sentence structures, and various patterns of arranging ideas, all through reading. How easily you translate what you read into what you write depends, in part, on how practiced you are as a reader and a writer. Throughout this text and your writing course, you will be asked to pay special attention to your reading skills to help build your writing skills. As you write more, your reading will become more focused, too.

BEING A READER

We'll be looking at some articles about bicycles later in the chapter. Practice reading and writing by noting in your journal how you feel about bicycles. Answer some of these questions:

1. Do you own a bike? If so, do you ride it regularly?
2. Do you think of a bike as a primary means of transportation or is it simply a "toy" for leisurely relaxation?

3. Have you ever been scared to ride a bike? When?

4. Have you ever hit anyone while riding a bike? When?

5. Have you ever been hit by a bicyclist? When?

6. What's the most memorable bicycling scene you can recall from a movie or TV program?

7. What's your most memorable bicycling experience?

Now turn to a pair of readings on bicycles by Lance Morrow and Frank Trippett. Think about the different attitudes expressed in the two articles. How do the readings reflect your attitudes toward bicycles?

THE GREAT BICYCLE WARS   Lance Morrow/ TIME Magazine

When New York Mayor Edward Koch visited China last winter, he was beguiled by the sight of a million Chinese gliding harmoniously through their streets on bicycles. "I was swept away," Koch said later, "by the thought of what could be." Traffic back home, of course, is a lot denser and meaner than in Peking, but for a time Koch thought that the vision might translate at least partly to New York. A transit strike there last spring swelled the ranks of the city's commuting bicyclists to nearly Chinese proportions. Like Toad of Toad Hall discovering the motorcar, Koch seemed to conceive a passion for the bike. As an expression of his enthusiasm, he spent $300,000 from the city's depleted treasury to install 6-ft.-wide bike lanes along two avenues in Manhattan.

But Koch's passions are sometimes ephemeral; last week, after the lanes had been open for only three months, the transportation department sent crews out to tear them up—at a cost of $100,000 more—while bikers disconsolately demonstrated and tied up traffic. The lanes did not work, the mayor said, because bikers did not use them—his own bureaucrats' statistics contradicted him, but never mind—and everyone else thought they hopelessly slowed motor traffic that even at the best times inches along in a fuming stream of steel through midtown. Koch's decision was both premature (the lanes should have been tried for at least a year) and a bit scatterbrained, but it was also calculatedly political. In the street wars among cyclists, motorists and pedestrians, the mayor judged that he had been backing a loser.

The bicycle, formerly a Christmas-tree item or a Sunday diversion, has become a serious vehicle of transport in some American cities. But when bikes move into heavy traffic, problems of incompatibility arise. The circulatory system of the metropolitan U.S. is designed for cars and trucks, with pedestrians granted their margin on the sidewalks. In the culture of freeway or gridlock, the bicycle is a fragile but aggressive intruder. Today around the nation the shaken fist and flourished finger are exchanged between bikers and cabbies and bus drivers and commuting motorists—and, above all, pedestrians who chance to step in the path of a ka-mikaze ten-speed scorching silently up on the blind side. Bicycles, those sweet chariots of the old Consciousness III, now flourishing under the flag of narcisso-fitness, are becoming a distinct source of urban tension.

More and more bikers are demanding their share of the American street and road. In 1972, bicycles outsold cars in the U.S. for the first time. Five years ago, an average of 470,000 Americans commuted to work on bicycles on any given day, and Washington hopes that by 1985 as many as 2.5 million will be on the streets, saving as many as 77,000 bbl. of oil a day. OPEC and the huge American self-regard coincided to persuade millions of Americans that the bike makes both financial and cardiovascular sense.

But its virtue has not made the bicycle welcome in many U.S. cities. New York is a serious cyclists' town—but also one of the most dangerous. Still, if it now lacks bike lanes, Manhattan at least has the advantages of being both comparatively flat and geographically compact. Terrain must be right. The sheer distances of Los Angeles rule out anything but neighborhood cycling; San Francisco's hills discourage all but the most muscular. The Federal Government is firmly and officially on the side of the bicycle (healthy, energy-saving and the most efficient means of transportation for millions with short commutes, said the 1978 Energy Conservation Policy Act), but Washington, D.C., itself belongs pretty much to the fuming motorcar. Only a few smaller communities in the U.S., like Davis, Calif., and Eugene, Ore., have welcomed bicyclists with special lanes and bicycle parking areas.

The poor urban cyclist inhabits a hostile world. He regards the car as incomparably more homicidal than the bicycle and more profoundly antisocial—rocketing down the avenues like a bobsled, excreting carcinogens. Yet

bicycling is dangerous—905 cyclists died last year in the U.S.—and the unhelmeted are always merely a tumble away from disasters to the brain. The urban cyclist steers among the potholes with a fierce concentration. People have a way of abruptly opening car doors in his face. Cabbies are spitters of high caliber and range. Drivers flick hot cigar and cigarette butts at him. Some truck drivers with a pathological sense of fun like to see how closely they can blast by a cyclist. Pedestrians jaywalk; their eyes, programmed to see cars, are eerily oblivious to bikes. A man throwing his arm up abruptly to hail a cab can coldcock a passing cyclist. And when the bike is finally parked, thieves as dense and dispassionately professional as cockroaches descend with heavy-duty bolt-cutters that can bite through anything but expensive U-shaped metal alloy locks.

The noncycling creature, of course, sees the world with different eyes. Drivers who are not necessarily hostile to bicyclists are often simply terrified of hitting them and think that fragile frame with a person perched on it has no business trying to navigate such savage waters. The bike seems a sort of prissy intrusion, about as welcome as a rosy-cheeked second lieutenant from Princeton being sent in to command a filthy unshaved squad that has been in combat for a year. The veterans at the wheels figure that the biker is either going to get himself killed or maybe bring down mayhem on everyone else. Pedestrians see bikers as a silent menace—and with good reason. In New York just before Koch's bicyclical mood, bikers killed three people trying to cross the street.

Governments around the world have proved to be extraordinarily stupid about trying to reconcile bicycles and cars; they behave as if bikes merely contributed to the squalor of traffic instead of being a way to dissolve it—an anticoagulant. But reconciliations become harder and harder to finance: cities with their treasuries already bleeding away seldom have money to spare for anything as frivolous and unpopular as bicycle lanes.

Bicycles still zip around with an aura of childishness, of unseriousness. They still await the mass discovery that they are in fact splendidly functional. They will never replace cars, but they can provide quick, superior transportation for great numbers of people daily over short distances, at tremendous savings in fossil fuels and breathable air. The bike rider also knows that riding one as the day begins is a brief pure *aubade* of exertion and contemplation. Why else would cyclists risk it? Then, too, subconsciously, the bicyclist may be engaged in a long-term Darwinian wager: In 100 years, which mechanism will still be at work—the bicycle or the automobile?

SCARING THE PUBLIC TO DEATH   Frank Trippett/ *TIME* Magazine

On city streets and country roads, the war rages against cyclists

bicycle: lightweight, two-wheeled, steerable machine propelled by its rider; the bicycle is said to be the most efficient means yet devised to convert human energy into propulsion.—The New Encyclopaedia Britannica

A marvel of efficiency, the bicycle is also cheap, handy, nimble. It can sprint like a cat, then stop on a dime and give you nine cents change. It is easy to ride and speedy enough for any sane short-distance traveler. In the typical bumper-to-bumper city creepathon the bike can outrun a Porsche.

Unlike the car, truck, and bus, the bike does not spew stinky fumes and carcinogens. A bike is easy to park in a sliver of space, and of precious oil it needs only a smidgen to keep the wheels squeakless. Riders may turn rowdy, but the vehicle itself is quiet—a blessed virtue amid the squawk-bleat-scream-grind-growl-honk-toot-wail-shriek that is the voice of the big city.

Given such merits, the bicycle ought to be universally embraced by human-kind as a sensible way of getting about in the strangling, traffic-plagued city. Bicycles have long been a major mode of transport in Europe and Asia; there are as many as 230 million of them in China. Now they have taken to U.S. streets with a vengeance. According to Bill Wilkinson, director of the Bicycle Federation of America, roughly 2 million people commute to work on bikes, up from approximately 500,000 a decade ago.

Still, though Americans have always liked two-wheelers as a child's plaything, and currently own 111 million of them, they have never truly welcomed the bike as a serious vehicle. In fact, wherever it appears in numbers, the bicycle provokes tension, annoyance, outrage or hostility. This year bikers from Manhattan to Denver, from Oregon to Missouri, have wound up in conflicts: bikers vs. motorists, bikers vs. pedestrians, bikers vs. runners, bikers vs. police.

In Washington the overlap of bicyclists and Pentagon-based joggers has turned the Arlington Memorial Bridge over the Potomac River into an anger zone. Last month bikers were banned from hiking trails in California's Santa Monica mountains. In St. Louis, where a motorist has been known to slosh a bucket of water on a cyclist in cold weather, someone sprinkled tacks on the route of a Labor Day cycle tour and flattened the tires of some 40 bikes. Motorist-biker tensions around St. Louis grew high last month after bicyclist John S. Reif Jr., 22, a nationally ranked triathlete, was fatally injured in a head-on collision with a car. Speaking of the current mood, Deeds Fletcher, 47, a municipal-bond dealer and a cyclist, says it often feels as if "cars are going after people. It's like the Christians and the lions."

In Boulder police in July snared and ticketed a flight of 55 cyclists racing past a stop sign, and Steve Clark, the city's bicycle-program coordinator, applauded the crackdown: "When one segment of the group creates bad p.r., it hurts all cyclists." In Eugene, Ore., according to Bicycle Coordinator Diane Bishop of the public-works department, police patrol university areas, especially in their annual autumn bike-safety campaign, in which, she says, "they ticket as many as 100 riders a month." Proliferating cyclists reduced Denver POST Sport Columnist John McGrath to epithet: "Look around: geeks in long black shorts are hunched over a pair of handlebars at every urban intersection, on every country road."

Nowhere has the bike provoked such a sustained and official skirmish as in New York City. Mayor Ed Koch, who suffered a pro-bike mood in 1980 and had bike lanes built, had them eliminated a few months later. By this year Koch had become so antibike that he banned the cycles from several major Manhattan avenues. The state supreme court in Manhattan overturned the ban last month, but did not overturn Police Commissioner Benjamin Ward's opinion about the city's pedalers. "They are scaring the public to death," says Ward, "and we've got to do something about it."

"It" means the free-form riding habits of 5,000 or so messengers. Inspired by the fact that more deliveries mean more money, many messengers whiz around the city in pseudo-kamikaze style, heeding neither red lights nor one-way signs, zagging on and off sidewalks, leaving behind a wake of screeching tires and cursing pedestrians. Many messengers even opt for bikes without brakes, to save on a few pounds of heavy metal.

There were 640 reported incidents of bikes colliding with pedestrians in New York City last year, up from 339 in 1981. Three New York City pedestrians were killed by cyclists in 1986, while nine bikers were killed by motorists. "They are like roaches," complains Anita Sockol, who was crossing Lexington Avenue in June when she was floored by a speeding cyclist. She suffered a broken hip and wrist, and now limps. "They come at you from all sides," she adds.

Even cyclists admit that some bike riders act like pit bulls on wheels, but enthusiasts attribute most accidents to impatient walkers, many of whom insist on waiting in crosswalks for the light to change. "Most pedestrians don't look before they cross the street," says Eric Williams, a Manhattan messenger. "I've pulled so hard to stop that I've got scars to prove it."

The numbers prove that Manhattan's reckless-bike-riding problem is not trivial. Even so, the ire stirred by the bikers is striking. Some argue (not too convincingly) that the antipathy toward messengers, who are mostly black, is racially motivated. But that does not explain the shouts of anger directed at white speed demons by startled white pedestrians.

Efforts are being made all over to educate bikers about traffic rules and to train motorists in the ways of bikers. In Los Angeles, state and county planners are even contemplating a 2½-mile-long overhead bikeway that would rise above the congested streets around UCLA. But the real culprit on American roads, as conspicuous among cars, cabs and trucks as among cyclists, is an arrogant, scofflaw spirit that sends vehicles—those with four as well as two wheels—streaking through red lights and stop signs, just as it tempts pedestrians into habitual jaywalking.

WRITING *Writing About Reading*

Answer the following questions in your journal:

1. List specific differences in attitude toward bicycles between the first and second articles.
2. How do the authors reflect your attitudes toward bicycles? Look back at the journal entries you wrote before reading these pieces. Did your attitude toward bikes and bicyclists change because of your reading?
3. What evidence do the authors use to support their opinions in these essays?
4. What is the most memorable word, phrase, sentence, and example in these readings?

READING AS A WRITER

Whenever you read—the morning newspaper, a college textbook, road signs, letters from friends—you read with a purpose. You may want to be entertained, diverted, reminded, directed, or informed, but you always read with a purpose. Reading as a writer adds a second purpose to your primary goal; you read not only to understand the material but also to see what choices other writers make to keep you interested and attentive. Reading as a writer means putting yourself in other writers' shoes to recreate their writing processes.

For instance, do you suppose Frank Trippett knew from the moment he began to think of "Scaring the Public to Death" that he should begin with a quotation and a definition from an encyclopedia? Some writers rework the beginning of an article several times before hitting on a particular opening. Reading as a writer requires that you evaluate how successfully the writer's opening gets and keeps readers' attention so that you can adapt the technique when you need a catchy opening.

When you read from a writer's point of view, you also let your reading stimulate ideas you might write about. You might not want to respond directly to either Trippett's or Morrow's essay, but reading what they have to say about bikes may inspire you to write about bikes as well. You might use data from these articles (properly documented, of course) or branch off and write from a totally different perspective.

Reading as a writer means staying open to possibilities whenever you read—possibilities to study techniques and to get ideas.

WRITING *Analyzing Reading*

Answer the following questions in your journal:

1. Where are Trippett and Morrow least successful in making their points? Why do the essays lose interest for you (if they do)? Where do the essays seem too long?
2. Who are the authors thinking of as their readers? What main purpose do they think their readers bring to these essays?
3. What ideas other than bikes vs. cars vs. pedestrians occur to you as you reread the bike essays? List several possible topics you might write about (for example, what makes people rude?).

WRITING AS A READER

You know yourself well enough to be aware of what keeps you reading. Sometimes, you may like funny titles and snappy openings, gripping details, or specific examples, as long as they meet your primary goals as a reader.

You may not be as aware of some other principles that readers generally use to process the words on the page before them. For instance, if a reader had to identify each letter to identify a word and then figure out how the word fit into the sentence, the reader would forget the first words in the sentence before finishing the last words. We simply don't read letter by letter and word by word. We read by *predicting* what is most likely to appear on the page and then sampling the print to confirm or alter our predictions.

How can such a method of reading work?

Think about what you know before you ever begin reading. If you pick up a newspaper, you know what to expect—articles on news events, perhaps a weather report, comics on certain pages, and want ads on others. You don't expect poetry. You don't expect *Moby Dick.* You don't expect calculus or geometry. On the other hand, when you pick up a literature text, you know you might get poetry or *Moby Dick,* but you don't expect the weather report.

Even before you begin reading, you start predicting what might be in the print, limiting the possibilities as quickly as you can. You check the title of the book first. If the title includes the word *Geometry,* then you narrow your expectations. You begin the first chapter, and there the headings and subtitles guide your predictions even more. Eventually, you must read the print, but you read it largely to confirm what you expect will be on the page. In a geometry text, you expect to see proofs with lines and other drawings; in a poetry text, you expect to see wide margins with lines of text, each beginning with capital letters.

Moreover, as soon as you see *Geometry* in a title, you focus your mental attention on everything you know about geometry. You bring to the foreground all your past experiences with geometry—good and bad—and use those to fit new information into your stored knowledge. The same is true of any topic you read about: as you begin reading you *activate* the knowledge you already have on that topic to help predict the information on the page.

Finally, you also predict based on the structure of a piece. If a writer begins by setting up a comparison between two items, you, as a reader, call upon your experience with comparing. You know how comparisons work, and you expect the writer to follow a familiar structure. The same is true of paragraphing, use of transitional words and phrases, even sentence structure. You draw upon all your experiences as a speaker and reader to help you read only what you absolutely must read to confirm your prediction about the text.

Let's consider the essays by Trippett and Morrow. By checking the titles, you knew before you began reading them that both dealt with bicycles. You also knew a good bit more about what might be in the essays from the first paragraphs that set up the focus of each essay. Certain cues—transitional words—told you that Trippett was about to give an example or to show a contrast. You knew from other cues—paragraph breaks—that ideas were related or going off in new directions.

In other words, readers create hypotheses about what they will read. Their predictions begin with the structure of the whole piece—poetry, news report, or textbook—and can move on to structure within the piece—comparison/contrast, narration, or classification. Equally important, readers predict content based on titles, thesis statements, headings, and other elements that highlight the focus of the writing. Readers also rely on other elements—transitions and connecting words—to help them predict the path a piece will follow. When readers need to know the specific details a writer has included, they fit those details into the larger picture their predictions have set up. We read as efficiently as possible, but we can do so only because writers build on exactly these same elements to help readers predict accurately.

When you become more attuned to techniques that help you read, you can adapt similar techniques to your writing. We'll talk about ways to get essays underway, but you should practice those that you find successful when you read. We'll also talk about the importance of focusing ideas so that readers know exactly what point you're making. Readers expect clarity, as you know from your own frustration when reading an unfocused piece. We'll practice using transitions and paragraphing, varied sentence structure and specific detail so that readers keep reading. The more you become aware of your own reading habits and processes, the more likely you will see connections between your writing and your audience's reading.

Read the following sample article, paying special attention to techniques you use when you write. Note also how Charlier uses the title and headings to help you predict exactly what's coming in the text.

OVERDOING IT   Marj Charlier/*Wall Street Journal*

In Name of Fitness, Many Americans Grow Addicted to Exercise

They Work Out to the Point of Harming Themselves; Socially Acceptable Habit

Escape From a Bad Marriage

Every time she lifted her legs to step over a curb, Lois Deville grimaced with the pain of her shinsplints. The Miamian, in New York City on business, was frantic over missing her daily aerobics classes. To compensate, she paced the streets for hours, even though the pain was so excruciating she couldn't put a sheet on her legs at night.

Back home, a month later, a stress fracture abruptly halted Ms. Deville's working, walking, running and aerobics classes. One night, she sat outside the aerobics studio near her home, crying as she watched others dance. Ms. Deville was an exercise addict, unable to stop running and doing aerobics even when it hurt. Now in therapy for her problem and holding her aerobics classes to three times a week, she ruefully recalls the recent past: "What kept me going was the panic of weight gain and facing what [else] I would do with my day."

Feeling of Worthlessness

A feeling of worthlessness, loneliness and a history of family problems drove Ms. Deville to her abuse of exercise, she says. She was far from alone. A national love affair with fitness—combined with the same psychological problems that cause the eating disorders of anorexia and bulimia—has spawned a growing health problem: obsessive, addictive exercise.

Doctors and psychotherapists aren't concerned with the millions of healthy Americans who insist on going to aerobics classes or the running track a few times a week. They *are* worried about the growing number of exercisers who are taking anti-inflammatory drugs to mask serious injuries and who are sacrificing their family lives and their jobs to the pursuit of impossible physical goals. These concerned doctors know that the stress fractures or shinsplints or tendinitis commonly incurred by obsessed joggers and aerobic dancers can persist for a lifetime. For women, additionally, the loss of body fat induced by too much exercise can lead to amenorrhea, or the loss of monthly menstrual periods. The long-term consequences of amenorrhea on female organs and general health isn't known, doctors say.

Seeking a 'High'

Exercise compulsion is a burgeoning problem among upper- and middle-class professionals, who abuse socially acceptable exercise as others abuse drugs, food, or alcohol. Many are seeking the "high" that prolonged exercise can produce, and many report the same kind of withdrawal symptoms when they don't exercise as alcoholics and drug addicts do when they stop drinking and taking drugs: depression, nervousness and insomnia. But many of these obsessed exercisers don't see the parallels with addictions to mood-altering substances. "These are people who wouldn't think of getting loaded in bars or copping drugs on the street," says Doris Denmark Zachary, a clinical psychotherapist and a director at the Center for Counseling Services, Plantation, Fla. "Exercise is the way they cope with conflicts inside themselves."

How many exercise addicts there are isn't known. Medical experts, however, report that between 50% and 75% of serious exercisers are potentially problem exercisers. "If you run more than three miles a day four times a week, you do it for something other than fitness," says aerobics guru Kenneth Cooper, head of the Aerobics Center in Dallas. And medical doctors have found that men who run more than 45 miles a week show abnormally high levels of stress hormones as well as increased orthopedic injuries.

Warning Label

Doctors have recognized addiction in joggers for some time. One medical writer once suggested in jest that jogging shoes carry a warning label much the way cigarettes do. But doctors and psychotherapists report the problem is growing—especially among women. Women today "want to feel stronger and more independent and competitive," says Robert Goldman, director of sports research at the Chicago College of Osteopathic Medicine and an adviser of many world-class women body-builders. That's fine, he says, but some women are just taking it too far. (On the plus side, counselors report that women exercise addicts are more likely to seek treatment than their male counterparts.)

The near-universal belief in the benefits of exercise makes exercise addiction tough to stop and to detect. The addict can rationalize that "the neighbor next door runs, and the woman across the street goes to aerobics, too," says Kathy Bowen-Woodward . . . at the Renfrew Center in Philadelphia, a treatment facility for eating disorders and addiction to exercise. "It's not easy to recognize when you're into it."

Furthermore, many corporations may be unwittingly contributing to their employees' addiction by providing benefits such as health-club fee reimbursements and in-house fitness centers. But some have begun to recognize the potential for problems. "We have people who are in here three times a day," says Max Morton, manager of Adolph Coors Co.'s Wellness Center. He tells Coors employees who exercise more than an hour and a half a day that they need to examine why they are doing it. "We're certainly trying to steer them to a more moderate approach," he says.

Experts make a distinction between obsessive exercisers and those who are training for real athletic goals, such as professional athletes and those preparing for an occasional marathon. The obsessive exerciser often has no concrete athletic goals, says John Durkin, manager of the fitness center for Mesa Limited Partnership in Amarillo, Texas. "There's just something they're trying to destroy or run away from," he says.

Consider Eric Bolton. Now a 30-year-old senior manager at a Dallas real-estate firm, Mr. Bolton says that a few years ago he was "absolutely obsessed" with running, logging as much as 100 miles a week. He cut out evening activities and got up at 4:30 a.m. to run, often wrapping elastic bandages around his knees to reduce the pain in his aching joints. He was sleepy by two or three o'clock in the afternoon. An auditor at the time, he says his reviews took longer and were less thorough as his running took over his life. "I wouldn't let anything interfere with my running," he says. Mr. Bolton ran because of frustration with a bad marriage, he concludes now. But he didn't realize he was obsessed, he says, until he moved away from his wife, got a new job and suddenly, "I found that running wasn't that important anymore." Hearing about other obsessive exercisers made him conscious of his own symptoms, he says.

'Good Little Girl'

Betty, a 44-year-old housewife, also became obsessed with exercise for family reasons. From childhood, she says, she was expected to settle family arguments, please her parents and quietly handle her own problems. Now she also tries to make a perfect home for her own family. "I am the pleaser, the good little girl," she says. Once anorexic—dropping to 74 pounds at one time—she turned to exercise a couple of years ago, running as much as 100 miles a week. "My husband was frantic—I was gone two hours a day," she says. In the past year, with the support of her husband, she started both individual and group therapy. She has cut down on her running, but her compulsion is still evident; now she often finds herself frantically dancing to music while ironing, vacuuming and mopping.

Another self-described good little girl is Alexandra Gordon, a Miami stockbroker. Struggling to be perfect, she says, she exercised constantly to control her weight. But eventually she wouldn't even enjoy a day on the beach with her fiancé because she would miss her aerobics and weightlifting sessions. Finally, he broke their engagement . . . and demanded that she get help if she wanted to repair the relationship. She is now in counseling with Ms. Zachary.

Counselors say that one factor in exercise addiction is control. "When they can't control what else is going on in their lives, they can control what they eat" and how much they exercise, says Shelly Wartman, who counsels young women with eating and exercise disorders at Florida's Center for Counseling Services. But, often, says her colleague Susan Cossack, exercise begins to run their lives. "Then they lose control and have no options whatsoever."

Relieving Loneliness

Frequently, what frantic exercisers need is better relationships with people, says Dr. Bowen-Woodward of Philadelphia's Renfrew Center.

Single professionals come home to an empty house, and they can't wait to hit the streets or dive in the pool. Emily, 38, a Florida real-estate saleswoman whose divorced parents sent her to boarding school when she was seven, swims at least twice a day and walks for hours. Emily has never had a boyfriend and has few friends. "Walking keeps me from getting lonely," she says.

William Glasser, a Los Angeles psychiatrist, thinks that exercise gives some "a way to avoid the social ramble" and the potential failure of finding friends. If the exercise addicts are exercising all their free hours away, the doctor says, "it eliminates the chance to satisfy the need for love and affection."

Doctors generally agree that a sure sign that a person is addicted to exercise is when he does it in spite of injuries. But not all doctors are inclined to confront exercise addicts with their problem. Betty, the housewife, says that when she was told by her doctor that her back and leg injuries were too severe to keep running, "I found a doctor who said he would keep me on the road." And Ms. Gordon, the Miami stockbroker, found a doctor who would prescribe anti-inflammatory drugs to keep down the pains in her ankles and knees so nothing would stop her exercise routine.

Some doctors and sports professionals maintain that the line between healthy and obsessive exercise is too fine to separate addicts from average exercisers. William P. Morgan, a University of Wisconsin sports psychologist, says he quit studying exercise addiction because it involved too many value judgments. And even those exercisers who know the problem firsthand aren't inclined to intervene in the lives of others with apparently obsessive behavior. Shannon, an exercise addict and a nurse at a South Florida hospital, says she sees people at her health club who she thinks are addicted to exercise, but she then looks the other way. "You can't approach them," she says. "They just think you're jealous."

WRITING *Writing as a Reader*

Answer the following questions in your journal:

1. Do you use headings, transitions, focusing sentences, repeated key terms when you write? Which are most successful for you?
2. What words, phrases, or sentences in the passage seem especially striking in this piece? Why?

Do the following activities in your journal:

1. You've now read about physical fitness and some of its disadvantages. List at least five other disadvantages of staying fit.
2. List ten advantages of fitness.
3. List additional topics you might explore based on the reading. Perhaps you were struck by the point Charlier made that exercise addiction strikes certain classes. Why? You might want to pursue why women, more than men, feel the need to be strong and independent and choose exercise to improve body image. Try to find at least five additional topics you might develop into essays.
4. Pick out a newspaper, a popular magazine, and a new textbook. Open each at random, and go to the beginning of the next article or chapter. Write down what you can predict about the content of each article or chapter just from the title and headings on the first page.

   Now read the first paragraph or so of each. Add more specifics to all three of your predictions.

   Next, compare the three sets of predictions. Which seems most thorough? Why?

   Would one of the three be more difficult to read because you don't have many past experiences or acquired knowledge to "activate" as you begin reading? Consider the role of what you already know as you continue reading one of the pieces.

WRITING FOR THE READER

Although your journal writing is directed to yourself, the writer, most of your other writing is directed to someone other than yourself. Writing to someone else means you have to be much more explicit. For example, if you were to leave a note for yourself, you might jot down just one or two words:

Pizza. 7 p.m. 555-0076.

That message might well be adequate to remind you to phone in for pizza for the club party. But if you were to leave the message for someone else, you'd need to add more detail:

> Sue,
>
> Please place the order for pizza for the Tech Club party. We need three pizzas to be picked up at 7 p.m. on Tuesday night. Use Panhandler's Pizza at 555-0076.

If you left the first message for Sue, you might not get three pizzas. You might not get them on Tuesday. You also might find that she called at 7 P.M. rather than earlier to have the pizzas ready by 7. In other words, when you write to a reader other than yourself, you need to fill in more than a rough sketch of an idea.

Many times you may do quite a bit of creating before you think about your precise audience. You might want to give yourself completely free range to generate and collect ideas without worrying who will read your final paper. That's a fine approach so long as you consider the audience later in the writing process (we'll look again at audience when we talk about shaping the drafts of an essay).

Sometimes, however, you need to visualize your reader to help you think of ideas to write about. In some writing situations, you will find that ideas occur much more quickly if you can "see" a reader who needs to know what you know. Think back to our example about the pizza, and think too about a person who always gets instructions wrong. If Sue is that sort of person, then you must keep her in mind as you write directions. You might want to add even more detail (who will pick up the pizza, for instance).

You might decide to write about a personal experience you've had. If you write the paper as a letter to your brother, you'll include different details than if you write it to a classmate who doesn't know much about you. By visualizing your brother, you can probably anticipate when he'll laugh at your detailed memories and when he'll get bored by details he already knows all too well. Similarly, by visualizing the classmate, you can anticipate where you'll need to fill in background information. The checklist on the next page gives questions that may help you visualize.

A Checklist of Questions to Help You "See" Your Reader

1. Why is my reader reading? To be informed? entertained? persuaded?
2. How old is my reader? What sex is he or she?
3. How well does my reader know me?
4. Does my reader share my background (age, location of birth, upbringing, education, and so on)? Outline differences.
5. Does my reader share my attitudes toward this topic? Outline differences.
6. Does my reader have special knowledge of this topic? Outline the areas of knowledge.
7. If I am writing to a group, can I name one person most representative of the group? If so, can I outline that one person's characteristics that affect him or her as a reader of my paper?

Writing for an audience means that you help your reader every way you can. Not only do you include detail that you know but that your reader doesn't, but you also provide a clear focus for your message. In fact, you might repeat your focus several times throughout a paper if it will help your reader see your point. In addition, you structure your writing so that your reader can proceed smoothly and efficiently. For example, although your ideas may have first come to you as a story you want to tell, perhaps narrative is not the most efficient structure for your reader. You need to put yourself in the reader's place to find the best structure to help the reader understand your message, and then you revise your first drafts accordingly.

Thus, writing for a specific reader can help you discover and collect ideas to write about. It can limit the other work you do in prewriting by helping you to focus and, ultimately, it makes your message clearer to the reader so that you communicate effectively. Whenever you think you will be writing to a reader who has specific needs, consider visualizing that reader even before you create the ideas that you'll communicate to him or her.

WRITING *Writing for the Reader*

Answer the following questions in your journal:

1. Make a list of at least thirty points on which you are an expert. Include hobbies, jobs you've held, chores you've done, travel, and so on. Don't forget to list life experiences such as being the middle child,

running a marathon, or undergoing a risky operation. You'll discover you are an expert in more areas than you might think, simply because you have experienced life from a unique perspective.

2. Now match the items in your expertise list with possible readers. For instance, if you are a coin collector, could you write about numismatics for beginners? for experts? for investors? Consider specific journals as sources for audiences. For instance, if you want to write about being a middle child, would you write to *Redbook* or *Psychology Today?* What are the differences in audience for those two magazines?

3. Choose one topic and the audiences you listed. Now describe in detail the differences between the audiences and what you would include in an essay to address each of the possible audiences.

4. Look back at your lists of detail comparing writing to some other process. How would you change your lists if you were writing to classmates, your writing teacher, a third-grader just learning to write essays, or a potential employer who would hire you for a job that required a great deal of writing? Add at least three details that would appeal to each of these audiences.

CHAPTER 3

Creating and Writing

Any writer who has struggled to write a good essay from beginning to end has undoubtedly also stared at a blank piece of paper for a long time. The writer hopes for divine inspiration to get the paper going and hopes the inspiration lasts long enough to fill the required number of pages.

Most good essays, however, don't appear magically from the writer's pen. Good essays depend much less on divine inspiration than on discovering, collecting, and generating ideas before beginning the essay itself. The writing and thinking that goes on *before* a writer drafts an essay is called *prewriting* or *creating*.

As part of creating, you may first need to determine what idea to write about as well as who will be reading your paper and why. You may need to ask yourself why you must write the paper in the first place. Then, having established a context for writing, you go on to tap ideas from personal memories, facts, reading material, and other sources to gather raw material for the essay.

Creating allows you to find new perspectives on topics rather than settle for the expected. Thinking before writing a draft also gives you time to discover what you already know and what you need to know to write meaningfully for a reader. Although it requires time and energy at the beginning of the writing process, creating pays off in more insightful essays. It also helps you find out what you think about a subject—to discover something about it—because often you see something quite differently after you write about it than you do before you write. In fact, it may turn out that just getting your thoughts down on paper produces clarity or insight that you wouldn't have had otherwise.

Realize that the writing you do while creating is *not* the essay itself; it is a collection of thoughts that will lead to the essay. You don't have to worry at this point about whether your thoughts are good or bad; you are exploring the subject to find something to say. What you put down now is tentative, disposable. You aren't trying to be clear for anyone else; you aren't making a final decision to write on any specific part of the subject. You are writing whatever comes into your head on the assigned topic—maybe a list, even a collection of disjointed thoughts—so that later, with an objective eye, you can read through your writing and find what you want to say to another person.

In short, creating allows you to

discover a subject to write about;

set yourself up to have ideas on the subject;

follow specific activities to get started on a writing assignment;

tap your total resources by putting all thoughts on paper without immediately evaluating their significance or importance;

discover what you know and think about a particular subject;

decide exactly what you want to communicate to another person about a particular subject;

determine who will read your paper and what's in it for him or her; and

determine why you want to write.

Remember, too, that creating never stops; it goes on even while you are drafting and revising. Don't hesitate to return to the creating techniques that we will discuss here and in the following chapters. The techniques can be helpful when you need a new stimulus while you are drafting your paper or when you need to revise a section or paragraph.

SIMPLE CREATING TECHNIQUES

You have been using simple *creating techniques* for years. Perhaps when you gave an oral book report in grammar school your teacher told you to answer the five *W*s—who, what, when, where, and why—and you found that these helped you think of what to say. Maybe you remember sitting down to make a grocery list and, as you wrote, thinking of a number of other items you needed that were nowhere in your thoughts when you began the list.

Simple creating techniques are thought-producing techniques and, while useful in many situations other than writing, they are a particularly valuable way to begin to probe your mind when you must write. Let's review these simple creating techniques.

THE REPORTER'S FORMULA

Newspaper reporters use six simple questions—who, what, when, where, why, and how—to discover the essentials of events on which they are reporting. You can use these same questions to remind yourself of details you know about a subject. Answering these questions will (1) set you up to write a complete account of your subject, (2) jog your memory to supply every detail and, therefore, (3) serve your reader. Readers always want a complete story, and this method is one way to be sure that they get it.

Tips for Using the Reporter's Formula

1. Answer all the questions, even if some don't seem obviously pertinent.
2. If one question has more than a single response, jot down several answers.
3. Include as much detail as you can in your responses (although you need not write in complete sentences). Plan to focus and cut irrelevant detail later.

BRAINSTORMING

Business people often have *brainstorming* sessions to discover ways to solve problems, create new products or services, or get a fresh approach to an old situation. Brainstorming is a group activity. Members of the group bring up ideas on a specified subject—ideas spoken by one person stimulate others to have ideas of their own. It is this back-and-forth play that causes new thoughts to come to mind.

Tips for Brainstorming

1. Do it as a group activity.
2. Call out every idea you can think of. Go for quantity.
3. Freewheel. The wilder the ideas, the better.
4. Build off other people's ideas. Don't wait until you have an original thought.
5. Be completely nonjudgmental. No idea should be ridiculed, discarded, or decided upon prematurely.
6. Jot down all the ideas as they are spoken so that you will have a list to use later. Or use a tape recorder so you can devote full attention to the activity.

After holding a brainstorming session on a writing topic you will probably have a long list of ideas. Go through the list and mark out all the ideas that won't work or that do not interest you. Then, of the remaining ideas, pick the one or two that you can see using as a subject for your writing. Finally, run these ideas through another creating technique. When you do the actual writing, you will discover that you are well on your way to knowing exactly what you would like to say about the subject.

MAKING A LIST

We all make lists in order not to forget. What about making lists in order to discover?

Making a List can be a valuable first step in many writing situations, especially those that require you to recall something you already know, or realize something new about a familiar subject. You might list the steps in a process detailing, for example, how to make a bookshelf, or the arguments for or against something, perhaps explaining why you support nuclear disarmament.

As you settle down to write, a list can (1) give you a definite purpose and activity to get you started, (2) cause you to come up with associations and thereby to think of something you might not have thought of before, or (3) provide a framework for your thinking at that moment.

When you have finished the list, you can do several things: select the items on the list that seem to have the most promise for your writing; put the items on the list in some order—say, most important to least important; cross out items that you don't like; expand one or two items; add new items. The important thing is for the list to serve as a source of ideas as you begin to write your paper. The most valuable use of the list will be what it reveals to you—what you see when you review it.

Tips for Making a List

1. Put a title at the top of your list so you will keep your purpose in mind and always remember why you are making the list ("Why I Deserve a Raise" or "Things Our Town Could Do for Young Adults").

2. Write as fast as possible and use single words or short phrases.

3. Don't be critical of any item on the list at this point; just collect as many points on the list as you possibly can in a limited time.

WRITING *Simple Creating Techniques*

1. Practice the three creating techniques discussed so far to collect ideas for these topics. Keep your notes in your journal.

   Keeping a pet while in college

   Holding a part-time job as a student

   Spending time

   Happiness

   Physical fitness

   Road courtesy

2. Read the following short article on physical fitness of children. Then use the Reporter's Formula to determine the audience DeVenuta might have had in mind as she wrote the piece. Be sure to note specific details from the article that show who the reader is, what the reader is interested in, and why the reader might be interested in the article.

FUTURE STARS AREN'T READY   Karin DeVenuta / *Wall Street Journal*

Better training may help the U.S. do well in the 1988 Olympics, but considering the crummy condition of the athletes of tomorrow, don't bet the mortgage on the games in the year 2000. American children are getting fatter and more and more out of shape, in large part because of cultural changes and technological developments that have turned them into watchers instead of doers.

Surprisingly, the fitness craze that sent their parents into the streets in jogging shoes and into health clubs in leotards has passed them by. Some items of interest:

■ Almost one third of American children between six and 11 are fat, according to the Center for Adolescent Obesity at the University of California. That's a 54% increase in the past 15 years.

■ In tests of children five to eight years old, 40% displayed at least one risk factor for heart disease, according to the President's Council on Physical Fitness.

■ Many U.S. children perform abysmally on various physical tests. Of 200 Californians who recently took a 30-meter Soviet swim test, more than half couldn't finish.

George Allen, chairman of the president's council and a conditioning fiend when he was a National Football League head coach, has been appalled to find six-year-olds who weren't flexible enough to touch their toes. The lamentable shape American children are in "came as a shock to everybody," he says. He vows to shape them up. "My objective is to work them out five days a week, an hour a day, under competent instruction," he declares.

He and the council, whose task is to promote physical fitness, have a long way to go. Physical education in many schools amounts to putting on gym clothes, taking off gym clothes, and standing around a lot in between. One major youth-fitness study found that while nearly all children go to a gym class, the average elementary student spends only two or three minutes a session in moderate to vigorous exercise.

In years past, that didn't matter as much as it does today. Children rode bicycles, played street sports, and had toys that required effort. Now they prefer bikes with motors and play video games instead of stickball. The toy trucks they used to push around are now electrically powered. "Children are living vicariously," says Joseph Zanga, chairman of the American Academy of Pediatrics' section on school health. "Instead of playing sports they watch sports. Instead of dancing they watch rock video."

Parents should turn off the TV set and get the children outside and moving, he says. Amen, says Mr. Allen, who adds: "They shouldn't be spending six or seven hours a day in front of the television eating popcorn and peanut butter."

Fine, but are the kids and their parents listening? Tune in to the Olympics in 12 years and find out.

3. Now use the Reporter's Formula to help you determine an audience for your own short article on physical fitness among those in your peer group.
4. Brainstorm about physical fitness with a group of classmates and then make a list of details you can use for your article on the physical fitness of your peer group.

CLUSTERING

Some people prefer to show how ideas are related to one another as they jot them down. Lists don't do that, but *clustering* can. In clustering, one idea becomes a central focus and related ideas are noted as branches from the main idea. With this technique, you may generate detail on one main point or several, and your mind can range freely to associated details as they come up. This technique tends to be loosely structured but can generate more related detail than brainstorming or making a list. Because clustering also generates a visual structure, some writers like seeing the "map" of ideas. A student developed the following clusters beginning with the idea "accidents."

falling on snow

bike

hitting a bike with a car

accidents

dropping valuable breakables

car

when dad was driving

no one else helped

dad saved a life

dad applied pressure

man covered with blood

lost consciousness after being thrown through windshield

now dad covered with sweat and dried blood

Tips for Clustering

1. Put your first main idea in the center of the page.
2. Show ideas connected to the main idea by lines.
3. As one idea brings up associated points and details, connect those with lines.
4. Consider all details—memories, sensory detail, analysis, examples, and so on.

BRANCHING

Branching is a creating technique that helps writers move from general points to specific details. Most often, it begins with a general subject that the writer subdivides into two or more subtopics. Then the writer continues subdividing each of the subtopics to get to more and more specific details.

Like clustering, branching gives writers a visual map of the way their ideas develop. The map also can suggest areas that need more detail or that might not be fruitful. Beginning with the general subject "My Dad," one student branched out into the ideas shown here:

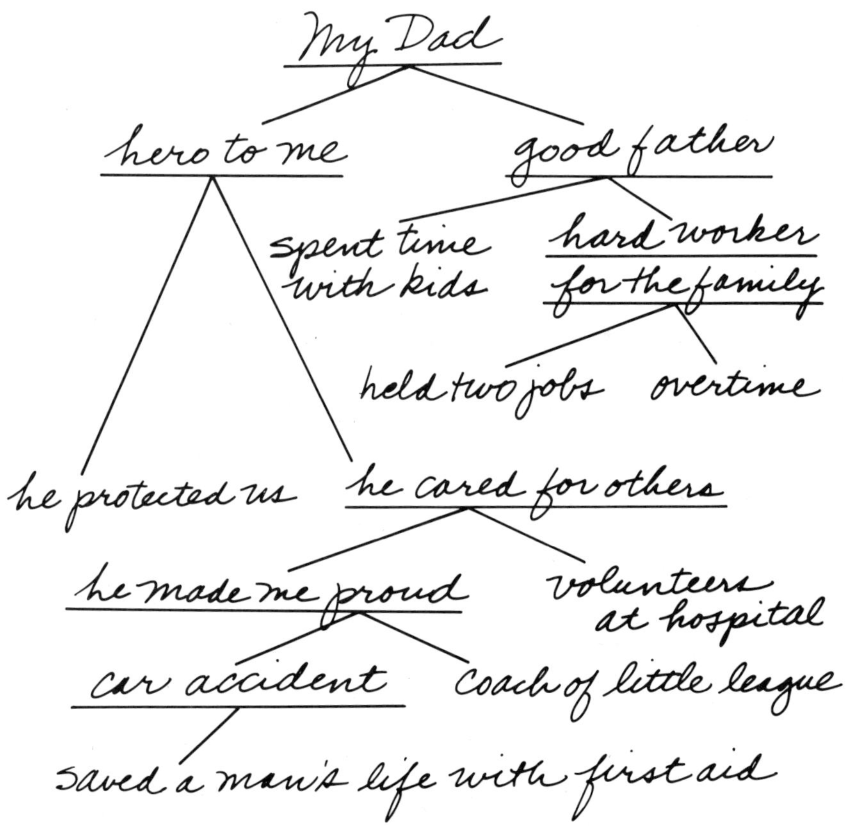

My Dad

hero to me   good father

spent time   hard worker
with kids   for the family

held two jobs   overtime

he protected us   he cared for others

he made me proud   volunteers
                        at hospital

car accident   Coach of little league

saved a man's life with first aid

Although the earlier example for clustering and this one for branching start with different ideas and generate different details, you can see how clustering and branching might lead a student to a similar focus for a paper.

Tips for Branching

1. Put your general subject at the top of the page.
2. Subdivide that subject into at least two subtopics. Draw lines to show the connection between topic and subtopics.
3. Continue to divide subtopics as they seem fruitful. Try to get to the point where you are giving examples or specific details.
4. If you have followed one branch for several layers, consider following at least one other branch to find another perspective on the topic.

STUDENT EXAMPLE   *Branching*

Tom knew he wanted to write about his father for a personal experience essay. Although he knew his subject, however, he wasn't sure of a specific topic that might interest his classmates who would read the paper. Branching helped him focus his ideas about his father. In the preceding branching example there are two general aspects of the father's heroism leading to a specific heroic action after an automobile accident.

Look at Tom's essay to see how creating helped him focus his main point and generate details.

THE ACCIDENT

The summer of '74 contained more than its share of excitement. My family had decided to move from a small, friendly community to a larger, more vibrant city. At the time, I was only ten years old and could hardly wait to meet new friends and move into a new house. This experience did not prove to be the highlight of my summer. Of far greater significance, I witnessed a near-fatal automobile accident. Never before had I been exposed to such pain and suffering.

The accident occurred on the sixty-mile stretch of highway connecting our town to the city. It was my Dad's day off, and he had asked me to accompany him as he drove the old Ford truck, loaded down with furniture, to our new home. I couldn't pass up the offer. Riding in the truck with my father was always enjoyable, even though I had become bored with the monotonous scenery of the trip. The traffic on the narrow two-lane highway was heavier than usual for a Saturday afternoon, but it did not seem to diminish Dad's ability to talk and drive at the same time.

Roughly forty miles into the journey the real action began. Several hundred yards ahead of us was the junction of our highway with the interstate that led into the city. As we entered the approach ramp, I remember Dad commenting on the excessive speed of a red car traveling in front of us. Out of reflex I turned my head to face the front window. It was at this time that a cold chill of fright grabbed my body. I froze to my seat, watching the same red car mysteriously vault from the highway, fly over the long, steep embankment, and vanish from my field of vision.

Without a blink of hesitation or fear, Dad slammed on our brakes, sending the truck into a controlled skid. We came to an abrupt stop on the shoulder of the road in the vicinity of where the car had become momentarily airborne. Several other cars also stopped, but I saw no one advancing to the wreckage. Then Dad turned in my direction, instructing me to stay close to the truck. Filled with fear, I watched as he fled from our vehicle and descended the steep embankment, twice losing balance and landing on his back. As Dad made his way to the crushed automobile, not one of the other bystanders responded in a similar manner. They all remained on the highway, watching the action from a distance.

A cloud of smoke and dust surrounded the site where the car had landed. From my location I could smell the fumes of gasoline and burning rubber, though I could neither see nor hear any signs of life. As Dad approached the smoldering wreckage, however, I became aware of the deathly scream of a young girl trapped within. Dad reacted quickly, attempting to jar

one of the twisted doors open. Being unsuccessful, he then crawled beneath the inverted car and pulled her to safety through the opening that had once been occupied by the front windshield. She appeared to be holding her left knee as she squirmed frantically on the ground. Hearing her screams, I could tell she was in great pain.

The driver had miraculously been thrown clear of the automobile, possibly escaping death by the shattered front window. I watched as he attempted to stand up, his face and chest dripping with blood. This attempt ended instantly as his wobbly body collapsed to the earth. He had lost consciousness. I began to panic as not one of the adults standing next to me responded to the crisis. Out of instinct I yelled at my Dad. Hearing my screams, he immediately switched his attention from the girl to the unconscious man. By applying pressure to the open wounds, he was able to stabilize the excessive bleeding.

Within a few minutes an ambulance arrived at the scene. The paramedics rushed down the embankment with their first-aid equipment and began emergency care of the victims. Sensing he was no longer needed, Dad made his way back to our truck. His previously clean shirt was now filthy with blood and dirt, and his face was sticky with sweat.

I had observed everyone's reaction to the accident from my position on the highway. I was amazed at how quickly my Dad had reacted. He had possibly saved another person's life. What confused me, however, was the reaction of the other adults who were standing alongside me. Why, I wondered, had not one of them offered assistance to my Dad? I could not understand how they could simply watch and not respond when other human beings were desperately in need of help. Perhaps they had been overcome with fear, momentarily paralyzed. Or maybe they preferred not to get involved, assuming my Dad had the situation under control. Whatever their reasons, I was perplexed at their behavior. If I had been older, I surely would have attempted to help.

I remember how proud I was as I watched Dad climb back into the truck. His shirt was ruined, but he did not seem to mind. As we drove the remaining twenty miles to the city, I sensed he was satisfied with how he had responded to the emergency; I know I was. From that day on I wanted to grow up to be just like him.

WRITING   *Clustering and Branching*

1. Use either clustering or branching to generate still more detail for the piece on physical fitness you started earlier.
2. Use clustering to find a new perspective on your fitness piece. Put your dominant reaction to exercise in the center of the cluster. Now cluster your emotional reactions to exercise and fitness. How might the new details change your approach to the topic?

CHAINING

Chaining is a simple creating technique that uses questions and answers to stimulate your mind and help you to make connections and see relationships. Chaining is particularly valuable as a method that allows you to build one thought off another and, in doing so, produce something new.

Chaining works like this: The first question becomes the first "link" in the chain. The answer to that question then becomes the second "link." Then a question related to the answer becomes the third. And so on. By asking and answering your own questions, you can produce a chain of thought that builds effortlessly on itself.

STUDENT EXAMPLE   *Chaining*

Here is an example of how chaining helps generate ideas on a subject.

Topic: Alarm Clocks

Q: Of what use are alarm clocks?

A: They wake people up.

Q: Is that good?

A: Most of the time, yes, because people have to get to work or school on time. People can't sleep all day.

Q: Why not?

A: If we slept all day, we wouldn't get work done, earn money, graduate, and so on.

Q: Are these goals worth giving up sleep?

A: Yes, but sometimes they are hard to keep in mind when we're tired.

Q: What do you think of when you're tired?

A: I think about how the alarm clock seems to be a beast.

Q: How is it like a beast?

A: It waits for its prey silently, then it springs with a howl.

Q: Just what does the alarm clock sound like?

A: A medium-sized nuclear device—no, a chain saw started up by my head.

Q: Why does that little box seem so vicious and violent?

A: Because it is small, I expect it to be mild-mannered and it surprises me to be awakened so mercilessly after a short night of sleep.

Q: Is the sound worse after short nights?

A: Absolutely, because then I want more than ever to sleep.

Q: So the clock capitalizes on your weakness?

A: You bet, that clock is after me!

TIME TORTURE

Don't get me wrong—I'm really not paranoid. I mean, my alarm clock *looks* like a typical generic style clock/radio. Nothing appears outwardly abnormal at all. In fact, it doesn't have any truly distinguishing features at all, and I'm tempted to say that it's an average, run-of-the-mill, nondescript clock/radio. But, since it's a cop-out to describe something as "nondescript" (if not outright contradictory), I'll give a quick rundown of it. I've owned this clock/radio, a Realistic Chronomatic 213, for a month now,

and it's still difficult to remember exactly what it looks like. There it is, a rectangular box sitting on my desk in the corner, six feet from my bed, with a bright red digital readout saying 9:39. The colon between the 9 and the 39—no, now 40—flashes on and off once per second, 24 hours a day. To the right of the time display is the radio tuning dial, set near 97 FM, probably KBCO Boulder. Also on the rectangular front face, just below the clock display and the radio tuning dial, is a row of four small round switches, used to set the time and the alarm. The top and the sides of the radio are an artificial wood-grain finish, trimmed with black and separated from the front panel by a chrome strip. Centered on its top is a small square speaker grill.

Yeah, this alarm clock would seem like a normal, well-adjusted appliance to most people, but that's because they don't have to live with it. Just by looking at it, a person wouldn't sense that this clock/radio carried a grudge and had general anti-social tendencies. Even I didn't notice anything strange until recently. First, small irritating things became apparent. For instance, the way it stares at night, annoyingly blinking its stupid red colon. After a half-hour of watching the clock gaze back, it's obvious that the stare isn't a benign one; it has the qualities of an unpleasant sneer, that certain executioner's look of someone in ultimate control. Then, I noticed how time always seemed to speed up at night while I slept. I could almost hear that damn blood-red colon flashing faster and faster, but as soon as I would open my eyes it would skid back down to once per second, once per second. The unnerving part, though, is that the clock speeds up in direct proportion to the amount of sleep that I need—so even if I go to bed early the night before a big exam, I still wake up with severe jetlag.

This clock's attitude problem doesn't become blatantly apparent until early morning, however. The hours of darkness slowly convert it into a remorseless predatory creature, primed to terrorize. Yes, terrorize. Remaining utterly silent and motionless so as not to stir its unsuspecting comatose victim, the clock waits. Mercilessly it savors its position of power as the final seconds slip by. And then it strikes. Noise and chaos, resembling the detonation of a medium-sized nuclear device in the corner of my room, slam out of its tiny speaker. At five in the morning. Actually, at five in the morning, the sound has more of a physical quality, roughly equivalent to a chainsaw being started in the left ear while a rake crashes into the jaw. Instinctively, my body, instantly brought from suspended animation to adrenalin overload, lunges in the general direction of the demonic box on the desk. My hand swats at every small knob—there are now millions of them—until it slaps the right switch in the right direction, snuffing out the noise and the pain.

Every morning, as I lie limply on the floor, I can see the clock display staring straight ahead, blinking its damn red colon in the morning sun, once per second, once per second, and I *know* it's trying not to snicker. I'm not paranoid—the clock really does hate me.

As you can see from this example, chaining can throw light on a subject which has reached a dead end or suggest a new perspective on an everyday topic. Asking and answering questions can help you explore a subject you want to write about.

Tips for Chaining

1. At the top of your paper, write the subject to be explored.
2. Begin by asking a question about this subject.
3. Let the answer to the question lead to the next question to be asked.
4. Keep asking and answering questions until you get an insight into the topic.

WRITING *Using Creating Techniques*

Practice at least one simple creating technique for each of these writing situations. Keep your "creating" in your journal.

1. You are a student whose teacher has just assigned the first essay: a description of your home town.
2. You are looking for a job; the employment counselor tells you to write a short paper in which you describe all the jobs you have had in the past and what skills you developed on those jobs.
3. You are a member of a sports or social club that will be listed in a newspaper supplement on "Things To Do." You are the person who will prepare the information about your club for the newspaper.
4. You have decided that bicyclists on campus endanger pedestrians. You need to write a letter to the editor of the college paper to gather support for banning bikes in certain parts of campus.
5. You have decided that students who drive to campus waste gasoline unnecessarily since most of them could walk, ride a bike, or take public transportation. Write a letter to the editor about banning parking on campus.
6. Write an essay on bicycling in your community or on campus. Create a specific audience, perhaps for a class in sports medicine or contemporary social phenomena, perhaps to classmates looking for specific problems in physics (controlling traffic flow), psychology (the devil-may-care attitude of some cyclists), sociology (interactions of bikers and pedestrians), and so on.

CHAPTER 4

Expanded Creating Techniques

In Chapter 3 we looked at an example in which something as simple as making a list could be a creating activity in the writing process. Unfortunately, creating devices such as lists or brainstorming sessions don't always produce the best or fullest ideas for a piece of writing. Writers find it useful to have a whole catalog of creating techniques they can choose from.

CREATING TECHNIQUES TO GET ANYONE STARTED WRITING

The following four creating techniques are designed to help any writer come up with something to say for any writing task. Practice the four techniques so that you can experience how they help you form ideas on any subject. Become familiar with them. Make them a permanent part of your own personal repertory of ways to get ideas. With such a repertory you should never again have to worry about not having something to say.

LOOPING

Looping is a writing activity in which you start with a subject and, without planning or consciously thinking, write anything that comes into your mind on the topic. This technique lets you explore a subject to see what you know or think about it without making any decisions about whether the ideas are good or bad, or whether they are important enough to do a paper on. The looping activity also gets other things that are on your mind out on paper so they don't block your mind as you work to come up with something to say on the subject.

Tips for Looping

1. Begin with a specific topic.
2. Write nonstop for X number of minutes.
3. Make no changes or corrections.
4. Write a center of gravity sentence for each loop before going on to the next one.

Begin with a Specific Topic. At the top of the page, put down the topic you are going to write on in the loop. This helps your mind focus on one particular thing at the beginning. As you write, you may discover that your mind gets off the subject and you are writing about something else entirely. When this happens, go ahead and finish what you are writing and then go back to concentrating on the subject you listed at the top of the page. Often, when you write off the subject, what you write will be something that is on your mind, perhaps worrying you. Or what you write may only look as if it is off the subject although it is connected. The aim of looping, however, is to come up with some ideas on a specific subject for a paper, and so it is best to stick to the subject as closely as possible.

Write Nonstop for X Minutes. This rule is simple but crucial. Set a timer or an alarm clock when you start. Give five minutes to each loop when you are first learning the technique. Later, you will want to vary the time, depending on the subject and on the amount of time you have. Part of the magic of this technique comes about because you must keep writing. Do not take your pencil or pen off the page. Keep it moving the whole five minutes. You can write things like "I can't think of anything on this topic," or "This topic is dumb," or "I despise this looping activity." You may even draw circles or make chicken-scratch marks on the paper, but you must keep the pen moving to keep your thoughts stirred up and your mind open to whatever ideas may occur on the topic.

Make No Corrections. Whether you follow this rule or break it will determine the success or failure of your looping. You cannot stop to think about whether a word is spelled right or whether a comma is in the wrong place. You cannot stop to make a judgment of whether a statement you have just written is stupid or smart. You cannot even stop to decide whether you want to say something or don't. *Any kind of correcting or deliberating will cause the looping activity not to work.* (There is a time to correct your work, but it isn't while you are creating.) The purpose of looping is to scare up ideas, and to do that you need to forge ahead, not to pause or polish. So don't mark anything out; don't change anything. Just keep writing until you run out of time.

Write a Center of Gravity Sentence for Each Loop. When you have finished each loop, stop, sit back, and scan what you have written. What are you most drawn to in this loop? What did your mind go back to as you wrote? What do you seem to be drifting toward in this group of sentences? If you had to pick out the thing that "weighs" the most—that has the most interest, the most potential for you—what would that be? This is your *center of gravity* for the loop.

The center of gravity may appear, perfectly stated, in the loop. Or you may have written around it rather than stating it directly in a single sentence. Look over what you have written and make a quick, unstudied decision about what your center of gravity is. If you don't find it or can't think of what it might be, just make one up. This isn't a test—it is merely a way to come back to home base after exploring uncharted territory. The center of gravity will ground your thinking for a few seconds before you begin to loop out again.

After you have written the center of gravity sentence for the first loop, do two additional loops to complete the creating activity. (Be sure to include a center of gravity sentence after the second and third loops.)

Usually by the end of the third loop you will have come up with an idea that can be developed into an essay. Something will have stirred you or excited you or interested you; it may have just barely cropped up in the loop writings, but there are strong odds that you will see something to use as a slightly more focused subject than what you started with on the first loop. If an idea has not surfaced by the end of the third loop, you might try writing an extra loop or two, or switch to another creating technique to see if it will work better.

STUDENT EXAMPLE *Looping*

Here are the loops and the essay one student wrote as she began exploring the topic "opportunity."

Topic: Opportunity

Loop 1

This may be the start of a bad habit. I bought this new pen today so I could write neater and now I'm doing a looping with it. Oh, well, I'll just be careful of my pen. First of all, to get some things off my mind before I write on opportunity (which is a very dumb topic). Excuse me, but my pen's messing up. First of all, the coach of the football team resigned today and that's pretty sad because he's a human being and what will he do and where will he go from here. Also, I'm mad at my best friend because I was taking a nap and she turned the television on. Later I found out she wasn't even watching anything. Now, to zero in on opportunity. I have had opportunities to sing, to dance, to jog, to be me. I've had lots of opportunities throughout my life. I was brought up in a nice home with neat parents who never fought in front of me and who will be married for 25 years this August. I went to a great high school with a rotten football team, but that's OK because I guess I learned a lot about people while I was there. I learned a lot about boys anyway! Ha. In high school they were all nerds. Oh, well, what will be will be. I also went to a nice church and we had lots of kids and a fabulous choir director. We put on musicals and went all over the United States. I almost didn't take that opportunity, though, because I hated choir at first. I never did want to go to rehearsals. I really didn't want to spend my Saturdays all day practicing music and choreography. I'm glad I did, though. That was a neat opportunity my parents made me do.

Center of gravity sentence: *I've had lots of opportunities in my life, and some of them my parents made me take when I didn't want to.*

Loop 2

I really have . . . I guess I'm glad my parents made me do those things. In fact, I'm more than glad; I'm ecstatic. Really, I think my best opportunity is myself, though, how I am. I owe it to my parents for bringing me up the way they did, though. They instilled values and personality into me. But right now going to college, planning my biggest opportunity is about myself—is myself. I guess that sounds conceited but . . . I'm thinking about something a former teacher of mine told me, that writing was an art and a writer didn't have to paint by number or follow lines. Well, that's the way I feel about my opportunities to get out there and make something of my life. See, I'm the artist; I hold the brushes and the oils and my parents' training is the . . . I have the opportunity to be anybody I want this person to be. Conceit, conceit, conceit. I better narrow this thing down further. I have grabbed opportunities and created opportunities by all the things I've done. One way that I've realized this and changed my attitude about myself in the world is by working in Colorado this summer cleaning cabins. I've always thought of myself as a city girl, but I've always loved the mountains, so when the opportunity came, I went to clean cabins. I look back on it now and think, man, what all different opportunities there were. I learned how to fly fish, how to flip gas refrigerators to make the freon circulate. I think, most of all, I had the opportunity to learn that it's people who make a feeling, not a place. A place can bring back memories, but it can't make you feel things. I don't know, I thought I was just going to clean cabins, and I ended up learning lots about business.

Center of gravity sentence: *My biggest opportunity is* myself, *and I proved this by working in Colorado this summer.*

Loop 3

When I was a little girl, we used to go to Taylor Park, Colorado, for vacation, and we found this rickety place called Holt's Guest Ranch. I'll never know what made me love that place so much except maybe it was the childhood memories I feel there. Fishing with my dad. Dancing at family night. Anyway, Mr. and Mrs. Holt always hired two college girls to work with them. I used to tag along behind them, and Mrs. Holt would always say, "Debbi, someday when you're in college, maybe you can come work for us." I had all my plans made when I was nine. . . . I realize as I write this that what looked like an opportunity last summer wasn't just a fluke or just good luck. I, myself, brought that opportunity about by keeping in touch with Mrs. Holt, even after they sold the ranch to the Speers who almost ruined it, and then when they bought it back. And, especially, I caused that opportunity to happen when I told Mrs. Holt last year to call me if they kept the cabins. I wonder how many things we call opportunities are really like this; we do things that make the opportunities happen. I feel real encouraged by thinking about this. If I—myself—made that opportunity happen last summer, can I do it again? And I am really proud of what I learned by taking advantage of that opportunity. I remember that first night there. I slept in Dad's flannel pajamas, long Fruit-of-the-Loom underwear and lined ski socks. We had two beds, but the thermal coupling in the heater was broken, so my roommate and I slept in the same bed to keep warm. Also, I didn't want to sleep in my bed because there was a dead mouse in it. (Squiggles) I don't know what else to write. I'm tired of thinking about opportunities. I wish the timer would go off and I could stop this loop. Great, there it is.

Center of gravity sentence: *I made my own opportunity.*

When Debbi finished these three loops, she had a subject for her essay. She decided to write on the idea that occurred in her second loop. "My biggest opportunity is *myself,* and I proved this by working in

Colorado this summer." Now read the essay she wrote on this subject. You will easily see the connection between her creating activity and the content of the essay itself.

CONFIDENCE

Last April my telephone rang early in the morning, and it took me a full thirty seconds to recognize Mrs. Holt's voice. She wanted me to come to Colorado that summer and clean the guest cabins at her ranch. I thought about it a while and decided to go. I told myself, "This is a great opportunity to make money." What I learned during the summer, however, was that there is a bigger opportunity than making money. That opportunity is having confidence in yourself.

I flew from my hometown on May 19. When we arrived in Colorado, the temperature was 38 degrees. I got off the plane and realized that I had to carry both my suitcases and my clothes bag myself. This was just one of the things I was to discover during the summer that I had to do for myself. All the way up the drive in the canyon to the ranch, I kept thinking, "Don't forget how much money you are going to make. It will be worth it all." I was scared.

It is true that the summer was a great opportunity to make money. I saved $500. My salary was $250 a month plus room and board. With all the baked potatoes and gravy and even some boiled cabbage that I finally learned to swallow, I felt I came out on the good end of the room and board part of the deal. I was able to save almost all my salary because there was nothing to spend it on except maybe an occasional tube of toothpaste at Sherm Cranor's Taylor Park Trading Post.

Sometime during the early summer, I quit thinking about the opportunity to make money.

I began to experience the opportunity of proving myself and accomplishing hard and new things by myself. It was really rough running a guest ranch. There was always a pilot light that had gone out or a toilet that wouldn't flush. There was always a beaver to clog up the irrigation ditch or a guest who needed dry bath towels at the strangest moment. I learned all about leaky pipes and the parts of a toilet. I spent hours plunging with my plumber's friend. I even learned how to run a "snake" through sewer pipes. I made beds in three minutes flat, and I washed three million dirty bath and tea towels every day. I set thousands of mouse traps. I learned how to light the pilot on cooking and heating stoves. I helped flip refrigerators so their freon would circulate, and I exploded them when they wouldn't draw the air up. I painted signs and cleaned the fireplace and dusted furniture and even helped lay linoleum in the laundry room. (It got a big wrinkle down the middle. We nicknamed it the Continental Divide.)

So, what I had thought would be just an opportunity to make money turned out to be an opportunity to grow with myself. I found out so many things about me. I became very proud of myself and what I was able to learn and do. I found out I really liked people. It made me feel good to work hard and accomplish things. I even learned to like cabbage.

Someday, I'll go back. By then I am sure that I will have grabbed a lot more opportunities to make myself proud of me. And I will probably even make money on top of it.

WRITING *Looping*

1. Pick one of the following topics and do three five-minute loops on it:
   Families
   Music
   Travel
   Include a center of gravity sentence at the end of each loop.
2. Read over everything you have written during this looping activity. If you were required to write an essay on some idea that occurred to you during this loop writing, what would you write on?

   Be prepared to discuss the topic you picked with the class. Were you surprised when you hit on it? Was it something you hadn't thought about for a long time? What do you like about it? What makes it seem like a good subject for an essay? What is there about the essay that you think would interest other people?
3. Write three five-minute loops on frustrations and rewards of learning something new.

CUBING

Often writers can't get going on a subject because they are locked into a single way of looking at the topic. That's when *cubing* works well. Cubing is a technique for swiftly considering a subject from six points of view represented by the six sides of a cube. The emphasis in this technique is on *swiftly* and *six*. Cubing lets you have a single point of view for only 3 to 5 minutes, then moves you on to the next point of view. When you've finished cubing, you've spent 18 to 30 minutes deliberately varying your point of view.

Use All Six Sides of the Cube. For the cubing technique you analyze a topic from six perspectives that make up the six sides of the cube.

1. *Describe it.* Look at the subject closely and describe what you see. Colors, shapes, sizes, and so forth.
2. *Compare it.* What is it similar to? What is it different from?
3. *Associate it.* What does it make you think of? What comes into your mind? You may think of similar things as well as different

Tips for Cubing

1. Use all six sides of the cube.
2. Move fast. Don't allow yourself more than 3 to 5 minutes on each side of the cube.

things, different times, places, people. Just let your mind go and see what associations you have for this subject.

4. *Analyze it.* Tell how it's made. (You don't have to know; you can make it up.)

5. *Apply it.* Tell what you can do with it, how it can be used.

6. *Argue for or against it.* Go ahead and take a stand. Use any kind of reasons you want to—rational, silly, or anywhere in between. Then switch to the other side of the issue and argue that.

You need to use all six sides because cubing is a technique to help you learn to look at a subject from a variety of perspectives. Consequently, doing just one of the sides won't work. You may decide after doing all six sides that you do want to focus on only one side; but by then your decision will be meaningful and intelligent, based on your realization that one side presents the best approach. So remember, cubing takes all six sides.

Move Fast. Don't allow yourself more than 3 to 5 minutes on each side. The energy in this creating technique comes from frequently shifting your perspective on the subject. By moving around the cube, one side after another, in rapid succession, you see that you can look at your subject from different angles and that you can talk about it in different ways. You are not hunting for something to say from each perspective; you are taking a quick run into your mind for whatever presents itself on that angle, and the quickness of the run is important. It is the switch from angle to angle that makes cubing work.

STUDENT EXAMPLE *Cubing*

In the cubing that follows, the topic, fire, is addressed from each of the six sides of the cube.

Topic: Fire

Describe

Fire is orange, red, blue, and yellow. It has spires, peaks, valleys and is broad in some places and narrow in others. Pieces of it split off from the main portion. It seems to come from a reddish-orange base and go into a yellow-to-blue tip. Its flames tend to vary in size— some or a few of them are high and pointed and others are low with scoops and dips out of the middle of them. Fire crackles and breathes as it burns and throws the sparks off to all sides as it rants, raves, and rages forward to engulf the air and physical surroundings in its presence—leaving them smoldering in its wake.

Compare

Fire is similar to the sun. It has a center and its heat goes out into the surrounding space. Fire is similar to the heating element of a stove. It generates a great deal of heat in a localized area. Fire is also similar to a chemical reaction in terms of the heat that is produced by both. Fire also provides light and is again like the sun in this way. Fire is like an atom bomb in that it inherently contains the potential for both benefit and destruction.

Associate

Fire is associated with Robby burning the back of a chair; and smoking my mother's cigarettes. The fire I caused in the field back of our house. The fire Robby set in the garage, the fireplace at Nana and Grandad's, the fake fireplace at my grandparents' house. I also associate fire with cooking marshmallows, roasting acorns, Christmastime, coffee drinking with my mate, the wonderful smell of burning pinon wood and the onset of snow, the winter games and the ensuing hazards and troubles of the winter months.

Analyze

Fire is made of energy released from the impact of many atoms, traveling at tremendous speed, with each other. Fire comes from wood in a fireplace, from lightning that strikes in the woods. Fire needs oxygen to exist and survive. Different fires burn differently. For instance, grease fires burn only where the grease is and will continue to burn if not smothered. Wood fires burn all over the wood and jump from place to place when the wind blows.

Apply

Cooking, heating, destroying, purifying, cleaning, warning, safety, growth, clearing. Fire can be used to make jewelry, cut metal, sterilize equipment, light cigarettes, cigars, etc. Fire can be used as a light in a cave or to light a candle where there are no lights; fire from the spark of a spark plug causes the energy necessary to drive the engine of a car and in turn make the car move; the same for trains, lawn mowers, etc.

Argue For

Fire is a great tool and should always be available to man. Man can clean his instruments, cook his food, heat his home, and many other things with fire. It makes the grass grow in springtime. Fire is the source or originating idea behind many of our present machines and technologies. Fire has given humans many things that were not possible before its presence. Fire, in one form, saves lives and allows life to go on.

Argue Against

Fire also destroys the creations of humans, and takes life. Fire can be used to harm people and to perform criminal acts, such as cutting through the metal of a safe to steal the money or jewels within; or lighting fuses of dynamite, which blow things up; or as a weapon in war. Fire can easily destroy many years of tree growth in the woods—in only a matter of hours it can take away that beauty. Fire in the hands of a pyromaniac makes people and buildings in danger of destruction. Fire is too potentially destructive.

Here is the essay that resulted from this cubing. Notice how the writer pulled ideas from each side of the cube.

A LEGACY FROM PREHISTORIC TIMES

At first, it's a little bit like wandering into a landscape on another planet: the valleys are orange, the mountains tipped with incandescent blue. In that strange clime, bodies and other solid things undergo a kind of metamorphosis; they shimmer in the air. At the valley's base is something primitive, urgent, like ancient dancers swaying in the wind, leaping wild, leaping high, climbing endlessly up the blue-tipped spire. Who, in this eerie terrain, can survive?

Our ancestors survived it—and, for the most part, tamed it, used it for warmth in winter, light during night, fuel for cooking, a place for gathering, a fortress against wild animals.

Fire. Without it, our society would not be what it is.

Our ancestors began thinking about how to harness fire's energy, and we have been thinking along the same lines ever since. Many of our inventions have fire as their basis, in one form or another. Given the existence of fire and the presence of their desire to warm their homes, early humans put those two things together. The wood-burning stove emerged as a refinement of that original idea. Later on came floor furnaces and space heaters. The notion that fire could be used to heat an area was behind these relatively recent inventions as well as their older prototypes.

And then there was cooking. Early humans got the notion that most food tasted better cooked than raw—a notion they probably got when someone's raw dinosaur chop fell into the fire by accident and emerged not ruined but actually tasty. Later on, the wood-burning stove improved on the fire pit as a dual-purpose heating/cooking apparatus. Nowadays, gas and electric stoves, and even microwave ovens, use modern technology to produce heat; and certainly they are safer than an open fire. Yet we need to recall the origin of even our fanciest cooking devices.

The fireplace, too, has its origin in times past. Where once it was the campfire that functioned as a central gathering spot, today the fireplace is where people get together. They cozy up in front of the fire in couples, they congregate in groups for cheery drinks and Christmas carols, and they even cozy up to their thoughts and reveries while staring at the flames. And, as realtors can attest, the presence of a fireplace (all other things being equal) can make or break the sale of a new home. So in both tangible and symbolic ways, the fireplace is a status symbol in our society.

Fire continues to provide us with light, as well. Camping trips depend on kerosene lamps to light the way back to the tent. And the candle, while no longer essential to the persistence of civilization past sundown, still lightens our nights during stormy blackouts, inevitable power failures, or romantic dinners.

In this day of high technology, it's probably worth our while to remember the humble beginnings of so many of our current heating, cooking, socializing, and lighting conveniences. From fireplaces to space heaters, from wood-burning stoves to microwave ovens, fire continues to influence our lives and society, just as it did for our ancestors. We can appreciate the warmth, fuel, cooked food, and beauty that fire offers us. And perhaps our ancestors, once they were warmed and well fed, also had the luxury and ability to appreciate the strange, intense, multicolored beauty of that soaring, wind-dancing, spire-climbing element: fire.

WRITING Cubing

1. Pick a topic familiar to you: A family holiday celebration; the personality of your sister, brother, aunt, best friend; the den in your house. Cube this subject; you will be surprised at the "new" thoughts you have during this creating activity about an "old" subject.
2. Use the topic you chose in the looping application—families, music, travel, or frustrations and rewards of learning something new. Put the same subject through the cubing creating technique. This is one of the best ways to discover what each activity has to offer—how each differs in bringing ideas to your mind. In light of what you discover, for what kinds of subjects do you think cubing is most useful?
3. Try cubing on one of the topics you listed after reading the passages in Chapter 2 on bicycling and exercise.

TRACK SWITCHING

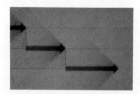

When beginning to explore a subject, we all tend to put down familiar words running along their familiar track. *Track switching* makes use of this automatic tendency of the mind.

To direct your thinking about a subject in ways that are not automatic, you can begin wherever your mind wants to begin—no matter how ordinary, automatic, or unoriginal that place is—and then you can

Tips for Track Switching

1. Begin by making any statement on your subject.
2. Write on that track for five minutes.
3. Switch to Track #2. Make another statement about your subject, as different as possible from the one you just made.
4. Write on this track for five minutes. Stay on the track.
5. Repeat the process until you have five tracks.
6. Write a fresh idea track, in which you trace the fresh idea you see emerging from or standing around the fringe of the tracks you've just written.

deliberately switch tracks. You can intentionally change the angle or approach you took originally by writing about the subject from an entirely different viewpoint.

Switching tracks works like this. Begin by making a statement about your subject—any statement. This statement does not have to be anything you believe in or care to be held to. It's just a place to start. Each time you switch tracks, you make a new statement about your subject—again, any statement. Each time you change to another statement, you just use whatever pops into your head. You do not have to deliberately say the opposite of what you have just said or say anything connected with any angle you have taken so far.

As you are writing along on each track, don't worry about having to say anything smart. If you can't think of something new to say, just repeat what you have already said until you do think of something else to put on the paper. Don't try to be profound, just let the words run along the track and see what turns up.

At some point in writing these variations on your subject, a fresh idea will come—something you do want to say.

STUDENT EXAMPLE *Track Switching*

Let's look at this student example to see how track switching turns up something fresh and interesting on a potentially overused subject.

Topic: Jogging

Track #1—Jogging is boring.

Have you ever run by yourself around a track? Such monotony. Nothing to see but the same old thing. Putting one foot in front of another. You stay on the track. You do the same thing over and over again. And it's just the same thing day after day. Put on your shoes—go outside—run. No variety, unlike tennis in which the ball might go any way any time it comes toward you. Or football, during which you always have to anticipate what other people are going to do. You don't even have the variety of swimming—you can vary your strokes in that exercise—how much variation can you put into the way you run? Yes, jogging is about as boring as any sport can be.

Track #2—Jogging is an exciting sport.

The challenge of jogging is all inside you. You can make up the game—how long will you run—how far—how fast? When you just start to jog, you can make up a game called "get out the door." The excitement in jogging is internal, not external. You can get excited about how much better shape you're getting into. You can create excitement when you jog by changing your route and changing the time of day you run. You can become very excited about learning how your body functions in different circumstances—how long can you run in the heat—how long in the cold. Jogging is a very exciting sport if you make it that way.

Track #3—Jogging is not something everyone can do.

Babies can't jog. People in wheelchairs can't jog. People riding in cars can't jog. People sitting in chairs can't jog. People with no discipline over themselves can't jog. Anybody not intending to jog or not aware enough to jog or not physically able to jog can't jog. Looks like all other people can jog, if they want to.

Track #4—Jogging is a lifetime opportunity.

One of the great things about jogging is that you never get too old to jog. And by getting in shape at one stage in life and continuing to jog, you can only build on being in shape. Contrasted with some sports, age is not a factor. So you can make it a sport for the rest of your life.

Track #5—Jogging is a national phenomenon.

Why? It is easy to do. You don't need equipment. You can be any age. You can do it on the road. You can run everywhere. It also shows the spirit of individual responsibility and choice. You can be yourself. Is there anything else? Are we learning to be with ourselves more?

When you have finished switching tracks, look to see what you've uncovered for yourself. After the last track, write a capsule fresh idea track.

Fresh Idea Track

In these five tracks I see this idea emerging: jogging allows people to be in charge of their own lives, to play alone, to take themselves as a project. People can build a sense of control over their own lives by jogging and can display commitment at the same time they are doing something valuable for their health.

Do you see how much more individuality and freshness is potentially present in this fresh idea track than was present on the first track the student wrote—a track that began with an automatic, unoriginal idea? As you read through the tracks you may not see a clear statement of the fresh idea. You may see only the fringe of the idea—a faint shape of the idea—the hints and first appearances. With careful reading, however, you can watch the mind at work, beginning to think for itself rather than just running along on an automatic track.

Here is the essay which resulted from the track switching.

JOGGING TO A GOOD JOB

It was the spring of 1984, my last months in high school. All of us seniors were counting the hours until the senior prom, graduation day—and then freedom. None of us had much to do in our last quarter's classes, so we were mostly breezing through.

Then Coach Marshall had his bright idea. Our boys' physical education class would take up jogging. Serious jogging. We *started* at two miles and went up from there. Coach Marshall had never heard of running some and walking some. He certainly had never heard of starting with something as simple as one mile.

We jogged five days a week, rain or shine. The two miles soon became four and then five and then six. Every day, I hated it when it was time to get out on the track. I hated every step of the way. The only thing I didn't hate was the feeling of pride and satisfaction I had at the

end of every gym period when I had completed the jog.

It wasn't until the summer after we graduated that I found out how valuable that last quarter's physical education class had been. I needed a job to help pay my college tuition in the fall. I had been planning all year long to work at the docks, unloading fish and shrimp from the trawlers. High school kids had always been able to get summer work doing that.

When I started making the rounds of the fishing fleet in early June, though, there was no job to be found. The red tide had come in and ruined fishing. Nobody had any jobs on the docks. This meant that I had to find some other work, and in a town where fishing is the main economic activity, that wasn't easy.

I went out every day that first week. Every-time somebody told me "no," I screwed up my courage and just knew that the next place would be better. But day after day I had no success. By the second week I was ready to call it quits—but I really didn't have the choice to do that. I had to find a job.

Then I remembered jogging. I knew that if I had gone out jogging day after day when I didn't want to that I could keep looking for work. I also knew from that jogging class that things didn't have to start out easy, that I was capable of doing more than I would have ever believed if left on my own. I also remembered the satisfaction I got from jogging—even though I would never in a million years let Coach Marshall know that.

I guess the most important realization that kept me looking for work was that hating something didn't have anything to do with doing it, even doing it well. So, I put what I had learned from jogging to good use. I went out every day that second week and then the third.

It was on Thursday of the third week that I got work in a place where I would probably never have thought to look if things hadn't been the way they were. Almost as a last resort I went to the police station to see if they had any kind of summer work. They did—helping clean the beaches of the dead fish and scum from the red tide. So, I got to do something that made me feel good inside—cleaning up the environment—and something that paid me well.

I guess you might say I jogged myself to a good job.

WRITING *Track Switching*

1. Choose one of the following subjects to practice track switching:

   Parent/child relationships
   Staying in shape
   The value of a college degree

2. Imagine that you are applying for a job. You need to write a letter about yourself to accompany your resume. Do a track switching exercise to discover something fresh to say about yourself and your work capabilities.

3. At two of the commercial breaks during televised college football games, there is a spot on each of the colleges playing that day in the game. Sometimes this college description is about how many students go to the school, what the school is noted for, where the school is located, and so on. Imagine that your school is playing in a game and will be featured in one of the commercial spots. Do a track switching exercise to find something provocative and interesting to say about your school.

4. Use track switching for one of the following:

   A paper to persuade
   An advertisement
   An annual report for a company
   A resume and an application letter to get a job

CLASSICAL INVENTION

In ancient Athens there were people who gave speeches in public places as a way of life. These speeches were designed to persuade listeners on controversial subjects, and the arguments were often intense and always serious. One of the most distinguished of these ancient orators, Aristotle, decided to write a "how-to manual" for these speakers. In it, he covered subjects like how to make emotional yet ethical appeals to the listeners and how to deliver a speech most effectively; he also passed on valuable hints about how to find the "best" thing to say. Aristotle's advice summarized the best that was known in his time. Not only has his work survived through the centuries, but it also continues to be valuable today. His question-and-answer technique for finding ideas is today known as *classical invention*.

Classical invention suggests that when you are trying to get ideas for your writing, you consider different ways to approach the subject. The five common ways to view your subject, as suggested by Aristotle, include *definition, comparison, relationship, circumstance,* and *testimony.*

When you first begin to use the modern version of classical invention, you will want to move methodically through the following checklist, asking questions from each perspective to see if that point of view gives you something to say. After a little practice with this creating technique, however, finding the perspective that suits your subject may become more instinctive and you may not have to go through the entire checklist to determine which perspective will give you the best ideas.

Checklist for Classical Invention

Definition

1. How does the dictionary define _____?
2. What earlier words did _____ come from?
3. What do I mean by _____?
4. What group of things does _____ seem to belong to? How is _____ different from other things in this group?
5. What parts can _____ be divided into?
6. Did _____ mean something in the past that it doesn't mean now? If so, what? What does this former meaning tell us about how the idea grew and developed?
7. Does _____ mean something now that it didn't years ago? If so, what?
8. What other words mean approximately the same as _____?
9. What are some concrete examples of _____?
10. When is the meaning of _____ misunderstood?

Comparison

1. What is _____ similar to? In what ways?
2. What is _____ different from? In what ways?
3. _____ is superior to what? In what ways?
4. _____ is inferior to what? In what ways?
5. _____ is most unlike what? (What is it opposite to?) In what ways?
6. _____ is most like what? In what ways?

Relationship

1. What causes _____?
2. What is the purpose of _____?
3. Why does _____ happen?
4. What is the consequence of _____?
5. What comes before _____?
6. What comes after _____?

Circumstance

1. Is _____ possible or impossible?
2. What qualities, conditions, or circumstances make _____ possible or impossible?
3. Supposing that _____ is possible, is it also desirable? Why?
4. When did _____ happen previously?
5. Who has done or experienced _____?
6. Who can do _____?
7. If _____ starts, what makes it end?
8. What would it take for _____ to happen now?
9. What would prevent _____ from happening?

Testimony

1. What have I heard people say about _____?
2. Do I know any facts or statistics about _____? If so, what?
3. Have I talked with anyone about _____?
4. Do I know any famous or well-known saying (e.g. "A bird in the hand is worth two in the bush") about _____?
5. Can I quote any proverbs or any poems about _____?
6. Are there any laws about _____?
7. Do I remember any songs about _____? Do I remember anything I've read about _____ in books or magazines? Anything I've seen in a movie or on television?
8. Do I want to do any research on _____?

1. Take the questions one at a time, thoughtfully.
2. Write brief notes about the answers.
3. If you get stuck or have nothing to say, move on.
4. When you finish the questions, reread the answers and star those that are most useful in generating material, information, or energy. Make a list of the major points that emerged from the classical invention.

Take the Questions One at a Time, Thoughtfully. Following this rule is the key to using classical invention successfully. The power of classical invention comes from its relationship to common, ordinary patterns of human thought. Probably a number of times each day you discover the meaning of a new term (definition), compare one thing to another, consider relationships, decide whether to accept or reject some advertiser's claim, or weigh whether some action will or won't be possible (circumstance). Taking the questions one at a time and thinking about the answers (for example, giving more than a yes or no answer) will strengthen that particular way of examining the subject. When at work on questions in the definition section, you strengthen your mental skill of defining in exactly the same way a weight lifter or violinist will practice specific movements to develop one specific physical skill. Some of the categories may be less comfortable than some of the others. Remember that few of us can juggle, water ski, or type without a lot of practice. In addition, you may be exercising a kind of thinking that is entirely new. So be kind to yourself, and allow this new mental skill to develop at its own rate, even if it means working slowly, thoughtfully.

Write Brief Notes About the Answers. It will be necessary to have some kind of notes so that you can re-create your thinking later. Because our minds range widely—especially on a question that seems particularly stimulating and appropriate to our subject—we also need notes, outlines, and key words or phrases that will let us retrace our thoughts. Keep the notes brief—otherwise, you'll be writing long, sometimes exhaustive (and exhausting!) answers.

If You Get Stuck or Have Nothing to Say, Move On. Although it takes a reasonable amount of time to come up with an answer for every question—and sometimes several answers—there are some questions that simply don't apply, or that you don't want to deal with. For example, questions under the Testimony point of view ask what sources you've looked into. Those are useful questions if you need ideas on places to look for testimony, or if they jog your memory about something recently read or heard. Unless you intend to do research on a subject, however, it's best to use Testimony questions as memory aids and let it go at that. If other questions clearly don't apply, pass them by. Remember, though, that surprises can happen; sometimes a seemingly useless question can provide a subject that you had never dreamed you would be interested in writing about.

When You Finish, Reread and Star the Most Useful Answers.   Make a list of major points that emerged after doing classical invention. Your brief notes will have already started to reveal your thought patterns connected with each of the different categories or questions. By starring the answers that promise the most for your future writing and making a list of the major points that emerged in this creating activity, you will be in the position to take the ideas to their next level. You can follow up, perhaps by looping, to develop in more detail and depth the questions and answers that hold strong possibility for the writing you are going to do.

Take a look at how the following student example uses classical invention.

STUDENT EXAMPLE   *Classical Invention*

Topic: Going Back to School as an Adult

Definition
1. How does the dictionary define this?
   (I have to find one word for this concept. The closest I can come up with is "reentry" student.)
   Reentry: (1) a retaking possession;
   (2) a second, or new entry;
   (3) a playing card that will enable the player to regain the lead;
   * (4) the action of reentering the earth's atmosphere after *travel in space.*
2. What earlier words did _____ come from?
   Middle English *entre,* Old French *entree*—both mean "to enter."
3. What do *I* mean by _____?
   Going back to something after an absence. Doing something else in between.
4. What group of things does _____ seem to belong to?

Animals that go back to a certain place—birds migrating south in winter, salmon swimming upstream to spawn; the prodigal son in Bible story.

How is _____ different from other things in this group?

Different from animals—for them it's biological; for people, reentry is
∗ a *choice*. Different from prodigal son—reentry students didn't necessarily do anything wrong by leaving.

5. What parts can _____ be divided into?

Older students who return, after their kids are grown, to continue their original path of education; older students who return in order to change careers; younger students who took time out, or dropped
∗ out, to travel or work, etc. and are *ready to be serious about getting an education*.

6. Does _____ mean something now that it didn't years ago? If so, what?

What's new is that the term "reentry student" applies now to many students. There are enough reentry students that this group of people gets to have a category all its own.

7. What other words mean approximately the same as _____?

Return; come back; (and, making "re" words of synonyms for "en-
∗ try") repenetrate; repierce, *reprobe*.

8. What are some concrete examples of _____?

Me! (and many others)

9. When is the meaning of _____ misunderstood?

When people accept a stereotype instead of finding out the facts. Many people think the typical reentry student is in her mid-40s, has two boring, obnoxious teenage kids, and has kept her mind totally submerged in dirty dishwater since leaving school.

Comparison

1. What is _____ similar to? In what ways?

It's similar to coming home, coming back to church, attending a family reunion—returning to something larger than just yourself, some-
∗ thing that connects you to others. Being *welcomed back* into the fold.

2. What is _____ different from? In what ways?

It's different from being a rebel; from being a provincial who never ventures out of your territory; from being in a rut; from giving up.

3. _____ is superior to what? In what ways?

∗ *Superior to never having left*—leaving for "real life" gives you valuable life experiences not obtainable by perpetual students, and gives you a chance to clarify what you really want to learn. *Superior to never coming back*—reentry students are more *mature,* and they learn in more mature, goal-directed ways.

4. _____ is inferior to what? In what ways?

Inferior to going all the way through school when quite young, and thereby having the knowledge and degree to use earlier (more expertise, professionalism, status, money in one's career).

5. _____ is most unlike what? In what ways?

(I'm blanking here) Most unlike a 16-year-old college freshman; a moss-covered stone (opposite of a rolling stone); an anti-intellectual.

6. _____ is most like what? In what ways?

Most like a rolling stone; a ripe fruit; a Talmudic scholar; a knight seeking the Holy Grail; a smart cookie.

Relationship

1. What causes _____ ?

Eagerness to learn; dissatisfaction with present job and/or state of knowledge; boredom; curiosity.

2. What are the effects of _____ ?

✳ Excitement; disorientation; *fears of inadequacy; feelings of confidence;* appreciation for learning; *appreciation for one's own experience.*

3. What is the purpose of _____ ?

To get knowledge of a particular field of study; to get a degree.

4. Why does _____ happen?

It happened to me because I only discovered my real interest after spending many years doing something else.

5. What is the consequence of _____ ?

A degree; new job skills.

6. What comes before _____ ?

Leaving school; other jobs (including the job of homemaker and mother).

7. What comes after _____ ?

Staying in school; persisting; getting the degree.

Circumstance

1. Is _____ possible or impossible?

Possible.

2. What qualities, conditions, or circumstances make _____ possible or impossible?

Having a high school diploma; having decent grades your last stint in

✳ school; having time and *money* to go back to school; having good babysitters (and/or a spouse, parent, friends who'll sit and maybe even cook).

3. Supposing that _____ is possible, is it also feasible? Why?

Yes, for me. I have the time, the money (student loan), and a husband who is willing to do childcare and defrost TV dinners.

4. When did _____ happen previously?
   Never for me. For others, it's probably been happening since there have been colleges. (A guess—I don't know for how long, but certainly it *has* happened before.)
5. Who has done or experienced _____?
   Many people from all walks of life, all races, all ethnic backgrounds, both sexes.
6. Who can do _____?
   Anyone with a high school diploma, decent college grades (if they
   ∗ went to college), and the *motivation* and stamina to return to school.
7. If _____ starts, what makes it end?
   Getting the degree, or dropping out again.
8. What would it take for _____ to happen now?
   For people to want to return to school, and for them to be accepted by a school of their choice.
9. What would prevent _____ from happening?
   Thinking it's too hard to get accepted, to get financing (loans, etc.), to keep up with the work; undefined learning and/or career goals; lack of interest.

Testimony

1. What have I heard people say about _____?
   That it's sometimes hard at first; that it can take time to adjust; that in
   ∗ some ways it's *easier* to be in school as a reentry student than it was the first time around.
2. Do I know any facts or statistics about _____? If so, what?
   I don't know any exact figures, but there are many more reentry students now than there used to be. Some schools even have "over-40" programs for reentry students.
3. Have I talked with anyone about _____?
   Yes—several friends who've done it; college deans and advisers; my family.
4. Do I know any famous or well-known saying about _____?
   "It's better the second time around."
5. Can I quote any proverbs or poems about _____?
   "'Tis better to have loved and lost than never to have loved at all."
   (This isn't exactly on the subject, but if you substitute "gone to school" for "love" it sort of works.)
   "Experience is the best teacher."
   "A little bit of knowledge is a dangerous thing."
   "I am woman; I am invincible."
6. Are there any laws about _____?
   You have to pay the tuition, attend most of the classes, turn in assignments on time, take the exams.

7. Do I remember any songs about _____?
   "The Whiffenpoof Song"
   "Sweetheart of Sigma Chi"
   "Sock Hop
   "Varsity Rag"
   "Teacher's Pet"
   Any books or magazines I've read?
   Books: *Ella Price's Journal,* by Dorothy Bryant. Magazines: Probably some articles in *Ms., Redbook* (don't remember distinctly).
   Anything I've seen in a movie or on television?
   No, but I sure would like to. Maybe Shirley MacLaine would play the lead . . . ?
8. Do I want to do any research on _____?
   Not really, although maybe a few statistics on how this population has grown in the last ten or so years wouldn't hurt.

After going through the classical invention technique, the points that follow emerged most strongly.

- A reentry student has been somewhere and done something in between (something of value, although student may not see this right away).

- Going back to school as an adult is a *choice*. Kids who go to college straight from high school aren't always acting from pure, voluntary choice. Older people usually are.

- Reentry students are serious about getting an education. They usually are there for more defined reasons (having to do with career or what they wish to learn) than for ambiguous or social reasons.

- "Reentry" carries a subtle stigma, as if people have been wasting time in between, or doing nothing important, or didn't have what it took to persevere through college for four straight years in their teens and early twenties. But in fact this usually isn't true: reentry students are often more mature, more insightful, more able to learn, more able to make practical use of what they learn.

- "Reentry" means *reprobe*—to explore again, this time from a different vantage point.

- Does one reenter school as a prodigal son (sinner) or as a confident, valuable person who is shifting focus? Does the reentry student feel stigmatized or welcomed back?

- There is a value in having left school, and in coming back to school.

- Reentry students don't always appreciate their own contributions to the teacher and the rest of the students. They need to see and appreciate the value of their life experiences in a school setting.

- It's harder to be in school when an adult, in some ways, but in other ways it's easier.

- Motivation gets you through obstacles in coming back to school.

GOING BACK TO SCHOOL AS AN ADULT

Some people may think of reentry students as befuddled-looking, middle-aged women wandering dazedly around a campus, trying to keep their books in their arms and a mess of facts in their brains, while all around them younger students in designer jeans and off-the-shoulder sweatshirts cavort in the cafeteria and still manage to pull straight A's. But this is the Hollywood, Grade-B view of adults who come back to school. In truth, the situation is very different.

There are two categories of reentry students: those who never completed their undergraduate work and return to get a B.A. or B.S., and those who completed their undergraduate work, spent time out of school, and are now coming back to graduate school. The majority of adults in either category return to school not because they couldn't make it in the world—often, they have been quite successful as lawyers, homemakers, teachers, secretaries, and social workers—but because the experience of living and maturing has helped them realize what they really want to do with their lives. As one woman in her late thirties said, "When I was eighteen and starting college, all I knew was that I *didn't* want to get a blue-collar job, I *didn't* want to be different from my friends (all of whom were going to college), I *didn't* want to be out in the world yet, forced to fly before my wings were quite dry. However, I didn't

know what I *did* want—being in college was just marking time. So I dropped out—I went out into the wide world, tested my wings, fell down some, and flew some. Now here I am, ready to be serious about school."

This is a common story. Many people, who left school (or who stopped with their B.A. or B.S.) because they didn't really have the motivation to continue, find that when they return to school as adults it's by *choice*. The act of *choosing* to return to school seems to go a long way: reentry students are full of enthusiasm, motivation, stamina, and a wealth of life experience that can enrich discussions of many subjects, in many classes.

Unfortunately, reentry students don't always realize their own value. They sometimes feel too old (compared with energetic teenagers), too insignificant ("*All* I did was raise two children."), too rusty ("I haven't taken an exam in 14 years—I've forgotten how!"), and too disoriented ("How can I tell one classroom from another? They all look exactly alike!"). This "reentry shock" afflicts even very bright and competent students. It's a bit like the "culture shock" experienced by travelers returning to their own country: Suddenly the native language sounds foreign, the customs seem odd, the normal routines seem, at best, anthropological. So during this reentry period, adult students must bridge the gap between their earlier experiences of school and the nonschool, adult world they have been living in. Experiencing confusion, anxiety, and feelings of inadequacy during this period is not pleasant; but it is normal, and it eventually does pass.

One thing that helps to shorten this awkward period is for reentry students to realize that for all they have yet to learn, there's a lot they already know. This knowledge isn't limited to facts, either. Reentry students tend also to know:

1. *The relative importance of things.* For example, they can now tolerate getting a B rather than an A. The "failure to be perfect" is no longer a cause for thoughts of the Foreign Legion.

2. *How to learn what they don't yet know.* Teenagers don't have the experience to evaluate what is and isn't important to them. This can make being in school an overwhelming experience; young students may *accept* all the information (and end up feeling stuffed or confused) or *reject* it all (and end up feeling angry and isolated). Adult students, however, have lived through, and survived, real-life events—from losing loved ones through getting the mortgage paid. This experience of surviving the normal vicissitudes of life can make adult students more able to take in and evaluate new information.

3. *How to pursue a goal.* Nobody forces adults to come back to school; reentry students are inner-directed. They already have some idea of what they want and how to get it. School isn't molding shapeless clay—it's helping the adults refine and challenge their already developed notions and fill in the holes.

4. *How to satisfy themselves, instead of worrying about what others think of them.* Teenagers inevitably care so much about how others see them. While this preoccupation never goes away entirely, by adulthood it has receded into a more realistic perspective. Adults tend to be more concerned about whether an activity satisfies them than about whether it gets the approval of someone else. This inner-directedness makes it easier to be in a classroom, to risk offering the wrong answer, to study with interest, to write papers, and, in general, to have the experience of becoming educated.

So adults who go back to school have both a harder time and an easier time. And they enrich not only themselves by being back in school but also the people around them—by their experience, their sense of priorities, and their ability to hone in on their goal. Reentry students have nothing to be ashamed of; they are not prodigal children. We do ourselves a service by welcoming them back into the fold.

WRITING *Classical Invention*

1. Using the Checklist for Classical Invention, explore one of these subjects to see what you have to say about it.

   Independence
   Loneliness
   Hunger

2. Using the Checklist for Classical Invention, explore how addiction to exercise is like other forms of addiction.

WRITING *Starting an Essay*

1. Review all the prewriting you've done up to this point on bicycling or on physical fitness. Choose one focal point and determine an appropriate audience for an essay on one of the topics. Draft the essay.
2. Review your notes (collected from exercises in Chapter 1) on your writing habits and your observations of others writing in public. Do three five-minute loops on "writing." Then try cubing, track switching, or classical invention on a major point that appears in one center of gravity statement. Finally, draft an essay on writing for new students planning to enroll at your college.

CHAPTER 5

Enhanced Creating Techniques

The simple creating techniques—like listing, brainstorming, and chaining—and the expanded creating techniques—like looping, cubing, track switching, and classical invention—are multi-purpose ways to discover what you want to say. They are like a coordinated wardrobe; you can mix and match the creating activities for different audiences and different kinds of writing, to achieve various results. The following two creating techniques, however, are *not* designed for *all* kinds of writing. They are designed specifically for the occasion when you have time to do informal or formal research.

CREATING TECHNIQUES FOR RESEARCHERS

Let's say you know a week ahead of time that your final exam is going to be an essay on a particular subject. You can, of course, use any creating technique with which you are already familiar to prepare. *Noticing Inside Purpose,* however, will help you take full advantage of those seven days to get new ideas.

What if you have a research paper to do? What creating technique will help you know what you want to write about? *Reading and Researching* is a creating technique that will help you focus on potential ideas every time you read or do research.

These discovery methods are called *enhanced creating techniques* because they heighten and intensify normal activities like noticing (just looking around) and researching (finding things in the library) and result in unexpected new thoughts and ideas. With these enhanced creating techniques you can be productive much sooner than ever in the past; things will start "coming together" in ways that both surprise and encourage you.

NOTICING INSIDE PURPOSE

If you were building a birdhouse, someone once said, you would have more thoughts about carpentering than you would if you were putting together a stamp collection. This is how the human mind works—where there is a particular purpose or focus, the mind pulls in thoughts, sights, ideas, memories, and connections that are related to that purpose. The purpose—the focus—serves as a magnet for what your mind and eye notice. You can deliberately use this tendency of the mind to your advantage, getting ideas for something you want to write.

Noticing Inside Purpose works like this: imagine that your assignment is to write about the economy of a Third World country. You would set up Noticing Inside Purpose as part of the creating stage for the assignment. Setting up involves simply writing the purpose of your assignment at the top of the page. Over time, you fill up the page with things you

Tips for Noticing Inside Purpose

1. Buy a small (pocket-size) notebook and label it "Noticing Inside Purpose Notebook."

2. Write the purpose and subject of your notices (the subject of your future writing) at the top of the page. (Important: This is the purpose of the assignment—"Write about the economy of a Third World Country"—, not the focus of the paper you will write later—"The economy of Brazil is weaker than that of Argentina for three main reasons"—. You won't know the focus of the paper itself until after you've done some prewriting.)

3. Keep a running record of everything you notice that is connected with the subject on which you are going to write.

4. Every time you notice something new connected with this subject or assignment—or have an idea associated with it— turn to the next page in your notebook and record the observation or idea.

5. At least once before beginning to draft, deliberately go on a "noticing expedition." Have as your express intention to observe and watch your subject and to take notes of your watching and observation.

notice as you go about your daily activities. If your subject is Brazil, for example, your list might include such things as:

1. I noticed two articles in the newspaper today about the economy in Argentina and Brazil. (I've cut these out to read later.)

2. I noticed there was a guy from Brazil in my geometry class. I've set up a time to meet with him tomorrow to discuss the economy of his country.

3. I noticed today, much to my surprise, that the school library subscribes to a Brazilian newspaper in English!

This creating technique allows you to pay deliberate attention to and keep a record of those things that usually go unnoticed. When you have a particular purpose to accomplish, you naturally and automatically notice things connected with that purpose that you never would have noticed otherwise.

You can use Noticing Inside Purpose intentionally. Set aside a set amount of time on a specified day to go out noticing or observing your subject, and then record your observations on paper or in your journal. When you set out to notice things that are related to your subject, you will be surprised just how much there is to see.

This creating technique lets you hold onto observations in written form—observations that you otherwise might lose record of. The notes serve as a structure to hold the particles of information, ideas, plans, and possibilities for this piece of writing.

WRITING   *Noticing Inside Purpose*

1. Practice this creating technique even before you are assigned a paper in advance. You will be astonished at how many things seem to show up when you deliberately focus on one particular topic. Choose a purpose like one of these.

   Finding out how to save on energy bills

   Discovering what the current styles are in clothes

   Learning about Middle Eastern cooking

   Knowing what stocks are hot now on the stock market

   Start keeping your Noticing Inside Purpose notebook, even though you are not planning to write a paper on this subject. You'll be surprised how many times you see and hear something about this subject—just because you have set yourself a purpose that focuses what passes through your awareness.

2. Use this technique for a paper you need to write for another class.

READING AND RESEARCHING

You already know that *reading and researching* are necessary activities for many types of writing, particularly research papers and technical reports.

You may, however, be surprised to think of these common activities as techniques for the creating stage of the writing process, not as something you do prior to the writing process. Once you start thinking of Reading and Researching as part of the writing process, your mind will start connecting ideas for the writing long before you sit down to draft.

To set up Reading and Researching as a technique, put your reading and researching (as well as the note taking that is part of it) into an overall framework of "writing the paper." To do this, ask yourself questions—which you will answer twice—immediately before doing the reading and researching, and then again afterwards. The Reading and Researching technique uses questions like these:

Questions to Answer Before Reading and Researching

1. What is my specific purpose in doing this reading and researching?
2. How is the reading and researching I am about to do a part of writing the paper or report?

Questions to Answer Immediately After Reading and Researching

1. What specific ideas do I now have for writing my paper?
2. What did I come upon in the Reading and Researching period that will probably be the most valuable in my writing?
3. What are points/facts/ideas I got out of this reading and researching for my writing?

Tips for Reading and Researching

1. Consider each time period you spend reading and doing research as a distinct creating session for the paper or report you are going to write.
2. For each Reading and Research session, write answers to both the advance and the concluding questions.
3. Keep a running log for each Reading and Researching session with the date and questions noted above.

The power in Reading and Researching is that, from the start, you relate each Reading and Researching period to writing the paper. Each Reading and Researching period will yield different types of information, some more valuable than others; you identify the information that is most valuable. You may not hit the jackpot every time you read or do research, but putting these activities inside a creating technique will ensure that you get the most out of every session.

WRITING Reading and Researching

1. Think about how unfocused and time-consuming your library research may have been in the past. Then, to prove to yourself, even before you have a research paper to do, that there has to be a better way, do one Reading and Research session on a topic like one of these:

   A current career interest

   Sports in the 1800s

   A place you would enjoy going on vacation during spring break

2. Use Reading and Researching to prepare a laboratory report in a science, computer, or engineering class—even though all your research is going to be done in the laboratory or in your room (rather than the library). How does this creating technique work with material that is in your text or other supplementary sources?

SUMMARY OF CREATING TECHNIQUES

You have now practiced several distinctly different creating techniques, and you may already have a favorite among them,—one that works best when you are searching for ideas. You will certainly have noticed the ways the techniques are different. Some work like a fishing expedition—you lower a net and catch whatever thoughts you have on the subject. Some work like a reminder or checklist to help you think up things you already knew but had forgotten. Some let you invent something new by rubbing together thoughts, ideas, and information you already had, to come up with new combinations, insights, and relationships. Some work best when you don't have a single thing to say; others work best when you already have several ideas on a subject and need to decide which is the most promising. Some of the techniques are unstructured and loose; some are tightly controlled. No single one is inherently better than another.

Learning what each technique will do for you may be trial and error at the beginning, but as you become more and more familiar with the ways to create, you will develop a feel for which one to use when. The unique mix of subject, your knowledge about the subject, your mindset on a particular day, and many other variables will affect which creating technique works best for you for a given writing assignment.

WRITING *Double Creating Techniques*

1. Taking the same subject through more than one creating technique is an excellent way to see which techniques you find most beneficial for which kinds of subjects. To get practice in knowing the characteristics of various creating techniques, choose one topic from groups A and B below and run each through two different creating techniques. Be ready to discuss with the class what you discovered in this process, what one technique did that the other didn't, which you found more beneficial, or what idea(s) you came up with that you could write on if you were required to do so.

A. *Choose One*	*Choose Two*
Getting along with (parents, children)	Cubing
Finding work	Looping
Problems of growing up	Classical Invention
What you want in a relationship	Chaining
Why courtesy is vanishing	Track Switching
A landscape that appeals to you	Reading and Researching

B. *Choose One*	*Choose Two*
Things wrong with holidays	Cubing
A skill you have and are proud of	Looping
A problem you had and how you solved it	Classical Invention
	Noticing Inside Purpose
Ways people act that you don't like	Reporter's Formula
A movie you just saw	Brainstorming
How reading opens doors	Writing a List
Soap operas	

2. Review one of the essays you have drafted to this point. Identify where you need more material to flesh out the ideas in the essay. Use at least two creating techniques to help you generate more material for the essay.

PART 2   *From Creating to Drafting*

As you continue in your writing process, this section will help you to

- define in detail your audiences for writing
- consider purposes for writing
- move from prewriting on a topic to drafting a paper
- refine your focus through a thesis statement
- organize effectively for readers through the form of your papers
- review principles of paragraph structure and function
- clarify paragraphs in your writing

CHAPTER 6

Writing for an Audience

As we noted in Chapter 2, knowing precisely who will be reading your writing makes it easier to write. If you can visualize a single person you would like to entertain, enlighten, inform, engage, anger, or persuade, you can be more effective in reaching your goal. Even if you don't know a specific person in the audience you're writing for, try to imagine a person reading your paper. Writing to that person will help you focus your ideas and energies.

FOCUS ON A TARGET AUDIENCE

Often, writers ignore this advice and write to a faceless group—classmates, teachers, sports fans and others. Sometimes writers never even think of an audience and simply write to "anyone who might want to read this paper." The problem with writing to such general audiences is that you tend to scatter your efforts broadly rather than focus them. It is crucial to note who your *specific audience* is at the outset (or to invent an audience if the choice is yours) because your audience will determine your approach to the subject.

Just suppose that you were writing an essay to inform your readers about the vacation attractions of the town you live in. If you live in a place like San Francisco or Las Vegas, the essay may well be easier to write. But any town can be appealing—if you bother to work out the appeal for a specific audience. What would the differences be in how you approached the subject if your audience were composed of any of the following?

people your own age

people already living in your hometown

people with small children

out-of-state visitors

foreign travelers

retired people

If you were writing for someone your own age, you would likely emphasize the things you like to do; you could probably count on your audience liking these things too. You could also be more informal; the words you used might sound like your normal conversation with friends. However, think of how differently you would write the essay if you were praising your hometown as a vacation spot for foreign travelers, as contrasted to the way you would write it for people who already live there. Foreign visitors would need more background, directions, and reasons to choose your hometown over a hundred other places they could visit while in America. If you were writing for people who already lived in your hometown, however, you could skip much of the description, location, and directions and instead write about the places to go and things to do that even residents might have overlooked. For this audience, your purpose would be to write about the possibilities "right in their own backyard."

Not only the approach and purpose in writing are influenced by the audience, but also the content of the writing itself—what points you make, what examples you use. Deciding who your audience is gives you a place to start when you begin to write.

WRITING *Working with Audience*

As we talked about earlier, think of writing an essay that would describe your town as an attractive vacation spot. Make a list of things you would talk about for each of the following audiences:

people your own age

people already living in your hometown

people with small children

out-of-state visitors

foreign travelers

any other group you can think of

When you finish your six lists, look at the ways each list differs from the others because of the specific readers. Which audience seems easiest to write for? Which is hardest? Why? Which would you most enjoy writing for? Why?

USING THE AUDIENCE TO SHAPE AN ESSAY

How can considering the makeup of your audience in real detail shape what you write? Let's take a look.

Four Audiences, Four Writing Shapes

Naomi was asked to write four articles on gardening, with four different audiences. Here are the facts about her four target audiences:

Prevention: America's Leading Health Magazine
Four-color, journal-format monthly magazine aimed at health-conscious adults. Topics center on nutrition, fighting and healing illness through natural means, and keeping fit. Sample articles include "Surprising Facts about Snoring and Health" and "The 25 Top Superfoods." Length of article: About 1,500 words.

Parade: The Sunday Newspaper Magazine
Four-color weekly tabloid aimed at adults reading the Sunday paper (*Parade* is an insert in many Sunday papers nationwide). Topics relate to news (especially celebrities) and entertainment. Sample articles include "Jerry Lewis: Sometimes He Cries" and "Sex in a Permissive Society." Length of article: About 1,500 words.

Cricket: The Magazine for Children
Four-color monthly magazine aimed at children ages 6–12. Focus is on nonfiction and fiction. Sample articles include "Listen to a Book" and "Miniature Tropical Houses for You to Make." Length of article: 200–2,000 words.

Horticulture: The Magazine of American Gardening
Four-color monthly magazine aimed at experienced gardeners. Topics focus on horticultural advice, gardens of people around the country, and new ways to look at gardening. Sample articles include "Gardening on the Rocks" and "Northern Know-How." Length of article: 500–5,000 words.

Why Does Audience Matter?

Now, let's study the pieces Naomi wrote, looking at how targeting the audience helps her pull material together from creating. Depending on who the audience will be, certain facts and ideas from creating appear in the drafts of the article, while others do not.

STUDENT EXAMPLE *Article for Prevention Readers*

Here is how Naomi used looping for an article on gardening for *Prevention* magazine.

Topic: Gardening and *Prevention*

Loop 1

Gardening I know something about—but what is being prevented? I found a copy of this magazine in the library, and it's full of articles about what to do to prevent, or deal with, sickness—how to be or stay or get healthy, using vitamins and exercise and organic foods and stuff like that. So I guess what's being prevented is sickness. But how is this magazine's angle different from medical advice? It seems to have something to do with its readers wanting to be careful about what happens to their bodies. This includes what they eat, being careful about what they eat. So the link between gardening and prevention is that if you do your own gardening, you can have control over what goes into your body.

Center of Gravity Sentence: *Doing your own gardening means you have control over what you put into your body.*

Loop 2

Who cares about having control over what they eat? People who are skeptical of what other people claim is good for them. Maybe they've been "burned"—maybe their bodies don't react well to adulterated chemical foods. Maybe they've paid a lot of money to doctors and hospitals and feel angry about it—and are going to "take matters into their own hands." Or maybe they were sick and now they seriously want to get well. Or they're well and want to stay that way. Maybe they feel "the world is too much with us," that the bad things about civilization—noise pollution, air pollution, food pollution—are getting to them, and they want to create a better life for themselves. But they haven't all given up their city jobs to go live in the woods. Lots of them must work right in the heart of civilization—that's where most of the jobs are in cities. Look at any downtown of a major city, you see tall buildings, concrete sidewalks, and so on. A tree or two planted here and there, but the general color scheme is not green. Whoops, am I getting way off the track? What's all this got to do with gardening and prevention? Civilization—cities—downtowns—in the heart of urban life—oh yes! What if the reader of *Prevention* cares about keeping healthy but lives in an "unhealthy" environment? How can such a person have control over his/her own body, own life? And what does this have to do with gardening? Maybe the size of the garden doesn't matter. Maybe the size of the crop yield doesn't matter. Maybe health has some thing to do with the act, the process of gardening. If so, then I guess gardening could be done just about anywhere.

Center of gravity sentence: *Health has something to do with the process of gardening.*

Loop 3

It isn't just what you eat from your garden that keeps a person healthy; it's also the process of interacting with the soil and with what grows from it. Gardening is good exercise. (I remember how mom used to tell dad, "You go jogging! I have my garden to work out in.") All that bending, rising, kneeling, lifting—natural aerobics! And it's relaxing, too—it's hard to garden at breakneck speed. There's really no gardening in the fast lane—it's slow work. Something nice about slowing down that way—after a while the bird sounds seem louder, and the traffic sounds get softer. You can feel the sun on your back. And the colors of the flowers are so gorgeous. And the smells! I always end up breathing in more deeply around gardens—of course, all that good oxygen they breathe out! So relaxing. So—so healthy.

Center of gravity sentence: *Gardening is good exercise, and it's relaxing, too.*

After Naomi had done the looping and a discovery draft, she asked herself questions such as these about her audience.

How do I see the audience that reads *Prevention* magazine?

What kind of language and vocabulary will be particularly appropriate to them?

What kind of examples would fit the reading level and specific interests of this audience?

Are any explanations of the material necessary for this particular audience? If so, what kind?

What aspects of the subject would be most interesting to this particular group of readers?

How much development of my basic idea will I need for this particular audience?

In response to her first question—the nature of her audience for this essay—Naomi made the following assessment of the people likely to read *Prevention*:

> They will be mostly adults interested in and committed to good health. They want to be self-reliant. They are interested more in natural than chemical health/medicine alternatives. They may include retired people, middle-aged to elderly, although certainly not exclusively. This audience will be familiar with stress and interested in stress-reduction alternatives.

Now, whether her assessment is completely accurate or not, it was extremely valuable in guiding her thinking as she drafted her article. Using her description of her readers, look through the draft of the article for *Prevention* to answer the other questions Naomi asked about her audience (jot your responses in your journal).

GARDENING IS GOOD FOR YOU

Picture a middle-aged couple in their garden. The sun beats down on their orchard, their trees bearing almost-ripe oranges, plums, and apples. Tomato plants curl up thick stakes, and snow peas ($1.99 per pound at the supermarket!) inch their way up a trellis of string. The couple, holding hands, pause a moment to inhale the sweet aroma of rich soil, newly watered plants, and fragrant flowers. Then they straighten up slightly, as if actually nourished by their surroundings, even without having eaten the fruits of their labors.

"It's a wonderful life," they agree.

Wealthy retirees? Farmers checking out their acreage? Not exactly. This couple lives in a one-bedroom apartment in a high-rise condominium. Their "orchard" and vegetables and flowers are all dwarf varieties planted in containers on their 4 × 10 foot terrace.

Why do they do it? Because they are committed to being and staying healthy.

How can gardening help keep you healthy? Here are some of the ways:

1. Food. Home-grown food is better for you. Since you can control exactly what goes into the soil and onto the plants, you can make sure that you add nothing that goes against nature. Supermarket produce, on the other hand, is often grown with excessive chemical help and is picked prematurely to withstand the long trip to market. When you grow your own, you can harvest it when it's ripe and not a moment before.

2. Exercise. Maybe you like to do aerobics with Jane Fonda at 8:00 AM, and maybe you don't. If not, there are real-life activities that are just as good (maybe better). When you think

about it, gardening offers a variety of exercise positions—stooping, kneeling, bending, rising, lifting, reaching and, as a result, deep breathing!

3. Purer air. Outside of our homes we may be helpless against air pollution; but our homes are our castles, and we can ensure that around our homes we get clean air to breathe. Not by buying a negative ionizer, but by planting plants. Remember, plants breathe in carbon dioxide (which we breathe out) and breathe out oxygen (which we breathe in). And their oxygen smells wonderful, too!

4. Relaxation. Most of us are busy so much of the time. We move so fast. Well, gardening is definitely a slow-lane activity. You can rush it, but why bother? For one thing, slowing down is physically and mentally good for you. Medical studies prove that the ability to relax has physiological benefits; yoga practitioners have made this claim for thousands of years.

For another thing, slowing down by gardening is a little bit like taking a vacation. Your mind stops worrying, and you begin to notice things you hadn't seen before: a browning leaf lying on a stone; an ant crawling up a twig; a flower like an open hand that only last week was a tight fist. The ordinary wonders of nature come into view. Life seems less boring, more full of magic.

So when you think about planting a garden, think about your health. Then pick up your shovel and dig in.

Did you discover as you read and analyzed her article that Naomi tailored her article to the designated audience? Let's go on to look at how the other audiences reshape Naomi's thinking and writing on this topic.

How a New Audience Changes the Writing

What happens when the same subject is the focus of an article for a completely different kind of magazine?

STUDENT EXAMPLE *Article for* Parade *Readers*

Here is the cubing that Naomi did for the article about gardening she planned to write for the Sunday-supplement magazine.

Topic: A Garden

Describe It

A garden is an area of dirt with plants growing in it. These plants can be edible (fruit, vegetables, herbs) or ornamental (flowers, trees, shrubs, etc.). Gardens are planted by someone for some purpose, whether food, beauty, convenient exercise, or whatever. They can be extremely colorful (red tulips, pink azaleas, etc.) or kind of mono-tone (all green leafy vegetables). They can be tall or low. They can be huge (acres and acres) or tiny (a little balcony full of potted plants). They can also be a recreational area.

Compare It

A garden is like a house (for gophers, snails, and others). Also like a painting (all those colors—especially from a distance, it looks like a living canvas—especially by a French impressionist painter like Monet or Renoir). Like a lake (smooth green lawn). Like a factory (nature producing all that growth). Like a warehouse (bulbs store flowers for next year). Like a piece of writing (first it's an idea, then it's something tangible). Like Hawaii (well, maybe).

A garden is not like: a wilderness (someone deliberately planted it); a zoo (animals are there, but they aren't caged); a refrigerator (the food doesn't need to be kept refrigerated while it's still attached to the roots); a city of concrete and steel; a nine-to-five job; an exercise machine (you get natural exercise working in it); smog (it smells great, and the oxygen is really good for you).

Associate It

I haven't planted elaborate gardens on my own, but I've read about gardening (I love to look at pictures of flowers), and I've visited many parks, and some botanical gardens. And my mother did a really nice garden—I remember her all rosy-cheeked, with her hands so brown I had to tell her to wash under her fingernails! Sure wish I had time to plant a garden—I'm too busy (or lazy?) right now, but I sure do love to look at flowers, and to be around growing things. Something about the air they breathe out? I just always love the feel of it—like I'm a part of Nature too. Like a cousin to a tree (not a poison sumac tree, though—whoops, that's a plant, not a tree). Also, when you pass a house with a garden out front, it's like a big sign that says "Somebody who cares about this place lives here."

Analyze It

Dig up the ground so the dirt isn't packed down hard. Adding bits of organic stuff—amendments—helps soften the soil. Which helps water drain out, so the plant's roots don't get parched, or soggy. After you have gotten the soil ready you level it. Then you dig some holes (for bulbs, or transplants), or you sow seeds. Then you cover it all up with more soil, and add fertilizer (plant food). Then you water the plant. Then you have to take care of your garden regularly—watering, fertilizing, weeding—and harvesting!

Apply It

You can eat your garden. Fresh food is the best! No preservatives or chemical junk. Also, big agribusinesses that supply supermarkets and places like that pick the food before it's ripe (so it doesn't get rotten by the time it reaches the store). Premature picking affects the taste (as I know from experience, when I visited my aunt's friend in Nebraska and ate corn on the cob right off the stalk. Talk about sweet!) Other uses: A garden is good for attracting animals (kids like gophers, and ladybugs are fun). A garden is a terrific place to goof off—swinging in a hammock tied to a big tree (two trees). Kids wading in cheap plastic pools, or running through the sprinklers (mmm—the feel of soft grass on bare feet!). Gardens can be used for privacy (hedges as fences). For teaching kids about the wonders of nature, and about ecology.

Argue For or Against It

Who could argue against gardens? Gardens are a mainstay of modern life—and of ancient life. Once upon a time this whole earth was a garden. Where would we be without the Garden of Eden? And how about the Hanging Gardens of Babylon? Without gardens, we'd all be in concrete city. We'd be breathing carbon monoxide from car exhausts. We'd be philistines, cave folk (but they did have gardens—in the wild). If we had no gardens, we'd have no food—no onions to go on the Big Macs, no corn to pop, no cherries to sing "Life Is Just a Bowl of . . ." about. To be without gardens is to live in some futuristic nightmare. Gardens are wonderful. I say, let's have more gardens! and more! and more. . . .

How will the audience of *Parade* shape the writing of this article? Naomi's notes on this audience:

The readers of *Parade* will most likely be homeowners, regular people, trying to relax on a Sunday, reading the papers, the funnies, the gossip column. I will want to give them information, but in an entertaining way. Relaxation and enjoyment should be the central theme for this audience. I think I'll focus on aspects of the senses—things that will immediately appeal.

Use Naomi's analysis of the *Parade* audience to answer other questions about her article as you read it:

1. What kind of language and vocabulary will be particularly appropriate to this audience?
2. What kind of examples would fit the reading level and specific interests of this audience?

3. Are any explanations of the material necessary for this particular audience? If so, what kind?

4. What aspects of the subject would be most interesting to this particular group of readers?

5. How much development of the basic idea will be necessary for this particular audience?

FOR A SENSUOUS SUMMER VACATION—PLANT A GARDEN

Now that it's almost spring, summer will be coming soon enough. It's never too early to start planning your garden. After all, you need something to hold up your hammock.

Imagine yourself horizontal for the summer. Gently rocking in the warm breeze, a glass of iced lemonade in hand, you can hear your heartbeat laying back: "Lub-ah!-dub, lub-ah!-dub." You lie there in the shade of your sycamore/eucalyptus/pine tree and think contentedly, "This is the life."

Haven't got time to wait for the tree to grow to shading height? Then take up lying down directly on the grass. A super summer activity, grass lying is nevertheless harder than it looks. You are constantly distracted by the soft, brushy texture of grass against your unclothed parts; by the almost edible aroma of new-mown lawn; by the flirty calls of birds out for a lark, as well as by the annoyingly joyful shrieks of children running through the sprinkler or splashing in the plastic wading pool. Really, it's enough to make you lose your place in the latest best seller.

Flowers are a distraction, too. They really get in the way of your ability to keep focused on stock reports or final exams. They pose a double-whammy allure: fragrances that outdo the perfumes of even the most expensive stores, and colors that no color TV can duplicate. It's hard to be a good worrier if roses, lilacs, and jasmine are close by. And there's nothing like looking up from your novel set in exotic Bora Bora and catching sight of vivid purple fuschias, saucy yellow daisies, and bright pink azaleas, to make you think that you, too, lead an exotic life.

Don't forget about that other sense—taste. Summer is a good time for eating, and if you were smart enough to plant something edible, now's the time to reach over—slowwwwwly—and pluck your harvest. Anyone for a ripe peach, or plum, or cherries? Run a little hose-water over your pickings and then pop them in your mouth. Yum. (It does take a little bit of effort to stone plums and cherries; yup, this kind of exertion is the pits.)

So why pay all that money to go to Hawaii or Mexico or Bora Bora, when you can have enough sensuous experiences to satisfy all your senses right in your own backyard?

Why not start planning a garden today?

(On second thought, maybe better make it tomorrow.)

STUDENT EXAMPLE *Article for* Cricket *Readers*

Using the same cubing technique as for *Parade,* Naomi extracted different elements—elements that she thought would appeal to children—for an article in *Cricket* magazine.

> What are the characteristics of this audience?
>
> The readers of *Cricket* are kids—ages 6–12 or so. Kids like to do things. So I'll write about something they can do. Kids also like to have fun. It's fun to make something new out of something you already have—especially food. So I'll take an idea from my cubing and my discovery draft and write about planting seeds left over from a meal. I'll also make things funny whenever I can.

How did this audience shape her writing? Let's consider once again:

1. What kind of language and vocabulary will be particularly appropriate to this audience?
2. What kind of examples would fit the reading level and specific interests of this audience?
3. Are any explanations of the material necessary for this particular audience? If so, what kind?
4. What aspects of the subject would be most interesting to this particular group of readers?
5. How much development of the basic idea will be necessary for this particular audience?

PLANT FOOD SEEDS FOR FUN

Did you know that you can turn yesterday's breakfast, lunch, or supper into a brand-new plant? No, you can't make a pizza plant or a hot-dog plant. But you can make new plants from the seeds of oranges, lemons, grapefruits, avocados, and other fruits. You can also use carrots, sweet potatoes, and other root vegetables (vegetables that grow under the ground) to make cuttings (pieces of the plant that will grow into whole plants).

You will need the following ingredients:

Seeds and/or cuttings

Container for planting

Container for rooting (use only with cuttings and avocado seeds)

Soil

Toothpicks (use only with cuttings and avocado seeds)

Water

Planting Seeds

1. Collect seeds from your favorite fruits. Wash them off, and let them dry.
2. Get a container for planting the seed in. This can be a store-bought flowerpot, or a food container that you have washed clean. (Yogurt, milk, and cottage cheese containers work especially well.) If you use a food container, take a fork and punch a few holes in the bottom so that extra water can drain out. (Plants don't like too much water—they get soggier than you do when you stay in the bath too long.)
3. Put some soil in the container. Not dirt—soil. Soil is dirt that has really healthy nutrients in it (like vitamins; in fact, soil is dirt that has taken its vitamins). Ask a parent to buy you some—you can get small plastic bags of the stuff in lots of places, even in supermarkets.
4. Use a pencil or your finger to make a hole in the soil to put each seed in. Don't crowd the seeds—each container should have one seed (okay, okay—two). Make the planting hole about one inch deep (down to your first or second knuckle).
5. Place the seed in the hole. Cover up the hole with soil. Press the soil down firmly with the palm of your hand (but don't squoosh).
6. Get some water from the faucet—cool water, not cold or hot. Pour the water into the soil, a little bit at a time. The seed will be thirsty and will drink the water right down. You can see the water disappear into the soil. This means that the seed is getting ready to grow roots soon.

Planting Cuttings

1. Get a container to hold the cutting. You can use any kind of container, but the most fun is to use one that is transparent (see through), so you can watch the roots form.
2. Fill the container with cool water almost to the top.
3. Stick three or four toothpicks into the side of the cutting or the avocado pit. (Space them all around—don't put them all next to each other.) This will look like a kind of fan, and this fan will keep the top of the cutting out of the water, and the bottom of the cutting in the water.
4. Keep the container in a light place, like a window sill. When you can see roots that are so long they can wiggle, your seedling (new, tiny plant) is ready for transplanting (to be planted someplace else).
5. Now, follow the directions for planting seeds.

Caring for Your New Plant

Your seedling needs plenty of sun and water. Put the container on a window sill, or someplace else that gets a lot of sun. Water the plant every other day—baby plants are almost as thirsty as baby people. In a little while—a few weeks or even less—you will see something green start to come out of the top. This is the shoot (the first growth). It has two roundish-shaped seed leaves. After that, the true leaves will appear. The shape of these leaves depends on what kind of plant you have planted.

Once the plant has a few true leaves, it is ready to be transplanted into an outdoor garden. Or you can keep it indoors in a sunny place. (Transplant it into a bigger container if it starts to get too big.)

It's too bad that these seeds and cuttings won't produce fruits or vegetables you can eat. But they will produce beauty—and fun.

STUDENT EXAMPLE *Article for* Horticulture *Readers*

Finally, Naomi used the same cubing technique for a third time, this time for an article for *Horticulture*. Here, the audience is made up of serious, nonprofessional gardeners. When asking herself questions about the audience of *Horticulture,* this is how Naomi saw the audience shaping her article:

What is the audience for *Horticulture* like?

Experienced gardeners, although probably not professionals. More likely devoted hobbyists. They don't need to be told what gardening is all about—they know the basics. In fact, they would be bored with the basics. They need a new twist on an old theme. Something to catch their interest.

What language and vocabulary is likely to strike this audience's fancy?

How about nature-as-painter imagery and words? Like decorating, monochromatic, colors, Picasso, brushstrokes, canvas, hint, contours, shapes, still life.

What examples might be fresh for these readers?

From art—artists by name, periods of art, comparing gardener to artist, sculptor. The basic image of gardens as canvas on which to paint, with bulbs.

What particular aspects of subject should be covered?

Decide on color scheme for garden; decide on design scheme for garden (formal vs. spontaneous, straight vs. curved). Then, how to plan to produce this picture in the garden.

Now let's see how her analysis translates into her fourth piece on gardening.

BULBS PAINT A BRIGHT PICTURE FOR SPRING

It's just about spring—the time for Nature to get out her paintbrush. But why remain just an admiring bystander? You can join in with a palette of your own: bulbs.

Bulbs have many virtues: They are easy to plant, they don't need extra-special treatment, they flower for years to come, and they offer a wide spectrum of colors. Bulbs will help you do some exterior decorating—match your garden to your house, your mood, or simply your personal likes.

Consider a monochromatic effect (all one color, or shades of one color) in white, pink, peach and salmon, yellow, red, purple and lavender, or blue. (Consider Picasso's Blue Period for inspiration.) If you want color-coordinated combinations, try yellow and orange, or pink and red—or the striking lavender and orange (think of Kandinsky). Or add more colors still—use spontaneous brushstrokes à la the French Impressionists—a dab of yellow daffodils here, a cluster of red tulips there, a hint of purple violas in the underbrush, a soupçon of green gladioli off to the side—and the canvas breathes.

A bulb garden, unlike a painting, has three dimensions. The shape of the planting bed is up to you; it depends only on your taste and the contours of your land. If you like formality, try neat beds of tulips, irises, hyacinths, and anemones. If you prefer a more spontaneous look, naturalize your bulbs by tossing them, then planting them wherever they land. Bulbs good for naturalizing include narcissus, tulip, amaryllis, hardy cyclamen, and crocus (what is spring without the first crocus?). Or you can choose a middle way—planned but not rigid. Consider arcs, curves, and free-flowing shapes. (Remember Art Nouveau. Remember how Nature has no straight lines.)

Once you have decided on which bulbs to plant, get your site ready. The ground will need to be softened up, especially if it has just thawed out after a winter frost. Add some compost or other organic amendment, and dig it in to about two inches. This will enrich the soil and help it drain well. Good drainage is crucial for bulbs.

Next dig the planting holes and put fertilizer into them directly. Bone meal is good; so is superphosphate. Putting the fertilizer right into the holes helps the bulbs' roots reach their food easily.

After planting the bulbs, cover the holes with soil, tamp the soil down firmly, and water well. Really well—the water needs to reach all the way down to the roots. Thereafter, water regularly, waiting until the surrounding ground is dry. It will take a little while for the leaves to emerge, but once they do you know the flowers aren't far behind. Before long you will be surrounded by a colorful array of flowers for your garden and your table.

Anyone for a still life?

AN AFTERWORD: WHAT DIFFERENCE DOES AUDIENCE MAKE?

You may never wish to write four—or even two—articles on the same subject. But the illustrations presented here show how different—and how uniquely appropriate to the particular readers—two pieces of writing on the same subject can be when you use the audience as a magnet to pull your ideas into a coherent, cohesive shape. The more you identify the specifics of your audience, the more the audience will shape your writing for you.

WRITING   *Working with Audience*

1. Pick a subject from the list on the left and three different audiences from the list on the right. Imagine that you are going to write an essay on this subject for each of these different audiences. Make as complete a list as you possibly can of the ways the audience will shape your essay—discuss words that might be most appropriate for each audience, the particular aspect of the subject that might appeal most to each audience, what examples would be the strongest for each audience, and the characteristics of the audience itself that would be valuable for you to be aware of before you start writing.

Subject (Pick One)	Audience (Pick Three)
Bringing up children	A children's magazine
Being healthy	Your local newspaper
Learning a new subject	The Sunday supplement magazine in your newspaper
Learning how to do something new	Your church newsletter/bulletin
Dating	A specialty magazine—e.g., *Sports Illustrated, Travel, Prevention, Bon Appetit,* etc.
Divorce	
Celebrating holidays	
Action-packed vacations	The people who watch the local talk show on television in your town
Participating in sports	A civic or service club
Cooking	A magazine for retired people
Managing money	A magazine for people over 40
	A magazine like *Ultra* for the very rich

2. A good way to practice adapting your writing to a specific audience is to write about one topic for two or three different audiences. Pick a common object in the room you're now in. Now, in one paragraph, describe that object to (1) a four-year-old, (2) a junior-high schooler, (3) a classmate. Be sure to include adequate and appropriate detail so that each reader can visualize the object.

3. Practice audience adaptation by telling a brief story to three different audiences. You might want to have different purposes for telling the

story. For instance, you might tell a teenager a story with a moral, but you might tell your father the same story to amuse him. Pick three quite different readers to tell your story to.

4. Practice audience adaptation one more time by explaining a brief process (write a how-to paragraph or short essay) to someone totally unfamiliar with the process, someone who has completed the process and needs to be reminded of the fine points, and someone who is an expert in the process but disagrees with your "method" of getting the job done.

5. Take out the essay you are currently working on. Review your most recent draft for appropriate audience cues. Look specifically at definitions of terminology, word choice, detail, tone.

   a. What kind of language and vocabulary will be particularly appropriate to this audience?

   b. What kind of examples would fit the reading level and specific interests of this audience?

   c. Are any explanations of the material necessary for this particular audience? If so, what kind?

   d. What aspects of the subject would be most interesting to this particular group of readers?

   e. How much development of the basic idea will be necessary for this particular audience?

CHAPTER 7

Writing with a Purpose

Although people write for many reasons, most of their purposes for writing can be roughly classified into three main categories: to express, to inform, and to change.

Writing to Express conveys a personal experience or way of thinking. In this category, you, the writer, are the focus. For the *personal experience essay,* the emphasis is on your own experiences and feelings about your experiences. For the *personal perspective essay,* the emphasis is on your thoughts, insights, and perspectives, backed up by personal experiences.

Writing to Inform involves letting your reader know something that you know. The main emphasis is on the material itself, rather than on the opinions or reflections or experiences of the writer. We'll look in some detail at three kinds of Writing to Inform essays, each of which deals with a different kind of informing: the *how-to essay* which teaches the reader how to do something; the *problem-solution essay* which pinpoints a problem or a solution (or both); and the *information essay* which educates a reader about a subject the writer knows well.

Writing to Change intends to make the reader different in some way. Writing to Change provides information, but does it in such a way that the reader thinks or acts in a certain way as a result of reading. Again, we'll look at three kinds of essays in this category: the *assertion-with-evidence essay* which takes a stand and backs it up; the *evaluation essay* which compares one or more things, products, or ideas and directs the reader toward the best (or away from the worst); and the *persuasion essay* which attempts to get the reader to do something differently as a result of reading the essay.

A word of warning. Categories are neat, simplistic, and convenient, but they don't show the full picture. The purpose for an essay almost

94

never fits into only one category. For instance, a Writing to Inform essay may also produce actions in the readers, even though the writer did not specifically request that anything be done. A Writing to Change essay which contains a lot of facts to support its argument will inform readers, as well as challenge them to do something the writer thinks should be done. Similarly, a Writing to Express essay may inform readers about the writer's perspective and convince readers to act on their new insights.

In each of the following sections, however, we will discuss the most important characteristics of the three main purposes for writing. We'll look specifically at subcategories of each purpose, at possible writing assignments, and at student-authored examples to see just how writers identify their purposes to help communicate effectively with readers.

WRITING TO EXPRESS

Writing to Express focuses on you, the writer. You are the subject. Your sensibilities, experiences, thoughts, feelings, and realizations take center stage. But although Writing to Express may take on certain elements of Writing to Inform or Writing to Change, Writing to Express is distinct because it is a personal mode—you are educating your reader about yourself.

Unlike Writing to Inform, where the writer/reader relationship is "informed person" to "less-informed person," and Writing to Change, where the relationship is "person who wants *X*" to "person who could do *X*," the relationship here is friend to friend, or host to guest. Because of this relationship, Writing to Express has a personal voice—the reader can hear and know the person behind that writing.

The Personal Experience Essay

Personal experience essays come from writers' sense of their own worth. These essays are enjoyable to readers for many reasons. Readers may gain insight from the stories told or may recognize their own experiences in the writer's experiences; they can be inspired to do something or be stimulated to think about their own lives. Readers may also enjoy personal experience essays just because human beings are a story-telling species and they appreciate good stories.

Is an experience interesting to the reader simply because "it happened to me"? Why should a reader, who may not even know you, care about your experiences? Readers will care—often deeply—about your feelings, impressions, and experiences if you make the effort to write about your experience in such a way that readers have a living sense of that experience and can relate it to similar experiences. When you write about yourself, it isn't just to hear yourself talk—it's to express your understanding

Writing the Personal Experience Essay

Summary

1. Think of a personal experience essay as an opportunity for your readers to know more about you.
2. Choose an incident, occasion, event, or situation that you recall vividly and that will be interesting to other people. Make it the focus of your essay.
3. Use examples, illustrations, and details that will put the audience right inside the story.
4. Use the most vivid language you can find—go for description of taste, smell, touch, sight, sounds. Create your world for the reader.

of your experience and thereby to enrich the readers' understanding of their experiences. The words, examples, and illustrations you choose will be important for drawing in your readers.

A personal experience essay is more often narrative than analytical since you are basically telling a story. As with any story, appeal to all the reader's senses—sight, smell, touch, hearing, taste. Be specific. Select the details you want to include so that they give one main impression of an object, scene, person, experience. Moreover, be sure to give the reader a clear time order; let your readers feel the action of your story; and decide on a point of view.

Thesis. While your thesis or main point will have something to do with your experience, it won't be simply a presentation of the experience itself. The thesis says something about the experience—evaluates it, judges it, determines its significance or importance. "I had a great time in the mountains" is not a thesis; "I discovered that doing something difficult—climbing mountains—made me aware of strengths I hadn't known I had" is a thesis. You need to have a thesis, and you need to make that point clear.

WRITING *The Personal Experience Essay*

1. Your family is putting together a history, and each member is to write something about his or her life. Write a personal experience essay to go into this scrapbook, based on some incident that you would like the family to know about or to remember you by. Be sure to consider the diversity of readers even in your own family.

2. Many teenagers decide to drop out of high school or college without getting a diploma. Write to one such teen about a personal experience that shows why staying in school is a better approach than dropping out.
3. Students often have to work in "project teams" to complete assignments in engineering, physical sciences, technical writing, and other disciplines. Yet often students complain that they don't know how to pick team members with complementary skills. Write a personal experience essay that will show off the skills you can contribute to a project team in your major discipline.
4. All of us face crises in our lives, and we often turn to family, friends, church members, or other support networks to weather the crisis. Write a personal experience essay that shows how you have faced a crisis and now have the experience to support someone else through a similar crisis.

The Personal Experience Essay WILL MOM STILL LOVE ME?

Goal: To explore personal relationships
Audience: Classmates

"Mom, can you come here? I need to talk to you."

"Sure, Susie. I'll be there in a minute."

Sitting on my bed I could not even look at my mother when she walked into my room. All the trust she had in me was soon to be broken, giving way to anger and disappointment. I could feel my sense of security falter before I spoke. I had always been able to count on Mom's love and understanding, but this was different.

"What did you need to talk about?" I am sure she thought I wanted money for school, or that I was going to tell her I was failing a class. Instead, out of my mouth came: "Mom, I think I'm pregnant. If so, I'm about six months along."

I heard those words, but I felt as if I were in a daze. I was suddenly very hot and I could tell my face was flushed; I thought I might faint. Fear and humiliation were the only emotions I felt worthy of. And sadness. Sadness because of the disappointment I knew my mother felt.

She had given me so much and I was about to ask for more than she might be willing or able to give. Now, more than ever, I needed her help. I knew I did not want to keep the baby. I needed to know who to contact to arrange an adoption, I needed to get in touch with a doctor, and I needed money for the bills I would incur. Not only that, at the time I was in ninth grade so I had my education to consider. Most of all I needed to know that I was not alone and Mom still loved me. I was so afraid that she would reject me after what I had done.

The words I had spoken still lingered in the air between us. It seemed like an eternity as we sat facing each other, both waiting for my words to soak in. Did she know what I needed of her? Would she still love me?

Before my questions were asked Mom answered them. Together we cried and she embraced me with the arms of a mother who truly loved me. We talked about my alternatives, and she assured me that she would stand by the decisions I made.

In the two months that I was not able to attend school Mom picked up my schoolwork every week. Every Saturday morning she faithfully got me to my appointment with the doctor. In addition she helped me keep my pregnancy from my friends and arranged to have someone from Social Services counsel me. During most of the counseling sessions Mom was there lending me added support.

Since I had already decided to give the baby up for adoption, Mom tried to find the easiest way to go about it. Through pure luck she came in contact with a man who knew a couple that wanted to adopt. Mom met with her lawyer, who in turn got in touch with the couple's lawyer, and the adoption papers were drawn up.

At one point I remember Mom telling me, "If I could have this baby for you I would." She could not, but she did the next best thing. She was there for me throughout my pregnancy.

At 4:30 one morning I woke up and went into my mother's room. "Mom . . . I have cramps."

"Come lay down with me and see if they go away."

"They are not going away."

"Get up and walk around. If they go away then it is false labor." The pains did not go away.

We got to the hospital around 6:00 a.m. Mom sat with me in the labor room. She later told me that she wanted to come hold my hand but was afraid we would both start to cry.

My contractions came quicker and grew more painful. Soon it was time to go into the delivery room. There was Mom, all decked out in hospital green—mask and all. It was so comforting to know she was there. Even in the delivery room she never stopped supporting me. She was allowed to administer laughing gas to me. It made us both feel like she was really helping out. Although I did not weep uncontrollably in the delivery room, she wiped away the few tears I shed, all the while comforting me with her words. "Just a little longer, Honey, then you'll be all through. You're doing fine," I heard her calm voice say. She took away my fear, and I knew I would make it.

Afterward, she sat with me in my hospital room until I was too tired to stay awake. I told her to go home and get some sleep. That evening she returned with my sister and they gave me a stuffed Garfield toy. I think it was a way to say that it was O.K. for me to go back to being a teenager again.

In my mother's eyes I could see no shame, no resentment, no anger. Only love.

Ever since then I have known that no matter what, my Mom will always love me.

The Personal Perspective Essay

The *personal perspective essay* focuses on the writer's own opinion or perspective. It is different from the personal experience essay, where the focus is on your *experience*. In the personal perspective essay, the focus is on your personal perspective—your *opinion*. This kind of writing doesn't have to be researched, documented, or proven.

You don't have to be famous to write a personal perspective essay. You just have to say, "This is how I see the world; this is what I think." The reader may or may not agree, which is okay—agreement isn't necessary. The writing exists because you want to say something about your view of the world.

When writing the personal perspective essay, you need to find some topic about which you have strong feelings you wish to share with other people. When you find a topic you know and care about, you write from a strong position.

Think about audience for the personal perspective essay. Always keep the reader in mind. Anticipate what a reader will want or need to know. If you are using your Uncle Joe as an example in your essay, it's not enough to say "Uncle Joe says that. . . ." Your readers, not being members of your family, need to know who Uncle Joe is and why what he says should mean anything to them. So clarify—add the details that make your information as important to the reader as it is to you.

Matching your essay with the right audience can come from either of two directions. The first involves focusing on a particular publication and asking yourself, "What opinions do I have that the readers of this publication are interested in?" The other is to focus on the subject of your writing and to ask yourself, "What kind of person would be concerned about and affected by what I am writing about?" Once you have identified your readers, you can identify that audience's characteristics and write accordingly. For example, if your subject is "Television depicts too much violence," you will slant your material one way if your readers are TV watchers, another if they are TV-station owners, another if they are parents, and another if they are clergy.

*Writing the
Personal
Perspective
Essay*

Summary

1. Choose a subject that already interests you, something you have thought about for a while.
2. Take your own perspective—don't borrow the opinions, views, or positions of others.
3. Write with your readers in mind, anticipating what they might want or need to know.
4. Develop your perspective in a logical, clear, and orderly way.
5. Use many examples and illustrations—but only those that apply.

WRITING *The Personal Perspective Essay*

1. A course in literature sometimes helps students gain some insight into problems people face. Choose any piece of literature that you feel addresses a problem—finding and keeping love, happiness, success, or peace. Write about that problem and the insight you gained from the piece of literature.
2. Historians and other writers like to remind us that if we don't learn from the mistakes of others in the past we are condemned to repeat those mistakes. Choose some historical incident that sheds light on a contemporary political, social, or economic problem. Write an essay in which you use the historical event to explain your perspective on the current problem.
3. For a long time you have been wondering why relationships between men and women are so often rocky. Recently you had an insight that makes many things seem clearer, especially in light of your own past and/or current relationships. Write an article about your insight for a mass-market magazine (for example, *Redbook, Ladies' Home Journal, Seventeen, MS.,* or *Esquire*) whose readers are eager to learn about improving their relationships.

Personal Perspective Essay WHY THE HOLDUP?

Goal: To express one man's opinion about women's grooming habits
Audience: Classmates

What takes them so bloody long? Here I sit, foot impatiently tapping to the abstract humming coming from the bathroom, pondering this same question for the umpteenth time.

What is it that makes women, even under pressure, take so much longer than men to get ready? I had even called Beth from work to remind her of the importance of this work-related dinner and to tell her to please be ready by 7:00. I was to make a presentation, and punc-tuality was of the utmost importance. So there I sat, waiting, and I began to examine exactly what takes her so much longer than myself to get ready. I could think of at least three things where just being a woman makes a difference. Because of her personal hygiene habits, application of make-up, and concern for fashion, I was going to be late, again.

Glumly watching a rerun of Gilligan's Island and contemplating future career options, I listened to her take a shower. While I only spent ten minutes in the shower tonight, Beth spends an average of twenty to twenty-five minutes. When confronted with this, she merely replies,

"What would you rather be, late or going out with an ape?" I could see her point. She does her shaving in the shower. Whereas I would simply look rough after not shaving for three days, Beth would look like a Neanderthal. The stubble could destroy a pair of pantyhose or a person's first few layers of skin if rubbed too hard. Okay, I'll allow her this, but why spend so much time fussing with her hair?

I understand she wants to look her best, but are all the little extras necessary? My hair requires little in the way of attention. I simply shampoo, apply conditioner during the dry times of the year, blow dry and go. Not only is the conditioner a must, but so is the mousse, curling iron, and hairspray before Beth can be seen in public. Frustrated, I listen to her use each with a seeming unconcern for time. After finishing, I hear her open the cabinet door, knowing what is coming next.

The science of applying makeup is, with a few bizarre exceptions, completely unknown to men. This is the part I become the most hypercritical about. We complain about things like time and shake our heads, not daring to comment aloud about their vanity. Yet we fall in love with the finished product, not what is underneath. How many men think women look better without makeup? So we wait while they apply a layer of base, pencil on eyeliner, and lightly brush on eyeshadow, and put on rouge and lipstick, all the while being grateful that we do not have to do the same thing. Hearing the cabinet door close, I wonder how long the next step will take this time.

If I do not have to wear a suit, my most agonizing decision is which T-shirt I should wear and what pair of jeans it would go best with. Here, my choice is gratefully limited due to a simple lack of variety in Levi styles. Usually I would put on the basic blue jeans; if, however, I needed something a little nicer, the stone-washed would be my choice. Bars having a dress code do not allow faded denim, so the black stone-washed jeans would be appropriate while the lighter, grey ones are more suitable for parties. Tonight, however, I must wear a suit, and this is even easier to decide on than leisure wear as I only own three. Women, on the other hand, seem to enjoy creating their own frustration, and mine, as they sort, choose, and discard each item in turn. The sheer volume of choices is what proves to be confusing.

There would be no problem at all if women simply did not have so many clothes. Counting all my shirts, jeans, and suits, I do not have enough to fill a whole closet. Beth, however, does not have enough closets to fit all of her clothes. Hangers, drawers, and chests are all filled with her collection while my modest wardrobe would fit inside of a single box. Filing through skirts, dresses, slacks, and blouses, ignoring my opinion on each, she mumbles, "I haven't a thing to wear." I am told that I simply do not understand fashion: what style is appropriate for which occasion, what color coordination is, and what is not in style any longer. Fine, I already knew that, just get dressed! Finally, picking something out, she disappears into the bathroom again.

Realizing that the end is near, I glance at my watch and my mood improves by leaps and bounds. Only 6:30, we just might make it to dinner on time. At last, she emerges from the bathroom and my jaw begins a steady descent to my shoes. Whereas I look like I do every day, Beth stands before me, looking more lovely than I had thought possible. Her hair, the color of the sun and the feel of silk, lays neatly arranged in an ordered confusion of curls. Her face is more perfect than anything Michelangelo could produce (though he could come close in half the time). And her dress—a black, floor-length gown with a subdued sparkle, like that of captured stars—is sure to attract the attention of my co-workers and the envy of their wives. She answers my question with a single glance. Why do women take so long to get ready? Because the end result is definitely worth the wait.

WRITING TO INFORM

Writing to Inform allows you to present readers with valuable information that they probably do not have. This is different from Writing to Express, which intends to educate the reader about you and your personal feelings, experiences, and perspectives. It is also different from Writing to Change, which intends to make the reader see or do something in a certain way and take action. In Writing to Inform, you lay out or teach the reader something you know: you convey facts rather than opinions, hypotheses, positions, or personal experiences. Therefore, in Writing to Inform, what takes center stage is not what you think or how you feel about the subject, but the subject itself.

This means that you need to write about a subject you know well. And this, in turn, means that your writer-reader relationship is one of "informed person" to "uninformed person." This doesn't mean that you are superior to the reader; it just means that you know something that might be of value to your reader, and that you wish to make this information available.

The form in which you convey your information depends on what it is you want to tell, and what kind of result you intend to get. If you want to teach the reader how to do something—build a birdhouse, begin a stamp collection, solve an algebra problem—you will write a how-to essay. If you want to alert the reader to a particular problem and to suggest a solution, you will write a problem-solution essay. And if you simply want to let the reader know about the existence of something, you'll write an information essay.

The How-to Essay

The *how-to* essay is straightforward. You introduce the subject to the reader, explain it step by step, and then conclude. The purpose of writing such an essay is to communicate your knowledge about the chosen subject in such a way that readers can carry out the process you describe in your essay. Generally, the thesis of a how-to essay can be summarized as: "It is useful for you to know how to do *X, and so here are the steps for doing *X.*"

Be sure to think about your audience so that you can choose the style, tone, and details that will make a difference. Are you writing your essay for rank beginners, enthusiastic amateurs, or experts in the field? Will your readers be urban or rural, fifth-graders or senior citizens, stay-homers or jet-setters, and so on? The more you know about your audience, the easier it will be to direct your writing to those particular readers. After all, it isn't productive to teach auto maintenance to car mechanics (unless you have a new angle or a new development to report), but it is productive to teach this subject to new drivers, or to "all-thumbs" car owners.

*Writing the
How-to Essay*

Summary

1. Choose a process you know thoroughly.
2. Know exactly what audience you are writing for, and tailor your discussion of the process to that particular group of people.
3. Anticipate anything the reader might not know; define terms.
4. Make every step clear and orderly.
5. Use precise language and complete detail.
6. Put the information into an interesting framework.

By the same token, don't teach cake-baking to experienced cooks—teach it to 10-year-olds or to kitchen-shy singles.

If you are writing for people who know virtually nothing about the subject you know a lot about, assume that more information is better than less. If the subject is basic auto repair for readers who know nothing about cars, it isn't helpful to say merely, "Using a lug wrench, remove . . ." You need to explain what a lug wrench is and how to use it. Think through every step of your process, and anticipate anything the reader might not understand or might overlook.

In a how-to essay it's important to arrange steps in a clear and orderly way so that the reader can understand and follow the procedure. Include all the steps your reader will need to complete the process.

WRITING *The How-to Essay*

1. You have recently attended a workshop on the subject of "How to Get More Out of Life." Several friends, knowing that you went to the workshop, have called you (one at a time) to find out what the workshop was about and how to put its principles into practice. You didn't mind the first two calls, but by the sixth call things are getting too hectic. You don't want to spend the rest of your life on the phone, repeating the same thing. So you decide to distill the ideas and instructions from the workshop into a brief how-to essay, which you will photocopy and distribute to your friends. Write this essay.

2. You are seeing a career counselor to find out what kinds of job skills you have, and she suggests that you review your experiences to see what you have expertise in. By "experiences," she means not only paid jobs but also volunteer jobs and the skills you have developed without realizing that you developed them. For example, if you are a

working parent, you might write "How to Interview a Babysitter." If you have helped out at church dinners, you might write "How to Cook for 100." Find a skill you have that you have never looked at as a skill, and write a how-to essay about it.

3. You have worked at the same summer camp for the last few years, and this year the director approaches you with a request: the camp wants to start a file of camping skills so that new counselors can benefit from the expertise of the more experienced counselors. Subjects include teaching arts and crafts, swimming, making fires, and music. Pick an idea you know something about, and write up a how-to guide for counselors to help them teach the subject to their campers.

4. Imagine that a former employer of yours calls to tell you that you did such good work for him or her that you have been chosen to write up some how-to-do-it instructions for new employees (for a fee, of course). Choose one aspect of the job (for example, did you make pizza? complete credit-card transactions?), and write about it in the how-to format.

How-to Essay WRITING SOAPS

Goal: To explain "How-to-do-it" instructions for new workers caring for injured birds of prey

Audience: New volunteers at the raptor center

Keeping clear, concise, and up-to-date medical records on active bird cases is important to any raptor program. In effect, these records are a manual of each bird's problems. They inform the volunteer of everything about an individual case from the first day the bird arrives until the day it is released, euthanized, or designated as a teaching bird. In addition, the records contain pertinent information about when and how to treat the birds. Records help to communicate the bird's problems, or rather, a human being's interpretation of the problems. Since your interpretation plays a large role, it is vital that it

be as accurate as possible. You need to take great care to read past medical records thoroughly and to continue good care by writing excellent notes for the next person to review.

A good format for writing medical records, and the one that we use in our raptor center, is called the SOAP method. SOAP stands for Subjective, Objective, Assessment, and Plan. These are the four elements to include in good medical records. The first step is the subjective. This is *your* personal opinion of the bird. Take a few minutes to observe quietly; if possible, observe him without his awareness of your presence (i.e., from a distance, from behind a small viewing window, etc.). You can best observe the animal when he is under minimal stress; thus your obvious presence would only further his discomfort and anxiety. After a few minutes of close observation, jot down how you felt the bird looked and behaved. A common response for a relatively normal bird is "bright, alert, and responsive," or BAR. This is a good positive description. However, if you feel that the bird is depressed or lethargic, do not hesitate to voice your opinion. Your observations can only help the bird.

Next is the objective description: what you actually did to the bird or for the bird. This should include cage cleaning, feeding, watering, what was left of yesterday's food, and how many casts were removed. The objective entry should also show what medications you gave and in what quantities. A sample objective entry might be: "removed ½ mouse, removed 0 casts, cleaned cage, and fed 2 mice on the fist."

The third step is the assessment. This is an overall opinion of the bird—how did she behave while you were working with her? Generally, this is a time to combine the subjective and objective viewpoints. This step is important because it includes more detail, and others working with the bird may place special emphasis on your opinions in this section. Take enough time to think about each action you took and how the animal responded. A good assessment would be: "I found the eagle to be a little jumpy, but she remained on her perch while I removed casts and leftover food. She was extremely alert and observant. I left two mice which she immediately began eating." Taking a few minutes to watch her movements after leaving food is sometimes helpful because an animal's eating habits strongly indicate her overall health. Progress is much more positive if an animal is eating well. However, if the animal is overly stressed by your presence, then you may only hinder her appetite. Use your own good judgment and lots of common sense to collect details for the assessment section.

The last step of a SOAP is the plan, that is, what should be done the next time the bird is treated. The next person to treat this bird will read the previous few SOAPs and follow the direction left in the last plan. This is an extremely important step! Since the birds are checked regularly twice a day, the previous plan is most often accurate. Unless otherwise noted, that plan is continued until one of the doctors or the director signifies a change. A well-written plan might read as follows: "Continue treatments with 3c.c. of amoxicillin once each A.M. Clean cage in A.M. and feed two mice both in A.M. and P.M."

Don't just copy the previous plan without thinking about what it says. Make sure that you understand what you are writing, and do not hesitate to raise a question if you think something is incorrect. People are fallible; we all make mistakes. It is important to be aware of your actions so that mistakes are not left to be repeated, whether they be yours or those of someone else.

The following is an overall example of a SOAP:

S: BAR, looks good

O: removed 1 whole mouse, 1 cast. Cleaned cage and left 2 mice on floor of cage.

A: The bird is active and seems to be improving. He is showing a little more movement in left shoulder joint. Remained on perch as I worked in cage. Stepped easily onto my fist and transferred to Dianalee as I cleaned cage. Very well behaved.

P: Feed 2 mice twice a day. Clean cage in A.M. Weigh once a week on Friday.

Writing SOAPs is an extremely important aspect of our program. However, it is not a difficult job if you remain sensitive to the animal. Take pride in the SOAP that you write, for you are playing a vital role in the care and rehabilitation of this wild animal.

The Problem-Solution Essay

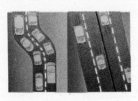

Much of the writing we are required to do in life has to do with pinpointing problems and suggesting solutions. We may be asked to come up with a report that suggests more efficient ways of using employees' talents; we may want an organization to implement a new procedure that would make things run more smoothly; or we may want to write a letter-to-the-editor that would make something happen differently. Certainly, there is no scarcity of problems about which to write.

It's tempting to take on a large, impressive, complex subject—like "Ending War" or "Balancing the Federal Budget"—but it is virtually impossible to write something meaningful about these broad subjects because it is so difficult to focus on such a wide picture. And if essays on such topics are unfocused, they usually turn out to be collections of abstractions and exhortations that nobody wants to read. For example, what do you make of this?

> Freedom is something that everybody wants, because freedom is a political and economic right, which our forefathers put down in writing. No one doesn't want freedom, and all sociologists and historians can attest to this. Freedom is the basis of everything, and no one wants to be oppressed. Slaves didn't want it, or Lincoln either, and inflation makes freedom harder to get but even more necessary than before, during the Revolutionary War and after.

What in the world is this writer talking about? The subject is too large and too unfocused; the writer doesn't pinpoint a specific problem or solution. Nor does the writer indicate any expertise about the subject, or even any interest. Without genuine insights into the real-life problems of "freedom," the writer has begun this paper with nothing more than a series of boring, unrelated platitudes.

So although you may be tempted to tackle the big problems—conservation, the environment, health care, war, world peace—the truth is that you are apt to flounder in these deep waters of abstraction. If you don't know a good solution for the problem from first-hand experience or reading, don't write about that problem. If you write what you know, then you are an expert, and therefore you have something of value to offer your reader.

Choosing a Focus.   In writing a problem-solution essay, you don't necessarily have to give detailed information on both the problem and the solution. You, of course, give both components equal attention, but you can also choose to focus only on the problem, in order to get the reader to think about it more. On the other hand, you can touch on the problem only briefly (especially if it is one with which your readers are familiar), and concentrate on the solution instead. Whether you emphasize the problem, the solution, or both depends on your purpose.

If the focus is on the problem, answer these questions.

1. What is the problem?
2. Why should the reader care about this problem?
3. Write a full description of the problem, with several examples. Now will the reader understand the problem?

If the focus is on the solution, answer these questions.

1. What is the problem?
2. Why should the reader care about this problem?
3. Write a full description of the solution, with several examples. Now will the reader understand the solution?
4. Why will this solution work?

If you focus in on both the problem and the solution, answer the following questions.

1. What is the problem?
2. Why should the reader care about this problem?
3. Write a full description of the problem, with several examples. Now will the reader understand the problem?
4. Okay—then what's the solution?
5. Write a full description of the solution, with several examples. Now will the reader understand the solution?

Writing the Problem-Solution Essay

Summary

1. Choose a problem and/or a solution that is the right size. It should not be a grand-scale abstraction, but something that you know about through first-hand experience or reading.
2. Decide whether you want to discuss the problem, the solution, or both.
3. Know your audience. Make sure the subject will matter to your readers.
4. Use many examples and illustrations throughout the essay. Be specific. Choose ones that will make sense to your audience.
5. End with a conclusion that tells your readers what to make of your presentation—clarify what they now know or should think about as a result of reading your essay.

WRITING *The Problem-Solution Essay*

1. You are running for a student government position. All candidates are preparing position papers to discuss some problem and solution facing students on your campus. Choose a problem you think your audience will feel is most pressing in their lives—parking space, library hours, quality of the food, lack of equal sports facilities for women and men. Write an essay describing the problem and your solution.

2. You are a new employee in a firm, and you see many things that could be improved. Perhaps you notice that the other workers' skills aren't used as fully as they might be, or that bureaucratic procedures are creating needless inefficiencies, or some other problem that no one else seems to have paid attention to. Write to your supervisor, identifying the problem and suggesting a solution.

3. For years you have been plagued with (1) a problem around the house, (2) a problem with a friend or relative, or (3) a personal problem (being overweight, smoking). Suddenly you come up with the perfect solution. It's so simple, obvious, or workable that you can't imagine why it took you so long to think about it. You think other people could profit from hearing of your experience. Write a problem-solution essay to an appropriate audience.

4. While shopping at the supermarket, you discover that the price of nearly every item in the store has gone up by about ten percent since the week before. You are outraged, and demand an explanation from the checkout clerk. The clerk tells you that this inflation is to cover the cost of stolen shopping carts—the carts have been disappearing from the store at a rapid rate. You go home fuming, and then, hours later, come up with a way for the store to prevent the theft of shopping carts. Write a problem-solution essay to the manager of the store.

Problem-Solution Essay SUICIDE: THE ROAD TO PREVENTION

Goal: To inform readers about problems with teen suicide prevention systems and to present one solution

Audience: Teachers

The will to survive and succeed had been crushed and defeated. I was like a general on a battlefield being *encroached on by my enemy and its hordes: fear, hate, self-deprecation, desolation. I felt I had to have the upper hand, to control my environment, so I sought to die rather than surrender. . . .* (qtd. in Sheidman 56)

No, this isn't a line from a soap opera; this is a quote from a young man who attempted suicide. Suicide among those fifteen to twenty-four years old has nearly tripled in the last thirty years, thus gaining notoriety as the second highest cause of death among teens and young adults. The problem has finally come to the forefront and the search for effective prevention is on. I support the proposed solution which entails mandatory training of public school teachers to spot suicidal individuals. By illustrating the problems with the current system of suicide prevention, pointing out the need for intervention, and examining the reasoning behind choosing teachers as the potential rescuers, I hope to bring to light the need for such suicide related education among the faculty of this nation.

Many believe that the current mode of dealing with the rising teen suicide rate is the best method possible. However, this is far from the truth. Currently, suicide hotlines, psychiatrists, and psychologists constitute the backbone of suicide intervention. As pointed out by Dr. Barry Garfinkel, Head of the Department of Child Psychology at the University of Minnesota, the current system of crisis hotlines has no measurable effect on the number of suicides because those teens who do call are not the same ones who are really serious about taking their lives (Strother 758). Following this same line of thought, the number of psychiatrists and psychologists within a community has no effect on the number of attempted suicides. Why is that? The root of the problem lies within the characteristic withdrawal of the suicidal individual from those closest to him. Such an introverted individual who avoids his friends and family is very unlikely to seek help from a total stranger or anonymous voice on the telephone. Presently, the suicidal youth is expected to seek out help and counseling on his own. Does it make sense to expect such a troubled individual to actively pursue counseling? The answer is a resounding NO! Granted, psychoanalysts do counsel those who have attempted suicide once, but this is too late for the other five thousand

young adults who succeed in taking their lives. What is needed to alleviate this problem is a system which involves another coming to the rescue of the potential victim of suicide.

The need for some form of intervention is illustrated by this quote from Mohammad Shafur, University of Kentucky psychiatrist: "We believe that completed suicide in children and adolescents does not occur on the spur of the moment or as an impulsive act of an otherwise healthy child. . . . suicide is the final outcome of serious emotional disorders which, in most cases, were not recognized or not treated" (qtd. in Holden 839). From this quote we can draw three conclusions: 1) there is a need for detection of such emotionally distraught individuals, 2) the claim that suicide is not prethought is a fallacy, and 3) the detection of suicidal characteristics is not an easy chore; therefore it takes training to learn what to look for.

What are the characteristics of an individual considering suicide as the only way out? These symptoms include neglect of personal appearance, sudden weight change, poor performance in school, trouble concentrating, loss of energy, and lack of interest in friends (Colt 221). These symptoms make it clear that the only persons likely to intervene successfully are parents and teachers because they have the contact necessary to detect such symptoms. Some may believe that it is the responsibility of parents to pick up the warning signs of suicide. However, this is relatively impractical for a number of reasons. In today's society we find more divorced, separated, and working parents than ever before, thus reducing the amount of time that a teen spends with his/her parents. Also contributing to the infeasibility of this belief is the fact that educating millions of parents would be impractical due to the cost and the fact that, in most cases, such knowledge would not be utilized to its full extent because of the small amount of time spent in the presence of the teen. What is needed to alleviate this problem is someone who has the contact and could utilize their knowledge of symptoms to the fullest. Who fills this description better than the teachers of America? There are several reasons for placing educators in this position. They come into contact with hundreds of students daily and are at least relatively familiar with most of them. In comparison with two parents per every three to four children (on average), only one teacher could effectively monitor the actions of hundreds of students. Teachers are also in contact with other students who may be overheard talking of how someone is acting differently or abnormally. Faculty members can also compare their beliefs with other members of the faculty concerning suspicions of a potentially suicidal youth and generally are in the position to confront the youth and direct him to authorities for help. Programs instructing faculty members to detect symptoms and to refer youths to the proper avenues have already been implemented and are showing positive effects on the war against suicide.

As I have illustrated, the current mode of dealing with the rising suicide rate among the young is ineffective. Someone has to come to the rescue of the suicidal teen for "If we fail to notice their problems, the troubled young people may try to command our attention in potentially lethal ways" (Strother 759). For a multitude of reasons, faculty members of our public schools would be the most effective in hearing the pleas from those crying for attention. Currently, we have our ears plugged to their plight in the sense that we are not effectively dealing with the problem. The call for a rescuer of these troubled young people has been broadcast. It is my hope that this plea will be answered by the teachers of our nation.

Works Cited

Colt, George Howe, "The Painful Riddle of Teen Suicide." *Seventeen* April 1985: 185–187, 221–222.

Holden, Constance. "Youth Suicide: New Research Focuses on a Growing Social Problem." *Research News* Aug. 1986: 839–841.

Shneidman, Edwin. "At the Point of No Return." *Psychology Today* March 1987: 54–58.

Strother, Deborah Burnett. "Practical Applications of Research." *Phi Delta Kappan* June 1986: 756–759.

The Information Essay

In writing the *information* essay, you are conveying certain information that you know well and that you believe will be of value to your reader. You are not teaching how to do something (that's the province of the how-to essay), nor are you pinpointing a difficulty and offering an alternative (that's for the problem-solution essay to accomplish). Instead, you are describing the subject so that the reader comes away as informed as you are.

Why might you write an information essay?

- to tell readers something they don't already know—something they might find educational, important, or interesting
- to enlarge the readers' knowledge about something they are familiar with, by giving them inside information or little-known facts
- to teach new information that readers want to know (for example, about a new theory, trend, or product)
- to record events that are happening in the present, or that occurred in the past

- to explain ideas, concepts, principles, or situations that readers might find hard to understand otherwise (without having education or training in specific fields)
- to present information and/or facts that will add to or broaden the readers' general knowledge

In effect, you are promising your readers that "I will tell you, teach you, or explain to you about X in a way that enables you to understand X and its importance to you." But remember that no audience wants to be bored. You need to offer your readers more than just a dry, solemn recitation of facts and figures.

Using Information Effectively.   Always keep in mind that readers can process your information most effectively if you observe these guidelines to make your writing:

Interesting.   You've heard the saying, "A picture is worth a thousand words." This is particularly true for the information essay. Since we think in mental pictures, use description (colorful words, analogies, images, and so on) to help your reader develop mental images of the facts you are presenting.

Understandable.   Even the smartest reader will find it hard to understand and make use of totally foreign material. To assist your readers, do all you can to help them relate the new information to something with which they are already familiar. This means giving familiar examples or references, as well as specific details and colorful word-pictures, so that the readers can assimilate this new information into their existing store of knowledge.

Significant.   Readers will want to know why it is important to know about this information you are presenting. When you draw comparisons

Writing the Information Essay

Summary

1. Make the information itself (not your opinions, insights, and feelings) the center of attention.
2. Present the information in as interesting, understandable, significant, and valuable way as possible. Dry facts are boring and hard to pay attention to. Use colorful words and images to help the reader make sense of the new information.
3. Do all you can to relate the new material to what the reader knows.

and contrasts between the new material and what the readers already know, you help them understand the significance of what they are reading.

Valuable.   Readers always want a good return on their investment of the time, attention, and effort they put into reading what someone has written. So let the readers know that you are taking them somewhere worth going—stick to the point, refrain from rambling, and avoid unnecessary details.

WRITING *The Information Essay*

1. You're taking an introductory course in world religions. Your instructor is putting together a set of supplementary readings which will give students a different perspective on various religions. The instructor has assigned an essay on this topic: "Write an essay about the religious influences on daily life in your family, neighborhood, or hometown." An alternative topic is "Write an essay in which you discuss the characteristics of the religious organization you know best." Every student will receive a set of the supplementary readings, which will be the basis for class discussion. Write your essay.

2. The teacher of a sixth-grade class in a local school wants your help in preparing a learning package on hobbies to be used to get the students interested in taking up some hobby for themselves. He has asked you to write an essay for the package which will inform the students about your hobby. He wants you to give the pupils enough information to let them know what the hobby requires, why it is fun, and what benefits can be gained from it.

Information Essay   *JOLLY ROGER FLIES AGAIN:* *RAMPANT PIRACY ON THE SOFTWARE SEAS*

Goal: Written to inform readers about software piracy
Audience: Classmates

In 1964, the United States Copyright Office registered the first commercial computer program (Chapman 789). With that first program, software pirates—those illegally copying software—set sail. By 1984, software amounted to a $100 billion annual market for the United States, and piracy was blasting an annual one- to three-billion dollar hole through its side

(World Press Review 57). Losses to Britain's software industry amounted to almost $200 million in the same year. Most other countries in the software market experienced similar losses: all software markets incurred some loss to piracy. By 1984, as many as ten pirated versions of a popular program were made for every legitimate copy sold (Lauer 26). Today, a vast sea of software exists, and every piece of it is vulnerable to pirating. As losses to piracy in the software market grow steadily higher, the problem rages beyond control.

Software pirating is copying a commercial computer program without the author's or publisher's consent. An illegal copy of a program is as unlawful as an illegal copy of a novel, a photocopy of a sheet of music, or a music album recorded onto an audio-cassette tape. A pirate is no particular age or type; he or she may range in age from six to sixty and in occupation from kindergartner to lawyer. Anyone old enough to read and to perform basic skills on a computer is capable of some level of piracy.

Most of the computer-using population is not a substantial threat to the industry, however. Rather, the threat comes from the people who copy programs in large quantities and sell the copies either publicly or in secret. In October, 1985, the Federal Bureau of Investigation uncovered illegal copies of Ashton-Tate's Dbase III and Lotus' 1-2-3, among other four- to five-hundred dollar business programs, being copied by Morris Shamberg and Gregory Howard, computer programmers in California companies. The two men sold the illegal copies through the *Los Angeles Times* classified ads for as little as $125 each.

Less damaging, but still a threat to the software industry, are casual pirates. These include employees who copy their company-bought programs for personal use and junior-high and high-school students who trade computer games with each other like record albums. These people constitute a large part of the personal software user market and they greatly reduce its profits by pirating.

A number of causes contribute to software piracy. Chief among them is a casual disregard for copyright laws by American society. Most people think nothing of photocopying sheet music or a magazine article. They aren't bothered about copying record albums illegally either: a Billboard survey conducted of 445 people at a concert revealed that 45% of home-tapers are most likely to borrow albums they record (Billboard 80). The same attitudes exist toward software. Often users support their "right to copy" with the claim that software companies are too rich and can afford to lose a little profit because they are practically stealing from the average consumer with their high prices anyway.

Another problem with copyright law is that it is impossible for software companies to monitor every user all the time to ensure his compliance with the laws. Also, the Supreme Court has ruled that a simple copying misdemeanor "cannot be the basis of a felony conviction." (Martin 15) If pirates do get caught, the maximum punishment they can expect is one year in prison and/or a $1000 fine. Software copyrights do nothing in themselves. Legislation, as well as the magnitude of the piracy problems, prevents an effective deterrent against individuals: pirates are hard to catch and harder to punish.

Another cause of software piracy stems from the introduction of disk-based copy-protection codes in the early 1980s in an early attempt to stop illegal copying. Software vendors put special codes in their software to prevent it from being copied. This created two problems. First, it tempted users to try to find a way around the codes. A new mindset came of this as successful code crackers made a hobby of it and called themselves hackers. Code cracking was ideally suited to high-school students who then set up clubs and networks for the sole purpose of cracking the newest protection codes.

Second, it prompted the creation of commercial programs to work around the codes. Not only had code-cracking become chic, but it had also become profitable; vendors now had to fight each other as well as the hackers. Locksmith, Nibbles Away, and Wildcard were only a few of the popular copy programs which entered the market. Since then, the industry's copy codes and society's ways of circumventing them have evolved at a rate similar to that of the Influenza virus. Copy-protection has itself become a multimillion dollar industry. Copy protection is self-defeating for the software vendors—no code has been discovered that can't be cracked or gotten around—and creates additional problems for legitimate software buyers who cannot easily make backups of their programs to keep in case the originals fail or become damaged.

Software piracy affects everyone from software writers to vendors to users. It hits vendors directly, decreasing their revenues. In response, vendors contend they must raise the prices of the software they do sell so they can regain the lost profits. Jean-Michel Paris, of Logo Computer Systems in Canada, said "the . . . consumer pays for it in the end. The price has to be that much higher to recover our costs." (Lauer 27) Affected almost as strongly is the program writer, who depends on royalties from his program for income. He works as hard as any novelist, but gets less reward because his work is copied illegally. The user is affected the most because any extra costs incurred by vendors are passed directly to him. Copy protection costs alone add an additional $1.50 to each disk (Pepper 54). Legitimate software consumers must contend not only with difficult copy-protection codes but with prohibitive prices.

Continued piracy causes an increase in software-related difficulties and costs both for the software industry and for the consumer. Current legislation is ineffective against it, and there is no feasible way to enforce copyright laws. We cannot strip the pirates of their cannon or halt their rampages over the software seas. A new solution must be found to eliminate, or at least reduce, piracy so that the seas may once again be safe for all.

Works Cited

Chapman, Michael T. "Copyright Law: Putting Too Many Teeth into Software Copyright Infringement Claims." *Journal of Corporation Law* Summer 1987.

"Computer Software Piracy." *World Press Review* Nov. 1984.

Lauer, R. "Fighting Computer Pirates." *Macleans* 23 July 1984.

Martin, James A. "FBI Charges Alleged Software Pirates as Crackdown Continues: Third in String of Recent Cases Probed." *Computerworld* 18 Nov. 1985.

"New Home Taping Study Published by Billboard." *Billboard* 16 Aug. 1986.

Pepper, Jon C. "User, Software Firms Continue to Debate Copy-Protection Issues." *PC Week* 8 April 1986.

WRITING TO CHANGE

What distinguishes *Writing to Change* from other purposes is that it intends to make something happen—to have the reader look, think, or act in a certain way as a result of reading the writer's words. Writing to Change uses some aspects of each of the other modes. Like Writing to Tell, it conveys information, and like Writing to Express it speaks in the writer's own voice. But its purpose in delivering information is not merely to inform but to convince the reader to do something differently, and its purpose in revealing the writer's voice is not to share experiences but to support the writer's assertions about what needs to be changed and how to make those changes.

A Writing to Change essay may take several forms. If you want to change what the reader knows, thinks, or believes about a particular thing, then you will write an *assertion-with-evidence* essay. If you want to change readers' abilities to judge by helping them be informed, then you will write an *evaluation* essay. And if you want to change readers' minds and perhaps persuade them to act, then you will write a *persuasion* essay.

The Assertion-with-Evidence Essay

In this kind of essay, you are not simply giving the reader objective information; you are giving the reader evidence to prove that what you assert—stated positively and confidently—is true. If you want your readers to consider your assertion and make some change, you need to back it up with researched documentation, carefully developed logical discussion, or examples and references that readers can check for themselves. The stronger your evidence, the faster the reader will accept your assertion.

In this kind of writing, clarity is crucial. This is not the place for elusive concepts or evocative phrases. You want to make your claim in no uncertain terms and say, in essence, "This is the way it is, and here is why." A good way to proceed, therefore, is to do the following:

1. State your assertion clearly, early in the essay: "Television soap operas give viewers an unrealistic view of life."

2. Give your evidence quickly, and make sure it supports your assertion. "A survey of TV soaps reveals that X% present uncommon crimes—kidnappings and espionage, for example—as if they were commonplace, Y% present casual sex without consequences, and Z% of the action takes place in hospitals or law offices."

3. To offer the reader convincing evidence, give facts, examples, illustrations, or other information that the reader can check, if desired. Or present a discussion that is so logical and convincing that the reader is willing to accept it without argument.

4. Acknowledge any weaknesses your evidence might have (or at least be aware of them yourself).

5. Mean what you say—be committed to it.

Audience for the Assertion-with-Evidence Essay. With all persuasive writing, targeting a specific audience is crucial. Your writing is almost doomed to fail if you try to convince jobless factory workers that robots are better workers than human beings. However, if the focus of your assertion is that anyone can be retrained to do a new kind of work, and that this new work might actually be a better deal for the former factory workers, your claim is more likely to get a real hearing. In general, then, tailor your assertion so that you appeal to the audience you are writing to, or choose an audience that will at least give your assertion a fair reading.

Writing the Assertion-with-Evidence Essay

Summary

1. Choose a subject you feel strongly about and can support with facts and examples or with logical, convincing evidence.
2. State your assertion early in the essay, and put forth your evidence clearly.
3. Choose your audience with your assertion in mind (or vice versa).
4. Be aware of what you want your readers to know, think, feel, or do as a result of reading your essay.
5. Flesh out your essay by means of concrete details—examples, illustrations, analogies. Facts are important, but give more than the facts; add attention-grabbing detail, too.

The more you know about the reader for whom you are writing, the greater your chance of making the appropriate assertion and of finding the appropriate supporting evidence.

WRITING   *The Assertion-with-Evidence Essay*

1. You are the parent of a small child; the two of you have just returned from the grocery store where he did nothing but whine and cry for the latest junk food cereal that was advertised on the Saturday morning cartoons. You know this cereal is coated with sugar and is not good for children, and finally, you have had enough. You sit down and write an assertion-with-evidence essay that you plan to mail to the network president. This essay will center on what you believe television commercials are doing to children. You also plan to send a copy of the essay to your local newspaper.

2. You are a newly appointed athletic coach at a local high school. You are surprised to learn that the previous coach used pain-killing drugs to enable athletes to perform even when injured. You know this is illegal and dangerous to team members. You decide that under no circumstances will you administer pain killers to team members. You must prepare a detailed statement that will appear in the newspaper, be read in the locker room, be sent to team members and their parents, and be posted on the school bulletin board. You want no doubt as to your position and the reasons for it. But you are aware of a "winning-at-all-costs" tradition in your school that most students and parents support. Take careful account of your audience as you write your statement.

3. Someone you know has smoked cigarettes since before you were born. You are aware of the health risks. You are sick of smelly ashtrays, and it worries you to hear all the coughing that goes on. Finally, you decide you have had it—it's time to convince this person to stop smoking. Write an assertion-with-evidence letter to this person. Give objective (and, if you wish, also subjective) evidence for your assertion.

4. Martin Luther turned history around the day he wrote a list of statements telling exactly where he stood on matters of religion and then nailed the list to the church door. Imagine that you have the opportunity to present a declaration of rights for some minority group (students, an ethnic group, the physically challenged, and so on), to be published in your local newspaper. Remember, you must back up your assertions with evidence, or else no one will read past the first paragraph. Write this declaration.

Assertion-with-Evidence Essay MANDATORY AIDS TESTING FOR JOB APPLICANTS

Goal: To argue that AIDS testing should not be mandatory for employment
Audience: Workers and employers

AIDS is a rapidly spreading disease that is reaching epidemic proportions. According to a brochure entitled *Facts About AIDS* put out by the Public Health Service, AIDS was first reported in the United States in 1981 (*Facts*). By early 1987, an estimated 1.5 million Americans had been infected with the AIDS virus, more than 30,000 had developed AIDS, and 17,000 had died from it. Researchers are predicting that by 1991, these latter two figures will be ten times as high ("AIDS: What We Know Now" 143). An issue evolving from the AIDS problem is that of whether or not employers can require job applicants to take a blood test for AIDS before the employers will consider hiring them. Although many workers feel they have the right to refuse to work with an AIDS victim because they do not want to risk contracting the illness, and although an employer might not want to invest in a person whose condition ends in death, these tests should not be made mandatory. They will only lead to discrimination in both the workplace and with insurance, and they are an invasion of privacy.

Once an AIDS test for a job applicant has come back positive, discrimination is likely to start. Many employees feel they do not have to work with a person infected with AIDS because they risk contracting the disease. This shows ignorance because over and over the U.S. Public Health Service has assured the public that AIDS cannot be transmitted through casual contact ("AIDS: No Need" 51). The only ways known to transmit the virus are through sexual contact, the sharing of needles for intravenous drugs, blood transfusions, and rarely, a mother's breast milk (*Facts*). One cannot contract the AIDS virus from a toilet seat or from sharing someone's eating utensils. These concerned employees have no logical or medical evidence to support them, only emotional input.

An employer might also want to require AIDS testing so he'll know if he wants to invest in a person whom he expects always to be sick and to have a short life expectancy. But in the *Facts About AIDS* brochure, it is stated that it might be up to five years after a person is infected with the virus before he starts experiencing symptoms. So even though he may have several good years to live and work, the employer will probably label him an AIDS victim and not hire him. This is discrimination because a person's life should not end the moment he or she is diagnosed as having AIDS. As long as he can, he should be allowed to lead a normal life, including working for as long as he is able. Fortunately, according to the article, "Workplace AIDS," most authorities feel that people with AIDS are included in the laws that protect the handicapped from discrimination. So if they don't have any symptoms that interfere with their work ability, they cannot be fired ("Workplace AIDS" 30). In all fairness, this should apply to hiring as well.

Discrimination doesn't remain only in the workplace, though. If job applicants' test results are passed on to insurance companies, they sometimes discriminate also. Fortunately, as stated in a *U.S. News and World Report* article, "contract law forbids insurers from barring newly diagnosed AIDS patients from group health plans" ("AIDS: A Time of Testing" 58). Yet, according to another *U.S. News* article, a man in Colorado sent a copy of his negative AIDS test to his insurance company, and they still refused him "on the basis that the fact he got tested at all made him too great a risk" ("Mandatory Tests" 62). These companies are presently fighting bills that would keep them from refusing AIDS victims ("AIDS: A Time of Testing" 58).

Along with causing discrimination, the AIDS tests are invading persons' privacy. Employers, by testing job applicants for AIDS, are prying into their personal lives. Employers don't test prospective employees for other diseases that aren't contagious through casual contact such as cancer, syphillis, and cerebral palsy, and for that matter, for diseases that are more easily contagious, such as hepatitis and pneumonia, so why should AIDS be an exception? Besides, once employers explore all aspects of applicants' health and discover positive AIDS tests, what's to stop employers from looking into causes and discriminating against the applicants, not necessarily because of AIDS, but perhaps because they are homosexual? That is quite a generalization, and perhaps most employers are more unbiased than this, but it is certainly possible that discrimination could become this out-of-hand.

Yes, the population of AIDS victims is rapidly growing, and it is frightening because everyone is afraid of contracting this dreadful illness. But if we refrain from the activities known to transmit AIDS, we have no need to worry, even in the workplace. AIDS victims—like everyone else—have the right to live normal lives, and as long as they are able to perform their job duties, they should not be discriminated against. So, until the medical community finds any evidence that AIDS can be transmitted through casual contact, I don't see any risk with an AIDS victim in the workplace. Therefore, mandatory blood tests to check for AIDS in job applicants are unnecessary.

Works Cited

"AIDS: No Need for Worry in the Workplace." *Newsweek* 25 Nov. 1985: 51.

"AIDS: What We Know Now." *McCall's* April 1987: 143–44.

Facts About AIDS. U.S. Dept. of Health and Human Services, Spring 1986.

"Mandatory Tests for AIDS?" *U.S. News & World Report* 9 March 1987: 62.

"Workplace AIDS." *Nation's Business* Nov. 1986: 30.

Works Consulted

Altman, Dennis. *AIDS in the Mind of America*. Garden City, NY: Anchor Press/Doubleday, 1986: 61, 69.

"A Consumer Guide to Testing." *U.S. News & World Report* 20 April 1987: 61–62.

Koepp, Steven. "Living with AIDS on the Job." *TIME* 25 Aug. 1986: 48.

"Labor, Mergers High on Supreme Court's Agenda." *Industry Week* 13 Oct. 1986: 32.

Taylor, Stuart, Jr. "Rights of Disease Victims Backed; Those with AIDS Could Benefit." *New York Times* 4 March 1987: A1, A21.

"A Testing Experience." *U.S. News & World Report* 20 April 1987: 58–59.

"Unleashing Bias." *The Nation* 5 July 1986: 3–4.

The Evaluation Essay

When you write an *evaluation* essay, you compare and contrast one thing with another: which restaurant has the best hamburgers, the drive-in or the dine-in? Which car is more fuel-efficient, the domestic or the import? Or, you compare something with a measuring rod of quality: Is the movie playing downtown any good? We evaluate things, people, products, ideas, and experiences hundreds of times in a single day.

The evaluation essay fits the Writing to Change category because with it, you intend to have an effect on or to direct which choice the reader makes. To evaluate is to judge something in such a way that the reader will recognize the value of the path you point to and take that path.

Implicit in evaluating is the conviction that there are standards against which to judge what is being evaluated. There are two kinds of standards: external and internal standards.

External standards are specific, objective, measurable reasons for our ultimate decision. For instance, "Car A is better than Car B because it gets better mileage, it costs less, and it has more accessible repair shops than Car A." In other words, these features can be observed and tested by anyone who makes the effort; thus, the standards are external or objective. The only subjective element is the evaluator's assumption that good mileage, low cost, and availability of service shops are more desirable than poor mileage, high cost, and scarcity of service shops.

Internal standards come from the writer's own values, based on personal experience, knowledge, and feelings. For example, "Don't bother seeing this movie because there's too much action, there's not enough plot, and the dialogue is awful." The writer obviously believes that a lot of action is bad, that a minimum of plot is a disadvantage, and that dialogue is important; the reader does not necessarily believe the same thing. Usually we like an evaluation if the writer uses our standards of what's important. It can, however, be broadening to read evaluative writing done by people who evaluate according to different standards.

When evaluation criteria are internal, the reader assumes that the writer has some special expertise, knowledge, or experience—otherwise, why take the writer's verdict seriously? Readers want to evaluate their evaluators: "What are the writer's qualifications for making this evaluation?" they will invariably (although sometimes not consciously) ask. If, in writing an evaluation essay, your criteria are internal rather than external, you risk having your audience disagree with you. The only way to counter this is to tell the reader clearly and convincingly why your personal standards are worth following, or at least worth considering.

As you focus on the criteria, or standards, by which you will do the evaluating, be sure to cover these points:

1. Let the reader know right away what specific criteria you are using to make the evaluation. If you are using external standards, list them so that readers can determine if the criteria are appropriate for evaluating your subject. If you are using internal or subjective criteria, explain them so that readers can determine if they accept your standards and thus your evaluation.

2. Use criteria that are fair, logical, and consistent. Evaluate in terms that are appropriate for the thing being evaluated.

3. Tell your readers how to use the criteria, unless you can safely assume that they will know without being told.

4. If you have many criteria from which to choose, pick the ones that are most likely to convince your specific audience. If you're evaluating a children's film, you'll use one set of criteria to evaluate for the children (pace of the action, straightforward plot, crisp dialogue) and another set for the parents (clear moral values, absence of violence or foul language, clear distinctions between good and bad characters).

5. Let the reader know why you are qualified to make your evaluations. With external standards, your qualifications might resemble

Writing the Evaluation Essay

Summary

1. Choose a subject that you are qualified to evaluate.
2. Let the reader know your qualifications.
3. Choose criteria that are fair, logical, and consistent.
4. Choose criteria that fit your audience's needs and interests.
5. Let the reader know your criteria (external or internal).
6. Evaluate your subject against all of the standards that are important to your readers.
7. Help the reader make sense of your findings.
8. Support your examples with details, facts, and illustrations.

a resume: "As a former pilot, I know what conditions make traveling difficult. . . ." With internal standards you will need to disclose something about yourself: "As a parent who talks to her children about values portrayed through films, I appreciate films that reinforce my teachings at home. . . ."

6. Use many details, facts, and examples to support your evaluation. Not only do they add interest and color, but they add a concrete dimension which helps the reader identify with what you are saying.

WRITING *The Evaluation Essay*

1. You have been invited to be the guest (book, music, dance, food, or film) reviewer for the local newspaper while the regular reviewer goes on vacation. This delights you because you have been wanting to see a variety of types of (those things) reviewed, and you welcome the chance to see your standards and preferences reflected on the review page.

2. You have a friend who resisted the idea of using computers for a long time. Now, however, he decides that he is ready to buy a personal computer. But when he glances at the ads, he feels overwhelmed by the amount and variety of brands, types and configurations of computers that are sold. He doesn't know where to begin. He thinks of you as a person who knows how to judge things. You have had a computer for some time and decide to help him out by evaluating several models you think will suit his needs and finances. Write the evaluation essay you would give him.

3. One of your cousins who lives in another state is almost ready to apply to college. You have been requested—by your aunt, uncle, mother, and father—to help your cousin choose a school that will fit her personality and interests. Moreover, her parents are concerned that she not go too far away and that the school teach her something. With the characteristics of your cousin's personality in mind, write her a letter about your recommendations.

4. You belong to a young adults' group that has its own monthly newsletter. The editor has asked you to write a piece for the next issue about the comparative advantages and disadvantages of living in a dormitory versus an apartment. Since you have done both—and, in fact, have had pleasant experiences with both living situations—you are a good choice to give a balanced evaluation.

Evaluation Essay A DRASTIC DIFFERENCE

Goal: To evaluate progress in a writing course by weighing first and last papers according to criteria important in good writing.
Audience: Writing teacher and the writer himself

If someone were to say that the difference between my first essay and my in-class essay were like night and day it would be an understatement. I can find nothing worth complimenting in my first essay, whereas my in-class essay, though far from perfect, does have its strong points. There are certain components crucial to a good essay which I have applied to both essays to judge and compare them. Based on these comparisons it is obvious to me that I have greatly improved my writing and deserve to pass this writing course.

The aforementioned components on which I evaluated my essays were collecting, focus, development, coherence, and conventions. The first, collecting, is most important because a paper needs good evidence to back up and support the author's claims. Without it the paper loses its clout. My first essay had almost no collection. I merely related the bare facts without much support. My in-class essay, however, had much supporting evidence and did back up the paper's claims. It told of "the first time my parents were separated" (page 1), "nights when my father would come home drunk" (pages 3-4), and my own problems with school and drinking. The evidence clearly gave a strong base to the paper. Without it the paper is merely a skeleton.

Focus is another important component in addition to the collection of data. If a paper is not well focused, the reader will lose interest and the paper will fail to do its job. This is where my first essay failed miserably. It seemed to just ramble on about "walking down the main street of Cancun, Mexico" (page 1), "gringos whooping it up" (page 1), and other things that had absolutely nothing to do with my topic. In comparison my in-class essay did not ramble on with the irrelevant. All the facts presented were clearly linked to the "dimming of my hopes and expectations for life" (page 6). It was clearly focused and did not allow the reader's mind to wander and lose the point of the essay.

Even if a paper is well focused, it will lose its power without proper development. It must allow the reader to see and feel what is described so he can relate to the situation. The reader cannot read the writer's mind. It is the writer's job to paint a picture for the reader. The length of my first essay will attest to the fact that there was absolutely no development. It tells of events but does not expand on them and expects the readers to fill in the gaps. Fortunately, I learned of this flaw during the course and was able to develop my in-class essay. The paper goes in-depth when questioning my father's decision, "How could he choose a bottle over his wife and kids?" and his subsequent stage of melancholy when I wrote of him being "disillusioned" (page 3). It also tells of times when "he talked to me of his younger glory days and the fun he had" (page 3) along with memories of his late father. All this adds richness and color to the paper like no other technique can. I truly believe development is the lifeblood of a quality essay.

In addition to the preceding components, an essay must be coherent. The paper must flow, not only chronologically but transitionally too. My first essay is a good example of this. Even though it was in chronological order it was hard to follow due to the absence of paragraph hooks. It was choppy and unpleasant to read. I believe my improvement in this area is displayed in my in-class essay. The paragraphs seem to relate to each other by allusions to the preceding paragraph and overall relevance to the main point.

Even if an essay includes all the aforementioned components, it will not be effective without using proper conventions. It sounds redundant to say you must know how to write an essay to write an essay, but it's true. Proper format is essential to a good essay. Selecting correct words and sentences, choosing proper punctuation, and proofreading are all very important to an essay. All of this will come if two or three drafts of a paper are made before writing the final one. A good example is the difference between my essays. My first essay was my only draft while my in-class essay at least had an outline. Practice, in everything, will improve skills, and that is what rough drafts are for.

In conclusion, I believe I deserve to pass this course. A testament to how much I have learned was revealed to me when I read my first essay at the beginning of this test and realized how lousy it was! I clearly remember turning it in in January and being happy with it; now I cannot believe I wrote it. Although I have much to learn, I believe I have taken a giant step toward being a better writer.

The Persuasion Essay

The *persuasion* essay is the most direct, overt form of Writing to Change. You may be writing to support a certain candidate for office, to promote a certain philosophy, or to get a law passed—but whatever the content, the purpose is always to persuade the reader to act on what you urge in your writing. In the assertion-with-evidence essay, you intend to make a strong statement, back it up, and thereby change what the reader knows about that subject. In the evaluation essay, you intend to influence—even change—which choice the reader will make. But in the persuasion essay, you intend to cause the reader to do, think, or believe something different after reading your arguments—in other words, to change their course of action or inaction.

All of us have ideas or beliefs that we hold valuable. Caring about your cause—being committed to it—allows you to move your readers to act. If you received a leaflet that said "Vote for Joe Schmoe, um, because, well, he's kinda good on the basic issues," you would not be inspired to vote for Joe Schmoe. To convince the reader, the writer must be convinced.

In the persuasion essay, the writer-reader relationship looks like this:

Writer	*Reader*
person who sees	person who hasn't seen yet
person who is committed	person who isn't committed yet
person who has a vision	person who doesn't have a vision, or who has a different vision

Therefore, to find a topic you feel committed to, ask yourself the questions that appear on the following page.

What have I seen that I want others to see?

What do I care about so strongly that I want others to care about it too?

What action would make the world better, in my opinion?

Once you have a topic, you can locate an audience more easily by asking yourself the following.

Who are the people who need to be persuaded, so that this desired change will be made?

What are their current needs?

What form of writing will best reach this audience, so that they can act on my appeal?

In writing a persuasion essay, you are entering into a partnership with your reader. Persuading is nothing like cornering an innocent passerby on the street and delivering your harangue—that's called "taking advantage of a captive audience." Persuading is the art of arranging your words so that they convey what matters to you and the readers too begin to care—and do something different about—what you care about.

The following steps will help you tailor your essay to your audience.

1. Tell your reader right away what it is that you want them to do, believe, or act on.

2. Focus on a single area of change—don't overload your readers with a shopping list of "things to do."

3. Be aware of the readers' needs, and appeal to those needs.

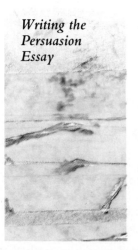

Writing the Persuasion Essay

Summary

1. Choose a subject you care about so strongly that you want to urge others to take action on it.

2. Keep your focus to a single area to be changed.

3. Choose an audience that is in a position to carry out the intended action.

4. Make your qualifications clear, and give personal experiences and other data from reading and research to help the readers identify with you and the situation you are describing.

5. Use many illustrations and examples. Support your generalizations with concrete details—the more the better.

6. Tell your readers exactly what action you want them to take.

4. Let the readers know that you know your subject thoroughly.

5. Use your own experience, as well as the experience of others and information gleaned from reading and research, to make your stand more convincing. Readers need to identify with you, or with the situation you describe, in order to see your solution as one that might apply to them.

6. Choose a tone that will not "turn off" your reader, and choose language that fits that tone.

7. Make it clear to the readers what they should do as a result of reading your essay.

WRITING *The Persuasion Essay*

1. You have just bought a used car, appliance, or other product. You were given a warranty certifying that the product was guaranteed for six months. Unfortunately, you have had nothing but trouble with the product. Even worse, the dealer who sold the product now claims that the warranty does not cover what has broken. You are furious—you want the product repaired at no expense to you. You plan to write to the state Consumer Protection Agency, reporting the dealer and asking that the agency investigate him and see that your warranty is honored. Write the letter you will send.

2. You are a student who has just completed a speed-reading/memorization course (or some other study plan). In one hour, you can now read, understand, and recall what required four hours before. You are totally sold on this method; and when you look at your fellow students, you know they could benefit from the same techniques. Write either (a) an open letter of persuasion to your fellow students for the school paper or (b) a letter to the school curriculum committee requiring the course for all incoming students.

3. Your brother, who is young, progressive, and well qualified, is running for office—in the student government or for a city, state, or national position. You have agreed to seek support for him among your peers. In a short, informal essay, persuade the members of your class, your church group, or the people with whom you work, to vote for your brother.

4. While working in a supermarket or restaurant, you notice how much food gets thrown out. You wonder whether such waste happens in other places as well, and whether the homeless and needy in your community could somehow benefit. You begin to have strong feelings

about this—strong enough that you want to help put a stop to it. Write either (a) a letter to your employer asking for his help in distributing the food to the needy, (b) a letter to your city council asking for a city policy on such food distribution, or (c) an article for the local paper about the situation and your recommendation.

Persuasion Essay **PLEASE EXTINGUISH ALL SMOKING MATERIAL NOW**

Goal: To effect a ban on smoking on airplanes
Audience: Air travelers

Straining to see my way clear, I emerged from the jet, my contact lenses dry and coated with a smoky film, my throat and nose irritated, not to mention the smell that would cling and follow me the rest of the day, just because the people seated around me decided to light up. Fortunately, I don't have asthma, allergies, or heart disease. Nevertheless, passive smoke endangers even my health. Although some people contend that smoking has become a right that does not present health or safety hazards to others, because of the confined space of an aircraft cabin where ventilation and air quality become a major concern, smoking should be eliminated from commercial aircraft. The trend in society away from smoking justifying nonsmoker's rights, new studies showing the harmful effects of passive smoke, and the safety and air quality issues inherent in air travel warrant a smoking ban.

First, the issue of rights inevitably arises in the smoking controversy. Smokers claim possession of an individual right to smoke whereas nonsmokers contend they are entitled to breathe fresh air. Lee S. Glass, a doctor and lawyer, while questioning whether a person can even claim smoking as his/her right, states that people "ought not be able to smoke in an airplane, when to do so may leave an asthmatic 10 rows away gasping for breath" (18). Common courtesy to others should always prevail. A right is not guaranteed when it proves harmful to others. Additionally, rules and regulations in general are intended to benefit the most people in society. Thus, smoking in public, airplanes included, becomes a matter of the rights of an individual versus the rights of the majority. The trend in society today moves away from smoking as the norm toward nonsmokers as the emerging majority. According to William U. Chandler, senior researcher at Worldwatch Institute in Washington, D.C., the United States has experienced a drop of more than a third in the percentage of males who smoke (57).

The time has arrived to recognize nonsmokers as the prevailing interest. Because of the confining quarters of an aircraft, with most passengers seated together in an open cabin, nonsmokers have no means of escape from the drifting and circulating smoke. Thus, outdated regulations favoring smoking on aircraft, fast becoming a habit of the past, should be eliminated and new ordinances established to protect the rising interests of nonsmokers.

Besides protecting interests of the majority, recent studies have exposed health hazards associated with passive smoke. Joseph Califano, former Secretary of Health, Education and Welfare, places the toll of Americans who die yearly of complications attributed to secondary smoke at 5,000. He cites involuntary smoking as contributing to lung cancer, pneumonia, asthma, bronchitis, and heart disease ("Restrict Smoking" 65). Keep in mind that these are *nonsmokers* dying as a result of smoke generated by others. In his article urging the banishment of tobacco, Chandler stresses that "Sidestream smoke—which wafts from a smoker's cigarette to an involuntary smoker—puts into the surrounding air fifty times the amount of carcinogens inhaled by the user." Accordingly, he states that passive smokers face a risk of succumbing to lung cancer three times higher than if the exposure was avoided (56, 60). Eliot Marshall, in an issue of *Science,* reported the findings of the National Research Council appointed to study the issue. They found young children brought up in smoking environments are highly susceptible to respiratory problems, nonsmoking adults married to smokers are more prone to lung cancer, and many nonsmokers suffer severe eye, nose, and throat irritation as a result of passive smoke (1066). These alarming discoveries and statistics illustrate the harm inflicted on innocent people. These are people who have chosen not to smoke, whether out of pride and respect for their health, simple distaste for the habit, or realization of the inherent risks. Yet to see these same adults and children, however careful they have been in this respect, suffering and dying from the effects of smoke created by others illustrates the need for action in this matter. When seated in an airplane, then, should it be so difficult to consider the health and well-being of those around you? Most domestic commercial flights reach their destinations within an hour or two, some with layovers to provide a break. Smokers, while in flight, could make use of commercially available alternatives such as smokeless cigarettes or nicotine gum to tide them over. As more

facts arise about the risks of secondary smoke, clearly measures should be taken to eliminate smoke from airplanes, where close personal contact cannot be avoided.

Additionally, airplanes themselves harbor exclusive safety and air quality problems not found in other public places, making a smoking ban essential. First, at the top of safety concerns, in the event of fire caused by a careless smoker, there clearly exists no escape from a cruising aircraft. Also, an article by Pepper Leeper cites conclusions drawn from a study done by the National Research Council committee on federal standards in air travel as mandated by Congress. With ventilation and air quality their primary concern, the committee released information that new aircrafts recirculate as much as half of the stale cabin air for greater general efficiency of the plane. Most of the ventilation systems are set to provide the minimum airflow rate allowable, before any tobacco smoke or contaminants are introduced into the pressurized compartments. Thus, the committee believes that smoking causes a drop of air quality in planes below federal standards (30). According to Thomas C. Chalmers, chairperson of the National Research Council committee and president emeritus of Mount Sinai Medical Center in New York, present filters in the ventilation system do not dispel those pollutants resulting from cigarette smoking, so those gases remain free in the cabins for a long period (5B).

Not only does the smoke recirculate, but it causes mechanical problems as well. Speaking to a maintenance supervisor of an airline, Lee S. Glass found that smoke accumulates in the metal tubing of the ventilation system, not only inhibiting circulation through the network, but requiring money to clean and restore the system (18). These statements indicate that because of the design, pressurization, and ventilation requirements of airplanes, no solution now exists to safely rid the smoke and ash from the cabin air. The only acceptable answer is a complete ban on the source of the pollution, tobacco smoke.

In response, the opponents of a smoking ban present various "resolutions" to the problem, none of which satisfy the core issue. While current seating may seem adequate, separate seating sections for smokers do not improve air quality for nonsmokers, but instead aggravate the condition. The research committee declares that separating smokers into one section concentrates the smoke so that it becomes too intense for the ventilation system, and cloudy air results. However, dispersing smokers among nonsmokers to lessen concentrations would meet overwhelming opposition from the public (Leeper 31). Other suggestions considered by the committee according to Chalmers included erecting physical barriers or air curtains that would interfere with safety standards and escape routes, redesigning cabin layouts that prove too costly, and increasing the flow of outside air into the aircraft that would rob the jet engines of their power (5B). Clearly, a feasible solution does not presently exist to warrant safe smoking aboard airplanes. The general nature of airplanes themselves, where balance and stability dictate design, limited and restricted public quarters exist, requirements for a pressurized and sealed compartment arise, and safety and air quality become critical, does not allow support for the threat that smoking aboard clearly imposes.

In ending, hustle and bustle along with a general lack of concern characterizes today's society. The days have vanished when people on the streets greeted one another with a smile and a "hello" and when people actively acquainted themselves with neighbors and other citizens. Presently, society consists of corporate executives, industrialists, capitalists, merchants, wage earners, and ordinary people so wrapped up in their own problems that a general disregard

pervades. The nearest airport measures the essence of this hubbub, where everyone seems to be jockeying for some crucial position. With airports working to their limits to meet the demand, meeting safety and health criteria becomes an intricate but vital endeavor. In this respect, smoking has no merit aboard airplanes. Until the time that enough people realize on their own the value of respect and consideration for others and show genuine interest, regulations will have to intervene. For these reasons, smoking should be banned on airplanes.

Works Cited

Chalmers, Thomas C. "Ban All Smoking on Planes." *Denver Post* 5 Sept. 1986: 5B.

Chandler, William U. "Banishing Tobacco." *Transaction Social Science and Modern Society* May/June 1986: 56–64.

Glass, Lee S. "Fly the Smoke-Free Skies." *Newsweek* 16 April 1984: 18.

Leeper, Pepper. "Cleaning Up the Air in Commercial Airlines." *The Air Conditioning, Heating and Refrigeration News* 13 October 1986: 30–31.

Marshall, Eliot. "Involuntary Smokers Face Health Risks." *Science* 28 Nov. 1986: 1066–67.

"Restrict Smoking in Public Places?" *U.S. News & World Report.*

Works Consulted

"Air Canada Smoking Ban Retained for Some Routes." *Wall Street Journal* 1 Aug. 1986: 22.

Bruning, Fred. "Drawing the 'Smoking' Battle Lines." *Maclean's: Canada's Weekly Newsmagazine* 12 March 1984: 13.

Engler, Nick. "Cigarettes and Jet Lag." *Omni* July 1986: 29.

McGinley, Laurie. "Ban on Smoking Sought for Flights By Airliners in U.S." *Wall Street Journal* 13 Aug. 1986: 6.

"Murky Hazards of Secondhand Smoke." *Consumer Reports* Feb. 1985: 81–84.

Otten, Alan L. "Sharpest Attack Yet on Passive Smoking Issued in New Study by Surgeon General." *Wall Street Journal* 17 Dec. 1986: 8.

Preble, Cecilia. "Academy Urges Smoking Ban in U.S. Commercial Aircraft." *Aviation Week & Space Technology* 18 Aug. 1986: 31–32.

"Psst! Wanna Smoke?" *Fortune* 4 Aug. 1986: 9.

"Study Expected to Urge Smoking Ban on All Domestic Flights." *New York Times* 13 Aug. 1986: A16.

WHY CONSIDER PURPOSE?

Many students taking writing courses or writing papers for other classes wonder why purpose is so important to consider when writing a paper. Unfortunately, most academic writing has a single purpose ("show my teacher I know the material") that students never question. But writing that comes from *your* need to write will always have a purpose beyond getting a grade or finishing a course requirement. Writing that you care about wouldn't happen at all unless you wanted to express, inform, or change.

Moreover, readers read with a purpose (remember what we said about the reading process in Chapter 2). Readers look for information, diversion, argument, inspiration, and enlightenment whenever they read. The most exciting match occurs when a writer, knowing his or her purpose, connects with a reader having the same purpose.

And so as you go on to consider other elements of the writing process, remember that readers and writers don't just stumble into communicating. Each partner in the communication process has a goal, and as a writer you can best meet your goals if you understand why you are writing and why your reader will care enough to read what you have written.

CHAPTER 8

Drafting

Writing is rarely, if ever, a straightforward process. Rather, a writer jots down notes or completes a creating activity, thinks about a good introduction to the paper, considers audience and thinks of a new intro, goes back to creating to get more ideas, drafts a paragraph or two for the body of the paper, revises them and goes back to creating to get more ideas. Each writer tends to have his or her preferred ways of getting words on paper, and each writing assignment puts constraints on the writer's methods.

At some point, though, writers must begin to *draft*—to write preliminary versions of their papers. Some writers prefer to get the introduction just right before going on. Other writers begin in the middle and write the body of the paper first, then come back and write the introduction after finishing the rest of the paper. Some writers skip back and forth between parts of the paper, writing a paragraph for the body, then two lines for the intro, then more of the body, then the conclusion.

Whatever your approach, you must begin to draft. The most important point to remember about drafting is that the writing is temporary. Try to think of a draft as one step toward a final paper. If you leave yourself enough time, you can do several drafts, making each one closer to the piece that communicates exactly what you want to set forth to a reader.

STARTING A DRAFT

When you begin your first draft, you will already have thought and written about your topic. Keep all your prewriting handy to remind yourself about details, examples, audience characteristics.

If you are working on a word processor, copy material that you might use in a draft from your prewriting files into your drafting file. Don't worry about having too much material in the first draft: cutting down a first draft is much easier than adding material later.

If you are working on a long paper, you might try drafting sections of it at a time, especially if you are doing research or data collection for each section.

Begin your draft by putting three things at the top of the first page: your goal in writing, a short description of your audience, and the general idea you want to communicate. These won't appear on the final paper itself (although we've left goal and audience on most of the student essays that appear in Part 2), but when you're drafting, these points will remind you of the reason you are writing and the person or persons to whom you are writing. They will set your mind in the right channel as you begin.

The beginning, middle, and end of an essay each play a specific role in achieving your goal. Sooner or later, the opening paragraph or paragraphs of your paper will have to

get your readers' attention;

reveal or suggest the message you intend to send in the essay; and

ease your readers into the aspect/perspective of your subject you want them to think about.

The middle paragraphs or body of the essay will have to

stick to your thesis;

deliver the message as promised; and

get the idea that was in your head into your readers' heads.

The ending of the paper will have to

remind your readers of what you said;

give your readers at least one new thing or twist on the subject to think about; and

provide a gentle completing of the paper so that your readers are not left hanging in mid-air.

It isn't likely that you will be able to accomplish all these goals in an initial draft, but keeping the purposes of each basic part of the essay in mind will often feed your creativity and help you make spontaneous, even unconscious, decisions about what you want to say and how you want to say it.

Set a deadline for completing a first draft. Give yourself plenty of time between this deadline and the deadline for the finished paper. Then start writing.

THE DISCOVERY DRAFT

Because many writers are not entirely sure about what they want to say even after prewriting on a topic, a discovery draft can help the writer see the directions his or her mind is taking.

Quite simply, you write a discovery draft to see how the paper is going to turn out. Remember that you may not know what you think on a subject until you write about it. You often need to continue to write to see how you want to say what you think. The discovery draft, then, has many positive results: getting something, anything, down on paper; learning what you really feel about a subject; seeing how your mind approaches a certain issue.

Sometimes when you write a discovery draft, you may find that the paper is almost writing itself, and sometimes you may find that nothing is working. There is no question that a discovery draft can be uneven, imperfect, and rough, but it can also be revealing. It can make you see new things you are thinking or a clear direction in which the writing is taking itself. Most importantly, it gives you a beginning. So just jump in and write the first draft of the essay.

How to Write the Discovery Draft

When writing the discovery draft, it's important to keep the following in mind.

Get Started on the Draft Itself. Start putting words on the page. Don't get caught in the cycle of writing and crossing out. If necessary, set a timer and write to complete the draft before your timer sounds.

You already know that an essay always opens with some kind of introduction, so start there. Think of anything that can serve as an introduction. Tell a story; give a quote; ask some questions—anything that leads into what you want to discuss with the reader. If all else fails just write *Introduction* across the page and go on to the middle.

Aim to Involve the Reader from the Start. Keep reminding yourself that you are writing to a particular person. You will be amazed at how many decisions you can make about what details to put into your paper and how to arrange them if you will only keep this reader in mind. At the same time, remember that your reader won't be seeing your discovery draft, so you can concentrate on expressing your ideas without worrying about how they are presented.

Write More Instead of Less. Write every idea you can think of to communicate what you want your reader to know. This is the main part of your discovery draft. Your reader has not been thinking about your subject and certainly hasn't done the creating activities you have done. The reader probably has a different background and set of experiences from yours, too. So write plenty of details that will help your reader understand your subject as well as you do. Make all the points you can think of to convince, inform, or explain. And when you suppose you have given enough information for your message to be clear, add about ten percent more.

Don't Get Bogged Down. Don't worry at this point whether this example should come before that one or if you can't spell some of the words, or if you can't recall specific details. You have to keep moving on. You can worry about all the rest later—you can take out, put in, fix up, skin down. Right now, however, you have to get the material onto the paper. Until you do, there simply isn't anything to revise.

Wrap Up the Essay. Go on and finish it, even if you think it is the worst thing you ever wrote. What was the main idea you originally wanted to leave in your readers' heads? Even if you are sure you didn't achieve your intention, put that idea down again now. Having written the discovery draft, you may have a better idea of what you want to communicate than you did when you began writing. This restatement may help you revise later on. Some writers have to write the last paragraph of the discovery draft before they know what they want to say in the opening paragraph of the revised draft. (This often happens because the idea grows and even changes during the discovery draft.) You may have insights now that you didn't have when you started. Don't lose them.

Put Your Discovery Draft Aside to Cool. Whatever the faults of this draft, you have at least tested your idea and done a preliminary version of your writing. Sure, it looks rough. But you do have a complete paper, something you can work on later. Put the paper aside with a sigh of contentment—or at least of relief. Leave it for several hours or more.

If you are working on a tight schedule and don't have time to let the paper cool for a few hours, at least do this: find a friend and read the paper out loud to him or her. Ask what message the person hears in the paper. Watch your listener's face and see if he or she looks confused as you read the paper. Listen to yourself and notice if you stumble anywhere as you read it. (Research shows that wherever you stumble you might well revise.) Ask your listener if the paper was boring. In general, get another person's response to what you have written.

Let's consider an example of a discovery draft to see how it helps the writer "discover" what he wants to write about.

STUDENT EXAMPLE *Discovery Draft*

Goal: To discover one change in growing older
Audience: Younger classmates

I saw a picture of a go-kart in a catalog. I was 5 or 6. I knew it would be fun. It looked *dangerous!* My mother and father foolishly encouraged my idea, thinking it would help me learn to save money. I saved half, and with their help for the other half I was the proud owner. The only one on the block. It was sleek, and it was just a little bit dangerous. Just enough to be the beginning. I've been spending a very significant part of my time and energy ever since pursuing ever increasing thrills and chills, never mind the spills. But the last few years I've noticed some other beginnings. Or, rather, I fear, endings.

Following the go-kart came a full succession of motorized mini-bikes, snowmobiles, motorcycles. My hometown was a wonderful area for snowmobiles and motorcycles. I would often ride with "the pack." In the winter, all on our snowmobiles, a dozen or more kids, racing across a frozen lake seeing who could go the fastest, jump the farthest, execute the most daring coup. In the summer with motorcycles it was the same, always discovering some new kind of excitement. I remember a track through the dirt alongside the county highway (97) and twelve miles long across the rolling hills. I would race as fast as I could, jumping driveways where they would turn in from the highway. I would try and pass the cars (going 65 mph) on my back wheel. Perhaps a mile or more along a particularly flat stretch. For an endless minute I would navigate a 1 foot wide strip of clear path at 65 mph on my back tire, just to see the look of surprise on the driver's face.

It was a gusty day, which I had never dealt with before. I tipped the nose up, and the wind caught me. I was wrenched off the ground, experiencing a power I had never felt before. Instead of gliding serenely down, as in my early short flights, I pitched and rocked violently. I concentrated to the utmost to maintain my heading away from the mountain. My knuckles were white on the control bar, the circulation cut off by my deathgrip. Five hundred feet below, or more, was the ground I had so recently departed. With only a loudly flapping rag of Dacron strung on a startlingly creaking web of aluminum and a few loosely attached and very thin wires keeping me from rejoining it all too quickly. Praying with a new fervency, I swore that if I landed alive, I would *never, never* do something, anything unreasonable, which included hang gliding. I landed alive, unscathed and so exhilarated, so supercharged with my realization that I made it that it took all my self-control not to go up for a second flight. And so it went with hang gliding. Each new wave of adrenaline washing over the one before. Hang gliding and high excitement are so enmeshed in my psyche that nowadays even when simply talking about flying my hands begin to shake and my voice rises and cracks. But lately a new feeling has slipped in as well. An uneasiness. A fear. A few months ago I called a friend that has a hang glider identical to mine. I needed some advice with some tuning adjustments. His sister-in-law answered. My friend was dead. He made a simple error in a launch. One wingtip brushed the ground. His hang glider turned into a rock. And now I'm wondering what it will feel like when I hit the rocks, *again*.

I've read that scientists have confirmed by their experiments that high risk sports' participants become addicted to adrenaline surges. I know from experience it's true. I've also read that scientists have discovered a chemical that drives people, especially abundant in young men, towards dangerous activities, and that these secretions die out towards middle age. I would like to believe this too.

But I don't. I think these scientists are just like me. They want some kind of good excuse, something they have no real control over, to act different than when they were younger, and life was full of excitement and they weren't afraid then like they are now. Just like me.

As you can see from this beginning, Max had an idea he wanted to communicate—that the "thrill" of adolescence becomes the "fear" of middle age. In this discovery draft, however, he doesn't focus the main point as clearly as he would want to in revised drafts. He did, however, have some good experiences to work into the paper and some good details to draw readers into the essay.

After writing the discovery draft, Max began looking at specific "thrill-seeking" experiences. He reorganized his ideas, and even jotted down a rough outline to help himself revise. He also did some additional creating to come up with specific incidents for his paper.

Let's look at a later draft to see how Max capitalized on the strengths of the discovery draft while adding and rearranging material.

Final Draft   FEAR OF FLYING

Goal: To explain one change in growing older
Audience: Younger classmates

"Conley's dead," the disembodied voice over the phone told me. I hung up, stunned. What did it mean? We flew together often, or at least used to. Just last month we had dodged in and out of clouds together, playing tag with a rumbling thunderhead at 16,000 feet. We knew that we were risking our lives; that's why we were there. We landed after an hour and a half, whooping and shouting about our daring adventure. As we broke our kites down, the wind began to scare up dustdevils alongside the road and fat raindrops started to splat off our helmets. Electricity crackled in the air, threatening, exhilarating, as we hurried to load our gear. Every weekend we clipped our lives to seventy pounds of aluminum and Dacron, trusting our luck and skill. Flying was our opium, the thing we lived for. "Air junkies" we called ourselves with a nervous laugh, swearing we would never quit until it killed us. Conley had just quit. And me? I secretly hoped to quit before it killed me as I had done with motorcycles and skiing. But I wondered if I dared cut it so close this time.

Motorcycles gave me my first lessons in brushing up against death. Motorcycles were what life was about when I was 16. I would ride with "the pack," a dozen or more kids like me, racing along the trails through the woods and down the dirt roads that crosshatched the midwest countryside. An abandoned gravel pit on a Saturday in July was heaven on earth. Up and down the vertical walls we would spin our wheels, around and around the old piles of sand, or straight up over the top. We would stop and critique riding styles or the latest bikes from our expert viewpoints, and after a short rest we would kick our beasts to life and ride again. Who could jump the farthest, ride a wheelie the longest? Whoever executed the most daring coup of the day was always held in high regard. I had a favorite stretch of trail that paralleled the county highway. When a car came up over the hill I would pull alongside, flash a smile at the startled driver and pull away, all the while riding on my back tire!

Accidents, of course, were commonplace. One cool dewy Minnesota evening a friend and I hit the asphalt at sixty miles an hour. The engine suddenly froze and we skidded and fell. "Look at the sparks," I thought, seeing tiny flashes coming off the rivets of my friend's jeans as we fanned out along the center-line. All the next week I wore the pain like a badge of honor. I limped down the school halls knowing that my friends were talking about my close call. But I paid a price each night when I would pull my clothes off oozing scabs that formed each day. Still, I never considered quitting, until years later. We rooted back and forth across the high school practice field relishing the huge chunks of turf being excavated by our rear tires. I opened the throttle and jerked up on the handlebars. The time was ripe for one of my renowned wheelies. Shifting from second to third my front wheel held its graceful loft. I caught fourth gear doing fifty—just as my rear tire hit the curb at the end of the field. The back wheel ricocheted upwards, the front slammed down and I sailed a perfect trajectory out onto the parking lot, greeting the asphalt once again. When everything came to rest, what had been a back wheel was now a pretzel. I felt the same way. It was weeks before I could walk normally again. That was the turning point in my motorcycle career. I've owned other, bigger, faster bikes, but I've never been able to ride the same. I had met fear.

Skiing became my new passion as I lost interest in motorcycles. I even moved from Minnesota to Colorado in pursuit of the "ultimate experience." The wind whistled past my ears and brought tears to my eyes; my skis chattered wildly as I careened downward, finally stopping with a flourish. Steep was not steep enough. Fast was still too slow. I escaped the dreary realities of the world the instant I stepped into my skis. The realities caught up with me again, though. The snow was later than usual one year, and when enough finally came to open the mountain I was ready. I skied with even more than my usual aplomb, endeavoring to make up for lost time. I swooped off the groomed trail, through the trees, tempted by the untracked snow. But the snow was just a thin veneer this year. The front of my skis struck a hidden stump. Slamming against a boulder and bouncing like a rag doll, cartwheeling and summersaulting, I finally stopped on my back, unable to move or even breathe. The ski patrol arrived and loaded me onto a toboggan like so many others I had sneered at. Foolish skiers, incompetents. Me. This time the weeks of my recovery seemed long, slow, painful. I was learning. I still ski occasionally, but not with my former sense of invulnerability, and the feeling of freedom has changed to ennui.

Hang-gliding succeeded skiing as the next step on my quest for adrenaline and has certainly been satisfying in that respect. Unfortunately, the razor is as sharp as always. Friends ran back and forth, yelled for help as I lay unconscious. Only seconds before, I stood at the edge of the hill, smiling. The sky was brilliant, dotted with a few fat, lazy cumulus. The wind was blowing straight in. Friends were already a mile overhead, tiny bright specks wafting and darting in the breeze. Anxious to join them I picked up my glider and ran off the hill. The kite started to turn, and I couldn't correct. The mountain that belonged behind me veered into my path. "Not again," I thought as I hit.

Until now, I've always been unwilling or unable to change my flying. I've never considered stopping, perhaps because I have nothing to replace it with. If I fold in my wings for good, I'm saying goodbye to a way of life. I'll be replacing adventurousness with discretion, daring with prudence. I'll be giving in to responsibility once and for all, shouting to the world, "I'm 30 now; I'm old and afraid." But Conley's dead. I feel old and afraid.

Max grabs the readers' attention with the opening line of this draft and moves quickly into his first example. He lets the examples *show* readers the thrill-seeking, but he also sets up his point about fear by referring repeatedly to death. This draft is much more effective, partly because Max used the discovery draft successfully to find out what he wanted to write about and how he might best arrange his ideas and examples.

You may not always want to write a discovery draft. Often, your prewriting will have helped you to narrow and organize your ideas adequately to begin a more focused draft. But however you begin writing the paper itself, think of early drafts as starting points, as material to revise in later drafts. Postponing your commitment to final form may make starting to write much easier.

DRAFTING *Getting Started*

1. Review your prewriting on any of the topics you've covered in your journal or on a topic you're considering for another class. Set a timer to allow yourself 20 minutes for each 250 words required in the final paper. Write a discovery draft.

2. Put your discovery draft aside for at least half an hour. Then reread the draft to find a main point you can continue to write about as you complete the paper. Prepare for a second draft by noting at the top of a clean page (or screen) the audience, goal, and main point you focused on in the discovery draft.

CHAPTER 9

Focusing Through a Thesis

As we saw in Chapter 8, writing a discovery draft can help writers discover what they want to write about. By this we mean not just the topic—writers will have a topic in mind even before they begin a discovery draft—but a *thesis* for the paper. Although many writers mistakenly believe that the topic and thesis for a piece of writing are the same thing, the thesis, in fact, includes not only your topic but also the assertion or point you want to make about the topic. The thesis may be contained in a single sentence or it may be implied within a whole paragraph, but whichever form it takes, it is important that the thesis appear as early in the paper as possible.

Why is a thesis so important in writing? A thesis helps writers communicate effectively with their readers. It also focuses both the writer's and the reader's attention on the perspective a paper takes on a given idea, guides the writer about what to include in the paper, and helps the reader see how best to read.

The most difficult part about writing a thesis is that the thesis commits a writer to a narrow focus on a topic. While a narrow focus is an important advantage for both reader and writer, some writers feel limited once they've jotted down a thesis. Other writers feel they can't write a paper until the thesis is perfect. Almost all writers, however, find that their thesis changes as they write drafts of a paper because writing about an idea clarifies their thinking on that topic. Thus the thesis represents the writing process in miniature—it helps writers (and readers) to focus, to generate and organize material, to stay on track, and to revise. Because a thesis can do all these things, it's complicated to get the thesis right. We'll spend this chapter demonstrating the importance of the thesis and ways to improve your thesis statements.

As you complete your first draft, a thesis—or some hint of a thesis—will probably show up. This first thesis is not usually as clearly focused or fully developed as it will be in later drafts of your essay. You need to think of the thesis in two phases—a *working thesis* that acts as a preliminary focus to get you started writing, and a *revised thesis* that guides your readers through your final paper.

THE WORKING THESIS AS A PRELIMINARY FOCUS

As you know from the prewriting you've done, much of your focusing occurs even before you think of a specific thesis. In effect, what happens is something like this: you get a general idea to write about and you brainstorm for possible approaches to that topic. Once you determine who your reader will be, you discover that several of the perspectives you uncovered in brainstorming may be appropriate. Then you try other creating techniques to see which of the perspectives is most interesting for you and for your reader. You might discover that although one perspective interests you, you don't know enough about that topic or you aren't expert enough to show details that support your point. Throughout the prewriting process, you are focusing your idea by throwing out those topics, approaches, and perspectives that just won't work in the paper you have in mind for your specific reader.

Once you've collected enough details through creating, you may have a pretty good idea of what the main point of your paper will be. If you do, this is the time to write a preliminary or working thesis to help you focus still more. You need not agonize over this thesis, because your main goal at this point is just to state your idea as clearly as you can *now*. You know that this working thesis won't be polished and ready for readers; you are only going to use it to guide you through the rest of the paper. This preliminary focusing statement will help you select appropriate material from your prewriting and may help you see when you are going off into territory not covered by your main point.

You may not be ready to draft a working thesis before you draft the entire paper. That's fine too. Many good writers draft the complete paper before they draft a working thesis. They write all of the ideas and related material they have collected into one draft, look at them on paper, and then extract the main point they have unconsciously used to guide them through the draft. Basically, that's how a discovery draft can help writers see a working thesis.

The main point is that you need to put a preliminary thesis on paper to help you see just what you are promising to readers. Only after you have a thesis on paper can you polish and sharpen the working thesis into a revised thesis that will guide your revision of the rest of the paper.

Let's step through a sample to see how one student moved through this process. Patti wanted to entertain her classmates with her experiences as a sunbather. She drafted this early version of the paper with a working thesis to guide her. The working thesis is underlined.

STUDENT EXAMPLE *Working Thesis*

Goal: To explore a personal experience
Audience: Classmates

Laughing in the face of adversity has been my saving grace for all those curve-balls life has thrown to me. Probably the truest test of my good nature came a couple of years ago when I stayed at a beach house in Japan, for a weekend, with my boyfriend and his family. I had been sick with strep throat just the week before, and therefore I was faithfully gulping down antibiotics every morning. This, of course, would not have been a problem if I had realized the side effects of being in the sun for hours on end while taking these pills. The first day I was there everything was truly wonderful, and I basked in the sun all day. Needless to say, it could not last, and the problems occurred the next morning. I could not believe my eyes when I first spotted a glimpse of myself in the mirror. My face truly looked like a well-done character in a Frankenstein movie. My forehead protruded as if I had reverted to Neanderthal times, and the bridge separating my nose and eyes no longer existed. I let out a small gasp as I stared unbelievingly at the creature that was now my face. Images quickly sprinted through my mind. I could be kidnapped, just disappear, or even kill myself, anything to avoid facing the guy I was trying so hard to impress, as well as his parents. But, I decided I had to handle the situation and shakily I walked down the stairs, but before anyone saw me, I laughingly said, "Are you all ready for a big surprise? Now do not scream!" I carefully explained the situation, and by laughing with them, saved myself from a potentially devastating experience.

Another sun-filled catastrophe happened to me while I was on vacation in Hawaii. I had just gotten a cherry red bikini I was incredibly proud of, and I had sauntered down to the beach to show it off. I had been lying in the sun for hours when I finally saw him, the muscular, tanned body that I was determined had been the missing piece of my life. I walked seductively past him and, when I received an incredible smile, thought I had succeeded in my intentions to be irresistible. It was not until I gazed down to see that I had sun poisoning and had acquired ever-growing red blotches on my legs, arms, stomach, and face, that I realized why I had been given such a smile. Later that day, sauntering through the hotel lobby, fully covered, I saw him again, and we laughed and joked about the scene. By laughing at my own misfortunes I have managed to live through some of life's most heated moments.

As you can see from the working thesis, Patti has focused on "adverse" moments when laughter saved her from prolonged embarrassment. The working thesis keeps her on track throughout this draft. In support of her thesis, she includes two examples of incidents when her sense of humor has carried her through trying situations. As a working thesis, this one is successful.

Before Patti gives this paper to a reader, however, she might polish the thesis still more. We will return to Patti's thesis shortly but now think about what she can do to improve this thesis. First, she needs to consider just how her reader will use the thesis to guide reading processes, and then she can see how best to serve the reader by focusing still more narrowly and choosing more precise words.

HOW READERS USE A THESIS

In Chapter 2 we described reading as a process of prediction. A reader sets up a hypothesis about what will appear in the reading and then samples the text to confirm or revise the hypothesis. Giving your readers a clear thesis, in effect, gives them a specific hypothesis to work from. If you have focused clearly and precisely, you take much of the guesswork out of reading and help readers predict and confirm easily. As a result, readers can pay more attention to your perspective on a topic, to the details you give, or to the style of your essay rather than spend time and energy just figuring out what the essay is about.

Think of your thesis as a promise to your readers. You promise to cover a specific topic from a specific perspective. You also promise to include all the details that readers will need to understand your main point, but to avoid extra details that take the focus away from your main point.

Now look again at Patti's working thesis.

Thesis: Laughing in the face of adversity has been my saving grace for all those curve-balls life has thrown to me.

What exactly is Patti promising to cover? Do readers know precisely what experiences Patti is leading up to? Not yet. Here's the first way she can improve her thesis. She can specify just what experiences ("curve-balls") she will address in the paper. What idea can she retain from the working thesis? Her reaction to adversity—laughter—surely needs to stay in the thesis because it promises readers that they will see humorous situations. The promise of humor is important because Patti's intention is to entertain her audience.

Here is the revised version of Patti's introductory paragraph. What does it now promise to readers? Can you find her thesis and explain why she revised it the way she did?

> For most people, basking in the sun for hours on end leads to the bronzed, beautiful bodies that women, as well as men, all over this country try to impress the opposite sex with. For me, I'm afraid the results are never this rewarding. Praying to the Sun God all afternoon only seems to lead me into embarrassing confrontations with people that I'm trying to impress. Thankfully, I have always been able to laugh my way out of these unfortunate situations.

Now readers have a much better idea of what to expect from the paper. Readers can see what Patti will focus on: she has narrowed "curveballs" to sunbathing excesses, and she has further specified the embarrassment she has laughed away. With this thesis—this promise—readers can predict and read the paper with greater ease.

WRITING *Using the Thesis as a Promise to Readers*

1. The following student essay is missing a thesis as promise. Read the essay and then without looking back at it jot down what you think the main point of the paper is. Then revise the introductory paragraph to include a thesis you draft for this essay.

ME AND MY BACKPACK

Goal: To retell a memorable incident
Audience: Classmates

It was the week before finals during spring semester. My friends were all partying and I really wanted to be prepared for finals. I had a strange feeling when I left the university that day: I had to drive some 80-odd miles to my hometown, where I could get away from the partying scene.

I drove south on Interstate 25 to reach my destination. Being the only occupant, I realized how roomy my brown Chevette was. A backpack full of books consumed the other occupied space. I had the stereo turned up slightly, singing along to the latest tunes. Then it happened;

my car wasn't accelerating anymore. The car died and I pulled over to the side of the road. There I sat with my backpack, stranded on I-25.

While wondering what to do next, I became aware of my surroundings. The car sat in the far right lane of the road as semi-trucks zoomed by. The trucks would shake my car as they passed. All alone, I wondered what to do next. There was nobody to discuss the situation with, so I had to determine a resolution myself. There was a small frontage road to the west. I thought I could walk along that road until I came to a house or small town. But that road was abandoned, not one car drove by. The farmers probably only used the road when they drove their tractors home from the back fields. I thought if anything happened to me nobody would ever know, so I sat in the car and didn't walk down the road.

The thought of walking down the highway crossed my mind, but the sun was setting and I wouldn't have been easy to spot. I kept wishing I could talk to somebody to help the time go by faster. I thought about hitchhiking, but my mother always warned me not to do that.

In my silent car I sat, wishing it would start. I prayed to God, but nobody else was with me, so why should He have been there?

Then suddenly it happened. A couple in a red Honda Civic pulled over. Suitcases and other things I couldn't quite decipher were crammed in the car. A blonde woman, in her late twenties, stepped out of the car and walked towards me and my spacious vehicle. I didn't know what to think. All of a sudden I was a child again, listening to my mother say, "don't talk to strangers." There I was stranded on I-25 with a stranger approaching. Not only was she a stranger, but an out-of-stater as well. What was I supposed to do? Could I trust her? She and her husband offered to drive me to a phone; I accepted.

At last I had some company, so I presumed. My backpack and I squeezed into the back of the Honda. I became frightened; for the first time in the past hour I didn't want anyone close to me. The couple tried to converse with me, but I was extremely reluctant. We finally found a phone and they dropped me off. Even though relieved to be out of the car, I thanked the couple for the ride.

I called my roommate since I was closer to the university than to my home. She said she would pick me up in a half-hour. So there I sat in an empty parking lot, once again just me and my backpack, waiting.

2. Look at the entire essay about sunbathing as Patti revised it and note exactly how the thesis sets up readers to expect the body paragraphs. Underline text and write notes in the margins to show how Patti follows through on her promise to readers.

SOME OF LIFE'S MOST HEATED MOMENTS

For most people, basking in the sun for hours on end leads to the bronzed, beautiful bodies that women, as well as men, all over this country try to impress the opposite sex with. For me, I'm afraid the results are never this rewarding. Praying to the Sun God all afternoon only seems to lead me into embarrassing confrontations with people that I'm trying to impress.

Thankfully, I have always been able to laugh my way out of these unfortunate situations.

Probably the most embarrassing tan-seeking experience came a couple of years ago when I stayed at a beach house in Japan, for a weekend, with my boyfriend and his family. I had been sick with strep throat just the week before, and therefore I was faithfully gulping down antibiotics every morning. This, of course, would not have been a problem if I had realized the side effects of faithfully continuing to seek that eye-catching tan by lying in the sun for hours while taking these pills. The first day I was there everything was truly wonderful; I basked in the sun all day and later saw the beginnings of that rosy color on my cheeks that I was sure would be golden brown by the next morning. Needless to say, the results were not quite what I had hoped for, and I could not believe my eyes when I first spotted a glimpse of myself in the mirror. My face protruded as if I had reverted to Neanderthal times, and the bridge separating my nose and eyes no longer existed. That wonderfully rosy color from the night before now resembled blood red. I let out a small gasp as I stared at the creature that was now my face. Images quickly sprinted through my mind. I could be kidnapped, just disappear, or even kill myself, anything to avoid facing the guy I was trying so hard to impress, as well as his parents. But I decided I had to handle the situation and shakily I walked down the stairs, but before anyone saw me, I laughingly said, "Are you all ready for a big surprise? Now do not scream!" I carefully explained the situation, and by laughing with them, saved myself from a potentially devastating experience.

Another sun-filled catastrophe happened to me while I was on vacation in Hawaii. I had just gotten a cherry red bikini I was incredibly proud of, and I had sauntered down to the beach to beautifully tan the body I was trying so hard to show off. I had been lying in the sun for hours when I finally saw him, the muscular, tanned body that I was determined had been the missing piece in my life. I walked seductively past him to show off my new tan, as well as bikini, and, when I received an incredible smile, thought I had succeeded in my intentions to be irresistible. It was not until I gazed down at my supposedly bronze body that I saw I had sun poisoning and had acquired ever-growing red blotches on my legs, arms, stomach, and face. Then I realized why I had been given such a smile. Later that day walking through the hotel lobby, fully covered, I saw him again, and we laughed and joked about the scene.

My two beach experiences were unfortunately not the only humiliating examples of my tanning quests. Not learning my lesson from my previous encounters with the eyes of the sun, I ventured to get a tan the day before the prom. I had just gone shopping and bought a beautiful baby blue dress, that I was convinced needed a rich, dark tan to elicit the desired look of excellence. Because of this, I returned home and proceeded to encase myself in layers of suntan oil, and then I ventured to the lawn chair in my backyard. It was a wonderfully sunny day, and I was so relaxed that before I knew it I had fallen asleep. The next thing I remember I was opening my eyes with the realization that I could not move any part of my body for fear of excruciating pain. I had managed to sleep for three hours and had burnt the entire front of my body a deep shade of crimson. Thinking quickly, I decided I should inform my date of the half-red catastrophe that was now my body. Hoping I was still going to have an escort to the dance, I hurriedly called my date. He decided he still wanted me, red or not, and we laughed at the picture elicited by my story.

I have finally seen that although laughing at my experiences in the sun has saved me many times, I need to find a way to learn a lesson from those swollen faces, red blotches, and burnt bodies. I would like to be able to avoid those earth-shaking moments altogether. In the future I will be sunbathing in the shade, with clothing that covers my entire body.

3. Take out an essay you have worked on recently. See if you can trace your thesis promise through the essay as you just did with Patti's essay.

REVISING FOR A STRONG THESIS

We've discussed how readers expect writers to show exactly what will appear in the paper—how readers think of the thesis as a promise. Now let's consider ways to revise the working thesis to make sure it states a clear promise to readers.

Narrow Your Topic to a Workable Size

The thesis works in much the same way as a microscope which puts objects into focus. When we use a microscope at 10 power, we can see relatively small objects, but not necessarily in great detail. When we raise the power of magnification, we can see less of the whole object, but we see much greater detail. A thesis performs the same function for readers and writers. A relatively narrowed thesis can allow writers to explore larger topics, but usually only with few details (unless the paper is considerably longer). A more narrowly focused thesis allows writers to use much greater detail. And detail gets and keeps readers going.

Read this opening paragraph, noting especially what the thesis commits the writer to covering.

> Many Americans feel overwhelmed at times by the amount of advertising they are exposed to in an average day: radio, television, newspapers, magazines, and billboards! After all, total advertising expenditures in the United States amount to 2 percent of the GNP. However, some economists argue that the importance of advertising to the economy is much greater than the 2 percent figure would suggest, as this $61 billion investment generates much more economic activity. They maintain advertising molds consumer demand for new products, often by making existing products obsolete. This "contrived obsolescence" appears, for example, in the fashion industry where every season efforts are made to bring about fashion changes and new fads in clothing styles. Other economists, however, argue extensive advertising wastes resources. So is it worth it? In studying several positions on advertising's merits and pitfalls, one can conclude that advertising—wasteful or not—is necessary.

What will this paper cover? It promises to examine several positions on the merits and pitfalls of all forms of advertising. Do you suppose any writer can succeed in this task in a paper of only three pages? Probably not. The topic is too broad to cover quickly, especially when detail is the key to keeping readers interested and informed. This writer needs to narrow his topic so that he can focus his and his readers' attention. Compare his revised introductory paragraph and thesis.

While watching Monday night football last week, a friend of mine violently threw an empty plastic cup at the television set. He was not upset because his favorite team was losing; rather, the interruptions from advertising proved too much for him. He is not alone. Many Americans feel overwhelmed by the amount of advertising they are exposed to in a given day: radio, television, newspapers, magazines, and billboards! Last year, total advertising expenditures in the United States exceeded $61 billion—an overwhelming figure indeed. Although many Americans complain about the annoyance and inconvenience caused by advertising, few realize the benefits advertising provides in our society. Advertising benefits society by strengthening key industries through increased sales and effectively lowering the prices of consumer goods by providing better information.

Now the writer can concentrate on "key industries" he will identify in the paper. And he will address advertising only as it relates to increased sales and informed consumers. He is still tackling a meaty topic, but a narrowed, focused one that he can now address in a short paper.

Focus the Thesis with Precise Words

Sometimes a sentence can *look* like a thesis, yet because it is either too broad, or too muddy, or both, it doesn't serve either reader or writer. For example, "The beauty and splendor of the Great Outdoors is exhibited throughout the heritage of our country, and it is the exploration of this heritage that remains as one of the last frontiers." This looks a little like a thesis, but is it?

No. For example, "the beauty and splendor of the Great Outdoors" sounds like a topic, but what picture does it give you? There are so many kinds of beauty and so many varieties of splendor that just to list them all might take several days. Right away we can see that the topic is too broad. The last part of the statement comes no closer to making sense to the reader: ". . . exploration of the beauty and splendor of the Great Outdoors remains as one of the last frontiers." You can imagine exploring the Great Outdoors, but what makes the Great Outdoors like a "last frontier"? This particular statement doesn't focus readers' attention on a precise idea or workable topic.

Make an Assertion About Your Topic

Make a point. Your readers should never read your thesis and say, "So what?" If you state your perspective, show your stance, declare a position, you have made an assertion about the topic that will draw your readers into the writing. Early drafts of essays often lack pointed assertions. A good thesis for an effective essay must focus the topic into a clear, sharp assertion.

Look on the following page at the opening paragraph of a student's discovery draft on tourist attractions.

> What can I say about tourist attractions? Well, tourist attractions are famous, or people wouldn't go to see them. And some are interesting (although some are boring). Many are in cities, although small towns have them, too—not only museums and tall buildings but also old forts, monuments. Elementary school field trips are often to tourist attractions—I've had my share! They are often so crowded, and people are bustling around with their cameras and soda bottles—sometimes it's hard to get to see the attraction for the crowds. Sometimes the crowd itself becomes the attraction.

This is fine for a first discovery draft. But it is clear that this student doesn't yet recognize the point of what she wants to say. She has a topic without an assertion.

For this writer to draft a thesis, she must answer, "What about tourists?" One way to do this is to read the discovery draft for an assertion—something upon which to focus everything else you have to say.

When Carla, the student who wrote the paper on tourist attractions, looked over her discovery draft to spot a possible assertion, she realized that what interested her most in the writing was the statement about how tourists themselves can be the attraction. She would write about how you can get the benefits of traveling just by being with tourists. Her new introduction looked like this.

> Ever find yourself squiring out-of-town relatives to your local tourist attractions? Ever find yourself waiting in line just to squeeze into some dark museum and see rusted-away eating utensils from some insignificant dynasty? Ever get elbowed black and blue by all the other tourists snapping their photos and buying their souvenirs? Well, if the museum, monument, or scenic sandlot doesn't thrill you the way it does your Aunt Sally, try focusing your lens on the tourists themselves. Sometimes they're the ones who really provide the interest. Visiting a local museum, for example, I've had the pleasure of eavesdropping on people from France, Sweden, England, Mexico, and Ethiopia. Even though in most cases I had no idea what they were talking about, just listening to the sounds of their languages, and looking at their clothes, movements, and gestures, gave me the sense that I was the tourist—that I could see the world right from where I was. The people don't have to be from far-away places, either, to enrich the touring-in-your-home town experience—listen for a Southern drawl, New York quick speech. See what you can notice—tourists let you do a bit of traveling without even leaving your doorstep.

This time the reader knows exactly what the thesis is—even if the thesis is not completely contained in a single sentence in the paragraph. The topic "tourists" has been further narrowed to "tourists who visit tourist attractions in your hometown." The assertion is clear, too: Tourists are attractions in themselves. In this paragraph, unlike the first, there is a point to the whole thing because the writer has made a focused assertion.

Be an Insider

After coming up with a clear thesis to discuss in an essay, you must ask this crucial question: "Am I an insider in this matter?" If you know something about the topic or thesis that the reader doesn't know, or if you have special expertise in the matter, you can present yourself as an insider.

Figure out and establish your special qualifications as an expert. For example, the student who writes about tourists doesn't need to be a world traveler, or to have logged 10,000 trips to the Statue of Liberty to be an expert about her topic. She does need to know a good deal about being bored at a tourist attraction. Concentrating on tourists as the point of interest, she can—if she has been to a few tourist attractions—discuss the tourists she observed there, and show what makes them interesting to her (and thus to the reader).

It's a point that can't be emphasized too much: if you can't write about something you're an expert on, if you can't give the reader the insider's view, you'll be staying on the surface and you'll wind up with a rehash of what you both already know.

State the Thesis Clearly

Make sure the reader knows exactly what your message is going to be. Get that message out clearly early in the writing. Sometimes the message is expressed in the thesis sentence; other times it may come across to the reader through several sentences or even a whole paragraph, as it did in the example about tourists. But whether the thesis is expressed explicitly in one unmistakable sentence or whether it is embedded in several sentences or a paragraph, let the reader know clearly what the rest of the essay is going to be about.

Here's an opening paragraph that shows not only what the topic is and what the paper will say about the topic, but also who the audience is and what the value to the reader will be:

> This last summer thousands of people stamped up and down hundreds of miles of backpacking and hiking trails all across the United States and Canada, putting their feet through such punishment and pain as they never had felt before. Blisters, corns, and painful swelling of joints plagued nearly everyone, including both the novice and the experienced trail guide. There is no sure way to prevent these discomforts, but the right type and fit of hiking boot can help make it a great deal easier, as I learned this last summer.

Who is the audience?
Anyone who hikes or is planning to hike.

What is the topic?
How to get the right type of fit in hiking boots.

What will the writer concentrate on?
Giving the reader information on how to choose hiking boots.

What is the value to the reader?
Information and, perhaps, more comfortable feet.

The thesis is expressed in the last sentence. The rest of the paper will expand on this thesis.

Here is another example, the first two paragraphs of a student theme:

Soft, intriguing music plays in the background. Martha, a pretty brunette, walks into the living room. Her husband, Paul, is sitting anxiously on the couch. "Martha, where have you been?"; then taking a closer look he adds, "You haven't been down at Ted's night-club again, have you?" She remains silent for a moment and then speaks defensively: "What difference does it make to you? You spend every night working at the clinic! What do you expect me to do, stay home and watch TV by myself?" And so another dramatic episode begins.

Each weekday, many stories similar to this one are broadcast on TV. These soap operas are viewed by thousands of people across the country. Men are also enjoying what used to be considered shows for women only, and new soap operas are appearing during evening hours. "The soaps" have become an American pastime. Why do people watch soap operas? Why have they become so popular?

Here the writer defers any hint of a thesis until the end of the second paragraph. Delaying presentation of the thesis as the writer has done, generates a certain measure of suspense. If that is the desired effect, a late thesis is fine as long as it is clear and reaches the reader in time to help him or her through the majority of the writing. In this case, it's evident at the end of the second paragraph that the topic is soap operas, that the paper will explore the reasons people like "soaps," and that the reader is probably someone who knows about soap operas and will be interested in an analysis of their appeal.

Check to See If the Thesis Will Matter to the Reader

It's always tempting to assume that anything interesting to you will also be interesting to the reader—but that's not always the case. Have you identified a reader who will learn from, be entertained by, or be persuaded by your thesis and your development of it? Checking your thesis against your intended audience in advance can help you present a topic

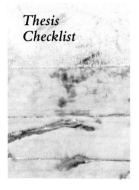

Thesis Checklist

1. Have I made an assertion about a narrow, workable aspect of my topic?
2. Have I used precise words to set up a specific focus?
3. Have I said something about the topic that the reader doesn't already know or hasn't already thought about—have I been an insider?
4. Have I stated the thesis clearly?
5. Am I reasonably sure this thesis is something that will matter to the reader I have targeted for this writing?

and approach that are exciting and satisfactory to you and that also connect with the audience you intend to communicate with.

SUMMARY OF THE THESIS

Asking yourself exactly what the paper is going to assert to your readers is absolutely necessary. To ensure that readers will be interested and that you'll tell them something they don't already know, you can run through the Thesis Checklist shown above.

WRITING *Working with Thesis Statements*

1. Read the following opening paragraphs from student essays. Answer these questions about them: Does each introduction have a clear thesis statement? If so, what is it? If a thesis statement is present, what assertion is the writer making? Can the reader know what he or she is going to get from reading the paper? What do you predict the paper will cover? How has the writer shown or indicated that he or she is an insider on the matter? Jot your answers in your journal.

    A. "Gee, Mom, it smells good in here! What's cooking?" asks a boy as he walks through the kitchen. Slam! Mom watches her son come in and walk by without even noticing her presence. In tears she looks on as he hunts through the refrigerator for a mid-afternoon snack and thinks, "You call this a family."

    B. It took me twelve years of school to finally realize that I did not know how to study. When I was in high school, I did about twenty minutes of studying a night (of course, excluding Fridays and Saturdays). Plus, for a test, I kicked in about thirty extra minutes.

Despite the lack of study I still pulled out a 3.325. Then came the shock of my life, college.

C. I cannot believe that it is all over. When I was little, all I ever wanted to be was a teenager. I longed for the days when I would do nothing but chase boys, talk on the telephone and blast my stereo. I wonder now, if I had not talked quite so long on the phone and had not listened to my loud stereo quite so avidly, if my high school years would have gone by any slower. I never really took the time to stop and say, "Hey! I am now one normal, 100-percent, full-fledged teenager!" Instead, it seems as if I made a transition straight from babydoll little girl life into womanhood without even stopping to think twice.

D. The serene atmosphere surrounding the neighborhood was pierced by an echoing scream. A teenager turned and ran in the direction of the noise. Rounding a corner he was confronted by a mother and father standing over their son. The teenager took note of the situation and immediately began artificial respiration. Within a few minutes the child was conscious and active. Why was the teenager able to save the child while the mother and father stood helplessly by? Were they overcome by the shock of seeing their son in trouble, or did they not know how to administer first aid? In either case their son might have died if it had not been for a total stranger. The teenager was able to save the child's life because he had been taught first aid.

2. All of the following opening paragraphs from student essays fail to meet the conditions for effective thesis development, effective adaptation to audience, or both. Read them carefully; then be prepared to discuss exactly how each fails and what could be done to improve it. When you've finished, pick two and rewrite them.

A. Man is, at heart, a cruel animal, injuring and attacking not for food or protection but for enjoyment. What is more, men do this fighting with each other. Those of the species who do not participate watch and cheer on their favorite, wishing all the time that they had the skill to be in his place. Of course I am speaking of man's sports, his vicious ways of recreating.

B. For many people, the idea of a restaurant brings to mind a place where one can relax and eat the food of his or her choice. Some people go to a restaurant to relax, have a few drinks and eat a good meal. After a hard day, nothing is better than to go to a quiet restaurant and let someone else, who is probably better than you anyway, cook the meal of your choice. You can also listen to the quiet music while you eat your delicious meal. With no interruptions like a telephone or a doorbell ringing, you can probably enjoy your meal more. You can take your time eating and enjoy every morsel of your delectable meal. Someone else will cook your meal to your specifications and will also serve it to you quietly and politely. The dishes will be taken away and you will not even have to clean them up.

C. There are many restaurants that specialize in certain types of food. My favorite varieties of food are seafood and Mexican food. One thing that annoys me is some people who go into a restaurant that specializes in one particular food and they order something completely off the menu. The customer should show some courtesy to the establishment. He could show this by leaving a tip for the waiter. A tip shows the customer's appreciation of a service which he considers the waiter deserved. In a few cases, I have encountered rude waiters who give no or poor service. But these cases have been few as I have been satisfied with most of the service I have received. A restaurant is still a good place to go to relax and enjoy the best food possible.

3. Look at these opening paragraphs from student essays and see if the writers seem to be insiders on the topic. Jot down the passages, words, and sentences that establish them as insiders (or outsiders, as the case may be).

A. I came to college with high and mighty, yet customary, goals. The excitement of everything about college seemed enough to keep me propelled forward forever. But, after two months, I worried. The excitement flew out the window, and I was left amidst the crowds of students sharing the same problem. Instead of something flashy and fairly easy, I found that college is dingy clothes and a D in Biology.

B. Dating is an important part of every young person's maturing process. One's social growth is very likely to be stunted by limiting himself or herself to a single steady date. Young adults are quick to believe they are in love and believe that marriage would be the only way to truly express it. True, some of these marriages work out fine but most result in divorces.

C. Racquetball is the youngest of the racquet sports. And, in many ways, it is the best. The game can be enjoyed at any level of competition. Almost anyone can hit a rubber ball against the wall, but few can do it with the power, velocity, and finesse of a racquetball champion.

D. "You know that class is awful. I never learn anything from it, but it seems to last for hours."

"I know what you mean. The lectures are so disorganized. He doesn't even know what he's talking about."

"Well, I won't be there next class. I have better ways to spend my time."

This conversation is often heard after many college classes. However, this attitude can be reversed through the efforts of the professor. By inspiring confidence in the student and through an organized and knowledgeable presentation of the material, a professor can make any class interesting as well as instructive.

DELIVER WHAT YOU PROMISE: STAY ON THE THESIS

Because one word can trigger another and one thought can lead to a different thought, it's easy to find yourself completely off the topic you promised your readers you would discuss. This happens not because you are a "bad writer," but because the mind's natural tendency is to have one thought follow another thought in whatever direction those thoughts are going. This tendency to drift is powerful in looping and other creating techniques, but by the time you start drafting your essays, it is necessary to start grouping and organizing your thoughts to make a whole.

The following essay illustrates what happens when a writer forgets what she promised:

Promise and Delivery TEST OF LIFE

Goal: To complete an application to college
Audience: College admission officials

"Ya'll, I'm scared of heights. I can't do this!"
"We're here for support; you can trust us, Mary."

I still remember this conversation vividly. It happened during summer camp in 1979, and it was during this camp that I learned the importance of trust and support.

[*The previous sentence is Sandy's thesis. She is promising the reader that she will write about a camp experience that taught her the importance of trust and support. This promise to her readers should help them predict precisely the content and direction of the essay.*]

The reason Mary needed to trust us was that she was standing on top of a pole which was six feet high, and her back was facing about ten people, in two rows, with their arms held tightly together. The frightening part of it all was that she was supposed to fall back into our arms.

No, this wasn't some kind of torture.

This was a game, actually, a group effort, in which the object was for everyone in the group to complete everything on an obstacle course. This wasn't just any obstacle course, either. It didn't even stress physical strength or ability but, instead, caused every one who passed it to have to work together.

To do this special obstacle course you had to go beyond fears which you might have had all your life. The one Mary was having trouble with was trusting that, when she fell off this pole backwards, the people below her would catch her and put her down to safety. Earlier in the game she had similar trouble crawling through a long, narrow tunnel which required you to let other people in the group support you completely in getting through the tunnel.

Mary finally jumped. Backwards she came into our arms. And we caught her. Everybody laughed and everybody cried. We all knew at that moment what it is to trust and support each other in moving through our fears.

I think that everyone who went to that camp learned many lessons that can be applied to life. Throughout life, all of us experience many hardships, and it is during these times that we often have to trust our friends to give us support. During that two-week period, my eyes opened up to see all of the times in my life when people came to my aid.

I will discuss one of these times, though there are many I would like to tell about.

[What is happening here? Sandy's thoughts on her experience at camp have triggered other memories of people coming to her aid. It is easy to see how the thoughts are related, how one has led to another. So, the thoughts aren't unconnected. They just aren't linked to the promise—the thesis—that Sandy has set up. She promised to discuss a time at camp when she learned the importance of trust and support. Therefore, she cannot branch off away from this promise, no matter how easily her mind has moved to the incident she is now about to relate. She has to deliver what she promised, because that was the hypothesis she put before the reader. She could, of course, change her thesis, her promise; but with this thesis she must stay on the course she sets at the beginning of this paper.]

There was a day that my family was the victim of a frightening accident, and we are lucky to have lived through it. I still remember looking up at the sliding glass door, and thinking what a big, funny-looking bug was on the window. (I was only four—what can you expect.) What it really was was the head light of a riderless motorcycle. The rider had jumped off a block away, but the bike kept going. It turned two corners and went between two parked cars in our driveway before it entered our house and turned our lives upside down.

When the ambulance finally arrived, it seemed as if all the work was already done. My father had lifted the motorcycle up off of me, and my mother picked me up and carried me outside. My father also picked up my sister Cindy and carried her out of the burning house. The ambulance attendant pronounced Cindy dead, but my mother wasn't going to believe that. She started to use CPR and saved Cindy's life. The miracle of it all was that the only demonstration my mother had ever seen of CPR had been the week before on "Romper Room." My sister and I were destined to spend over a month in the hospital.

In the fire caused by the accident we lost almost all of our possessions to smoke damage and everything was a complete mess. This was a time that my parents needed physical and emotional support, and their friends were nearby to give it. Cases like this are seen constantly in the news.

Many times, without friends and family to help us, it would be much more difficult for us to make it through a crisis. We all need to learn to trust our friends enough to lean on them when we need to, because they are always willing to help out. Just as we are willing to support them.

Because Sandy's essay falls into two parts, the focus of the communication is lost and the essay is much less effective than if she had used a thesis that would have let her tell both stories as a unit, or if she had delivered on the thesis that she set up.

In contrast, look at this example. Scott's essay makes a clear promise at the beginning—to explain how advertising benefits society by strengthening key industries. After he makes this promise, there is no point where Scott diverges from the predicted path.

Promise and Delivery ANNOYED BY ADVERTISING

Goal: To inform
Audience: High school students

While watching Monday night football last week, a friend of mine violently threw an empty plastic cup at the television set. He was not upset because his favorite team was losing; rather, the interruptions from advertising proved too much for him. He is not alone. Many Americans feel overwhelmed by the amount of advertising they are exposed to in a given day: radio, television, newspapers, magazines, and billboards! Last year, total advertising expenditures in the United States exceeded $61 billion—an overwhelming figure indeed. Although many Americans complain about the annoyance and inconvenience caused by advertising, few realize the benefits advertising provides in our society. Advertising benefits society by strengthening key industries through increased sales and effectively lowering the prices of consumer goods by providing better information.

By increasing the sales of products in key industries, advertising keeps millions of jobs secure, and secure jobs contribute to greater overall spending in the economy. The United States automobile industry estimates a successful advertising campaign is responsible for up to 40 percent of total sales in a given year. Without these sales, many auto workers would lose their jobs, and industries dependent on the auto

industry such as steel, rubber, and upholstery would suffer as well. In the fashion industry, advertising successfully reinforces fashion changes and new fads in clothing styles. Messages such as "mini skirts are coming back" and "last year's suits are out" stimulate economic growth, exemplified by the steady year-to-year growth in the garment industry. And one must not forget the thousands of retail outlets and accompanying jobs that also benefit from the increased sales.

In addition to increasing sales, advertising benefits the consumer by effectively lowering prices. By providing important pricing information, advertising enables consumers to compare the prices of competing retail outlets. Retailers realize this, and therefore must keep their prices competitive to survive. A current study provides support for this view. In some states, optometrists are not allowed to advertise the prices of prescription eyeglasses; when compared with states that allowed advertising, the prices were 55 percent lower in the states allowing advertising. A similar result occurred in the legal profession. Until recently, attorneys never advertised the price of their services. After they began advertising, fees for routine services such as divorce, wills, and bankruptcy declined by about 50 percent. No wonder many attorneys are upset at the prospect of advertising.

Clearly, advertising is a powerful and vital

institution in American society. Perhaps the worst aspect of advertising relates to the annoyance caused by the constant bombardment the public receives every day. However, the effects of strengthening industries and lower prices outweigh this annoyance. When I tried to explain this to my friend during Monday night football, he threw a plastic cup at me.

The thesis guides the reader by stating the assertion that the writer promises to develop in the essay. The thesis also guides the writer by focusing his or her ideas, helping the writer choose appropriate details that support the assertion, and suggesting the most effective arrangement of details within the essay.

As you continue to work on thesis statements for your essays, remember that the thesis is probably revised more than any other single sentence (or group of sentences) in an essay. But if you can revise your thesis successfully to focus precisely for readers, you will improve your chances of getting and keeping your readers' attention and communicating effectively.

WRITING *Thesis Statements*

1. Using your prewriting or discovery draft for a paper you are starting, write three possible thesis statements for your next essay. Did your assertion get more focused or more precisely stated as you wrote each version?
2. Take out an essay you have completely drafted. Before you look again at the thesis, read the body paragraphs only. Now write a thesis that sets up what you drafted in the essay. Next, look again at the original thesis. Use the checklist of questions on p. 151 to help you choose the better thesis and revise it. Now go through the essay and determine where the revised thesis helps you add, delete, or rearrange detail.

CHAPTER 10

Organizing Through Form

Writers generally do not set out to write an essay in a certain *form* or according to a predetermined structural pattern. Rather, knowing to whom they want to write and what they want to say, writers allow the form of the piece to follow logically. The forms most commonly used and those that we will cover in this chapter include narration, process analysis, description, examples, definition comparison and contrast, and causal analysis. For example, in the chapter on purposes, we saw that a writer used narration to express her feelings about a mother's love. Similarly, the writer who wanted to explain the problem of teenage suicide examined some of the causes of the problem before going on to suggest a solution. The writer of the information essay defined terms and examined causes and effects of software piracy, thus combining forms in that essay. In each piece of writing, the audience, purpose, and thesis *formed* the essay by giving it its direction and shape.

Why do we even talk about specific forms, then? Because these forms reflect patterns of thinking common to all human beings, everyone, no matter what his or her native language or cultural background, relies on certain patterns to organize information in the brain. We use the forms that readers already know simply because they have had experience organizing other data about the world through these forms.

You already know the forms because you have used them in everyday activities, but you may not have used them explicitly in your writing. One way to become more comfortable with form is to build up your reading and writing experience with the specific forms. Having read and written paragraphs and essays using these forms, you will be better able to develop essays with the appropriate form because all the forms will be in your writing repertoire.

Thus, even though you will rarely plan a paper beginning with form, this chapter will suggest writing assignments that allow you to practice some of the most common forms student and professional writers use. (Occasionally, you may find that a writing assignment specifies a form. Most often this happens because the thesis is also specified by the assignment; essay test questions often fall into this category.) Remember that most of *your* writing will begin with audience, purpose, and thesis—and those elements will dictate the appropriate forms to develop your message for your reader.

NARRATION

Narration means simply telling a story. We all know about telling stories. When we were children, stories began with "Once upon a time" and ended with, "And they lived happily ever after." Now that we're grown up, our stories have become more complex, but they still follow the same general pattern—we include details that show readers how an experience unfolded from the beginning to the end. More experienced storytellers know how to begin in the middle of the story, fill in the early parts through flashbacks, and proceed back and forth through time. Most of the stories you write will begin at the beginning and follow straight through to the end. To do this, you'll generally use certain cues for the reader—transitional words and phrases, such as *first, next, meanwhile, then, later,* and *finally,* that indicate the time sequence of the story.

If your purpose in writing is to tell about the space shuttle and capture the drama of its re-entry, you might have a thesis like this.

> *Thesis:* The story of the re-entry of the space shuttle Atlantis reads like a thriller.

And then you naturally begin

> First, the re-entry began . . .
>
> Then, the trouble developed . . .
>
> After that, the team . . .
>
> Next, this happened . . .
>
> Finally, . . .

and on to the end of the story. You close off the essay with some discussion of the significance of this story for the reader. Your specific pattern of organization or form here is narration, and you have not imposed it arbitrarily. The form has emerged from the thesis of your essay and your purpose in writing.

WRITING   *Warming up for Narration*

---

1. Freewrite in your journal for seven minutes about an experience that captures the essence of "home" for you. Perhaps you remember a specific holiday tradition or celebration; perhaps you recall a specific incident that shows family closeness; perhaps you see in your mind's eye a special place that signifies the emotional ties of home.

2. Use clustering or listing to gather details about a specific incident that evokes one of the following emotions: anger, sorrow, regret, gratitude, embarrassment.

3. We all have turning points in our lives that we might not recognize as such when they happen but are clearly important when we look back on the decisions we made. Freewrite on any major turning point in your life—perhaps a career decision, a choice about continuing or breaking off a relationship, or a decision to give up or continue an important activity. Focus as carefully as you can on the moment that captures the turning point.

READING

Look again at the narrative examples Max uses in "Fear of Flying" to illustrate his growing fear of death (from Chapter 8).

> Accidents, of course, were commonplace. One cool dewy Minnesota evening a friend and I hit the asphalt at sixty miles an hour. The engine suddenly froze and we skidded and fell. "Look at the sparks," I thought, seeing tiny flashes coming off the rivets of my friend's jeans as we fanned out along the center-line. All the next week I wore the pain like a badge of honor. I limped down the school halls knowing that my friends were talking about my close call. But I paid a price each night when I would pull my clothes off oozing scabs that formed each day. Still, I never considered quitting, until years later. We rooted back and forth across the high school practice field relishing the huge chunks of turf being excavated by our rear tires. I opened the throttle and jerked up on the handlebars. The time was ripe for one of my renowned wheelies. Shifting from second to third my front wheel held its graceful loft. I caught fourth gear doing fifty—just as my rear tire hit the curb at the end of the field. The back wheel ricocheted upwards, the front slammed down and I sailed a perfect trajectory out onto the parking lot, greeting the asphalt

once again. When everything came to rest, what had been a back wheel was now a pretzel. I felt the same way. It was weeks before I could walk normally again. That was the turning point in my motorcycle career. I've owned other, bigger, faster bikes, but I've never been able to ride the same. I had met fear.

WRITING *Narration*

1. Using any of your prewriting from an earlier writing assignment, continue prewriting or draft a piece about home, emotions, or a turning point in your life. Use narration to communicate your message as you tell your classmates a story.
2. You are probably familiar with Murphy's Law—*Anything that can go wrong, will go wrong.* We often use different versions of it to account for things that repeatedly go wrong or for things that just seem perverse. Murphy's Law appears in so many places and with so many variations that the following constitute only some of the possible variations of the "law":
   a. Bread always falls jelly side down.
   b. Left to themselves, all things go from bad to worse.
   c. Nature always sides with the hidden flaw.
   d. If everything seems to be going well, you have obviously overlooked something.
   e. If there is a possibility that several things will go wrong, the one that goes wrong first will be the one that will do the most damage.

   Think of several incidents that show Murphy's Law in action in your life. (You might try listing or brainstorming here.) Then freewrite on the most intriguing incident as if you are planning to tell a story about it at a party with friends.

PROCESS ANALYSIS

When we examine how things work or how to do things, we ordinarily call the analysis a *process analysis*. The process might be

   a biological process (how caterpillars change into butterflies);

   a chemical process (how chlorofluorocarbons break down ozone);

   a mechanical process (how an internal combustion engine works); or

   a political process (how federal judges are appointed).

The subject of your analysis might be the process of performing an action—how to tie a shoe or how to perform an appendectomy. Whether you want readers simply to understand the process or to perform the steps in the process, you use a pattern of organization that relies on chronological or time ordering of the details of the process.

> *Thesis:* Following these steps, a person can spend less for groceries even in these days of high inflation.

Do you see how the development that follows a process thesis will automatically follow a chronological order?

> First, you do this . . .
>
> Then, you do that . . .
>
> After that, you do . . .
>
> Another thing you can do is . . .

and so on to the end of the steps.

As in the narrative, you need to include all the steps in a chronological sequence. Also, you need to include all the instructions a reader might want to know. As we noted in Chapter 7, readers often follow the steps in a process analysis as they complete the process themselves. But even if you are examining a process that readers will not follow—for instance, how the Congress enacts laws—you need to include all the steps in the sequence so that the process is clear and complete.

Audience is always a first concern for writers, but writers of process analysis have to be especially careful to accommodate their readers. Make sure you know how much to expect of your readers. If they are unfamiliar with the process, you may need to define terms and give elaborate detail. If you are writing to readers who already know a good bit about the process, you can assume that readers are comfortable with technical terms and need less explicit detail in the sequence of steps, but you may want to take an unusual slant on the process (as will be clear in your thesis).

WRITING *Warming up for Process Analysis*

1. List several processes you complete every day—shaving, cleaning glasses, applying makeup, fixing meals, and so on. Star those that seem most useful to teach to a five-year-old.
2. We are surrounded by "things that work." Jot down several mechanical objects that you know enough about to analyze in a process analysis.
3. Consider biological and chemical processes that you observe in and around the house—the action of soap on grease, the combination of yeast and flour, the growth of trees and plants, and so on. Choose one such process that you know well and begin listing the steps in the process.

READING

Consider again how Naomi tells readers of *Horticulture* magazine to plant bulbs.

> Once you have decided on which bulbs to plant, get your site ready. The ground will need to be softened up, especially if it has just thawed out after a winter frost. Add some compost or other organic amendment, and dig it in to about two inches. This will enrich the soil and help it drain well. Good drainage is crucial for bulbs.
>
> Next dig the planting holes and put fertilizer into them directly. Bone meal is good; so is superphosphate. Putting the fertilizer right into the holes helps the bulbs' roots reach their food easily.
>
> After planting the bulbs, cover the holes with soil, tamp the soil down firmly, and water well. Really well—the water needs to reach all the way down to the roots. Thereafter, water regularly, waiting until the surrounding ground is dry. It will take a little while for the leaves to emerge, but once they do you know the flowers aren't far behind. Before long you will be surrounded by a colorful array of flowers for your garden and your table.

WRITING *Process Analysis*

1. Complete a draft of the process analysis describing some common daily process to a five-year-old. Assume that the child will try to complete the process without adult help.
2. Draft a process analysis about how a familiar item works to help a foreign visitor understand why Americans rely on labor-saving devices.
3. Examine a biological or chemical process and draft a process analysis to explain that process to someone unfamiliar with the scientific concepts underlying the process.

DESCRIPTION

When we write, we are constantly describing people, places, and objects. *Description* appears in almost all writing because writers try so hard to create word images of the ideas they convey. Description is a common way to present details, but it often appears with other forms or patterns of development.

Two elements are crucial for effective description. First, readers need explicit, specific detail if they are to create exactly the mental image writers have in mind. Vague words, general impressions, and skimpy details simply don't add up to concrete images for readers. Moreover, readers are better able to create a mental image if the details appeal to all senses— sight, hearing, taste, touch, and smell. Second, readers need a logical sequence of detail—a spatial order. A writer describing a person, place or object might work from top to bottom, bottom to top, right to left, clockwise, and so on. Having begun a pattern of movement, however, the writer must stick to that spatial presentation of details.

Finally, descriptions can be objective or subjective. If you want to describe a person, place or object as anyone might experience it, then you would write an objective description. You would use specific but neutral words that would not carry your personal impressions into the description. If you want to create an impression or a mood, as well as to describe, then you would write a subjective description that reflects your attitude toward the subject you describe.

WRITING Warming up for Description

1. Choose a common object in the room with you now and begin listing sensory details about that object.
2. Think of a place associated with strong emotional memories. Place a central emotion in the center of your page and begin clustering for details about the place.
3. Choose a memorable person and use the Reporter's Formula to generate detail that will describe the person in a characteristic moment.

READING

Look at how Jodi describes a memorable place.

> Bathrooms are generally one of those places where one spends an incredible amount of time never really paying attention to the essence of the room itself. Perhaps this is due to a lack of creativity on the part of lavatory design experts who tend to neglect basic human aesthetic needs. However, every rule has its exception.
>
> Near the heart of downtown Denver, in a skid-row neighborhood, on the second floor of a semi-dilapidated warehouse, is a

glorious exception. Within an artist's studio, hiding behind a tiny, barren kitchen, this bathroom is not simply to be seen but to be experienced. After closing the large windowed door on the rest of the studio, an enveloping sense of privacy is quickly crushed. There, a visitor beginning his rituals suddenly discovers that two of the four walls are sheer glass, uncurtained, unscreened, and hardly sheltering from the external world. Although the western view is beautiful, one cannot help but feel vulnerable as the eye catches two winos staggering across a rooftop below, sharing a bottle of some heartening spirit. City sounds and smells of rushing automobiles drift in the open window. The ancient claw-footed bathtub rests next to the western window giving any bather a feeling of being part of the world whizzing by outside. A gargantuan fern seems to float somewhere between the tub and the vintage sink which clings to the wall silently. The braided rug fadily blanketing the wooden floor gives the place a kind of earthy simplicity, further enhanced by the naked walls. An old porcelain toilet of the same era as the other fixtures balances the room out. From a position on this Olympic stool, a guest's only consolation is the incredible view.

Hardly the place for a modest individual, this water closet is clearly a reflection of a whimsical, eccentric mind. This is a bathroom oddly devoid of privacy, yet one can slip comfortably into the simple magnificence of its unconventionality. Where else could a person take a steaming bath caressed by sunlight, to an audience six sheets to the wind?

WRITING *Description*

1. Draft an objective description of the common object you listed details for in the warm-up activity.
2. To determine your impressions of him or her, freewrite on the person you chose in the warm-up activity. Then draft a subjective description.
3. Draft a description that moves from objective to subjective details to portray the place that holds emotional memories for you.

EXAMPLES

Writers use *examples* to show that evidence already exists for the position they take in the thesis. Examples might come from personal experience—in which case they can be short narratives or extended examples of incidents that support the main point. Examples can also come from observing the world, from reading, or from other people's experience. Writers use examples as specific support for a thesis statement.

Typically, writers will find that examples are the most convincing way to develop an idea that calls for real-world experience. For example, a writer hoping to convince fellow dorm residents to enact a study curfew might begin with a thesis like this.

> Anyone trying to study in the dorm between 8 and 11 P.M. will be greeted night after night with loud parties, hall hockey games, and other distractions that make concentration impossible.

The writer would then go on to give examples of loud parties—with specific details about at least one such party that disrupted his or her studying. Then the writer would give an example of the distraction of hall hockey, and finally the writer would include several shorter examples of "other distractions"—perhaps people running down the halls, loud stereos playing, roommates calling loudly about telephone calls, or residents making a lot of noise in the showers. All the examples would lead to the conclusion that stricter noise regulations would help students study in a quieter dorm.

Often, good examples will crop up in your prewriting or creating as you think about the subject you plan to write on. You need to choose the examples that will best support your point. If your readers will be convinced by your experiences, use those as examples. If your readers are more likely to be convinced by historical examples or examples from reading, use those. In short, consider not only your thesis but also your audience and purpose as you select the strongest, most convincing examples to include in your paper.

WRITING *Warming up for Examples*

1. We probably all see examples of folks not "following the rules" every day. List several such examples from your college experience. You might group the examples according to "classroom abuses," "dorm violations," "cafeteria culprits," and so on.
2. Freewrite about the last time you broke a rule and how you felt about it. Now list other instances of "bending the rules."
3. Political news often focuses on government officials putting themselves above the law. Brainstorm for as many examples as you can of illegal and unethical government actions, current and historical.

READING

Examine how a professional essayist, Frank Trippett, uses examples to support his point about law-breaking (excerpted from "A Red Light for Scofflaws").

> The dangers of scofflawry vary wildly. The person who illegally spits on the sidewalk remains disgusting, but clearly poses less risk to others than the company that illegally buries hazardous chemical waste in an unauthorized location. The fare beater on the subway presents less threat to life than the landlord who ignores fire safety statutes. The most immediately and measurably dangerous scofflawry, however, also happens to be the most visible. The culprit is the American driver, whose lawless activities today add up to a colossal public nuisance. The hazards range from routine double parking that jams city streets to the drunk driving that kills some 25,000 people and injures at least 650,000 others yearly. Illegal speeding on open highways? New surveys show that on some interstate highways 83 percent of all drivers are currently ignoring the federal 55 m.p.h. speed limit.

WRITING Examples

1. Use your prewriting about scofflawry on your campus to draft a paragraph modeled on Trippett's.
2. Based on your brainstorming about government rule-breaking, draft an essay in which you use examples to argue for stronger "ethics in government" policies.
3. Assume that you are writing to your teenage child about why he or she should follow the rules you set down. Use your examples about your rule-breaking to illustrate your point.

DEFINITION

Definition explains the essential qualities of the subject being discussed. If you are writing about how "commercial advertisements make people greedy," then you'll need to define "greed." You can define

> by synonym (gluttony);
>
> by class (it goes with the six other deadly sins);

by origin (some say that greed is an innate part of human nature); or

by description (it's not enough to own some good knives and a blender—the ads exhort you to buy a grinder, a breadmaker, and a food processor).

Or you might use

opposites (greed and selflessness);

comparison (greed far exceeds meeting one's basic needs);

derivation (greed comes from the Old English root *giernan* meaning to strive, desire, yearn);

history (Wall Street yuppies don't have a corner on greed compared to, say, Roman Emperors);

function (greed keeps the economy growing for certain segments of our society);

process (one learns to become greedier as one practices the art, as seen if we consider pampered children becoming adolescents who can't deny any shopping whim); or

whole-to-part relationship (greed fills out a pattern of egocentrism in the "me" generation and beyond).

In short, you let your reader know exactly what you mean when you use a specific word, especially if it is a technical term or a word otherwise unfamiliar to your audience.

Definitions often begin by placing the word in a larger context and then distinguishing the word from other elements in the larger class. For example, with the thesis, *Cajun cooking is not like other southern food,* the essay would begin with a discussion of the general subject, southern cooking, of which Cajun food is one type, and then move to a definition of the specific subject, Cajun cooking.

WRITING *Warming up for Definition*

1. Every discipline has its own terminology that insiders use to communicate efficiently with other insiders. Think about your academic major. List at least ten terms you had to learn as you began to study in the discipline.
2. Like academic disciplines, most sports and hobbies use terms that have special meanings for the sport or hobby. Jot down several words and phrases you have learned through such activities.
3. Many slang terms come and go in our language, often with new meanings each time they appear. Take, for instance, "cool." It can

mean composed, jazzy, or good. Choose a current slang term for which you know your parents had some other meaning. Cluster as many possible definitions as you can around the term.

READING

Consider how Patty uses various definitions to explain a concept in her field.

Neanderthal

Neanderthal man has suffered some low blows. Since their discovery in 1856, Neanderthals have been unfairly depicted as hunched-over, knucklewalking ape-men. Clad only in loin cloths, they violently clubbed tigers over the head and dragged them to their butchering sites. Neanderthals' communication consisted of grunts, growls, and snarls; these ugly, smelly, hairy beasts had no occupations other than eating and reproducing.

The work of paleoanthropologists and archeologists in recent years has spared the reputation of the Neanderthal culture by laying these unfounded misconceptions to rest.

Neanderthals (first discovered in the Neander Valley, Germany, hence, their name) lived during the Upper Pleistocene, from about 100,000 to 35,000 years ago. Widely distributed in Europe, Africa, and Asia, Homo sapiens neandertalensis outcompeted their ancestors, Homo erectus, by adapting to extreme environmental conditions. The Wurm glacial advance, geologically dated from 75,000 to 10,000 years ago, brought a frigid, moist climate to Western Europe; Neanderthals survived by using fire and seeking additional warmth in caves and rock shelters. With an advanced stone tool culture (including spear points, cutting edges, and burins), they hunted, ate, and wore the hides of arctic fauna such as the mammoth, woolly rhinoceros, bear, musk ox, reindeer, and fox. Neanderthals respected their dead kin and buried them with flowers; but first, as a ritual, they consumed the corpse's brain.

In response to the arctic climate, Neanderthals were built like modern Eskimos—short, stocky, and heavily muscled. A few anthropologists argue that if a Neanderthal walked today's city streets, no one would look twice; after all, some modern men also have large teeth and jaws and heavy eyebrow ridges. This image of Neanderthal man stretches the fossil evidence. Like modern humans, however, Neanderthals walked fully erect, as did their ancestors three million years earlier. The appearance of a chin first arose with Neanderthals, allowing freedom of movement of the vocal chords (i.e., speech). As remarkable, Neanderthals had a forehead, which meant that the frontal lobe of the brain was expanding; they manufactured tools according to a plan and specific intent, and were capable of past, present, and future thought.

The image of Neanderthal people as primitive, knucklewalking ape-men was based on a single fossil find, a curved femur, discovered over a century ago. Now we know that a curved femur is characteristic of squatting and is present in modern populations such as the Eskimos and Aborigines. Accurate descriptions of our ancestors require much fossil evidence. Today, with adequate skeletal remains and cultural artifacts, we are safe in assuming that the Neanderthals would have dominated the planet had not a more gracile population, Homo sapiens sapiens, appeared 35,000 years ago.

WRITING *Definition*

1. Draft a short essay to a general audience to clear up misconceptions they might have about a term you use in your academic discipline.
2. You've just made friends with someone who cannot understand why you enjoy the hobby or sport you like. Draft a letter in which you explain your hobby or sport by means of defining at least one key term your new friend will have to understand to share your fun in the activity.
3. Draft an essay to an audience of readers who are about your parents' age. Define a slang term so that the readers can understand how their teenagers are using the term in casual conversation with friends.

COMPARISON/CONTRAST

You use comparing and contrasting almost every day as you go about the regular routine of life. You have to decide, for instance, whether to pack a lunch or buy one, whether or not to take an umbrella, whether to watch a special television program or finish homework. In all these daily activities, you compare and contrast: Would a packed lunch taste better than one bought from a hot-dog vendor? Does the sky look gray enough to mean rain or just a haze like the day before? Will the television program or homework mean a happier evening—and next day?

Comparing (showing similarities) and *contrasting* (showing differences) are such a natural part of life that you may use them without realizing it when you begin writing. Imagine that the thesis of your essay was this:

> *Thesis:* City dwellers often fantasize about living in the country, but their fantasies are very different from actually living the rural life.

You would set up your paper to discuss two things: fantasies about living in the country and the reality of living there. Because of the contrast present in the thesis, it would be natural to follow the contrast form for your paper as you *show the differences* between the fantasy and reality.

Of course, a writer might also want to *show only similarities,* and then the thesis statement would set readers up to expect comparison.

Finally, a writer might want to compare *and* contrast in the same paper—show both similarities and differences. Consider this thesis for a paper you might write on renting versus buying a home.

> *Thesis:* The question of whether to rent or to buy your own home is becoming more complex every day.

This thesis clearly points you toward comparison and contrast of renting and owning. As the writer, though, you still have a major choice: will you cover all your points about renting and then write about owning, or will you alternate between renting and owning as you look at specific issues? For example, will you talk about a particular aspect of the thesis—say, tax relief—and, in the discussion of tax relief, talk about both renting and owning, and then go on to another aspect of the thesis—perhaps, initial investment—and talk about both renting and owning under that aspect? No matter which variation you choose, the basic form—comparison/contrast—is an organic part of the thesis itself.

WRITING *Warming up for Comparison/Contrast*

1. Think back over the last several dates you've gone out on. Which two stand out as being least like each other? Make two lists—one for each date—in which you note the major differences between the two dates.
2. List several activities you've participated in recently—shopping trips, pre-game (or post-game) parties, trips, or visits to museums, for example. Now pick one of the activities and pair the two instances least like each other. What was the main impression you have from each?

Use that as a central image and cluster for details of each instance of the activity.

3. Brainstorm for entertainment you've enjoyed in two forms—a movie and a book, a TV show and a book, a play and a movie, a record album and a movie, a play and a painting, a poster and a speech.

READING

Notice how Soviet historian Isaac Deutscher compares Stalin and Churchill as they approached the bargaining table in Teheran in 1943 (excerpted from *Stalin, A Political Biography*).

> One can think of very few instances in which men of such contrasting temper, background, and interests came together, as allies or partners, to decide issues of the greatest moment and gravity. What different worlds, what different outlooks and aspirations were embodied in these . . . men confronting one another across the conference table! The extreme antipodes were Churchill and Stalin, the descendant of the Duke of Marlborough and the son of serfs, the one born in Blenheim Palace, the other in a one-room hovel. The one still breathed the spiritual climate of Victorian and Edwardian England, whose imperial heritage he was guarding with the full vigour of his romantic temperament. The other had in him all the severity of Tsarist and Bolshevik Russia, whose storms he had ridden in cool, icy self-possession. The one had behind him four decades of parliamentary debate; the other as long an activity in clandestine groups and secretive Politbureaux. The one—full of eccentric idiosyncrasies, a lover of words and colour; the other—colourless and distrustful of words. Finally, the one had an empire to lose; the other something like an empire to win.

WRITING   *Comparison/Contrast*

1. Draft a humorous essay comparing two dates you've been on. Assume your audience will be other readers about your same age.
2. Draft an essay in which you compare/contrast any two instances of an activity you commonly engage in.

3. Draft an evaluative essay in which you compare and contrast the two forms of entertainment you noted in the third warm-up for comparing or contrasting. Be sure to explain which form was more enjoyable or more effective for you.

CAUSAL ANALYSIS—CAUSE AND EFFECT

A *cause* is a person, thing, or act that inevitably leads to a specific result or *effect*. When examining cause and effect, writers identify *what* brings about a particular result, and then show *how* the cause leads to that result. Of course, there has to be a real, not an invented, relationship between cause and effect. If you say, "Video games are the main reason that sales of books are down," you must make clear to the reader how you determined this cause/effect relationship. You must also remember that just because one event happens before a second event, the first does not necessarily cause the second. A simple time sequence is not an adequate substitute for the logical relationship of cause and effect.

You must also be aware of how significant either the causes or effects you discuss are for your audience. Your readers will not be convinced of the logic of a causal analysis if the causes and effects are not the most important or the most reasonable ones to examine.

Sometimes it is possible to identify a single cause/effect chain. But more often, writers will identify a single cause leading to several effects or several causes leading to a single effect. For example,

Thesis: The 1954 Supreme Court decision on *Oliver Brown et al.* v. *Board of Education of Topeka* caused American education to change.

To develop this thesis, you write about the cause—the 1954 court decision—in as much detail as you think your readers will need. Then you determine what effects you see in American education. You list those and show how they resulted from the Supreme Court decision. For each effect, you show a direct connection to the cause—the court decision.

As you look again at your cause/effect thesis, you'll often see a clear plan for organizing the paper itself. In the paper on *Brown* v. *Board of Education,* the paper will clearly follow the pattern set up in the thesis: first, the material on the court decision, and then the material on the historic effects of that decision. Consider how you might organize a paper with this thesis that presents an effect and then the causes:

Thesis: When youngsters don't meet academic standards in elementary school, we should look not at the students but at the teachers, parents, and school board for most of the blame.

Your paper would fall into a discussion of the effect first followed by a longer discussion of the causes of this effect—the teachers, the parents, and the school board—in the order they appear in the thesis.

WRITING Warming up for Causal Analysis

---

1. Most of us can identify some behavior that we would call a bad habit, including chewing gum noisily, drinking too much coffee or other caffeinated drink, fiddling with paper clips or pencils, or doodling. First list any bad habits you have. Then choose one habit and freewrite on how the habit is bad for you and those around you.
2. More serious than a bad habit is addictive behavior. Smokers addicted to nicotine and substance abusers addicted to alcohol, cocaine, or other drugs know that "quitting" is a lifelong commitment to fight the addiction. Make two columns, one for causes and the other for effects, and jot down all the causes and effects of addiction you can think of. Include not just the effects for the individual but also for society.
3. You've visited and partied at other students' apartments and you're surprised at how thoughtlessly some students destroy rented property. Freewrite on the effects of some students' attitudes toward rented apartments.
4. As you listened to or read the news today, you heard a cause-effect analysis that you just didn't agree with. Use chaining to help you get ideas about why the analysis you heard is wrong and why your analysis is right.

READING

Look at how Patti explains her inability to study because of her boyfriend

> . . . My first hot-tubbing date was magical, and for a night like that one a homework lapse could probably be excused. But even after those first weak-willed moments of beginning to date this man, my classes have continued to suffer. The next example that comes to mind is the night before my first chemistry test when I decided to take a fifteen minute break from excruciatingly painful chemical equations to go downstairs and watch TV with my boyfriend. This time away from homework, in theory, would have been good for me, but as I began staring at the big women wrestling on the screen in front of me, I carefully folded into the arms of my boyfriend. Approximately five hours and two and a half movies later the realiza-

tion of the upcoming "D" on my test began to affect me. Again I had let my comfort and happiness override my motivation to study. Nor is my chemistry grade the only one that has suffered. Not learning my lesson from my well-deserved "D" the week before, I dropped my biology book and again jaunted downstairs for a short break. Needless to say, I left the fifty pages of reading that I was supposed to be doing for my biology class sleeping upstairs below my desk. This time the feeling was similar to the week before as I lay in the arms of my boyfriend, thinking to myself that not hell, high water, nor biology reading was going to motivate me to leave my strategic spot in front of the TV.

WRITING *Causal Analysis*

1. Write an essay focusing on either the causes or effects of a bad habit you have. Assume that your reader is someone who has been annoyed by your bad habit and would like you to break the habit.
2. Write an essay in which you examine the social effects of addictive behavior. You might consider the political effects of addiction to nicotine (the tobacco lobby is one of the strongest—and wealthiest—in Washington). You might analyze the economic effects of alcohol addiction. Or you might focus on the consequences in schools of students who abuse drugs. Be sure to find additional resources to back up your argument on the most important effects.
3. You are a college student looking for an apartment to rent. You have searched for weeks for the perfect place—enough room, reasonable rent, and a good neighborhood. You are ready to sign a one-year lease when the landlord asks your occupation. As soon as you say "student," he shakes his head and says, "sorry, we don't rent to students." Write an analysis of why landlords hesitate to rent to students for your college *Renter's Rights* newsletter.
4. We hear about cause/effect relationships in the news almost every day. Yet we might disagree with the analysis linking cause and effect in the news. For instance, you might argue that increasing tuition will not expand student services as the chief administrator at your school maintains. You might argue that banning diesel cars will not necessarily lower air pollution in your town as your mayor claims. Or you might argue in good company on either side that having health clinics in high schools does/does not affect students' control of unwanted pregnancies. Choose any cause/effect relationship you have heard recently in the news and argue that your causal analysis is the correct one.

MIXED FORM

Suppose that you studied a group of essays that appeared together in a collection and were introduced as Essays of Definition. Then, when you started reading the essays, you saw that they did many things besides defining—they also described, compared, and narrated. Don't let this confuse you. Remember that terms like comparing, defining, analyzing, and the like are names of ways in which all human beings think. Any of these can be both the form of an essay and/or one of the several specific ways that the essay is developed inside that form. Just remember that although the general overall form of your essay may be, say, comparison, you will use several other patterns and kinds of thinking to develop that essay.

Read the following student essay by Ron and notice (a) how the overall form of the essay is determined by the writer's audience, purpose and thesis and (b) how other forms of thinking also appear inside the overall pattern.

Mixed Form THE GRIST MILL, A RESTAURANT YOU WON'T FORGET

Goal: To review an excellent, nearby restaurant
Audience: Readers of a restaurant review column in the local newspaper

Have you ever stumbled onto an unbelievably good restaurant in the middle of nowhere? Have you ever searched for a restaurant someone told you about, and that search took you hours? If you have, then you will have some reference for understanding about The Grist Mill. Hidden away in an old German settlement, The Grist Mill is not an easy place to find. But, believe me, it is well worth the search. Established in the ghost town of Gruene, Texas, The Grist Mill has to be one of the best restaurants anywhere. You won't forget an evening you spend eating at The Grist Mill. It's a restaurant to which you'll have to go back.

After parking the car, as you are walking up the long gravel and dirt road to The Grist Mill, the strains of country and western music hit you. The music is coming from the oldest dance hall in Texas, which is located right next to the restaurant. The dance hall is huge and is made out of stone and thick wooden planks, which were painted dark green years ago. Inside, the live band plays to a large crowd.

Just past the dance hall is The Grist Mill. It is three stories tall and also made out of stones and wooden planks. The big front doors are thrown wide open, and you can see all the people enjoying their meals on the first floor. The upper two floors have windows that extend from about 3½ feet up, up to the ceilings, and these windows are propped wide open to catch the evening breeze.

After giving your name to the hostess, you can walk over and get some lemonade or beer from the outside bar and sit down with everyone else who is waiting. They are all sitting on split-log benches, facing an entertainer who will sing or play a guitar for you. As you wait, you can go over and look at the river. It is just a few feet to the right. If you stand on the edge of the bluff that the mill sits on, you can see the greenish-blue water of the Guadalupe River rolling by.

Soon you are called to take a table. If you are really lucky, the table is on the third floor, facing the river. You can see miles of trees that seem to form a bushy green carpet below your eyes. Hectic life seems a thousand miles away.

Now it is time to order.

For appetizers, you must order bratwurst and potatoes. Fried bratwurst, cubed, on toothpicks. (Bratwurst is a spicy, thick German stuffed sausage, which squirts its delicious juices into your mouth.) The potatoes are fried like chips, but the slices are thick enough to still be moist inside, instead of crunchy. For the main course, I recommend the chicken-fried steak: a tender cut of beef, marinated all night long in a wine marinade, then dipped into a delicious batter and deep fried.

After the meal, it is time for dessert. For the best dessert, order the strawberry shortcake. It comes on about a 6- or 8-inch platter, but you won't be able to see the platter—it is too obscured by all the whipped cream and strawberries. There is a soft, spongy cake with the center taken out, in the middle of this delight. In place of the center, there is a scoop of vanilla ice cream, and on top of the ice cream comes the whipped cream and strawberries, piled about 6 inches high, and topped off with a maraschino cherry.

Finally, it is time for coffee. The Grist Mill grinds its own beans, so the coffee is always fresh and strong. If you don't have to be rolled out of The Grist Mill, you might want to go to the dance hall and dance off some of the weight you have just gained.

Then again, you might just want to go on home, in a contented stuffed stupor, wondering how soon you will be coming back. The evening at The Grist Mill—from the sounds of the tumbleweed and the music in the air to the melancholy sigh of the ancient river rolling by to the testimony of the old German building where you eat and the food you put in your mouth—will be an evening you will not forget. I bet you won't be able not to go back.

Inside the overall ordering form of description, Ron does many other things. For instance, he narrates the walk up to the restaurant, the wait before the meal, the parts of the meal itself, and the ending of the evening spent at the mill. He defines the bratwurst and chicken-fried steak. He analyzes the reasons why this will have been an evening you will never forget. He has written an essay that has mixed form.

REVIEWING FORMS OF WRITING

Here are some suggestions for you to remember about forms of writing.

- Be confident that a thesis will suggest its own form.
- Realize that although the overall form may be defined as one word

(comparison, definition, etc.), many patterns of thinking will appear in the essay. The form of almost all essays is a mixed form.

■ Become familiar with and conscious of the basic forms of writing, but don't make these forms the reason you write.

Don't worry about memorizing such terms as comparison, definition, and causal analysis, because you will rarely set out to write an essay according to form. We are considering this matter simply to demonstrate how thesis, purpose, and audience suggest a form for an essay and to show that these forms can be discussed. Knowing this form or that form, however, won't help you write unless you understand the central principle: your audience, purpose, and thesis will lead, especially the more you write, to an appropriate form for your writing.

WRITING *Analyzing Form*

1. Take out any essay you have completed this term and identify, first, its overall form and, second, the other patterns that occur within that overall form. Explain how your audience, purpose, and thesis led to the form of the essay.
2. Take out the draft of any essay you are now working on. Identify all the patterns of development that appear in the essay. Why do those patterns occur where they do? How do they relate to the essay's overall form? Now change the audience, purpose, or thesis of your draft and explain how the form would also have to change.

CHAPTER 11

Organizing Through Paragraphs

In ancient Greece, the word *paragraphos* meant a mark a writer put in the margin of a manuscript to set off part of a text. (*para* means "beside"; *graph* means "mark.") Since early writers didn't indent the way we do today, or write in paragraphs as we know them, they used these marks in the margins to draw the readers' eyes to certain points. Our contemporary use of paragraphs is not too far removed from this.

Think of a paragraph as a container that holds words and sentences that you want to keep together for some reason or other. To see how this works, examine the two basic kinds of paragraphs.

TWO KINDS OF PARAGRAPHS

A *Topic Sentence Paragraph* presents content within the paragraph in a way that defines or limits the reader's thoughts. It contains a chunk of thought and provides the reader with a feeling of completeness and satisfaction by the paragraph's end.

In a Topic Sentence Paragraph, you take one main idea and develop it. This paragraph tells the readers what you are discussing, focuses the readers' minds on that particular thing, and then provides enough information to prove, explain, illustrate, or otherwise develop that main idea. Thus it is possible to break a Topic Sentence Paragraph down into two parts: the topic sentence itself (the main idea, either stated or implied) and the additional sentences directly related to the topic sentence which develop the main idea. It is the Topic Sentence Paragraph that carries the information or content of the writing and is essential in getting the message across to the reader.

A *Function Paragraph* directs the reader in how to read the essay and helps keep the reader interested. It allows you to emphasize or elaborate on certain points and lets you show your style in writing.

The Function Paragraph is entirely different from the Topic Sentence Paragraph. In the Function Paragraph, you won't find one complete idea set forth and developed. In fact, at times a Function Paragraph may be only one sentence; it may be a "paragraph" only because it is indented. Often a series of Function Paragraphs, taken all together, does make up a single, related chunk of thought, but the writer chooses to break that chunk into smaller units. Some of the most common uses for Function Paragraphs are the following:

- to keep the reader's attention
- to make transitions
- to set off conversational dialogue and questions
- to break up a paragraph that seems too long (or to keep all paragraphs in the piece of writing about the same length)
- to emphasize a point, to develop an example, or to add details
- to introduce and conclude essays

Of course the functions of the two paragraph types are not exclusive. It's possible to have a Topic Sentence Paragraph that keeps attention or to have a Function Paragraph that adds details. There are qualities that both paragraph types share.

Let's look at a piece of writing to see how Topic Sentence Paragraphs and Function Paragraphs are used. This essay illustrates the individual ways to organize through paragraphing.

Types of Paragraphs GROWING UP

Goal: To relate a personal perspective on growing up
Audience: Classmates

[*Topic sentence paragraph*]

When I was a little girl, my father made magic. Placing his hands completely over his face, he slowly inched them up toward his forehead— and the sun radiated out, so bright was his smile! Then his hands slowly moved down toward his chin, and the world could have wept along, so sad was his face. Up and down went his hands, changing his face, changing the world, changing my hopes—up and down, down and up. From my crib, I watched my two-faced father metamorphose back and forth. My heart was, pass by pass, broken and healed, broken and healed. I could have gone on forever; I never grew tired of watching it.

[*Function paragraph—adds drama*]

But he grew tired of doing it.

[*Topic sentence paragraph*]

I did not give up easily on magic. I watched my mother's hair go from little snail-like squiggles to a luminous black sheath; I watched food appear on the table; I watched my father walk out the door all neat and energetic in the morning, and come back in the door all rumpled and tired in the evening; I lay on the back seat of the car (while up front my father—my chauffeur—did the driving) and watched the rooftops whisper to the blue, blue sky. Some day it would be my turn. I would turn a key in an ignition and a two-ton metal turtle would take me to the movies, the ice cream store; I would wear lipstick and high-heeled shoes and Prince Charmings would dismount from their horses to make for me a path of their royal ermine robes.

[*Function paragraph—*
makes transition]

I grew up. The magic wasn't there.

[*Function paragraph—*
emphasizes a point]

When I finally realized it, I felt furious, betrayed. Why hadn't it worked? Hadn't I done all I was supposed to? Hadn't I chosen a major, chosen a career, started a checking account, bought an appointment book, used the right lipstick, the right clothing, the right wine, the right aspirins? I had copied grownups the best I could. How, then, did I come to so resemble the White Rabbit, all fuss and bother and "can't waste time"? Where was the magic of my childhood? What was different?

[*Topic sentence paragraph*]

Some people call this change the "inevitable disillusionment" of growing up—that when we are children we see things in a magnified, highly colored way; that we imbue our parents, and grownups in general, with more power than they feel (or deserve); and that they necessarily must fall from their perch, and we necessarily must suffer disillusionment. That we must reenact The Fall of Man over and over . . .

[*Function paragraph—*
breaks up paragraph]

There is probably something to this. But could there be something else happening as well? Is it possible that the magic can be reclaimed? Is there something that grownups can learn, can do, to make real, conscious magic happen?

[*Function paragraph—*
makes transition]

What, really, was it about childhood that accounted for the magic? I think it has something to do with time. And timelessness.

[*Topic sentence paragraph*]

When we are children, we have all the time in the world. Time enough to spend hours watching an ant rappel down a twig, a butterfly make a dazzling three point landing, a twisted candy wrapper ride the crest of a rain-swelled gutter-wave on its courageous and daredevil way toward the sewer. We give ourselves totally to what is happening. There is no worrying about tomorrow's grocery list, no incapacitating regrets about the *bon mot* we neglected to say the day before. All there is, is now. We have attention for looking, for listening, for feeling the weight of the air, for sensing the true underlay of outward behaviors. We are masters of nuance, unwitting practitioners of zen. And in the moment, without past or present, disappointment or expectations, the magic—the rightness, majesty, and beauty—of what is is so. And is enough. And is made possible by our slow-motion attentiveness; our ability to not be encumbered with thoughts.

[*Function paragraph—*
sets of questions]

Can we be grown up and be similarly un-encumbered? Is this possible? Is it even sane? Doesn't being grown up mean being full of busyness and purpose, carrying briefcases, and wearing three-piece suits? Is there room for magic in a grownup's world?

[*Topic sentence paragraph*]

I say there is, and must be. I don't disparage all goals or the things we must do to meet our goals. But there are times for goals, and then there are times for no-goals. When we structure time into little slivers, little quarter-hour pieces, we become its slave; we forget that we imposed a structure on time for our convenience. We act as if time imposes itself on us like a nightmarish Big Ben sprawling on top of us and leaning down hard enough to make us deflate. But children aren't in danger of such deflation—they live in slower time, magic time.

[*Topic sentence paragraph*]

How to reclaim magic time? I think it comes in the allowing. Any moment can be slowed down enough to reveal its inner mystery. Whatever you are doing, there is always something incredible to attend to—the play of light on your freckled hands, or the miraculous way in which our bodies (no matter how we worry) continue to breathe in and out, to take from what is outside and make of that what becomes our insides. There is the magic of loving another, and the magic of standing quite still on an endlessly spinning orb, and the magic of the ideas of one person reaching the mind of another person through the medium of funny little squiggles on some stiffened wood-pulp. The magic is everywhere, when we make time for it. In the air, in the water, in the stars.

[*Function paragraph—adds drama*]

And in ourselves.

You can see from this essay that without Topic Sentence Paragraphs there can be no developed message. Without Function Paragraphs, however, the reader would probably be bored by the sameness of the writing and a lack of consideration for the reader's attention span. Topic Sentence Paragraphs have a clear logic; there is a main idea, either stated or implied, and a group of sentences that develop that idea. Function Paragraphs usually have no logic except the author's own. They aren't caused by a new thought, don't have main idea sentences, and don't develop a topic. They do, however, keep the reader moving, provide continuity in the essay, and often reflect the individual personality of the piece or of the writer.

We'll look at Topic Sentence Paragraphs in much greater detail in the rest of this chapter, considering especially those elements that make Topic Sentence Paragraphs most effective for readers. We'll come back to Function Paragraphs again in Part 3, Revising and Polishing, since writers often see the best ways to use Function Paragraphs not as they are drafting but as they are revising.

THE TOPIC SENTENCE PARAGRAPH

All essays must have several good Topic Sentence Paragraphs to focus and limit the reader's attention. The Topic Sentence Paragraph also provides the reader with a sense of satisfaction or completeness because it gives the content of your message. A good Topic Sentence Paragraph will never leave your reader guessing. It will also never let the reader's mind wander from your subject.

The success of Topic Sentence Paragraphs depends on four principles: *focus, unity, coherence,* and *development.* Let's look at these principles carefully, one at a time.

Principle 1: Focus

The Topic Sentence Paragraph is named for its chief characteristic: the topic sentence that clearly *focuses* the reader's attention on what the paragraph is about. The topic sentence expresses the organizing idea, and all other sentences in the paragraph relate to the topic sentence by explaining, developing, or giving additional information. The topic sentence helps a paragraph deliver a developed message because the topic sentence

- directs your readers to think about one particular aspect of your subject, and
- orders your own thoughts.

The topic sentence in a Topic Sentence Paragraph lets you put together those thoughts that belong together. Here is how it works. Imagine that you are packing to move, and you have one box marked "take," one marked "give away," and one marked "burn." As you go through the closet, you put everything in the "take" box that is going on the truck; anything you think someone else might use but that you don't want, you put in the "give away" box; and what you don't think anyone would want you throw into "burn." The label on each box determines what goes into that box.

The topic sentence in a paragraph works like the labels on those packing boxes. What the topic sentence says determines what gets put into that particular paragraph. Look at this example about the Anasazi Indians, who built the famous cliff dwellings in Colorado:

The Anasazi were builders and settlers on a large and permanent scale, and it is for this that they are best remembered. At a time many centuries before the European discovery and settlement of the Americas, the Anasazi had developed a complex civilization of large and closely related communities. They erected massive and multistoried apartment buildings, walled cities, and cliff dwellings of shaped and mortared sandstone. They were dedicated farmers who planted, tilled, and even irrigated their crops, putting by the harvest to see them through the year. They were creative craftsmen of pottery and jewelry, and practiced a highly formalized religion in distinctive ceremonial chambers. The permanence and stability that they saw in their lives was reflected in the homes they built, but for reasons not yet completely understood their civilization lacked the durability of the building. The Anasazi abandoned their homeland, leaving the great stone cities and familiar farmlands for other areas in the Southwest, eventually to mix in the amalgam of modern Pueblo.

—*Donald G. Pike*

Because the topic sentence is what it is—*The Anasazi were builders and settlers on a large and permanent scale, and it is for this that they are best remembered*—the reader can see immediately why the six other sentences in the paragraph belong there. The topic sentence is the label on the box, and gathered around it are the sentences that constitute the rest of the things that belong in the box. The topic sentence determines everything else that goes into that particular paragraph.

You can see why you must have a topic sentence for the paragraph. Without a topic sentence, there's nothing to direct the readers' attention, and there's nothing to hold the sentences together as a group. A paragraph without a topic sentence looks like this:

Jogging is a fast-growing sport. Sports really contribute to good health. There is a new sports magazine on the market this month. Playing ball was a sport done thousands of years ago in primitive societies. People get injured in sports every year. Tennis players do not have a wide variety of shoes available to them. Sports can be expensive.

Reading that jumble of sentences, you feel as though you were being pushed from this to that, never knowing what was coming up. There was not a single "leader" sentence in the bunch that directed your thoughts and served to hold all the other sentences together.

How could this paragraph become a good Topic Sentence Paragraph? In fact, it's impossible to use all these sentences in one focused paragraph; the best you could do is choose one of them, make it the topic sentence, and add the necessary sentences to develop the point.

Playing ball was a sport done thousands of years ago in primitive societies. In fact, at Chichen Itza, an ancient Mayan Indian ruin on the Yucatan Peninsula in Mexico, you can still see the long ball court, the rings through which the ball was thrown, and the murals showing the two teams playing the game. The guides at Chichen Itza will tell you, too, how the winner of the ball game was rewarded. He was sacrificed to the rain god because that god deserved the very best. And by winning the game, he had proven he was the best.

To repeat: the topic sentence lets the reader know what you are going to discuss and is the controlling idea for the rest of the sentences in the paragraph. All the other sentences are there because they add specifics about the focused topic that is set up in the topic sentence.

Because your whole purpose is to get a message across to another person, you need to do everything possible to make that message clear.

Topic sentences can do that for you. Remember that the reader gets impatient. He or she wants to know what you are going to talk about, and wants to know quickly. Remember that the topic sentence also sets up an expectation that the rest of the paragraph should fulfill. This expectation can order your thoughts as you write. The topic sentence reminds you about what you should be discussing.

WRITING *Paragraph Focus*

Here are some sentences that might be added to develop a topic sentence into a Topic Sentence Paragraph. Write the topic sentence that will tie each unit together.

A. Red makes you feel aggressive and alive. Blue, on the other hand, can be calming or it can be depressing. If you wear yellow, you will probably feel cheerful, if for no other reason than because people say, "You look cheerful today, dressed in yellow." Black can look smashing and chic, or it can look drab, depending on how you accent it. Probably the worst color to wear at all is gray. You just fade into the crowd.

Topic Sentence:

B. This is generally an excellent time, because you will be able to capture the attention of all those buyers who have been out looking at other open houses. Even though a Sunday afternoon open house does cut into the few remaining weekend hours, it is perhaps preferred by most because of the response gained. Buyers generally plan to set aside a certain portion of time during the week for their home inspections. Generally, they go out looking at a time when they will be able to inspect the most properties in the shortest amount of time. You might decide to stick with this trend.   —*Ronald W. Jensen*

Topic Sentence:

C. When the day is cloudy and gloomy, I get depressed. Even if I have a busy day planned, the gloominess of a day without sunshine makes it difficult for me to function effectively. But rainy days don't depress me at all. Sometimes, though, they make me angry—especially when I have to do a lot of walking that day. I hate to arrive at work soaking wet. Other times, rainy days cheer me up. There is nothing as refreshing as a rain shower after several days of hot, muggy weather. My best moods, however, occur on warm, sunny days. The brightness of the sun lifts my spirits; I feel energetic and ready to work. The only problem then is that I'd rather be outdoors than indoors.

Topic Sentence:

Placement of the Topic Sentence. Where does the topic sentence go in the Topic Sentence Paragraph? Usually in one of three places:

1. at the beginning
2. at the end
3. nowhere—it's just "understood"

1. *Placing the Topic Sentence at the Beginning.* By far the most common location for the topic sentence is at the beginning of a Topic Sentence Paragraph. It is easy to see the advantage of putting it there. The reader knows immediately what you are going to talk about. It also provides *you* with a constant reminder—from the start—of what you are concentrating on in this paragraph. The topic sentence will help you stay on the subject. Knowing how fast thoughts can come—often faster than you can write them down—you're only too happy to have a system that weeds out the unnecessary ones immediately.

Here is a paragraph written by a college student. The writer took pains to let the reader know immediately what she was going to talk about. See how the topic sentence signals readers about what is going to be discussed.

What happens when ducks swallow lead? The pellets pass through the digestive track to the gizzard where they are converted to a soluble form and absorbed by the bloodstream. Lead causes a reduction in oxygen supplies to all tissues. It interferes with the body's ability to break down glucose, leading to weight loss. Lead also disrupts the production of hemoglobin and anemia is the likely result. This imbalance in blood chemistry impairs the functioning of the liver and heart and causes severe damage to these organs. The external symptoms are an extreme loss of weight, wing droop, refusal to eat, a tendency to seek isolation and cover, and loss of the ability to walk or fly.

2. *Placing the Topic Sentence at the End.* One good reason for putting the topic sentence at the end of the paragraph is to keep the reader in suspense and, therefore, interested. If what comes first is compelling, the reader reads on to see what you are going to say when you get through. Catching the reader's interest up front, however, is critical. Imagine a business or professional person picking up a book that started, "You should learn how to type." Do you think the person would be interested in reading on? Imagine how it would be, though, if the writer approached the subject by beginning the paragraph differently.

> All around us, every day, hundreds of millions of units of information travel all around the globe. From Bangkok to San Francisco, from Paris to Perth Amboy, this information rides the electronic waves that are changing and permeating the modern world. Nowadays, most people would find their lives greatly simplified by the use of computers—the "airline" that transports this wealth of information. And there is only one factor, aside from money and the fear of trying something new, that prevents the average business or professional person from benefiting from the computer goldmine: not knowing how to type.

The reader is much more likely to be willing to read on because the writer built up to the main point.

Another reason for putting the topic sentence at the end of a paragraph is to build point by point toward the conclusion so that the reader will be prepared to agree by the time he or she arrives at the end. This type of paragraph is sometimes called inductive, since it draws the reader through a series of specific details toward a conclusion. Here is an example.

> The Tarzan legend interests us for many reasons, not the least of which is that this human child was reared by apes. Wolves also, according to documented accounts, have raised humans (who grew to be more feral, more wolflike, than human). And stories abound of abandoned cubs of one species being taken in by nursing mamas of another. I myself know a ten-year-old cat who routinely washes her kittens—one of whom is a large three-year-old collie. So nature herself tells us that it is "natural" to adopt a child of another race.

The first example, about computerized information, shows how a reader can be teased into reading further. The second example shows how a reader can be taken, one step at a time, toward a particular conclusion. The first sets out to trap interest; the second sets out to trap agreement.

3. Placing the Topic Sentence Nowhere—Having It "Understood."
Sometimes you may feel that the reader will know the main idea in the paragraph without being told. In other cases, you may feel that formally stating the main idea in a topic sentence is somewhat artificial and stiff. When you wish to imply your topic sentence instead of stating it directly, you may just disperse specific details throughout a Topic Sentence Paragraph. In the following example, the writer is describing New York City's subway system. There is no one sentence that says so; the main idea of the paragraph is just understood.

EXAMPLE *Implied Topic Sentence Paragraph*

It's a world unto itself down there—dark and drafty on the platforms, garishly bright and sweaty-hot (from all those bodies pressing together during rush hour) in the cars themselves. For some, the subway is "just a way to get from here to there," but for others it is, as they say, "an experience." Here is a typical subway experience: you spot an entrance and head quickly for it, glad for the chance to escape the rain/noise/pollution/what have you. Once inside, you convert your coins into round tokens with upside-down "Y"'s stamped out. You put your tokens into the slot of the turnstile, push mightily, and the arms of the turnstile allow you to enter. (On a bad day—i.e., when the crowd is massive, or angry, or just generally disgruntled—comparisons with the Gates of Hell are hard to resist.) You descend, or ascend, to the track on which your train will, eventually, come, steering clear of the gum that has not yet grown hard and stiff, the still-smoldering cigarette butts, the piles and puddles of questionable droppings—and you emerge on the platform. While waiting for the train, you have time to notice the visual decorations: giant ads that sport mustaches and various ingenious curses; general signs of decay that an old structure denied of daylight is probably entitled to; and, most blatantly, the train graffiti. Some people see this testimony to the invention of spray paint as shocking and vandalistic; others see it as art. Whichever side you're on, you may not be able to see out the windows, which bear just as many boasts, curses, and comic-book style decorations as the metal surfaces. Once on the train, you sit—if you're lucky—in a seat made of hard orange plastic (the older cars have wicker seats—these are unraveling, slashed by knives, or both). Or you stand, fighting openly or surreptitiously with other flailing fists for a handhold on the bar above the seats. If you lose out on the bar (or the straps that hang from it), you will have to use your sea legs to stay erect as the train lurches wildly from one bend to the next. Or, if you are in the thick of the sardine-can phenomenon known as rush hour, you will be kept vertical by the sheer pressure of bodies surrounding you. But you may not make it to—and out—the door when the train gets to your stop. (Assuming, of course, that you can see your stop from the painted windows.) Once you manage to get yourself out of there, you can try to get the brand-new wrinkles out of your permanent-press suit, dust yourself off, shake yourself into place, and ascend, or descend, the steps to the street—glad for the chance to be out in the rain/noise/pollution/what have you.

Please note: It's important to recognize the difference between a paragraph with an implied or understood topic sentence, such as the preceding one, and a paragraph that is just a collection of unconnected sentences. If you are in the slightest doubt, put in the topic sentence. That way you are certain not to go wrong.

WRITING *Topic Sentence Placement*

Finding the Topic Sentence: Pick out the topic sentence in each paragraph below. If the topic sentence is implied, compose an appropriate sentence that describes the paragraph.

A. The alcohol-drunk driver usually finds it hard to hide his condition, if stopped by the police. But the pot-high driver often believes he can "come down" and carry on a seemingly normal conversation with a police officer. This apparent ability to "hide their high" gives many pot smokers confidence that they can drive stoned.

—*Peggy Mann*

B. The room in which I found myself was very large and lofty. The windows were long, narrow, and pointed, and at so vast a distance from the black oaken floor as to be altogether inaccessible from within. Feeble gleams of encrimsoned light made their way through the trellised panes, and served to render sufficiently distinct the more prominent objects around; the eye, however, struggled in vain to reach the remoter angles of the chamber, or the recesses of the vaulted and fretted ceiling. Dark draperies hung upon the walls. The general furniture was profuse, comfortless, antique, and tattered. Many books and musical instruments lay scattered about, but failed to give any vitality to the scene. I felt that I breathed an atmosphere of sorrow. An air of stern, deep, and irredeemable gloom hung over and pervaded all.   —*Edgar Allan Poe*

C. We get home from church around 12:30. After a late lunch, the afternoon seems to stretch before us unendingly. We leisurely read the Sunday paper—there's always more to it than there is to the weekly papers. Usually, there's homework to do, but no one feels like doing it, so we postpone it, choosing to nap or to go for a ride instead. Occasionally, there's an old movie worth watching on television. And, of course, it's always nice just to sit in the shade sipping a Coke or lemonade while the afternoon wears on.

D. In democracies, by definition, all human beings should have a say about technological developments that may profoundly change, even threaten, their lives: nuclear power, genetic engineering, the spread of microwave systems, the advance of satellite communications, and the ubiquitous use of computers, to name only a few. And yet, in order to participate fully in discussions of the implications of these technologies one must have training in at least physics, psychology, biology, philosophy, economics, and social and political theory. Any of these technologies has profound influence in all those areas. Because most of us are not so trained, all discussion takes place among our unelected surrogates, professionals and experts. They don't have this full range of training either, but they do have access to one or another area of it and can speak to each other in techno-jargon—"tradeoffs," "cost-benefits," "resource management"—and they therefore get to argue with each other over one side of the question or the other while the rest of us watch.   —*Jerry Mander*

E. When we first saw the barracks apartments, I told myself I would never live there. Five minutes later, we were turning the key to an apartment in one of those horrible buildings. (None of the nicer apartments were vacant, and we needed a place that day.) The first thing I didn't like was the stove that faced the door as you entered the apartment. Walking right into the kitchen as you came in reminded me of the crowded ghetto apartments I've seen on television. Then the couch looked like something you'd find in a cheaply furnished, rundown bus station. It was a gaudy orange vinyl and had no arms, and only two people could sit on it at a time because it was so small. There was no backboard on the bed, and the dresser drawer was made of brown, ugly metal. In the bathroom sink, there were separate hot and cold water faucets. I hated everything about that apartment—but we lived there for three years!

F. I think the stature of humor must vary some with the times. The court fool in Shakespeare's day had no social standing and was no better than a lackey, but he did have some artistic standing and was listened to with considerable attention, there being a well-founded belief that he had the truth hidden somewhere about his person. Artistically he stood probably higher than the humorist of to-day, who has gained social position but not the ear of the mighty. (Think of the trouble the world would save itself if it would pay some attention to nonsense!) A narrative poet at court, singing of great deeds, enjoyed a higher standing than the fool and was allowed to wear fine clothes; yet I suspect that the ballad singer was more often than not a second-rate stooge, flattering his monarch lyrically, while the fool must often have been a first-rate character, giving his monarch good advice in bad puns.   —*E. B. White*

Principle 2: Unity

Make sure that every sentence in the Topic Sentence Paragraph is related to the topic sentence. In the process of writing, ideas can pop up anywhere, sometimes surprising even you, the writer. Often these surprising ideas are so original or intriguing that you veer off in happy pursuit of them. For example, this paragraph from a student paper shows how the writer's thoughts veered while the paragraph was in progress.

> The sand dunes on the Oregon coast are as much fun as a carnival ride. You get into a modified pick-up truck, and the driver, who is probably 35, acts 14. He races up the dunes, stops suddenly, then takes off so fast that the truck—and you—leap several feet into the air. One man in our truck lost his glasses and his cigarette lighter on one of those leaps. His wife got very angry because the man could not find his belongings. The sand was so white and the truck had gone so far before the driver could hear us yelling "Stop!" that the glasses and lighter were nowhere to be seen. The wife wouldn't talk to the man all the way back to the ticket office. The spirit in the back of the truck just wasn't the same after that incident. The man was mad at the truck driver, and his wife was mad at him.

What has happened here? The writer began with a good topic sentence: *The sand dunes on the Oregon coast are as much fun as a carnival ride.* The next couple of sentences give additional information about why the dunes are fun and like a carnival ride. But then the writer veers off course: after telling about the man who lost his glasses and lighter, the writer gets onto a different topic—the anger and resentment associated with loss of the articles. Suddenly we've been shunted from fun to anger. And although there is some connection—the articles got lost and the anger came up during the dune buggy ride—the writer has not stayed on the topic announced in the topic sentence.

The paragraph could be made to flow easily by giving some attention to the supporting sentences. Here's the revised version, with all the sentences relating to the topic sentence.

> The sand dunes on the Oregon coast are as much fun as a carnival ride. You get into a modified pick-up truck with a driver who is probably 35 but acts 14. He races up the dunes, stops suddenly, then takes off so fast that the truck—and you—leap several feet into the air. One man in our truck lost his glasses and his cigarette lighter on one of those leaps. The driver will also spot another truck in the distance. The two will run right toward each other, swerving only at the last minute to avoid a head-on collision. Once our truck ran to the top of a dune, and suddenly there was nowhere to go. The dune

went straight down so suddenly that you couldn't see the bottom at all. We all thought we were sailing off into the far-blue yonder and said our last goodbyes. When the ride was over, we all jumped off the truck saying, "I'll never do that again," but in fact we could hardly wait to get back in line to take the ride again.

Here the writer sticks to telling why the truck ride on the dunes is so much fun. The writer doesn't get sidetracked onto the story about the man's glasses or his wife's anger. Everything in the paragraph connects to the topic sentence.

WRITING *Paragraph Unity*

Determine which of the paragraphs below stay on the topic and which stray off. Rewrite the ones that go off the topic.

A. Successful cooking can't be done quickly. Good cooks read recipes carefully before using them, and reread them as they go along. They must assemble needed ingredients—or go out and buy them if they aren't available in the kitchen. They must gather utensils, and when the specified utensil isn't available, they must try to come up with a suitable substitute. As they begin the recipe, they measure patiently and exactly and add things in the order specified. They follow instructions exactly, beating, cooking, and mixing for specified periods of time; they know that failing to do this may result in a less than perfect product. Then, they cook the whole thing for as long as the recipe says—not five or ten minutes more or less. After everything is mixed and cooking, they take time to clean up right away. Bowls, measuring spoons, beaters, and measuring cups must be washed. Unused ingredients must be returned to their proper places. Sometimes the kitchen floor must be mopped to clean up spilled flour or broken eggshells. But for the people who enjoy cooking, all this is time well spent.

B. These days, deciding how to spend your leisure time requires wisdom. If you watch television, you must determine which programs are worth watching and which should be turned off. Sometimes I think the people who produce TV programs aim to insult the public. There's nothing on but silly, unrealistic "sitcoms," violent, unrealistic adventure series, or ridiculous game shows. Do the producers think we have no taste when it comes to TV viewing? Do they think we don't use our minds when we watch television? The least they could do is offer something realistic. Sometimes I get so mad, I seriously consider getting rid of my set.

C. What I like most about going to college is the chance to meet new and exciting people. My roommate is one of the nicest persons I've ever met. He is goodnatured, understanding, and generally easy to get along with. There's only one thing I don't like about him— he studies too much. He gets up early to study and stays up late. I can't sleep when his study lamp is on. And I don't appreciate being awakened at 6 A.M. by his alarm clock. I sure wish he'd ease up on his studying. He'll end up going through college without having any fun—and I'll go through college without enough sleep!

D. Many people today seem to be out of touch or out of reality. Psychiatrists and psychologists have many patients. The patients visit them regularly to return to reality and try to get problems out in the open and solved. The schizoid condition is a general condition of society. People take out loans at record high interests. Do these people really think that they will be able to pay these loans off? Some people think that a new car, boat or house is worth being in "hot water" for. Another problem that faces society today is the misuse of drugs. Many young people seem to want to be out of touch. For this purpose, they use mind-altering drugs. These people do not seem to know that natural highs are present throughout the universe. Professionals are not able to help all of the people in need. The entire world seems to be out of touch today. Wars are raging in the Far East today. Could not these people settle their differences and stop the loss of innocent lives?

Principle 3: Development

When developing the Topic Sentence Paragraph, always give the reader enough information. The danger is that the writer always knows more than the reader and can easily underestimate the reader's need to know. If you raise the expectations of the reader and then don't fulfill them with enough information, the reader resents what feels like a set-up.

Here are two versions of a paragraph that illustrate this principle. The first version clearly does not give enough information:

Cooking southern food is something anybody can learn to do. The most important thing the cook has to learn is to be patient. The cook must also learn to think imaginatively. Finally, someone cooking southern food must think big instead of small.

This paragraph is almost provoking in its skimpiness of detail! Why is patience important? What makes imagination necessary? And what on earth does the writer mean by "think big instead of small"? This is a beautiful example of a paragraph in which the writer knows more than the reader and isn't giving enough detail.

Now see what happens when the writer rewrites the paragraph, this time making sure that the reader knows what the topic sentence means:

> Cooking southern food is something anybody can learn to do. The most important thing the cook has to know how to do is to be patient. Almost all southern dishes cook for an enormously long time. Black-eyed peas simmer for half a day. Chicken and dumplings take hours. Green beans are cooked until they are pearl gray. The cook must also have enough imagination to use meat for seasoning, because almost all southern vegetable dishes are seasoned with meat. Green beans and black-eyed peas are cooked with fat-back or salted pork. Bacon grease is put into corn bread. Biscuits are made with lard. Finally, someone cooking southern food must think big instead of small. A southern meal is likely to have at least two meats, four or five vegetables, three pies, and several cakes. And the portions are large, too. So the cook has to make plenty. With these characteristics, however—patience, imagination, and willingness to think big—anybody can cook southern food.

The details added to the revision bring life to the paragraph. What makes giving the reader enough information such an important principle? There are two reasons.

First, readers do not remember general statements very long at all. What they do remember are images, specifics, "pictures" that the writer gives them. This is why the topic sentence is not enough by itself. There must be concrete details, examples, that the reader can hold on to. The same principle is at work when a set of instructions contains both written information and a picture or chart, giving you a much better chance of understanding how to put something together. This is what you are doing in paragraphs when you give specifics to show what the topic sentence means. You are giving the reader more than one way to get the message: through both the topic sentence and the specifics that paint pictures for the reader.

Second, readers are more likely to get the message if you give it to them several times. Not only are you sending it in two different ways—through a topic sentence and through back-up details—but you are also just plain sending it X number of times. You can hope that at least one of those times the reader will get it. This isn't because readers aren't smart. It's just because the communication process has to operate across space, time, and distance. If you send your message in just one sentence, just one time, just one way, the odds are stacked against you.

How Much Is Enough? How can you know what is enough information? No sure formula answers this question. Your readers provide part of the answer, because how much they already know or don't know will determine how much or how little you, the writer, have to explain. As you look at your Topic Sentence Paragraphs, see if you have given as much information as you can guess your readers will need to know.

Methods for Giving Enough Information. Here are some ways to add information to your Topic Sentence Paragraphs so that the readers will be satisfied.

Illustrations, Examples, and Details. Here is a Topic Sentence Paragraph that illustrates this method of providing enough information. Isabella Bird, an adventuresome Englishwoman traveling alone in the West in the late 1800s, wrote a fascinating account of her travels in a book called *A Lady's Life in the Rockies.* In the following Topic Sentence Paragraph she uses an example full of details to be sure the reader "gets the picture."

> But oh! what a hard, narrow life it is with which I am now in contact! Chalmers came from Illinois nine years ago, pronounced by the doctors to be far gone in consumption, and in two years he was strong. They are a queer family. . . . They have one hundred and sixty acres of land, a "Squatter's claim," and an invaluable water power. He is a lumberer, and has a saw-mill of a very primitive kind. I notice that every day something goes wrong with it, and this is the case throughout. If he wants to haul timber down, one or other of the oxen cannot be found; or if the timber is actually under way, a wheel or a part of the harness gives way, and the whole affair is at a standstill for days. The cabin is hardly a shelter, but is allowed to remain in ruins because the foundation of a frame house was once dug. A horse is always sure to be lame for want of a shoe nail, or a saddle to be useless from a broken buckle, and the wagon and harness are a marvel of temporary shifts, patchings, and insecure linkings with strands of rope. Nothing is ever ready or whole when it is wanted. . . .

Description. This method of adding information in Topic Sentence Paragraphs answers such questions for the reader as, "What does it look like?" "What does it feel like?" When you describe, you picture the object, person, or event for the reader. You draw it with words.

In this excerpt from *The Shirley Letters,* the writer—a cultivated woman—describes the interior of her log-cabin home.

> The room into which we have just entered is about twenty feet square. It is lined over the top with white cotton cloth, the breadths of which being sewed together only in spots, stretch apart in many places, giving one a birds-eye view of the shingles above. The sides

are hung with a gaudy chintz, which I consider a perfect marvel of calico printing. The artist seems to have exhausted himself on roses; from the largest cabbage, down to the tiniest Burgundy, he has arranged them in every possible variety of wreath, garland, bouquet, and single flower; they are of all stages of growth, from earlicst budhood up to the ravishing beauty of the "last rose of summer." Nor has he confined himself to the colors usually worn by this lovely plant; but, with the daring of a great genius soaring above nature, worshiping the ideal rather than the real, he has painted them brown, purple, green, black and blue. It would need a floral catalogue to give you the names of all the varieties which bloom upon the calico; but, judging by the shapes—which really are much like the originals—I can swear to moss roses, Burgundies, York and Lancaster, tea roses, and multi-floras.

Definition. At times you may want to define a term or process, to add information in a Topic Sentence Paragraph. Look at the way defining helps you understand the following excerpt; the Topic Sentence Paragraph defines in order to give the reader enough information:

The mountain dulcimer is a small, wooden, fretted instrument that is usually held on the lap while being played. The shape of the body may be a teardrop, a slender hourglass, or some unique variation. Likewise, the sound holes may vary in shape, from simple circles to hearts, clubs, or treble clefs. It has a raised fretboard—up to an inch from the body—on which three or four strings are tensed. These are attached at both ends—to stabilizing pegs at the bottom, and to tuning pegs at the top. Each string is tuned in relation to the other, according to the mode that one chooses—Ionian, Aeolian, Mixolydian, Dorian, Lydian, or Phrygian. The fourth string is often used as a drone—that is, it is tuned to the third string—which produces a haunting, resonant sound.

Explanations and Analysis. Here are two Topic Sentence Paragraphs that use explanation to give the reader enough information. They come from a *Road & Track* article on the best cars in the world. *Road & Track* had two categories for this article, "Best Cars in the World" and "Best Car in Each of Ten Categories." These two paragraphs explain what those categories mean. The topic sentence in each is underlined.

For the "Ten Best," we reasoned that some cars are "best" for one reason and some are "best" for another. So, if we established rigid criteria for the ten best, we would be restricting the final list in ways that would end up favoring one group or one type. And this, we didn't want. Each car that belonged on this list did have to be "best" for a specific reason, however, although it did not have to be a "best" for the same reason as another. We also decided that the cars on the Ten Best list need not be models that were sold in the U.S. Just because our benevolent and protective government has decreed that some of the world's best cars should be denied to Americans, we did not think this was a sufficient reason for a particular model's exclusion if we agreed that it qualified otherwise as one of the Ten Best.

For the "Best of Category," the criteria were more restrictive. Basically, the basic criterion was a judgment as to how well the car fulfilled the function for which it was intended in comparison with its direct competition. To make this decision it was of course necessary to include all the various facets that go into such an evaluation: engineering, assembly quality, handling, braking, reliability and so on. For the categories, we also restricted eligibility to those cars on which we had performed one of our normal road tests; that is, to those models that are available for sale in the U.S. at this time.

Facts and Figures. Another way to develop a Topic Sentence Paragraph is to use facts and figures when appropriate. The only purpose of any form of development is to give readers enough information so that they will notice and listen to what you say and then believe and agree with you. Statistics and factual information will often add weight to your assertions and swing the reader your way. Here is a paragraph which uses facts and figures to develop the topic sentence, *A food crisis exists in Ethiopia*.

> A food crisis exists in Ethiopia. As many as 10 million people in that country may be close to starvation as a result of the severe drought. The official government estimate of the number of people affected by the drought is 7.3 million. This figure is based on the number of people registered for emergency food aid. The 10 million estimate includes the hungry people of Eritrea and Tigre provinces, hard-hit by the drought and by heavy fighting, and others who are too weak to leave their villages and go to the relief camps. Many relief workers, including some government officials, estimate that by the end of 1985, more than 900,000 people will have died as a result of hunger and hunger-related disease in Ethiopia.

Repetition. You may be surprised to learn that at times repetition is an excellent device for developing a Topic Sentence Paragraph. Often, repetition merely bores, especially when writers repeat simply because they don't have anything else to say.

The kind of repetition we are considering here, however, is valuable development of the message you are sending. Readers do not have a long memory span for the points you are making, so repetition can reinforce your main points. The example here shows how valuable repetition can be when used in the right way:

> People who get fitted with their first pair of contact lenses are often very excited, delighted, and grateful to see so effortlessly after many years of wearing thick, heavy glasses. But they need to be responsible, too, especially in terms of cleaning their lenses. After a normal day of wear, lenses are coated with a film of natural chemicals secreted by the eyes. If this film is not washed off with a solution made for that purpose, the lens will get brittle and possibly scratched, making it unwearable. Also, the coating obscures clear vision, like a dirty windshield on a car. So it is really important to take care of lenses every night by cleaning them carefully with a lens-cleaning solution suitable for the particular kind of lens. Well-kept lenses are more comfortable, and last much longer.

Comparison and Contrast. A common way to help your reader "see" what you mean is to *compare* it to something else, showing how the two things are alike, or to *contrast* it with something else, showing how your idea is different from something else. Putting two things up together can throw light on the point that you, the writer, want to get across. Look at the way Annie Dillard uses a comparison of Nature with a children's puzzle to develop her thoughts:

> It's all a matter of keeping my eyes open. Nature is like one of those line drawings of a tree that are puzzles for children: Can you find hidden in the leaves a duck, a house, a boy, a bucket, a zebra, and a boot? Specialists can find the most incredibly well-hidden things. . . .

Narrative. "Once upon a time . . .": you can never fail to get a reader's attention if you tell a story. In addition, a narrative can help you explain or illustrate the point you are making in a Topic Sentence Paragraph. In the second paragraph here, Thomas Merton uses a story to let the reader know what he means by the paragraph which has come immediately before.

> The rain I am in is not like the rain of cities. It fills the wood with an immense and confused sound. It covers the flat roof of the cabin and its porch with insistent and controlled rhythms. And I listen, because it reminds me again and again that the whole world runs by rhythms I have not yet learned to recognize, rhythms that are not those of the engineer.
>
> I came up here from the monastery last night, sloshing through the cornfield, said vespers, and put some oatmeal on the Coleman

stove for supper. It boiled over while I was listening to the rain and toasting a piece of bread at the log fire. The night became very dark. The rain surrounded the whole cabin with its enormous virginal myth, a whole world of meaning, of secrecy, of silence, of rumor. Think of it: all that speech pouring down, selling nothing, judging nobody, drenching the thick mulch of dead leaves, soaking the trees, filling the gullies and crannies of the woods with water, washing out the places where men have stripped the hillside! What a thing it is to sit absolutely alone, in the forest, at night, cherished by this wonderful, unintelligible, perfectly innocent speech, the most comforting speech in the world, the talk that rain makes by itself all over the ridges, and the talk of the water courses everywhere in the hollows!

Nobody started it, nobody is going to stop it. It will talk as long as it wants, this rain. As long as it talks I am going to listen.

WRITING *Paragraph Development*

Each of the paragraphs in these two passages is undeveloped. Using any of the methods discussed previously, rewrite each paragraph so that the topic is developed fully for the reader.

A. Although a college degree is a form of success in itself, only the individual can determine if that degree is the beginning or the end of the road. A person must want success in order to attain it.

In today's highly specialized and technical society, a university education is practically the only way to open doors of opportunity. Most good jobs require college degrees. But once on the job, a person must be willing to work hard and be the best that he can be.

Although a university education is not the only requirement for success, it is a necessary part of the make-up of a successful individual.

B. Euthanasia would prevent prolonged mourning by family and loved ones. It would ease the enormous financial burden that a family must bear in order to keep a person alive on life support systems.

This financial strain combined with the worry and sadness of having a person in the family in this condition brings strains on the rest of the family. These combined pressures often cause breakups in family life and sometimes lead to divorce.

No family should suffer these misfortunes and in most cases if a family is close, euthanasia will prevent this problem.

Principle 4: Coherence

Make the paragraph hold together through order, transitions, and reminder signs. Readers expect ideas in paragraphs to hang together. Not only should all sentences support a topic sentence, but the sentences should lead logically from one to the next. This characteristic of writing is called *coherence,* and it is achieved in writing in three main ways.

1. We *order details* in paragraphs according to one of several natural patterns.
2. We use *transition words and phrases* to show connections between sentences.
3. We use *reminder signs* to help readers follow the flow of ideas.

Order Sentences in a Natural Pattern. When you think about how you organize your daily activities, you think of calendars, maps, and sometimes filing cabinets. Writers can use similar logical patterns to order their ideas in paragraphs.

One pattern of organization is chronological or time order. Paragraphs often pattern details in a clear time sequence because it is so common to all human activity. We note this pattern with transitional words such as *first, next, then, meanwhile.*

Another natural pattern is spatial organization. As you describe a room, for instance, you can move logically from right to left, left to right, top to bottom, inside to outside. Any such arrangement of details that consistently follows an orderly space pattern will help readers locate themselves—and the details in the writing—clearly. Common transitions with this pattern include *next to, above, under, moving to the left,* and so on.

You can also arrange details in a paragraph according to a general-to-specific order. A general statement is one that applies to many things and includes several instances or examples. A specific statement gives one particular example or incident. Paragraphs that move from the general to the specific help us understand new terms or concepts, for instance. Typical transition words for this pattern are those that introduce examples—*for example, for instance, in like manner.*

You might also use an order of climax to arrange details in a paragraph logically. If, for example, several of your daily chores turned out badly today, you might decide not to list them in the chronological or time order in which they occurred. Instead, you might order them according to how badly they went wrong and build to the most disastrous incident as the climax. With this pattern, you'll find yourself using transitions that show increasing intensity—*much/more/most, bad/worse/worst.*

Use Transitions to Show Connections. Transitions are specific words, phrases, sentences, and paragraphs that give readers signals about where a piece of writing is headed. You will probably find that you usually put transitions into your writing quite naturally and automatically. Check to be sure you have appropriate transitions to help readers move smoothly through your text. Here's a short list of the most common transitional words and phrases. Use sentences and paragraphs to signal changes in direction as well.

Transition Signal Words	Meaning
for example, for instance	illustration
because, consequently, since, therefore	cause or reason
in other words, that is, so	restatement or clarification
but, however, on the other hand, yet, nevertheless, on the contrary	contrast
similarly, likewise, in like manner, in the same manner, in the same way	comparison
also, too, in addition, and, furthermore, moreover	addition or expansion
first, next, then, last, before, prior, subsequently, earlier, later	time pattern
aboard, above, beyond, on top of, under, alongside, upon, beneath, to the left	space pattern
finally, at last, after all, in conclusion, to conclude, to sum up	conclusion

Use Reminder Signs to Show the Flow of Ideas. People generally have a short memory of what they read. Some recent research indicates that within twenty seconds, people forget the form of the message conveyed and remember only the gist of its content. Since a reader will tend to forget the order of the words themselves so easily, you must use reminder signs all along the way in your writing to refresh the reader's memory and to keep your subject clearly visible.

What are the reminder signs in writing? They are simply key words or phrases repeated throughout the writing. Sometimes it is the same word repeated exactly; other times it is a variation of the word, a synonym for the word, or a pronoun that stands for the word. The important thing about repeating is that it keeps the reader pointed in a straight line without looking back to rediscover what you're talking about. It's the principle of "courteous repetition."

Here's a paragraph that illustrates the principle.

Leaves fall in an annual *cycle,* and there is a natural *cyclical* pattern of normal *hair loss* on the human head, too. The greatest amount of *hair loss* occurs in November; the least amount in May. A single hair grows on your head for a little less than three years. Then it *rests.* After about three months of *rest,* it falls out and a new hair grows in its place in the same hair follicle, and the *cycle* begins again. This is the end of that *resting* period for old hair, so you can expect heavier accumulations than usual in your brush and comb. Up to *one hundred* hairs a day may fall out in the normal course of things, but healthy new hairs are growing as you read this. If you suspect that your *hair loss* is greater than normal, count the hairs that come out in your comb. If the total is higher than *one hundred,* take measures. See the hairologist at a good salon for treatments.

—*Vidal and Beverly Sassoon*

Examining this paragraph, you can see that the key words are *cycle, hair loss, rest,* and *one hundred.* These key words are repeated all the way through the paragraph, and the reader is never allowed to forget what the subject is, never is obliged to double back to pick up the thought. In your own writing, you have to beware of sounding monotonous and so will want to vary your wording, using pronouns or synonyms. You will, however, need to do a certain amount of repeating of the main word or words in your message if you are going to keep the idea directly before your reader.

WRITING *Paragraph Coherence*

1. In the two samples below, find all the transitions and reminder signs. List them and be prepared to explain how they keep the reader moving smoothly through the paragraph and how they keep the subject at the front of the reader's attention.

   A. Shopping around for a car loan is not as much fun as shopping for a car. But just as the savvy shopper checks out several car dealers before that final handshake, he should also check out competing lenders. To help him, the Federal Trade Commission has prepared a handy pocket *Credit Shopping Guide.* It includes tips on borrowing and a series of tables so you can compare the cost of car loans, home improvement loans and mortgages at various interest rates and over different time periods.

   The total finance charge on a loan can depend on where you borrow. Let's say you need $3,000 for three years to buy a new car. If you finance it through the car dealer, where the average annual percentage rate—the true rate of interest—is 13½%, that $3,000 loan is likely to cost you $665. But if you go to a bank, where the average rate is 11%, the loan may cost $536; and if you can borrow against your life insurance, the rate will average 6%—for a cost of $286. . . .

To get a copy of the free credit guide, write the Public Reference Branch, Federal Trade Commission, Washington, D.C. 20580.

—*Money Magazine*

B. Samuel Johnson has fascinated more people than any other writer except Shakespeare. Statesmen, lawyers, and physicians quote him, as do writers and scientists, philosophers and farmers, manufacturers and leaders of labor unions. For generations people have been discovering new details about him and reexamining and correcting old ones. Interest in Johnson is by no means confined to the English-speaking world, though naturally it is strongest there. In Asia, Africa, and South America, groups of Johnsonians meet every year to talk about every aspect of him. The reason why Johnson has always fascinated so many people of different kinds is not simply that Johnson is so vividly picturesque and quotable, though these are the qualities that first catch our attention. The deeper secret of his hypnotic attraction, especially during our own generation, lies in the immense reassurance he gives to human nature, which needs—and quickly begins to value—every friend it can get.

—*Walter Jackson Bate*

2. Here are two examples that show just how effective your writing can be when you constantly keep the subject before the reader by using reminder signs. The first is by Chief Joseph of the Nez Perce Indians (published in 1879). What are the key terms? How often are they repeated? How does this contribute to the force of this paragraph?

A. I have heard talk and talk, but nothing is done. Good words do not last long unless they amount to something. Words do not pay for my dead people. They do not pay for my country, now overrun by white men. . . . Good words will not give my people good health and stop them from dying. Good words will not get my people a home where they can live in peace and take care of themselves. I am tired of talk that comes to nothing. It makes my heart sick when I remember all the good words and broken promises. . . .

—*Chief Joseph*

This second example, by Don Fabun, is about the ways people use space to communicate. Examine it for two things: the way Fabun repeats the key terms he is discussing, and the way he signals the reader at the beginning of each sentence. Underline both repeated key terms and signals, and be prepared to discuss how Fabun uses each to lead the reader from sentence to sentence and to keep the main point always before the reader.

B. The way we use space is another way that we communicate with one another. The distance between you and someone else may determine the nature of the communication. If you are a few inches away from someone's ear, chances are that you will whisper and the nature of the communication will be "secret." At a distance of several feet, the communication may still be private, but its tone and nature will have changed. The change is even greater if you are speaking to a large audience. Here the nature of the message may be determined in part by the distance between you and the most distant members of the audience. —*Don Fabun*

WRITING *Paragraph Principles*

The following paragraphs do not follow the four principles about writing good topic sentence paragraphs. Determine what principle is missing in each paragraph. Then revise each paragraph so that the message has a better chance of getting across to the reader.

A. *No* is just a simple, one-syllable word used to express a negative answer. Agreed, the word *no* is easy to say, but to answer someone directly with it changes the entire situation.

B. Education concerning the harmful effects of smoking should be increased. This can be done through the schools, starting with health programs for children at an early age. Some schools have initiated such programs, but a more widespread and intensive approach must be employed.

C. Gardening of vegetables is one hobby that is money-saving; not many hobbies can claim this. It is also fruitful, literally. Gardening of vegetables is relatively easy if you approach it in the right manner. First, you must have the proper location and tools. Pick a site that gets plenty of sunshine, is wind free, and preferably enclosed. You then must have some tool that breaks up the soil. I would recommend investing in a small tiller. You will also need an efficient watering system and common tools such as a hoe and garden rake.

D. Jogging requires determination. When a runner first begins, a thousand reasons come up for not going out. It will be too cold or too hot. Or the runner won't have any spare time. It is quite difficult to run in hot weather, and a runner has to train for it. The best thing to do is to run in the cool part of the day, stay in the shade, run slower, and drink something cold upon the return from the run. Running in cold weather just requires bundling up warmly but be careful not to wear too many clothes because your body gets hot fast when you are jogging.

E. Although it was hard for the man working long hours and not getting paid a high salary, the woman's day was not easy. The average wife in the fifties stayed at home and cooked, cleaned and waited for her husband to come home. There is nothing wrong with this except for the fact that there was no diversion except for the radio. Television was not yet widely available. The average couple had only one car which the husband would take to work. This meant the wife was stuck at home all day. To buy groceries, the wife would walk and either carry the bags home or pull them in a small cart. Although a couple starting out in the 1950s had a hard financial struggle, they appreciated all they had worked for.

SOME FINAL OBSERVATIONS ON TOPIC SENTENCE PARAGRAPHS

With the exception of headings, paragraphs are the most obvious organizational units of your writing. You signal readers that ideas belong together by placing them in the same paragraph. You guide the reader's eye to new ideas or changes in direction by breaking paragraphs apart. You control the flow of the paper through the order and detail of your paragraphs.

Use these elements of your paper to communicate your message effectively. Even if the paragraphs seem to chunk themselves as you draft, scrutinize each paragraph carefully to check for focus, unity, development, and coherence.

PART 3   *Revising and Polishing*

As you continue in your writing process, this section will help you to

- revise your papers by re-seeing audience, form, paragraphs, sentences, and words
- edit and proofread your papers

CHAPTER 12

Revising: Re-Seeing
Your Writing

After you complete an initial draft, all the subsequent changes you make
in a text can be called *revising*. Revising, however, encompasses much
more than these changes. In fact, revising occurs throughout the writing
process. As you get ideas in your prewriting, you may reject certain ones
as unworkable—you may not jot down *every* idea you have while listing,
or branches may get dropped out of your branching as you go along.
Whenever you reject an idea as you prewrite, you are revising.

As you consider audience and purpose in writing, chances are that
you'll revise too. You may not have a single word on the page yet, but if
you decide to write to teenagers and then change your mind and decide
to write to parents about drunk driving, you've revised your audience.
Likewise, you may begin writing by assuming that a narrative of your
own experience will be the most efficient way to convey an idea, but
when you examine audience and purpose you may shift to a different
form of writing. Again, you are revising.

Later in the writing process when you focus, you revise even more,
because in essence you are cutting out areas of the topic that you won't
cover. Similarly, you are revising your thesis as you rework it to make it
say exactly what you want it to.

You often revise while you draft as well. Just as writing causes new
ideas to come to the surface, writing also causes you to sharpen your
focus on what to say and how to say it. You might change directions several times as we complete a draft. All these changes are revising.

Putting a section on revising in the later part of a textbook doesn't
take account of all the revising you do as you get ideas and draft a paper.
It is, however, the easiest way to remind you about the revising that occurs after the paper is drafted.

This section will guide you to some specific ways to revise your papers, looking first at the paper as a whole, then at individual paragraphs, sentences, and finally words.

RE-SEEING THE WHOLE PAPER

The revising you do when you have a complete draft of your paper can be the most difficult. Although not everyone enjoys this part of revising, most writers agree that it is the most rewarding. Re-seeing the entire paper provides your best opportunity to communicate your message to readers—and that's what writing is all about.

STUDENT EXAMPLE *Re-Seeing the Paper*

Let's consider revising the whole paper by looking at the first paragraphs of a paper planned to explain cell structure to high-school students.

Goal: To introduce cell structure and function
Audience: High-school freshmen

The Human Cell

Every cell has a specific purpose in maintaining the health of the body. Specialization occurs in the human, but each cell has the basic components of every other cell. The size of the cell does not diminish the complexity or specialization of the components of the cell. It has organelles, the specialized components of the cell, which provide very special services. The cell also has a membrane which surrounds the cytoplasm, the other major portion of the cell. The following paragraphs contain a description of the various parts of the cell.

The cell does not just conform to its surroundings nor does it remain rigid. The plasma membrane regulates the shape of the cell by completely surrounding the cytoplasm. The plasma membrane contains mostly proteins and lipids, but it contains some water, carbohydrates and other inorganic substances. The lipids form a bilayer with a space in between. The proteins reside mainly in the layer, but can protrude out of the lipid layer. This model for the plasma membrane is called the fluid mosaic model. The plasma membrane has four major functions in the cell. Obviously the plasma membrane must protect the cell from foreign substances. The plasma membrane makes contact with the other cells or substances and forms a communication link with them. The plasma membrane receives chemicals, hormones, nutrients and antibodies from outside sources. Finally the plasma membrane regulates what enters and exits the cell. This regulation is called selective permeability. The plasma membrane acts like a net. It has holes allowing small particles through while restricting the admission of others. Because the small particles can pass through without any energy, they use passive transport. If the particle is large or the particle must go the opposite way of the concentration gradient, it must use active transport. In active transport energy must be used. The mitochondria, an organelle, provides the energy needed for active transport. Both active and passive transport take place in the cell regularly. The plasma membrane provides both protection and a place of contact for the cell.

The plasma membrane keeps the cytoplasm inside the cell. The cytoplasm consists mostly of water, seventy-five to ninety percent. Proteins, carbohydrates and lipids compose the other part of the cytoplasm. The cytoplasm has five activities. First, most chemical reactions in the cell occur in the cytoplasm. It also receives substances from outside sources and converts them into viable energy sources for the cell. The cytoplasm also synthesizes new material for the cell. The cytoplasm can take these materials and package them for transport to other parts of the cell. Finally the cytoplasm eliminates wastes from the cell. The cytoplasm occupies a large area of the cell and is easily identified when seen. The cytoplasm also holds all the organelles except the nucleus.

The writer was hoping to explain cell structure and function to high-school biology students. Was the audience targeted well in the first draft? Here are several other questions asked of the writer as the writer and others read the first draft.

What do your readers already know about cell structure and function?

How can your readers use what they know to incorporate the new information here?

Which of these terms will be new to them?

Would high-school students be able to learn this material better if you made it more familiar and less formidable?

Why do you connect concepts the way you do? Do the concepts belong together? Can you make the logic of the connections clearer for your readers?

In short, other readers of the first draft agreed that it did not draw on what high school students might already know to help them learn new material. Furthermore, readers agreed that the writer didn't organize material in ways that would help someone learn this information for the first time. So by reconceiving the audience members in terms of what they knew and didn't know, the writer was able to re-see the whole paper. When the writer redrafted the paper, the same basic information was used, but it was repackaged completely. Several drafts later, this version developed.

THE CITY CELL

Every cell in your body functions like a small city, each producing special goods, but not all the goods necessary for a productive city, making it dependent on other cities. Every cell can satisfy its needs but not the needs of the entire body. A wall surrounds the city, and the cell has its own wall—the plasma membrane. Inside the cell exist different factories or organelles to produce different products or provide different services. Organelles in the cytoplasm resemble factories located along roads in the city, enabling easy transportation and communication. Although the size of the city overwhelms the size of the cell, the complexity and organization of both resemble each other.

The plasma membrane or wall of the cell composes the outermost portion of the cell. It keeps all the other portions of the cell inside the wall. Unlike the wall of the city, composed of wood and concrete, the plasma membrane contains proteins and lipids, two chemical compounds. The lipids form an outer and inner wall and the proteins solidify the wall from the space in between the two lipid layers. This organization of the wall is called the fluid mosaic model. The plasma membrane also possesses the property called selective permeability. The plasma membrane allows things to enter and exit the cell like gates in a city wall. Some particles can fit through the gate and require no energy to

move. Other particles are too large or try to enter when everything else is leaving (this is called opposing the concentration gradient). For these particles, entering the city is like climbing the wall, and energy must be supplied for the particles to enter the cell. Entering the cell without the use of energy is called passive transport, while those particles requiring energy move by active transport. Along with allowing particles to enter and exit the cell, the plasma membrane can make contact with other cells and receive nutrients, hormones and other chemicals from other cells like importing materials for a city. The plasma membrane provides both protection and regulation for the cell like a wall does for the city.

The city must have a basic layout and the cytoplasm fulfills this function in the cell. The cytoplasm contains the organelles. Most of the chemical reactions in the cell take place in the cytoplasm. The cytoplasm also receives substances from outside of the cell and converts them into viable energy sources for the cell. Also functioning as the receiving site, the cytoplasm packages materials and transports them to other parts of the cell. The cytoplasm has many functions including transport, synthesis, packaging and receiving.

In the middle of the city lies the headquarters; in the cell this place is occupied by the nucleus. The nucleus acts like the administration of a very dominant government. The nucleus regulates what, how fast, and how much will be produced by the organelles in the cell. Also included inside the administration building are plans for the next cities which are identical to the existing city. In the cell the plans are called genetic information contained in thread-like chromatin strands composed of DNA. These chromatin threads will later condense and become chromosomes which more easily divide and get placed into new cells. The nuclear membrane surrounds the nucleus and functions like the plasma membrane surrounding the cell. The nucleus is the headquarters for the cell and controls all the processes of the cell including plans for future cells.

Another organelle, ribosomes, composed mostly of ribose nucleic acid, acts like a factory. This factory produces proteins, a basic component of several larger substances—mostly enzymes or antigens for the body. The cell contains many protein factories. Those located in the cytoplasm are called free ribosomes. The free ribosomes produce proteins for use in the cell. Other ribosomes, attached ribosomes, produce proteins for use outside the cell like a factory that exports its goods. Ribosomes are like factories that produce parts for assembly in another factory which may be inside or outside of the city.

Factories like ribosomes must have some way to transport their products; in the cell this need is fulfilled by the endoplasmic reticulum. When the endoplasmic reticulum transports material it acts like a highway system. In the cell the highway system consists of a series of membranes acting like roads. The endoplasmic reticulum transports the proteins produced by the ribosomes, among other materials, throughout the cytoplasm. If ribosomes are directly attached to the endoplasmic reticulum, it is considered rough; without ribosomes attached, the endoplasmic reticulum is considered smooth. Both types help transport materials and absorb materials from the cytoplasm. The roads created by the endoplasmic reticulum can lead many places including storage areas for the cell, the nuclear membrane which allows contact with the nucleus, and the Golgi complex where packaging of materials occurs.

The Golgi complex is another factory or organelle in the cell. The Golgi complex acts like a packaging and export company. It has three major products to package and export for use outside the cell. The proteins transported to the Golgi complex by the endoplasmic reticulum are packaged in sack-like structures. Several proteins are placed in each sack and then pinched off from the Golgi complex and sent out of the cell through the plasma membrane like a truck released from the warehouse and sent across the country. The Golgi complex also takes lipids produced by the smooth endoplasmic reticulum and packages them in the same way the proteins are packaged for use outside of the cell. Finally the Golgi complex can produce some carbohydrates and package them. The Golgi complex operates as a packaging and export factory for proteins, lipids and carbohydrates.

Energy for all the factories in the cell is produced by the power plant of the cell—the mitochondria. The mitochondria has two membranes, an outer one which is just like an outer wall for the plant and an inner membrane which has many folds and acts like a furnace. Chemical reactions take place in the folds of the inner membrane and release adenosine triphosphate, the main energy source for the cell. The mitochondria is the only power plant in the cell and produces all the energy used by the cell.

The last organelle is the lysosome which acts like a garbage collector, picking up and eliminating everything used and discarded by the other organelles and nucleus. The lysosome forms from the secreted protein granules produced by the Golgi complex but not released from the cell. They are high-powered enzymes that destroy sick cells, parts of cells, and wastes in the cell. The lysosome travels through the cytoplasm and can eliminate things as does a garbage collector in the city.

Each cell operates independently from other cells, but they all have contact among themselves, just as cities are independent but trade and communicate with each other. Inside the city wall or plasma membrane many factories or organelles function to keep the city-cell running. But unlike a city, a cell is much more highly ordered and, for its size, is so complex that it can carry out all the functions of the body.

As you can see, the paper now organizes new information according to a plan high-school students know—the layout of a city. Using that analogy helped the writer shift information from paragraph to paragraph to make the entire essay clearer. By considering what the readers knew and what they needed to know, the writer was able to re-see the paper and recast it to be more effective in conveying the right message.

When you begin revising your papers after completing a draft, always think first about your audience and purpose. Do you still think your readers will care about what you've written and how you've written it? Look at other large elements of the draft—the thesis and what it implies about the paper, support, and arrangement. Do you need to refocus or reorder? Here are some other questions you might consider to help you re-see the whole paper.

Have I identified my audience carefully enough to let the reader guide what I include in the paper?

Will my reader care about this message?

Have I found a reader whose purpose in reading matches my purpose in writing?

Have I made everything clear? Do I give enough information so that the reader can see my point?

Do I relate the various elements to my main idea and to one another?

Can the reader always see where I am going in this piece of writing?

Does the thesis state a clear assertion—make a clear promise?

What form is most natural to use for this thesis? Have I followed through?

Does the introduction attract the reader immediately? Does it start "close" enough to the exact focus of the paper?

Does the conclusion remind the reader of what was said and give a sense of closure and completion at the end of the essay?

Let these questions—or others that help you step back and look at your paper as a whole—guide your revisions of the paper. Only when you've considered the overall message should you look at smaller elements: the paragraphs, the sentences, and the words.

WRITING Re-Seeing the Whole Paper

1. In your journal, jot down a list of questions you can use to help you re-see your papers. Be sure to consider audience, purpose, thesis, and form.
2. Now revise your list to make the questions pertain to the current paper you are working on. Generate new questions about the specific readers and goals of this paper.
3. Use your list of questions from 2 to re-see your paper.

REVISING PARAGRAPHS

We talked at length about Topic Sentence Paragraphs in Chapter 11. Many writers, however, don't worry about paragraphing while they draft. Instead they deal with paragraphs later as they revise. Let's first consider Function Paragraphs in more detail and then examine how they can help writers revise. Finally, we'll look at all paragraph concepts as keys to revision.

The Function Paragraph

It has been said that if the only tool you had was a hammer, you would tend to treat everything as if it was a nail. The same thing is true in writing an essay. If the only kind of paragraph you had to use was the Topic Sentence Paragraph, you would treat all your thoughts as if they were points to be developed.

Fortunately, this isn't the case.

As useful and necessary as the Topic Sentence Paragraph is, it isn't the only kind of paragraph in existence, even though it is the most commonly known. To get any developed message across, of course, Topic Sentence Paragraphs are necessary. But there are other kinds of paragraphs—and you see lots of them in magazine articles and books—that are not composed of a topic sentence plus development. They are Function Paragraphs, paragraphs that do things other than give the reader information about a topic sentence.

Function Paragraphs are amusing, quirky, fascinating—and useful. Knowing about Function Paragraphs, you aren't confused when you look at writing in books and magazines and find paragraphs that don't always begin with a new thought and give a developed message. More importantly, however, when you know about Function Paragraphs you are aware of the many more choices available to you when you write and revise. You can discover new ways of controlling your writing and directing your reader, and you will find new possibilities for putting energy and variety into your writing.

Function Paragraphs help you get attention, show what things you consider important to notice, and, in general, work like the time signatures and notations on a piece of music. They assist you in orchestrating the essay and in telling the reader how to read it. Following are some examples of what Function Paragraphs can do.

Function Paragraphs Get the Reader's Attention. Often when people are talking and want to get someone's attention, they may shout or say emphatically, "Listen to me!" They may use their hands in a dramatic gesture to keep the listener's eyes right on them. When you are writing, however, you can do none of these things, so you have to depend on other means to get the reader's attention. Function Paragraphs will do this for you. See how Isabella Bird uses a one-sentence Function Paragraph to set up the reader to anticipate what is coming next.

I shall not soon forget my first night here.

Somewhat dazed by the rarefied air, entranced by the glorious beauty, slightly puzzled by the motley company, whose faces loomed not always quite distinctly through the cloud of smoke produced by eleven pipes, I went to my solitary cabin at nine, attended by Evans. It was very dark, and it seemed a long way off. Something howled— Evans said it was a wolf—and owls apparently innumerable hooted incessantly. The pole-star, exactly opposite my cabin door, burned like a lamp. The frost was sharp. Evans opened the door, lighted a candle, and left me, and I was soon in my hay bed. I was frightened—that is, afraid of being frightened, it was so eerie—but sleep soon got the better of my fears. I was awoke by a heavy breathing, a noise something like sawing under the floor, and a pushing and upheaving, all very loud. My candle was all burned, and, in truth, I dared not stir. The noise went on for an hour fully, when, just as I thought the floor had been made sufficiently thin for all purposes of ingress, the sounds abruptly ceased, and I fell asleep again. My hair was not, as it ought to have been, white in the morning!

That first sentence is so catchy that we tend not to even notice that it is a paragraph all by itself. You read "I shall not soon forget my first night here" and dash on to find out about that night and what was so unforgettable about it. Of course, the author could have put that sentence with the next paragraph and thus have made one unit instead of two, but then the reader would have been denied the dramatic introduction to the experience.

Here's another example of a Function Paragraph used to grab attention.

After the tour I stopped at the refreshment stand at the base of Masada and found myself sitting across from a rather elegant-looking white-haired woman. "Excuse me," she asked, "would you happen to know where I can find some mud?"

Mud?

The one-word response to the woman's request dramatizes the speaker's incredulity and astonishment. We get it with a punch, which would certainly have been lacking if the author had replaced that single word with a sentence or two that explained how he felt. Furthermore, the single word contributes to the pace, the lean, swift movement of the passage, as contrasted with the loss of impact that would have resulted if there had been several lines of explanation. It's like the difference between someone who tells a joke and then lets it go, and someone who talks on for the next fifteen minutes to explain the punchline.

Function Paragraphs Make Transitions. In the following piece, the writer begins by discussing the role of fantasy in life. Then she prepares to discuss a new topic—how the dream of "togetherness" can turn out to be a nightmare when the couple is confined to each other's company only. To connect the parts of the essay, she had to write a paragraph that would work like a bridge to take the reader from one part of the writing to the next. Here is that paragraph.

So far I have talked about how much we need fantasies in order to live a life full of color, zest, and imagination. Without them, our days might be gray, humdrum, and lacking in adventure. I've mentioned other people's fantasies at some length. Now I'll tell you one of mine. One of my most persistent early fantasies was to travel cross-country in a small van with "the man of my dreams." We—I and this incredible, blank-faced lover—would skinny dip in silent, forested lakes, grab the fish that raced to jump into our bare hands, feast on them by the fire, and crawl into our little mobile love nest. Finally, stuffed with all the wonders that spot could dispense, we would take off for the next nirvana, kissing at all the stop signs. But that's not the way it really turned out.

By the time I met the man and we bought the van, life was down to a more realistic size. Meaning: It's hard to stand being with someone you love, day in and day out. Even couples who live together in a small apartment find ways to, sweetly, disengage. If, for some reason, there is no job or class to go to, at least there are errands to do, friends to visit, parks to walk in. But when all exit routes are blocked, and your mate complains about the quality of the map again, or picks his teeth with the bottom of a match again, or chooses to count the dead flies on the windshield rather than talk to you again, you might well find yourself wondering what better things the world might have to offer. (That's on a good day—on a bad day, you may despair that this is the best you'll ever get.) Truly, for van vagabonds, the honeymoon is over. If you think you're a perfect pair; if you think his refusal to cap the toothpaste is "cute"; if you think you've been through all that years ago and come out the other side, fine. But bring the salt. You'll need it to rub into each other's wounds.

Can you see in the first paragraph how the writer wraps up the earlier section of the essay and introduces the next? A transition paragraph like this is a courtesy to the reader. You can see, however, that the Function Paragraph that works like a transition does not have a topic sentence or main idea that is developed. The Function Paragraph serving as a bridge is *only* a bridge. It simply gets the reader from here to there; it does not present developed information. It isn't supposed to. Its function is merely to be like a road sign that says, "Turn here and now proceed in this direction."

Function Paragraphs Set Off Conversation. At times writers will use conversational dialogue to get the reader's attention and make a point by showing instead of telling. When such dialogue is used, each conversational response is put in a new paragraph. You may see multiple paragraph indentations simply because an oral conversation between two people is being recorded visually.

Here is a student essay that uses conversational dialogue:

"You know, this class is awful. I never learn anything from it, but it seems to go on for hours."

"I know what you mean. The lectures are so disorganized. The professor doesn't ever act as though any time has been spent in preparing for class."

"Well, I won't be here for the next class. I have better ways to spend my time."

This conversation is often heard after many college classes. These attitudes, however, could be reversed by a concerned professor. By inspiring confidence in the students and by organizing a knowledgeable presentation, a professor could make any class interesting as well as instructive.

All that you, as a writer, need to know about this use of the Function Paragraph is that conversational dialogues are indented so that the reader will know when one person finishes talking and the other begins. The Function Paragraph helps a reader know how to read the essay.

Function Paragraphs Break Up Long Paragraphs. Sometimes authors make new paragraphs simply because they think the reader's eyes will get tired if a paragraph is too long. Readers do need a break periodically—a psychological break if nothing else—and a paragraph indention can be just the break they need when the writing is long. When you look at the two paragraphs in the example below, you can sense that the writer divided them to avoid having one long paragraph. Of course we can't be sure that this is so, but there doesn't seem to be any other recognizable reason for the division of the two paragraphs except to break the length.

It's amazing how many people are convinced they "never dream." What they mean, actually, is that they don't remember their dreams. As numerous studies in "sleep laboratories" have shown, physiological changes associated with the REM (rapid eye movement) level of sleep take place even in subjects who swear they were "not dreaming." These studies reveal that dreaming occurs each and every night: We are witness to a private, often technicolor drama that plays for our benefit alone. Most of us do not take full advantage of this benefit, however. We relegate our night visions to the category of "only a dream," and then go about our daily life pretty much the same as we did the day before. But if we wanted to, we could actually use our dreams to better our waking reality.

How might this be? One thing is that our dreams provide coded messages on many very personal subjects—how we feel toward ourselves, our family and friends, our co-workers, and so on. Just knowing about our "real" feelings can give us an edge on dealing more effectively, less defensively, with other people. In addition, because dreams operate with a different kind of logic from the $2 + 2 = 4$ variety, they do not have to adhere to "what's possible." Therefore they may present solutions to "impossible" problems precisely because they are irrational—and creative. Many works of art, inventions, and scientific discoveries first came to their creators in a dream. Robert Louis Stevenson found Dr. Jekyll there; Isaac Singer discovered a vital component of the sewing machine there. Carl Jung, the Swiss psychoanalyst, so believed in the usefulness of dreams that he called them "the mystery that heals."

Function Paragraphs Emphasize, Develop, and Add Detail. In this use of the Function Paragraph, the writer will begin a new paragraph to emphasize or develop a point made in a preceding paragraph. Without the preceding paragraph, the reader wouldn't have a context for this Function Paragraph. The Function Paragraph with the details and examples must rely on the preceding Topic Sentence Paragraph for meaning.

Here is an example from Henry Boettinger.

The key to getting and holding attention lies in having something new happen continually. This calls for a sense of movement forward or backward, development, or the feeling of "something going on." Development suggests that what we are seeing now grew out of something before, and is going to turn into something else. Consider the difference between the attention a child gives to a basket of eggs on the kitchen table and his (her) concentration on an egg that is being cracked from the inside by a chick straining to emerge.

Another illustration, probably old when the pyramids were under construction, is the attention given to workers and their machinery on a large building project by sidewalk superintendents. The same project on a Sunday morning will hold no interest from passing crowds, because "there is nothing going on." Yet the structure's design is clear, and all the machinery stands ready, but silent. Clearly, the sense of development is dead, and with it dies attention. The fundamental aspect of development derives from its continuity with the past and the future. This unfolding of your presentation must parallel nature. Even the most spectacular and dramatic event in the story must be related to what has gone before. . . . Clear problem-statement is important because it allows a development related constantly to both aspects of any problem: that which exists and that which is desired.

Function Paragraphs Open and Close Essays.   The introductory and concluding paragraphs of essays also serve specific functions that we can examine in more detail.

Essay Introductions.   When used as an essay introduction, the opening paragraphs of your paper have got to do three things.

- *Get Your Readers' Attention.* This requirement of the introduction is easy enough to understand: you have to begin with an opening that will make readers listen to you. You must hook the reader immediately, probably in the first two sentences or 20 seconds.
- *State the Promise—the Thesis—You Are Making to the Reader.* After you have gotten your readers' attention, you must let them know what your purpose is, and what you are going to write about; you must point them in the direction in which you want them to begin thinking. The introduction must contain, either explicitly or implicitly, the thesis of the writing, and the promise you are making.
- *Ease the Readers into Your Subject.* This is a more subtle function of your introduction, but it allows you to use the opening of the paper for double duty. You could spend the entire introduction talking about your subject in general, but it is more efficient to go directly to your angle on the subject.

The following two examples will show you the difference between being general and being direct. Both deal with the same message—telling the reader that canning one's own pickles gives two advantages: the fun of canning and the pleasure of having good healthy food. Here is the first version, which starts out—as you can see—far, far too broadly.

> Health foods. Do those words make you think of seaweed cookies and sawdust-tasting soup? More and more people are beginning to learn that health foods can look and even taste just like ordinary food, yet they can really make a difference in length and quality of life. Health foods may be nothing more than ordinary foods grown or prepared in an organic and pure way, such as apples grown with no insecticide or peaches canned without additives. Realizing this, many people are more receptive to health foods and are willing to give them a try. A lot of people are beginning to do home canning. Pickles are a favorite thing to put up.

This introduction finally does get to talking about canning pickles, but readers have to wade through too much information about health food and the advantages of home canning in general. The writer is taking far too long to get to the subject and is not directing the readers' attention enough—or soon enough—to the specific aspect of the essay. They have to jump awkwardly from people's being willing to try health foods to home canning. Readers feel stretched and sense too big a gap there.

Let's look at the second version.

> Home canning used to be a drag. Women would slave over a hot stove, heaving large pots of boiling water and taking all day to put up perhaps just one batch of beans. Home canning now is a hobby for men and women alike, and a lot of the pleasure comes from the ease of modern canning processes and the satisfaction of knowing that you are putting up clean, healthy food with no additives or preservatives. The new inexpensive equipment available for canners and the new awareness of the dangers of many commercially canned products makes even a job like making pickles a real pleasure. . . .

In the second version, the writer gets immediately into the subject of home canning. The paragraph does a good job of moving right into the perspective of the essay. It gives the reader a clear focus to concentrate on; it lets the reader know right away why the essay was written and what he or she ought to be thinking about. The more a writer can do this for a reader, the better the writing will be received.

WRITING *Essay Introductions*

1. Read the following introductions to essays, some by professional writers, some by students. Notice how they (a) get the readers' attention, (b) tell the readers what the thesis of the writing is going to be,

either directly or indirectly, and (c) move quickly into the exact focus on the subject the writer wants the reader to think about. Be able to discuss the specifics of these introductions with your class.

A. We live in a country with the highest per capita income ever known to mankind; yet of every 100 of our citizens who reach the age of 65, 95 are flat broke! Of every 100 who reach their "golden years," only 2 are financially independent, 23 must continue to work, and 75 are dependent on friends, relatives, or charity.

  They lost the money game. The money game is not like any other game. You cannot choose whether you'll play. You cannot choose to sit out a hand or move to another game. For this game—the money game—is the only game in town.

  Since you have no choice but to play, then the only intelligent thing to do is to learn the rules and play to win! Losing means spending 20 to 30 years of your life in angry frustration in a state of financial insecurity.—*Venita Van Caspel,* The New Money Dynamics.

B. "What is my goal in life?" "What am I striving for?" "What is my purpose?" These are questions which every individual asks himself at one time or another, sometimes calmly and meditatively, sometimes in agonizing uncertainty or despair. They are old, old questions which have been asked and answered in every century of history. Yet they are also questions which every individual must ask and answer for himself, in his own way. They are questions which I, as a counselor, hear expressed in many differing ways as men and women in personal distress try to learn, or understand, or choose, the directions which their lives are taking.

  In one sense there is nothing new which can be said about these questions. Indeed the opening phrase in the title I have chosen for this paper is taken from the writings of a man who wrestled with these questions more than a century ago. Simply to express another personal opinion about this whole issue of goals and purposes would seem presumptuous. But as I have worked for many years with troubled and maladjusted individuals I believe that I can discern a pattern, a trend, a commonality, an orderliness, in the tentative answers to these questions which they have found for themselves. And so I would like to share with you my perception of what human beings appear to be striving for, when they are free to choose.—*Carl Rogers,* On Becoming a Person

C. Teaching ten-year-olds how to play tennis is like teaching them how to play the piano. The only reason they are out on the court is because "Mommy" signed them up. And since learning tennis takes many hours of repetition and concentration, this causes a problem. The ten-year-old has an attention span only long enough to allow his or her little mind to come up with something mischievous. After the first ten minutes are up, well, Billy and Jim start to fight, Terry puts gum in Nancy's hair, Nancy starts to push him, and the tennis teacher is ready to call it a day.

The trick to solving this problem is keeping the kids from thinking they are being taught. They could be at home watching television or riding bicycles which would be fun. So, the teacher must make learning to play tennis look like fun. That is the key to effective teaching.—*Rick Jones*

2. Read these opening paragraphs from student essays and notice how you respond as a reader. Are you interested? How can you tell what the writer is going to write to you about? What angle does the writer give you on the subject? Write your answers in your journal.

A. What will happen to you the first few days of college life? Once you have settled into your class and study routine, what will you do with spare time for social pleasures? Where will you search for new friends?

There is no need to look far. Even though most friends made at home and in high school are left behind, there will still be a lot of people around who are looking for friends just like you.

The first place you probably make a new friend will be. . . .

B. Chocolate-covered cherries have always been my favorite confectionery. They are always a special treat around our house especially around Christmas. This type of candy is, in my opinion, the best candy ever made. Plus it has a special kind of flavor made of ingredients that I do not particularly care for.

Christmastime around our house is something special . . .

C. "Do you want to go to the show tonight?"
"I don't know."
"Aw, come on. I don't have anybody to go with."
"Well, all right, guess I will."

Oops, has another *yes* slipped out again when a *no* was intended? Don't worry. It's a common problem many people share. *No* seems to be a word that sticks to the tongue while *yes* blurts right on out and past it. How does a person learn to say, "No"?

D. After waiting for what seemed like an eternity for my twenty dollar steak, I noticed a wisp of smoke float over my shoulder. I glanced behind me to see if the kitchen was on fire and caught a blast of poisonous smoke in my face. The effects of this attack were immediate; my eyes became red and watery and my once-hungry stomach suddenly felt sick and queasy.

I am sure all of you nonsmokers can empathize with my feelings that night as I was attacked by a foe who was wielding that omnipotent weapon, the cigarette. The physical and mental strain that nonsmokers get from smokers is intolerable. My anticipated pleasant meal that evening was ruined by an inconsiderate smoker. How can we nonsmokers stop this assault on ourselves?

E. Wouldn't it be super if you could just swallow a pill about the size of a vitamin and in a few minutes know everything there is to know about a certain subject? Jump into a machine and have it pop you into the middle of an atom to watch the electrons whirl about you? How about slipping back into the 1800s and seeing Abraham Lincoln and the way he lived his life? Just imagine how much time we wouldn't have to spend in school and how much more interesting learning would be.

Well, getting back to reality, I think learning is a difficult thing to get a hold of. It seems that a subject has to be interesting to enable it to sink into our head and stay there for a while . . .

3. Choose two of the introductions from 2 that need rewriting, and rewrite them.

Essay Conclusions. The ending of your paper ought to remind the reader of what you have said as it draws the paper to a close.

Since the whole purpose of your essay is to get a point across to your readers—some information that you wanted them to have, some opinions or experience of yours that you wanted to share—reminding them of what you have said and how it is significant (or what it means) is a smart thing to do at the end of the writing. You don't want to insult readers by simply saying what you have already said, using the same words. You *do* want to bring back into the readers' attention the gist of what you have taken the whole paper to tell, but you need only a few sentences because you have already explained it fully for the reader in the body of the essay.

As you re-present the main point of your paper, be sure your readers know that you are finished. Your readers are willing to move with you through the essay while you prove your point or develop your message, but at the end they want to be let down back to earth easily and told, "This is the end." Concluding your paper merely carries out the principle of closure which is central to human beings: you have opened a discussion and brought the readers into this discussion with you, so let your conclusion bring a gentle and clear ending to the exchange you began when you sat down to write.

Function Paragraphs in the Revision Process

As you can imagine, using function paragraphs in all these ways is almost impossible while a writer is drafting. Most writers find that they want to concentrate on getting the ideas down on paper before they worry about the best ways to move readers from one idea to the next. Often, you will not know that you need to use a Function Paragraph for added detail or emphasis until you can read the complete draft. Similarly, you'll recall that in Chapter 8 where we considered drafting, we noted that you may skip the introductory and concluding sentences on early drafts, simply because you need to know more about the direction of the whole piece before you set up and wrap up your papers. Thus, even the most obvious kind of Function Paragraph often appears only in a revised draft.

If you find that you can include Function Paragraphs in a draft of your paper, then you're one step ahead. Most writers, though, even the most experienced ones, still find that Function Paragraphs emerge through revising for emphasis and flow.

Use these questions to help you revise early drafts to include Function Paragraphs.

Where might you use a Function Paragraph to get the reader's attention? Why do you need to get the reader's attention at that point in your paper? What might that Function Paragraph look like?

Where might you use a Function Paragraph as a transition between major chunks or segments of your paper?

Where might you use a Function Paragraph to signal a major change in direction in your paper?

Where might you use dialogue and thus Function Paragraphs?

Where might you divide a long paragraph into two, making the second a Function Paragraph for emphasis or added detail?

How can you reconsider your introduction and conclusion for more effective Function Paragraphs?

Does your introductory paragraph get the reader's attention? Does it lead smoothly to your main point or thesis? Does it set clear expectations for the writing that follows?

Does your concluding paragraph round out your paper? Does it remind your reader of your main point?

Revising Topic Sentence Paragraphs

As we noted earlier, most writers worry very little about paragraphing as they draft, but good writers worry much more about paragraphing as they revise. After you look at the largest elements of your paper to revise it most effectively, consider each paragraph. Be sure to check for the vital elements—a focused topic sentence, detailed development, unity, and coherence in each Topic Sentence Paragraph, and a clear purpose for each Function Paragraph.

Let's look at one of the paragraphs from the first draft of the essay about cells to see what the writer would have discovered had it been revised for paragraph elements.

The cell does not just conform to its surroundings nor does it remain rigid. The plasma membrane regulates the shape of the cell by completely surrounding the cytoplasm. The plasma membrane contains mostly proteins and lipids, but it contains some water, carbohydrates and other inorganic substances. The lipids form a bilayer with a space in between. The proteins reside mainly in the layer, but can protrude out of the lipid layer. This model for the plasma membrane is called the fluid mosaic model. The plasma membrane has four major functions in the cell. Obviously the plasma membrane must protect the cell from foreign substances. The plasma membrane makes contact with the other cells or substances and forms a communication link with them. The plasma membrane receives chemicals, hormones, nutrients and antibodies from outside sources. Finally the plasma membrane regulates what enters and exits the cell. This regulation is called selective permeability. The plasma membrane acts like a net. It has holes allowing small particles through while restricting the admission of others. Because the small particles can pass through without any energy, they use passive transport. If the particle is large or the particle must go the opposite way of the concentration gradient, it must use active transport. In active transport energy must be used. The mitochondria, an organelle, provides the energy needed for active transport. Both active and passive transport take place in the cell regularly. The plasma membrane provides both protection and a place of contact for the cell.

Is this a Topic Sentence Paragraph or a Function Paragraph? Clearly, the writer means it to be the former, but is there one sentence that acts as an explicit topic sentence to hold the details of the paragraph together? One of the first revisions the writer should consider is focusing the second sentence more carefully to act as the topic sentence.

The writer should also look at detail. Does all the detail in the paragraph belong there? Toward the end of the paragraph the writer gets caught up in distinguishing active and passive transport. These concepts are linked to the plasma membrane, but in this paragraph they seem extraneous. The writer might want to cut those sentences before trying to formulate a new topic sentence for the paragraph.

Does the writer need additional detail that hasn't been included? This paragraph is brimming with detail, perhaps even overwhelming the designated audience. The writer might consider breaking the paragraph into two parts—one on structure and one on function—to make the reading easier for the readers.

Finally, does the writer repeat key words adequately for the readers? Are additional transitional words and phrases needed to show sentence connections and changes in direction? One problem with the paragraph is that short sentences sometimes cut apart ideas. The writer could easily revise for coherence now but might wait until after combining and revising sentences, as discussed in Chapter 13, to see how many gaps in coherence are left.

These, then, are the concerns of the writer revising paragraphs. Again, use our questions or ones you find effective in helping you spot appropriate revisions in your paragraphs.

Do I have a focused topic sentence for each Topic Sentence Paragraph (or is one implied so clearly that a reader cannot miss my point)?

Does each Function Paragraph serve a purpose that will be clear to the reader?

Do my paragraphs accommodate my readers? Should I break paragraphs apart for easier reading or emphasis? Combine paragraphs for flow?

Does each paragraph contribute to the overall logic of the paper?

Does each paragraph contain necessary information? Have I cut out all irrelevant details?

Have I chosen the best possible support? Could I replace a weak example with a stronger one? Could I find a more telling detail or fact?

Have I included adequate transitions and reminder signs to help readers move through my paragraphs easily?

Remember, paragraphs help your readers identify your main points and show the connections between those points. They cluster a general idea and the detailed support for that idea. They move the reader at the writer's pace through the paper. Be sure to use paragraph revisions to make your message clear—and as effective and dynamic as possible—for your reader.

WRITING *Revising Your Paragraphs*

1. Personalize a list of questions you can use to guide revision of your paragraphs. Concentrate first on questions that help you revise the areas you know you have trouble with. Then generate questions about focus, development, unity, and coherence for Topic Sentence Paragraphs, and about purpose and effectiveness for Function Paragraphs if you haven't already done so.
2. Now turn to your most recent paper. Use your set of questions to revise your paragraphs thoroughly.

CHAPTER 13

Revising: Re-Seeing Sentences and Words

After looking at the larger elements of a paper, you generally turn to the smaller elements. When writers begin working on sentences and words, they commonly feel that they can revise almost endlessly. Many students feel so overwhelmed by the possibilities that they cut short their revising at this level. But if you keep in mind a reader on the other end of your paper, you can more easily see the most efficient way to use your revision time in reworking sentences and word choice.

By this point in your revising, you should have a clear idea of your purpose, audience, and the main point of the paper. (If these elements are *not* clear, then you need to step back and review the entire paper again.) With your purpose, audience, and point in mind, read your paper aloud to hear the impression it makes, and tackle the paragraph that seems to be the weakest link. Rework sentences that are not crisp and clear; revise words that don't contribute to the specific mood and tone of your paper. By the time you're through the weakest paragraph, you'll probably see many ways to improve sentences and words in other paragraphs as well.

Then read the paper aloud to someone else and check your listener's reactions. Did you miss any glaring problems, any sentences that go awry or go on too long? Did you miss any words that jarred your listener? Did you have vague or wordy phrases that put your listener to sleep? Get some feedback to help you polish in this final phase of reworking the smaller elements that are so essential in making—or breaking—your point.

REVISING SENTENCES

Even when you have an intriguing message, how can you best keep readers attentive to your writing?

- ◾ You can rebuild some sentences: combining choppy sentences and adding details in the right places.
- ◾ You can deliberately vary sentences.
- ◾ You can emphasize important information through coordination, subordination, parallelism, repetition, and rhythm.

Rebuild Sentences

The following are different ways to rebuild sentences.

Combine Choppy Sentences.   You don't keep your reader's attention by sounding monotonous. Here is a passage from a third-grade book that shows how sentences that are too short and choppy can put a reader to sleep.

> Most of the ways to turn salt water into fresh water cost a lot of money. The Symi factory on an island in Greece uses a way that costs little.
>
> Right in the middle of the town are some long ponds. They are only a few inches deep. The men of Symi dug out earth to make the ponds.
>
> Over each pond is a low tent. It is made of plastic that you can see through.
>
> At night, sea water is pumped into the ponds. The next day, the hot sun shines through the tents. The sun's heat turns the water into vapor that rises from the ponds. The salt is left behind.

Of course, the short paragraphs and the simple vocabulary also contribute to the too-simple effect. But it is the repetition of sentence after sentence, each in the same pattern, each containing only a single unit of information, that makes that passage sound so childlike, immature, and undeveloped.

Now look at this passage from a college-level government book.

> John F. Kennedy's assassination on November 21, 1963, probably evoked—in the period that followed his death—greater feeling on the part of more people than the death of any other American. His assassination was as close to formal tragedy as is conceivable in a democracy. Kennedy had all the attributes of a hero: power, prestige, presence, the heroism of the warrior, affability, social standing, youth, physical attraction, religious belief, and wealth. He embodied

all of these qualities with a special grace, and his death seemed associated with the death of youth in America.—*Theodore Gross*

By comparing this passage with the earlier one, you can see immediately the effect of short, simple sentences and the effect of longer, more varied sentences. The short little sentences are perfect for the third graders in elementary school, but unless they are your audience, sentences that sound as though they were written for eight-year-olds may insult your readers. The more you combine short, simple sentences, the more sophisticated your writing seems to the reader—and the more information units the reader gets per sentence—which facilitates communication by making it seem effortless.

Add Details. To get more into a sentence—so that your reader can get more out of the sentence—you need to provide more than just a flat statement. When you add detail to a sentence, you make it come alive for the reader. For example:

The girl carried her lunchbox.

This sentence does tell the reader something, to be sure. But how much more information is provided when descriptive detail is added to the sentence?

The crying girl carried her broken lunchbox with a touching dignity.

Already, we know a great deal more from the added details. They set up questions that can provoke the reader: Why is the girl crying? How did her lunchbox get broken? Why does she react with dignity? When you give enough descriptive information, the reader wants to keep reading.

Put Detail in the Right Place. Detail can be placed in three different positions in a sentence: before the subject, between the subject and verb, and after the verb. For example:

before the subject	After I turned out the lights,
between the subject and verb	the child, who was scared of nightmares,
after the verb	tossed and turned with open eyes

This is a guideline, however, not a rule. It's generally not a good idea to put descriptors in all these places. You want to give the reader enough information to get excited about your sentence; you don't want to give so much information that the reader feels swamped and confused.

After I had completed my banking transactions, which I typically do at the branch nearest my home, although, from time to time, I utilize the branch nearest my office, which actually, is in the same building, an architectural concept that, as an office worker, I find admirable but, as an appreciator of beauty, I find often quite deplorable, I walked home.

This sentence is technically correct, but the writer has jammed in far too much irrelevant detail.

WRITING *Rebuilding Sentences*

1. Rewrite the following paragraphs by combining the choppy sentences.

    I was fortunate enough to be able to travel to Europe during my senior year in high school. We went during our spring break, March 17–26. The travelers consisted of eighteen students and two teachers. We traveled in a group known as the American Leadership Study Group.

    There was question of whether or not I would be able to go. During the Christmas holidays we had a family reunion. My parents asked me if I wanted to go on the European trip. I said no immediately because I thought it was out of the question. The trip was too expensive. I began thinking about the trip more and more, and I finally decided I wanted to go. I had done quite a bit of baby-sitting and saved the money.

    We proceeded to find out more information about the trip. My mother and I thought the only obstacle would be getting the passport in time. However, my teacher told me there was a waiting list for the trip. He told me he was an area representative for ALSG and that a friend of his owed him a favor. That information lifted our spirits. I would probably be first on the waiting list. My mother and I went to the post office to apply for a passport. We learned that we could receive a passport very quickly if we paid an extra fee. We paid the fee and received the passport in a week.

2. The sentences below are unrevealing, flat statements. Add detail to put life into these sentences.

    A. The man left home.
    B. By noon it was empty.
    C. Hereafter, I will not go.
    D. The bell rang.
    E. The woman held the door.
    F. The children looked out.

3. Choose the best locations for adding descriptive words to the following sentences. Consider what words to add as well as where to add them.

   A. The game was over.

   B. The night ended.

   C. Boys came over.

   D. The check bounced.

   E. The return was not audited.

   F. The candles sparkled.

   G. We saw stars.

Vary Sentences

Here are a few of the different ways that sentences can be varied.

Vary Basic Patterns. Linguists tell us that basic English sentence patterns are few and simple, like these.

Cows   eat.

Cows   eat   grass.

Grass   is   green.

Even though these are the basic sentence patterns of the English language, we rarely use such simple patterns in regular conversation or writing. Our sentences are longer and carry more information. We vary the basic patterns and add information to sentences through a process called expansion, adding single words or groups of words here and there.
This is an example of such an expansion:

John has a job.

Finally, John has a job.

After three months of hunting, John has a job.

John has a job after three months of hunting.

Although he spent three months looking, John finally has a job.

When you are revising sentences, check to see if you use the simple patterns over and over again. If you do, you can probably count on your readers getting bored. Give them some variety. For now, you can vary your sentences by modeling variations after some of the ones that follow. Take a simple, basic sentence like

Green pepper is good in spaghetti sauce.

Now look at the variations you can make of this basic pattern.

> To make good spaghetti sauce, you should add green pepper.
>
> With green pepper added, spaghetti sauce is much better.
>
> By adding green pepper, you can make good spaghetti sauce.
>
> Spaghetti is better with green pepper in the sauce.
>
> That green pepper which has been added makes this spaghetti sauce better.
>
> The spaghetti sauce, with green pepper added, is better.
>
> The spaghetti sauce, which has had green pepper added to it, is better.

Just for practice, see how many variations you can make of this sentence.

> A grocery list aids shopping.

Vary Sentence Openers.   Sometimes a sentence opener that works just fine on its own loses its power when it is repeated again and again. For example, look at this paragraph from the paper on the cell from Chapter 12.

> The city must have a basic layout and the cytoplasm fulfills this function in the cell. The cytoplasm contains the organelles. Most of the chemical reactions in the cell take place in the cytoplasm. The cytoplasm also receives substances from outside of the cell and converts them into viable energy sources for the cell. Also functioning as the receiving site, the cytoplasm packages materials and transports them to other parts of the cell. The cytoplasm has many functions including transport, synthesis, packaging and receiving.

In this paragraph, only one sentence begins with an element other than the subject. By varying the sentence openers, you can better sustain your reader's interest. For example:

> The city must have a basic layout and the cytoplasm provides one. Because the cytoplasm contains the organelles, it allows for systematic, predictable chemical reactions within the cell. Specifically, the cytoplasm receives substances from outside the cell and converts them into viable energy sources for the cell. Also functioning as the receiving site, the cytoplasm packages materials and transports them to other parts of the cell. Thus, the cytoplasm has many functions including transport, synthesis, packaging and receiving.

Which paragraph would be more likely to get your attention?

Vary Word Order.   Obviously, you cannot put your words in nonsensical order. "The ball red rolled into busy the street" won't get your message across effectively. But sentences whose words don't all follow the same pattern are more interesting than sentences whose words follow an identical pattern. For example, here is a paragraph in which sentences follow only a single order.

> He raised the window. He looked out the window. He saw his friend. He waved to his friend. He threw down the key. He did not see his friend. He listened for a sound. He heard the key turn in the lock.

By ordering each sentence identically, the writer ends up boring the reader. But what if the word order were varied from sentence to sentence? It might come out like this.

> He raised the window and looked out. He saw, and waved to, his friend, and threw down the key. No longer seeing his friend, he listened for a sound. In the lock, the key turned.

Varying the order of the words and adding a few transitions can turn a monotonous string of sentences into a connected, flowing paragraph.

WRITING *Revising Sentence Variety*

1. Rewrite this paragraph, consciously varying the basic sentence patterns you find there. See how many different kinds of sentences you can include.

> It was the last track meet of the season. The state championship. I was going to long jump and run the mile relay. Now the long jump is the first event at any track meet, so I got there early. The long jump started at 10:00 and went on until 12:30. Then the mile relay was at 5:00. I got to the field at about 8:30. I ran around the track four times to loosen up and stretch out. All this took about an hour. By 9:30 the stands were packed, and that's when this terrible nervousness hit me. I realized that over 2,000 people would be watching me as I would run down the runway and take my jump. I got a cold sweat; my entire body was shaking worse than jello in an earthquake. Then everyone started giving orders at once. My two other teammates were telling me what to do and what not to do. The official was telling me to get ready to jump. My coach was yelling at me to get a good jump the first time, and the crowd in the stands was going crazy because we were about to start. As I stepped out onto the runway, my entire mind and body went blank. I couldn't see anything or anybody except the long jump pit 104' 6" down the runway. My head was pounding, and all I could hear was the blood rushing through my body. I waited a second, said a little prayer and took off. It

felt like I was moving in slow motion. My legs felt like lead weights. My arms didn't want to move the right way, and I thought I'd never get to the end of the runway to the take-off board. Finally, I saw it closing in on me.

2. All the sentences in this paragraph begin with the same words. Re-write the sentences by varying the way the sentences begin.

The afternoon was hot. The boy felt lazy. The flies were buzzing in his ears. The fish were calling. The plow felt heavy in his hands. The sun was hot. The boy made a decision. The boy left the field and went fishing.

3. Every sentence in the paragraph below has the same order: first the subject, then the verb, then the object or prepositional phrase. Vary the order of words in these sentences to add life to the writing.

We left to go home. The others left to go to the game. Everybody agreed to meet at our house. Everybody came to the house after the game. We made pizza. Everybody had fun. We didn't know the whole story, though. A storm was in the wind.

Revise for Emphasis and Style

As you revise sentences to sustain reader interest, you have some stylistic aids at your disposal. For clarifying relationships of elements within a sentence, consider coordination and subordination. And for creating a style that says "This piece of writing is one of a kind," consider parallelism, repetition and rhythm.

Coordination and Subordination. Coordination and *subordination* help you show your reader which elements are more important and which are less important. *Coordinate* comes from the Latin *co-* (equal) and *ordinare* (to arrange in order). *Subordinate* comes from the Latin *su-* (below) and *ordinare.* Thus coordinate is of an "equal order," and subordinate is of a "lower order."

You can associate *coordinate* with co-partner or co-worker, someone you are on an equal basis with, someone in the same position as you. You can associate *subordinate* with subfloor or a substitute player in a ball-game, someone less important than the main players.

Coordination. Coordination links words, groups of words, or sentences of equal type and importance. We use a special set of connecting words to coordinate—*but, or, yet, for, and, nor, so.* Let's consider more closely how coordination links ideas.

Math and English are supposed to be the hardest subjects for freshmen.

Linking the two words math and English makes perfect sense—they have equal value in the sentence. Similarly,

> He spent the evening typing his essay and studying for his chemistry test.

Linking the two phrases, *typing his essay* and *studying for his chemistry test,* cuts out a lot of extra words and suggests that his evening was spent evenly divided between the typing and the studying.

You can also coordinate whole sentences:

> I had planned to spend the afternoon in the library.
> I took a nap instead.
>
> *Coordinated Sentence:* I had planned to spend the afternoon in the library, but I took a nap instead.

Adding the word *but* allows the reader to move more quickly through the information and makes the two sentences one thought. Coordination in your writing helps you do two things:

1. By combining words and groups of words, you avoid the monotonous repetition that steals energy from what you say.

2. By combining whole sentences, you reveal the relationship between the thoughts.

When sentences are joined together by a conjunction that shows that the sentences are equal, the reader knows that one sentence is as important as the other. The next example shows why the writer must determine the precise relationship between ideas. Here are two sentences.

> John doesn't plan to go to college.
> He believes that experience in the working world is more valuable than an academic degree.

Looking at them, we can infer that the second is somehow related to the first, but we have to produce the inference in our own imaginations—the writer gives no clues, merely sets forth two sentences, period. Look what happens, though, when the sentences are linked in a way that shows exactly how the two items relate to each other.

> John doesn't plan to go to college, for he believes that experience in the working world is more valuable than an academic degree.

In the combined form, you know that the second sentence explains the first and that the two ideas are of equal importance.

Subordination. By subordinating one sentence to another when you combine them, you carry your reader's eye to what you think is most important and show the relationship of one part of the sentence to the other.

This connection can only help the reader move easily and effortlessly through the essay.

For example, consider the pair of sentences we just looked at on the preceding page. We noted that when the two sentences are coordinated, the reader infers that John spent about equal time studying and typing. But what happens when we subordinate one sentence to the other?

John spent the evening typing his essay.
He also spent the evening studying for his chemistry test.

Subordinated Revision: Because John spent the evening typing his essay, he couldn't spend as much time studying for his chemistry test.

or

Subordinated Revision: When John spent the evening studying for his chemistry test, he couldn't type his essay until after midnight.

Each revised sentence shows a new relationship between the parts of the sentence. Through subordination, readers see cause-and-effect, time, or other relationships between sentence parts. Words such as *although, because, when, after, if, since, where,* and *as* can all subordinate one idea to another to let readers see exactly what is most important in a sentence as well as the logical relationship between ideas.

Consider again the difference between coordination and subordination. If we rewrite these sentences to subordinate one idea to the other, we imply different things about John.

John doesn't plan to go to college.
He believes that experience in the working world is more valuable than an academic degree.

Subordinated Revision: Because he believes that experience in the working world is more valuable than an academic degree, John doesn't plan to go to college.

Subordinated Revision: When he believes that experience in the working world is more valuable than an academic degree, John doesn't plan to go to college.

Subordinated Revision: If John doesn't plan to go to college, then he must believe that experience in the working world is more valuable than an academic degree.

Although a few other words are changed in the third version, the sentences are exactly the same as the original sentence except for the subordinating word and the clause subordinated. Yet the first sentence implies that John values work over academics, the second that John wavers between valuing work or academics more, and the third that someone thinking about John's decision is trying to understand the reasoning behind it.

When writers help readers see which ideas weigh more in the writing, readers get the message clearly and efficiently. Choose subordinators with care and help your reader see the logical relationships among your ideas.

WRITING *Revising for Emphasis and Style*

Coordination

Rewrite the following groups of sentences using coordination.

A. To save money, Andrew's parents have decided not to travel to Yosemite this summer.
They will spend a few weeks at a local lake instead.

B. Americans constantly criticize their leaders.
They don't make an effort to vote in national elections.

C. Many people consider a college education vital for success in the business world.
Few professionals have reached their positions without at least one degree.

D. Wearing clothes that are in style is important to some people.
Others don't seem at all concerned about their appearance.
They wear jeans and T-shirts everywhere.

E. Everywhere you look you see people jogging.
You see people walking.
You see people climbing stairs instead of riding the elevator.
More and more people are growing conscious of the importance of good health.

F. Julie knew she could easily get tickets to tonight's rock concert.
She knew that if she went she wouldn't study for Friday's big chemistry exam.

Subordination

Rewrite the following groups of sentences using subordination wherever possible.

A. Mary hates housecleaning.
She claims she's basically a neat person.

B. We want to visit the college campus next month.
We want to make sure we have chosen the right courses.

C. John's uncle may offer him a job in his grocery store.
John may have a job this summer.

D. The rain may stop soon.
We may have to cancel the picnic scheduled for tomorrow.

E. Most people seem willing to cut down on their use of electricity, gas, and heating fuels.
They don't want energy conservation to interfere with their established life-styles.

F. We spent the afternoon in the library working on our history project.
We all went out for pizza.

G. Old movies seem to get more popular every year.
They offer plot and drama that modern movies often lack.

Parallelism.   In writing, *parallelism* means that two or more words, phrases or even sentences use the same structure in close repetition. Parallels are used for a specific effect. Parallelism can be swift and punchy, as in this sentence by Malcolm X.

> In those days only three things in the world scared me: jail, a job, and the army.

The effect, likewise, can be formal and elegant, deliberate and thoughtful, as in this passage by Winston Churchill.

> We shall not flag or fail, we shall go on to the end, we shall fight in France, we shall fight on the seas and oceans, we shall fight with growing confidence and growing strength in the air, we shall defend our island, whatever the cost may be, we shall fight on the beaches, we shall fight on the landing grounds, we shall fight in the fields and in the streets, we shall fight in the hills; we shall never surrender.

Since the human mind responds to rhythm and order, the reader automatically responds to the rhythmic repetition of the parallel parts of sentences. Readers get started with the particular structured order you set up in the first part, then move on with you quickly and satisfactorily through the second, and even third, parallel constructions. You have also set up an expectation for the reader, at least by the second parallel item, and by continuing with that particular pattern you are fulfilling the reader's subconscious expectations.

Because the reader *does* expect repetition and order, you need to keep elements you coordinate parallel in structure. The elements joined by *or* in this sentence are not parallel.

> We not only have a Congressional mandate *to manage* our National Parks; we also have an ethical responsibility *to maintain* or *restoring* their natural qualities for future generations to enjoy.

The reader is jolted by "maintain or restoring" when "maintain or restore" is the parallel structure he or she expects. This revision makes the coordinated elements match and smooths the sentence for the reader.

> We not only have a Congressional mandate *to manage* our National Parks; we also have an ethical responsibility *to maintain* or *restore* their natural qualities for future generations to enjoy.

Repetition and Rhythm. As a drumbeat gives energy to music, *repetition* of words and phrases gives energy to your writing by carrying the movement along. Repetition is aesthetically pleasing—readers respond to repetition in writing as listeners respond to rhythm in music.

> So many urbanites have a country fantasy, spun from within windowless offices. They soothe themselves with images of wooded glens, blue ponds, and laughing cows. But they know nothing of the hard work of chopping wood from their own trees, and they know nothing of the hard work of draining their own ponds, and they know nothing of the hard work of feeding, sheltering, and milking those laughing cows.

Here, the writer leads off with two relatively short sentences, then builds a longer one with a series of three clauses, each introduced by *they know nothing of the hard work of.* This sentence could have been condensed like this.

> They know nothing of the hard work of chopping wood, draining ponds, and feeding, sheltering, and milking cows.

Certainly that would be correct enough, in terms of combining basic elements and compressing them into the most direct, least wordy message. Yet that would lose the ease of motion, the tone of speaking from experience, the picture painting in the original version. The rhythmic version sounds as if the writer feels passionate about the subject and has her own story to tell; the condensed version sounds as if the writer is a more distant, formal expert who is explaining something. The first is casual, approachable; the second is rather formidable. In both, it is the rhythm and the use of repetition (or absence of it) that produces the effect on the reader.

Here's a good example from a student paper of what can happen when an "ordinary" person uses parallelism and repetition.

> A hero is someone whom we all admire and respect. Either he has performed some spectacular task or he has set an example that is worthy enough for others to follow. Such a man needs not to have done something of earth-shattering importance, though he may be more easily recognized as a hero for doing so. He may be a man who

has walked on the moon, or he may be a father who is gentle but firm. He may have climbed Mount Everest, or he may be a patient school teacher. He may have saved the lives of his fellow soldiers in combat, or he may have cared for a child's scraped knee. No one says a hero has to have done something of world-wide significance.

The point of this passage is to contrast the two concepts of heroism. By using balance (he may be this or he may be that), and repetition of this pattern through three sentences, the writer effectively uses structure to reinforce meaning.

WRITING　*Revising for Emphasis and Style*

Parallelism

Transform each group of sentences below into a sentence that contains parallel elements.

A. My grandmother bakes cookies and cakes for all of our birthdays.
She rides horses.
She gardens.
She models.
My grandmother is a remarkable woman.

B. Studying requires determination.
It frequently means sacrificing fun times.
To study effectively, you must have a serious attitude toward your education.

C. A good teacher is someone who thinks of each student as a person.
He is willing to spend additional hours at school to counsel troubled students.
He doesn't care if class discussions veer toward a relevant topic not scheduled for discussion.

D. Walking whenever possible shows that a person is concerned with good health.
Exercising regularly shows a concern with good health.
Watching the kinds of foods you eat is important if you want to be healthy.

E. I expected to feel independent when I moved away from home to go to college.
I knew I would enjoy making my own rules.
I expected to feel grown-up about paying my own bills.

Repetition and Rhythm

Rewrite these sentences in a paragraph illustrating repetition for emphasis.

A. My grandmother was a woman of remarkable energy.
She canned the fruit and vegetables which grew in her garden in the summer.
In the early spring, she always planted a garden in her back yard.
When autumn came, she made fruit pies—some to eat right away, some to freeze and save for winter.
During the winter, she knitted warm clothes to give to her grandchildren as Christmas presents.
She even helped shovel snow when necessary.

B. It was an unprecedented time in the history of the country.
The President had resigned.
The office of the President had never before yielded so dramatically to public pressure.
The voting public had at no other time exercised its democratic privileges with such results.
Criminal accusations had never before tainted the President himself.
The public had never felt so deceived by the leader they had elected.

REVISING WORDS

When you begin to revise words, it's easy to imagine exchanging this word for that one, that one for another, just about forever. This section will suggest a few principles to help you revise efficiently and effectively at the word level. These suggestions will enable you to revise your writing so that your words will hit the reader squarely with exactness and directness.

Exactness, Specifics, Pictures, and Images

There is no doubt that you are writing for a television generation. This means that your readers are visually oriented; they are accustomed to seeing things instead of reading about them. To hold their attention—perhaps even to catch it enough to begin to get your message across—you are going to have to draw pictures for them, pictures in words. Readers remember specifics, so you should include as many detailed pictures, exact references, and precise images as is appropriate for your audience, purpose, and topic.

Do you recall this vivid opening from the essay in Chapter 8?

"Conley's dead," the *disembodied* voice over the phone told me. I hung up, *stunned*. What did it mean? We flew together often, or at least used to. Just last month we had *dodged* in and out of clouds together, playing *tag* with a *rumbling thunderhead* at 16,000 feet. We knew that we were risking our lives; that's why we were there. We landed after an hour and a half, *whooping* and *shouting* about our daring adventure. As we broke our kites down, the wind began to *scare up dustdevils* alongside the road and fat raindrops started to *splat* off our helmets. Electricity *crackled* in the air, *threatening, exhilarating,* as we hurried to load our gear. Every weekend we clipped our lives to seventy pounds of aluminum and Dacron, trusting our luck and skill. Flying was our *opium,* the thing we lived for. "Air junkies" we called ourselves with a nervous laugh, swearing we would never quit until it killed us. Conley had just quit. And me? I secretly hoped to quit before it killed me as I had done with motorcycles and skiing. But I wondered if I dared cut it so close this time.

This paragraph not only sets the tone for the paper but creates a vivid image in the reader's mind to help the reader and writer share an experience. The writer used specific, precise words and images to paint a picture for the reader.

Even in the business world there is room for colorful, descriptive writing. This excerpt is by George S. Odiorne, from *MBO II: A System of Managerial Leadership for the 1980s.*

Like *styles in clothing and office buildings,* styles in management change. Management by objectives, in addition to being a somewhat scientific system and a humanistic mode of managing, is a style of managing. That *style* is one that is *situational.* That is, we adapt our behavior and *our goals* to suit the environment, the culture, and the milieu in which we are operating. As one behavioral scientist suggests, you sing *hymns in church and bawdy songs at a party* and never mix the two, or you'll be *thrown out of both places.* Therefore, it is important to look ahead and try to assess what kind of managerial style will be prevalent during the coming ten to fifteen years.

The principle is clear: use specific, concrete words, and use them vigorously to give readers detailed, memorable ideas.

WRITING *Revising for Specific Words*

Pick out the words that contribute to the vividness of the passages below.

A. When my son and I arrived at the pigyard, armed with a small bottle of castor oil and a length of clothesline, the pig had emerged from his house and was standing in the middle of his yard, listlessly.

He gave us a slim greeting. I could see that he felt uncomfortable and uncertain. I had brought the clothesline thinking I'd have to tie him (the pig weighed more than a hundred pounds) but we never used it. My son reached down, grabbed both front legs, upset him quickly, and when he opened his mouth to scream I turned the oil into his throat—a pink, corrugated area I had never seen before. I had just time to read the label while the neck of the bottle was in his mouth. It said Puretest. The screams, slightly muffled by oil, were pitched in the hysterically high range of pig-sound, as though torture were being carried out, but they didn't last long: it was all over rather suddenly, and, his legs released, the pig righted himself.

In the upset position the corners of his mouth had been turned down, giving him a frowning expression. Back on his feet again, he regained the set smile that a pig wears even in sickness. He stood his ground, sucking slightly at the residue of oil; a few drops leaked out of his lips while his wicked eyes, shaded by their coy little lashes, turned on me in disgust and hatred. I scratched him gently with oily fingers and he remained quiet, as though trying to recall the satisfaction of being scratched when in health, and seeming to rehearse in his mind the indignity to which he had just been subjected. I noticed, as I stood there, four or five small dark spots on his back near the tail end, reddish brown in color, each about the size of a housefly. I could not make out what they were. They did not look troublesome but at the same time they did not look like mere surface bruises or chafe marks. Rather they seemed blemishes of internal origin. His stiff white bristles almost completely hid them and I had to part the bristles with my fingers to get a good look.—*E. B. White*

B. My first car ever was a two-toned '61 Rambler station wagon, green on bottom, white on top, and bounded by a dented strip of rusty metal. The front seat ran the width of the car; it had a tan criss-cross weave, something like the New York subway seats, and scratchy vinyl to the touch. On the passenger end, the stuffing was constantly threatening to burst and overflow, to dribble down onto the floor, surge up onto the dashboard, and riproar crescendingly through the windshield. Passengers could ride at their own risk.

I loved that car. We went through a major rite of passage together—my learning to drive. I wept when it died.

That was the car that sat so uncomplainingly in the snow drift the winter of '67—the winter it snowed so much that we wore our shades at night to protect the eyes from even the memory of the sun's glare on the icy white streets. The drift was what piled up, over days, around an innocent-looking fencepost meant to keep cows in and cars out. The cows had long since gone indoors to await the eventual rebirth of their pasture, now blanketed and sleeping. Only I, my hands lusting for the wheel (my brain sleeping along with the summer clover), thought it necessary to venture out of my warm, tousled, languorous bed; don my orange thermals, two pairs of socks, and every scarf ever knitted by my mother during her stopping-smoking era; thaw the Rambler's door lock with a lighter; and jubilantly jump on in to go out for a spin.

I spun; I twirled; I plowed right into that fence post disguised as a vanilla cotton-candy cone. It took the nearest farmer's plow to undo the suction and get me back on the road again. Rambler's soul was sweet—she forgave, but she got tired. There were a few more scrapes like that, and before the winter was out, Rambler's rambling days were over. No car since—no fuel-savvy Honda, no hydraulically magic Citroen, no Plymouth convertible of my teenage dreams, no matter how sleek or snazzy or expensive—has ever equalled my one, my only, my first love, that green-and-white Rambler. Rest in peace.

Three Basic Steps in Revising Words

Making your message as clear and crisp as possible comes down to three simple things.

1. Cut out every word you don't need.
2. Replace vague, general words with specific, exact words.
3. Use action verbs.

If you revise your words with these principles in mind, you will have power in your writing.

Cut Out Every Word You Don't Need.   Save your reader time and energy: cut out the flab. Make your writing lean. Nothing will steal your power more than extra, flabby words the reader has to wade through to get your message. See the difference for yourself.

Fat: There are many people alive in the world today who are living strange and unusual lives.
Lean: Many people live strange lives.

Fat: Modern men and women of today are both alike in similar ways; they repeat again and again their messages after they have already said them once.
Lean: Both men and women tend to repeat their messages.

Fat: Because of the fact that I don't have any money and am therefore flat broke, I don't go inside a restaurant.
Lean: Because I don't have any money, I don't go inside a restaurant.

Be sure you cut out all words that don't contribute to your message, including *very, really, actually, absolutely, quite*—intensifiers so overused that they don't intensify any more. Also question every phrase that can be replaced by a single word or a crisper phrase, such as

Wordy Phrase	Replacement
make an attempt to	try
reach a decision	decide
it is the belief of	believes
is in the process of being	is being
the question as to whether	whether
in a hasty manner	hastily
owing to the fact that	since/because
in spite of the fact that	though/although/despite
the fact that I had arrived	my arrival
the fact that he had not succeeded	his failure
of great importance	important
in connection with	with
fellow colleague	colleague
surrounding environment	environment
impending promotion that will eventually occur	impending promotion
carelessly discarded litter	litter
necessary prerequisite	prerequisite
long in size	long
blue in color	blue
of an indefinite nature	indefinite
by means of	by
end result	result
because of the fact that	because
final climax	climax
connect together	connect
in the event of	if
along the lines of	like, as
with the result that	so that
in order to	to
for the purpose of	to
on the basis of	because, since
in connection with	about

Replace Vague Words with Specific, Concrete Words. Look at the difference in these sentences.

Vague: The landscape is varied.
Specific: The landscape changes from high, old mountains in the east to flat, horse-raising country in the middle to river-bottom delta land in the west.

Vague: The people living in the housing project are diverse.
Specific: The people living in the housing project come from ten different countries on four different continents.

Vague: The pizza was great.
Specific: The pizza started with a crust made of fresh-baked dough on which was piled a layer of cheddar cheese, ground beef, mushrooms, anchovies, sliced meatballs, sausage, baloney, pepper, onions, green pepper, and finally another layer of cheese: mozzarella.

Whenever you supply a specific for a general word, you will add power to what you write. Remember, too, that specific images are more memorable for readers than general sketches.

Use Action Verbs.   Most texts take an unyielding stand against passive verbs. Passive verbs have gotten a bad reputation because students often use the passive voice to avoid taking a stand about anything, and because business and technical writing often lacks character and flavor because of excessive use of passive constructions. Occasionally, though, passive verbs are useful to the writer—as when a cause or agent is unknown or when sentence variety and paragraph flow require that words otherwise following the verb be shifted to the beginning of the sentence. But because passive voice can seriously slow reading, be sure to use it only where it is appropriate.

Even more important, use verbs that show action rather than forms of *to be* that simply link sentence parts. Often you can transform a word ending in *-ion, -ent, -ant, -ence, -ance* to replace a *be* verb as you revise for active sentences:

Lifeless Verb	*Active Verb*
indication is provided by	indicates
repayment will be made	we will repay
consideration is given	we consider
make an adjustment	adjust
has an appreciation of	appreciates
operation was performed	operated
investigation was undertaken	investigated
analysis has been made	analyzed

Similarly, *there is, there are,* and *it is* are sentence openers that simply take up space rather than add meaning to your sentences. Consider recasting all sentences that begin with these empty openers.

There are several reasons why some school children fail to learn to read, but the most important is that parents don't get involved.
Revised: Some school children fail to learn to read largely because parents don't get involved.

WRITING *Revising Words*

1. Each of the sentences below contains problems in word use. Identify the problem and then revise the sentence.

   A. Exercise is something that should be tried by everyone.

   B. In my estimation, the requirement of additional classrooms is an unwise move undertaken by the school board.

   C. It is expected by most of the members of the community that the abandonment of the drive to retain the trees will be detrimental to the city.

   D. The Congress's insistence on backing up the unfair demands by the President only resulted in the creation of an atmosphere of resentment and mistrust among the voters.

   E. It was agreed by everyone that a good time was enjoyed at the great movie last night.

2. Read the following passage, identifying problems in exact diction and wordiness. Revise the passage to make it more precise and less wordy.

   The choice of a particular university is very important in a student's college career. Prospective college students select a university by considering many factors. Every student has decided on certain qualities his or her university must possess. To some students, distance is an important aspect of their choice. They want to be close to home, far away from home, or just far enough so they will have some independence. Others view reputation as a vital factor. The college may have to be in the "Ivy League" class. Others may want to attend a private, religious university. Still others want the college of their choice to be well known academically. All of these factors are considered to a certain degree in making a decision considering which university to attend.

3. Rewrite the following sentences to reduce wordiness. Explain what causes wordiness in each.

   A. In our ultra-modern society of today, it is increasingly difficult to maintain the friendly easygoing outlook on life that was prevalent in the past.

   B. The style in this essay is very effective in achieving the purpose of the writer.

   C. One point that is often overlooked by many is the fact that Lee had given most of his slaves their freedom before the outbreak of the War Between the States.

D. A third reason which makes Howard Roark and his society a dream is the fact that nothing can keep him from achieving his goal.

E. In the late 1800s a scientist of some esteem put forth and had published a copy of what he believed to be an explanation of the origin of man—the scientist of course was Charles Darwin.

F. It is a common misconception among the feline owners of the world that the Siamese breed of cats is, without exception, the most unfriendly of their kind. Myself owning an example of living proof, I can readily disprove this common belief. My Siamese cat, Kohlou by name, is undoubtedly one of the most affectionate animals I have ever seen.

G. The first thought which comes to mind is one of shock.

H. Agronomists are very certain that there will soon be a food crisis. Many things are being discovered to help ease food shortages, such as polypropylene. However, it is difficult to carry out plans or to get the richer nations to help develop the poorer ones.

I. When people begin their lives as children, they are very heavily influenced by their parents.

WRITING *Revising Your Sentences and Words*

1. Rank the kinds of revisions you can best use to revise your sentences. Do you generally have more problems with choppy sentences or repeated patterns? Do you need to work first on varying sentence openers or combining sentences? Do you need to revise early on for clear logical connections between ideas (subordination)? Be sure to list questions that will help you zero in on the sentence problems you know you have.
2. Rank the kinds of revisions you can best use to rework word choices. Again, be sure to list questions that will help you zero in on the word choice problems you know you have.
3. Now turn to your most recent paper. Use your sets of questions to revise sentences and words.

CHAPTER 14

Editing and Manuscript Form

After all the hard work you have put into your paper to be sure that readers enjoy the writing, it would be irresponsible not to edit it. *Editing* requires a careful look at *how* you've presented your message to make sure that no superficial flaws or errors get in the way of effective communication. Look at some specific reasons for editing. You'll see for yourself that editing is the smart writer's last act.

WHY EDIT?

Editing is important for several reasons.

1. Certain conventions of propriety are associated with writing. If you violate these established principles—say, have no margins or write in choppy, incomplete thoughts—then you are asking for the same kind of rebuff received by a barefoot person who tries to go into a roadside restaurant that posts "NO SHOES, NO SHIRT, NO SERVICE." Editing gives you the opportunity to adjust your writing.

2. Editing cleans up your writing so the reader will be more receptive to your message. Readers have certain expectations of a paper—they want it to make sense, to be readable, to have an order that they can follow, to be correctly spelled and punctuated, to be neat. Because that's so, some readers will see only weaknesses—the smudges, the misspelled words, the confused sentences—and fail to see anything else in the paper, no matter how important that "anything else" might be. You may not think it is fair to equate mistakes in papers with sloppy thinking, but many people do just that. They pay so much attention to one or two faults that they miss the whole message. To give your message the best chance possible, you have to make it free of blemishes.

3. Editing removes the last sources of confusion. Perhaps the reader is tolerant; maybe he or she doesn't mind a smudge or is "understanding" about a misspelled word (although it's dangerous to count on that). But even if such flaws don't upset the reader, they may still steal the punch or cloud the clarity of the message you are trying to get across. Why spend hours on a piece of writing only to have it less effective than it could be simply because you didn't edit thoroughly to remove the last sources of confusion?

4. Editing lets you review what you've written and make sure that it says what you mean in a way you can be proud of. It's impossible, however, to check on the way it is said while the thoughts are still hot and rolling in. Only after the words are "cold" can you do the fine tuning that turns work from "OK" into "good" or "good" into "best." Editing carefully gives you a chance to (a) say what you mean and (b) put on any finishing touches that you want to make. It's your final chance to make the writing something you are proud of—both for what you say and how you say it.

THE EDITING EYE

Editing does not mean condemning. The *constructive* critical faculty of your mind allows you to evaluate and discriminate while editing. You are able to turn a critical eye—*an editing eye*—on your writing and spot possibilities to make your writing even better. You aren't looking to blame yourself for what you did badly—you merely want to see how your writing might appear to someone else. You edit so that your readers will keep on reading.

Although you might suppose that nobody would send out a paper without polishing and editing it, experience shows that almost all beginning writers tend to skip this stage. Many writers, especially when they are pressed for time, read over a paper and think, "Well, that looks all right to me," because it takes a specially trained eye to know what to look for and to spot the ways the writing might be improved. This section will enable you to develop that "trained eye," and practice will perfect your use of it.

Five Editing Steps

There are five steps to take in editing, and each step takes you closer to the goal of a perfect paper. Here are the five steps.

1. Get Distance
2. Read Aloud

3. Find the Errors
4. Make It Look Good
5. Proofread

Let's look at what you need to do to complete this five-step approach to editing your work.

1. The Get-Distance Step.   It happens to most writers, including professionals: they fall in love with what they have just finished writing. This euphoria is well deserved—but not particularly trustworthy. The relief of finally being finished may get in the way of your ability to see your creation for what it is and how well it communicates to the reader. When love is blind, disappointment may lurk in the wings. Writers who are "in love" with their latest creation are not likely to be entirely objective.

What to do? Love your writing all you want. But get some distance. There are several ways to get distance, and although you'll get by using only one of them, you'll profit by using all of them. Here they are.

Let the writing cool before you edit it.   Let at least a day go by—preferably two—before you reread to edit. Waiting will make a "new reader" out of you—your approach will be more like a reader's and less like the author's. You will see weaknesses you simply couldn't see before.

Pretend you are a (skeptical) reader.   This is another way to give you some distance from your writing. Pretend that you are the most disbelieving, skeptical, "show me!" reader you can dream up. Ask the writer (who, for the moment, is someone other than you) to prove everything: "Oh yeah? Why should I believe that? What's the connection between this paragraph and the ones that follow? What's the point?" Granted, this isn't the kindest way to get distance, but it will provide you with a rigorous critique—and also prepare you to accept the critiques of others.

Read your writing backwards.   No, not from right to left (unless you write in Hebrew or Arabic)—from last sentence to first sentence. This odd exercise is an aid to becoming objective. It gives you distance from your writing by disengaging you from the familiarity of it, from the flow of one line to another. Each sentence stands out, alone and naked, unprotected by its neighbors. If it's weak, or incomplete, or boring, you'll know. (This procedure works only with sentences, not with larger elements such as organization and structure of paragraphs.)

Use symbols to make quick, short-hand notes in the margins as you edit.   (Obviously, leave wide margins on your draft.) You need to see your writing as a whole, and you can't do so if you are constantly stopping to make changes as you read it. When you are all done, then you can go back to your symbols and make the needed changes. You can make up your own symbols. Or you can use these.

? a passage seems unclear

ss sentence seems awkward

ℐ delete a word, sentence, or passage

✳ insertion needed for further explanation or similar reason

2. The Read-Aloud Step. This sounds like a small step, but it could be the secret to finding mistakes in your work before you turn it in for final evaluation. You can be certain that if you stumble over something that you read, you need to fix the sentence. When students are reading their papers out loud to other members of the class, they are often overheard to say things like "Oh, I left part of that sentence out" or "I didn't say what I meant to say there." The best way to solve these problems is to read your writing aloud to someone else—you tend to notice what doesn't work when someone else is listening! You can even read it out loud to yourself (preferably into a tape recorder), and your ear will catch what your eye may have missed. If you find yourself listening with only half an ear and becoming bored, read the paragraphs out of order. It will perk up your attention and help your ear catch inconsistencies in development as well as weaknesses in word choice and rhythm.

If you can find a willing listener, ask him or her to answer these questions after hearing your paper.

What words do you remember? (Have your listener call these words out to you.)

In one *sentence,* summarize what I just read to you.

In one *word,* summarize what I just read to you.

Getting your listener's responses to these questions will let you know what you have communicated. You need only take note of what the listener heard. Since you are the writer and you are in charge, you can do whatever you wish with the information you receive. You will probably want to use the information to help you edit (or even revise more) because what your listener heard is most likely what you will be communicating to other readers.

3. The Find-the-Errors Step. Some errors occur more frequently than others, and most writers quickly discover which mistakes they are most likely to make. If you know what kinds of errors to look for, you are likely to find (and to fix) them. Make a list of flaws you need to watch out for as you edit your writing. (You can check the section on Special Problems in Editing for more detail.) Here are some of the most common problems students have.

Sentence fragments.   Be sure that every sentence has a subject and verb—unless you intended to leave out one or the other. As you saw in the discussion of Function Paragraphs in Chapter 12, sentence fragments are sometimes used intentionally for emphasis. Just be certain if you have sentence fragments that they are appropriate to the writing and are intentional.

Fused sentences or comma splices.   Don't fuse two sentences together when they *should* be separate: *Don't have one complete sentence like this the next sentence will look like that.* And don't fix that problem sentence with only a comma: *Don't have one complete sentence like this, the next sentence will look like that.* Always check for appropriate use of periods, semicolons, or commas *and* coordinating conjunctions to mark complete sentences.

Punctuation flaws.   Watch out for things like commas left out or in the wrong place; apostrophes left out or in the wrong place; one quotation mark missing (in a set of two); or semicolons used in place of commas (or vice versa).

Words that are commonly confused, such as **it's/its, affect/effect.** Check the full list under Usage in the section on Special Problems in Editing to compile your list of problem words to check.

Insufficient use of writing tools.   Use the dictionary as often as you need to (maybe more). It will tell you about spelling, hyphenation, and what the best word might be for a particular application. (You may also want to use a thesaurus for finding synonyms, and a word divider for checking hyphenation.)

Misspelled words or typos.   Look for typing errors.
As you compile your personal list of editing notes, add appropriate questions to the following list that you can use to check your final editing.

If I have any fragments in the writing, were they intended?

Did I run two sentences together with only a comma instead of a period between them?

Did I put a comma before the word *and* when two sentences were connected?

Do my verbs all agree with their subjects?

Do my pronouns match their antecedents? (The eagles . . . them.) (The women . . . who are)

Did I draw pictures with words—give my reader vivid images to remember? (Find eight examples.)

Can I find 25 words I could take out right now and not miss them? (Delete as many words at this moment as you possibly can.)

Would I know the passive voice if I saw it? If I have used passive voice, was it intentional and effective?

Did I use commas clearly and appropriately to help readers get my message?

Did I use clichés?

Did I put an apostrophe in *it's* when I meant *it is*? Did I leave the apostrophe out of its when I meant to show possession? How about other apostrophes?

Is every word spelled correctly?

Did I find and correct all the typos?

Do I have wide, even margins?

4. The Make-It-Look-Good Step. When you have checked your paper for flaws and oversights, you are ready to print out or type the final copy for presentation to the reader in manuscript form. Now you want to think about the way the writing is going to look on the page. As in editing, don't let carelessness or laziness cause you to do a halfway job. Nobody would spend hours building a beautiful walnut bookcase and then display it at a craft fair with sawdust all over it. The way your paper looks will have a considerable psychological effect on the reader. While a good-looking paper with no content won't get you anywhere, a paper with excellent content but a sloppy appearance usually won't either. You can't win either way on this one; it has to have both. Good content + good appearance = success with reader.

Whether your paper is typewritten or printed by a computer, there are some conventions that you should always observe.

1. Make your paper as neat as possible. If you need to fix an error on a typed or printed page, use correction fluid instead of an eraser whenever you can. Correction fluid is especially good for long corrections.

2. Use one side of the paper only.

3. Use standard size unruled paper. Do not use legal size, colored, or spiral-notebook paper or cheap typing paper.

4. Always number your pages.

Making a Typewritten Paper Look Professional.

1. Always double-space when you type. Single spacing is difficult to read.

2. Use good quality paper. It is difficult to read material typed on cheap typing paper or onion skin paper. Do not use erasable bond. Its finish, which makes erasure easy, also makes smudging more likely. Besides, unless you erase carefully and professionally, erasure will still be noticeable and will often be messy. If you plan to type most of your papers, invest in several hundred sheets of good quality typing paper bought at a book or office supply store, not at the local grocery store.

3. Use a good black or blue ribbon. Change your ribbon when it begins to look faint. Do not use italics or script characters except for special effects. See that the type in your typewriter is clean.

4. Leave at least one-inch margins all around. If you will bind your paper in a folder, the left margin should be slightly wider to avoid making that side of the page look cramped once it is in the folder. The top margin on the first page should always be about two inches. Type the title; then triple space before beginning the body of the paper.

Making a Computer-Printed Paper Look Professional

1. Always double-space as you would any typed paper.

2. Establish good margins and be certain that the top and bottom of your computer pagination is what you will want for your finished product.

3. Type in upper and lower case; don't put the CAP key down on the computer keyboard for convenience and forget to let it up when you are editing the final version.

4. Use a letter-quality printer, if at all possible. No matter what printer you use, be certain that it makes a legible page. Don't turn in an essay that looks like a spread sheet with funny computer marks all over it and signs and symbols that nobody but you will understand.

5. If at all possible, copy the paper and turn in the copy. This will allow you to avoid turning in computer paper which may be of a

lesser quality than copy paper. If you must turn in the copy directly off your printer, be sure that you tear off the perforations on each side of the page, and tear the sheets apart.

6. If your computer and/or printer allows for varying fonts, work at producing a close-to-typeset-looking copy. You'll be pleased with the outcome and will feel enormously creative in the process.

5. The Proofread Step. Your paper may be proofread by you or by someone else, but be sure that it does get proofread. A well-written, good-looking page replete with typographical and other errors is like a beautiful, well-dressed person with spinach on one tooth: the effect is marred—and a little hard to take seriously.

What is proofreading? It is a final read-through for the purpose of catching careless flaws. At this stage, you are looking only for typographical errors, omitted letters or words, sometimes even omitted sentences, misspellings, inappropriate punctuation, and so on. Use the following symbols to indicate the necessary changes to yourself or your typist.

capitalization needed
no capitalization
insert comma
insert semicolon
insert period
insert colon
delete
close up
∧ insert a word or sentence
insert a space
transpose letters

It's worth your while to become familiar with proofreading concerns and symbols, but for extra insurance have another person proofread after you do. You will always have more difficulty spotting mistakes in your own work than someone else will. Since you know what you mean to say, the words don't have to be there on the page for you to think them as you read. Also, you may not know every principle for, say, appropriate punctuation, and it may take you a few weeks to learn how to edit thoroughly. In the meantime, your papers have to be evaluated. So get someone who is good at proofreading to go over your paper with you before you turn it in.

Always try to leave yourself enough time to retype or re-print pages with significant numbers of proofreading changes. If you don't have time, make the changes clearly on the final copy you will hand in. If you do have time to retype or re-print, proofread once again to catch any flaws you might have missed the first time or new ones you introduced in retyping.

Remember, your reader will begin forming impressions and expectations about your paper even before he or she begins to read it. Those expectations will be based on how the paper looks. Give yourself an advantage by presenting not only clear prose but good-looking prose, too.

PART 4   *Special Applications*

This section will help when you have special writing projects

- writing a paper from sources
- writing essay tests

CHAPTER 15

Writing a Paper from Sources

You, like most writers, probably feel that writing a paper from sources is more complicated and time-consuming than writing from first-hand knowledge and personal experience. While in both cases you have to exercise all the skills involved in the writing process—getting ideas, deciding about audience, shaping, revising, editing—to write a paper from sources you also have to exercise several non-writing skills simultaneously.

What are the non-writing skills that you have to master to write from sources?

- First of all, writing a paper from sources requires a skill that you haven't had to use in other essays: finding material to supplement what you already know. Often that entails learning how to use the library.

  Fortunately, learning to use the library to find supplementary material is a skill which will stay with you for life. It is also a skill transferable to any kind of research you will ever want to do.

- Other "extras" required in writing a paper from sources include summarizing the sources, incorporating source material or quotations into the body of an essay, and giving credit for the information. Again, these are skills you haven't had to exercise in most of the other writing you have done, but summarizing, incorporating material into your own writing, and documenting information correctly are essential to acceptable research in any field.

  Once you learn a system for summarizing, citing information, and documenting sources, you'll know it for good. The same system that you learn now will work when you do research projects for your company, when you look up legal briefs for an appearance in court, or when you search for the latest information on the income tax laws to handle an IRS audit.

■Finally, there's the form of the paper itself. All outside sources must be documented where they occur in the paper and must also be collected in a bibliography. This, then, is a third non-writing skill that you have to know how to use.

Learning correct documentation form really means simply learning where to look something up. (It's never anything you have to memorize.) Good documentation also serves the readers by letting them know what books, articles, and other matter they could read if they wanted to know more about your subject.

Remember, though, that even as you practice non-writing skills while writing from sources, you are drawing on the same writing skills you've been practicing ever since you began school. Let everything you already know about the writing process put you at ease as you begin to integrate new skills required for writing from sources.

WRITING BEFORE READING

The most efficient way to get started reading on a topic is to write. By calling to mind everything that you already know on a topic, you will have "old" information you can incorporate with the new information you gather when you begin to read sources; you will quickly see connections between new and old material. You can use the creating techniques that you have learned—cubing, looping, classical invention, and others—to call forth information and knowledge stored in your memory. You might also discover new thoughts as facts, experiences, and information that you already possess interact during your prewriting. As you go over what you know, you can often find an angle that will interest you and that you can shape to interest your reader.

Moreover, in Writing from Sources, Noticing Inside Purpose will help you gather information about a subject as you go, and to see the underlying theme or surprising interconnections that a one-time-only glance at a subject would not reveal. This technique provides you with new information you can use later on (whether days, weeks, or months later) when you are planning and writing the paper itself.

To see how writing can help you start reading, let's begin to work on a topic we'll cover throughout this chapter—minimum-wage legislation.

WRITING　*Writing Before Reading*

1. Begin by writing about your experiences and knowledge about the minimum wage. Answer these questions as you freewrite, cube, track

switch, or use some other prewriting techniques to help you remember what you already know about the topic.

    a. When have you worked for minimum wage (or less)? Did you feel exploited or undervalued because of your wage? Why?

    b. What minimum-wage jobs do you know of? Who often holds these jobs?

    c. What arguments have you heard or read in favor of raising the minimum wage? Who advanced those arguments?

    d. What arguments have you heard or read against raising the minimum wage? Who advanced those arguments?

    e. If you had to leave school tomorrow to get a job, would you take one paying minimum wage? Why or why not?

2. Keep a notebook for Noticing Inside Purpose on minimum-wage legislation. Recall these tips from Chapter 5.

    a. Get a small (pocket-size) notebook and label it "Noticing Inside Purpose Notebook."

    b. Write this at the top of the first page: *Write about minimum-wage legislation.*

    c. Keep a running record of everything you notice connected to minimum-wage legislation.

    d. Every time you notice something new connected with minimum-wage legislation—or have an idea associated with it—turn to the next page in your notebook and record the observation or idea.

    e. At least once before beginning to draft, deliberately go on a "noticing expedition" with the express intention of asking people about minimum-wage legislation. Take notes of your observations.

READING

Having collected on paper what you already know about your topic—in this instance, minimum-wage legislation—you are now ready to begin reading. You will find that by writing first, reading will be much easier for you. You know before you begin reading whether you need to fill in background on an unfamiliar topic or whether you can immediately begin accumulating extensive data and complex arguments. You know how to deal with preliminary definitions and detailed cases as you come across them in your reading. You may even be able to select the most appropriate reading material without spending a great deal of time because you are aware of how much you know and how much you need to know. In short, you are ready to fill in gaps in your knowledge so that you become an expert on the topic for your readers.

    Again, let's see how the process works by reading a short article on minimum wage. Keep in mind that it comes from a business magazine geared toward readers interested in how minimum-wage legislation would affect their businesses.

ANTI-DARWINISM   *The Economist*

When the Democrats recaptured the Senate in 1986, many expected a rush of progressive legislation. With the 100th Congress half over, not much of it has been passed. A conspicuous example of inaction is the Kennedy-Hawkins bill to raise the minimum wage. Senator Edward Kennedy, the chairman of the Labor and Human Resources Committee and the Senate's leading liberal, had hoped to send the bill to the floor by last autumn. It is still in his committee. In the House of Representatives the bill languishes in a subcommittee of the Education and Labor Committee.

The legislation would raise the minimum wage, unchanged since 1981 at $3.35 an hour, to $4.65 in three annual steps. The sponsors had hoped to make the first increase, to $3.85, on January 1, 1988. After 1990 the bill would mandate automatic increases by indexing the minimum wage to 50% of average hourly earnings.

A federal minimum wage, of 25 cents an hour, was first enacted in 1938. Its scope has been broadened repeatedly. There are not many more workers to bring into the net, and perhaps not many who need this sort of protection from their bosses. Minimum-wage legislation now competes with bills to require employers to provide health benefits, to allow workers to take unpaid parental leave without losing their jobs, to require employers to notify workers of occupational health hazards and to restrict the use of lie-detector tests.

Some members of Congress fear that foisting extra costs on employers will make America less competitive and may also increase unemployment. Mr. Bill Brock, a former secretary of labor, argues that the way to make the working poor better off is to teach them skills for a market that offers fewer and fewer unskilled jobs. Even Senator Kennedy's staff acknowl-edge that raising the minimum wage would probably dry up some job opportunities for the unskilled, but they argue that the numbers are trivial. The minimum wage, they say, protects the helpless against the "ruthless Darwinism" of markets.

By 1986, according to figures from the Labor Department, the number of workers receiving the minimum wage or less had fallen to 5.1 million. Opponents of the legislation argue that many recipients are young people living with their parents and that few minimum-wage workers are the sole bread-winner of their families. Moreover, they say, the minimum-wage population changes as young people learn new skills and advance. Representative Tom Petri of Wisconsin, the senior Republican on the House subcommittee, says boosting the minimum wage is the wrong way to raise the income of the poor. He prefers a bigger earned-income-tax credit, a kind of negative income tax.

States may, however, set their own standards. California raised its minimum wage in December to $4.25 an hour, an increase of 27%, making it the highest in the country. Connecticut's is due to reach the same level next October, and several other states are considering increases.

Senator Kennedy has the votes to bring the minimum-wage bill out of committee. But it is doubtful whether the Senate would pass it without weakening it first. Senator Dan Quayle of Indiana, a senior Republican on the labor committee, plans to offer amendments to trim the annual increases, delete indexing and write in a lower rate for the young. Such a bill might divide the administration. "Reagan's gut is against it," says Quayle, but others in the administration, not to mention Republican candidates, would oppose a veto on the eve of the elections.

The Kennedy staff acknowledge that they cannot get their bill through the Senate unchanged. They know they must give up indexing and possibly trim the increases. But the lower rate for teenagers is anathema to organized labor, and Senator Kennedy will not accept it. The unanswered question is whether Senator Kennedy prefers a veto to enactment of a diluted bill. Since 1988 is the 50th anniversary of the minimum wage, Democrats may feel they are in a good position to hold out for their kind of bill and use the fight to rally low-income workers, civil-rights leaders, unions and liberals to a Democratic "social justice" banner. Then, if a Democrat wins the presidency, a minimum-wage bill could be the first order of business, just as it was in 1977 under President Jimmy Carter.

WRITING AFTER READING

As you begin your reading on a topic, you'll want to try several techniques for integrating the new information you learn through reading, with the knowledge you already have on a topic. One way to do that is through continued writing on the topic after you read each selection. Your writing can be unstructured, but you want to be sure that you play new ideas off old ones. Try working through some additional questions on the minimum wage to connect your preliminary thinking, writing, and reading on the topic.

WRITING   *Writing After Reading*

1. Without looking back at your prewriting from before reading the article above, what strikes you in this piece as most similar to your experience and knowledge? What strikes you as most different?
2. If you had to continue reading on the topic, what questions would you want to have answered?
3. If you had to write on the topic, what three angles could you take on it?
4. Now jot down any new information you gathered from this article. You'll probably want to look back at the article to list some of the more important facts—such as the statistics on loss of jobs and on the dollar increases under the Kennedy-Hawkins bill.

WRITING ABOUT READING

Some readers like to read through an entire piece just to get the gist of it before they go back and sort through the details they want to remember. Other readers like to understand exactly how all the details fit together to make up the "big picture" as they go along in their reading. Although they may prefer one approach over the other, almost all readers use a mixture of these strategies.

No matter which approach you prefer, sooner or later you will have to move from reading to writing. As you prepare to write a paper from sources, you will need to take notes simply because no one can keep the amount of information you will be gathering organized and catalogued without them. Sooner or later, you will ask yourself, "Where did I see that? Who said that? When did that trend start? Where did I come across statistics on this point?" and sooner or later you will need to turn to your notes on your reading.

When you are writing from sources, you need to read with several goals in mind. In your early reading, you will probably be trying to get a sense of the topic, an overview of what other people have written and said about the topic. You will have some attitudes and opinions based on certain information, but you may need to step back and get a wider view to find out just how big your topic is before you can see how much you need to narrow it. When you are reading for this goal, you will want to keep track of what you read, but you won't yet know which are the most important facts that will help you write your paper. *Summarizing* is a good writing technique to use at this point because it will help you remember the general content of what you have read, making it easier to go back and find specific details later.

In addition, your early reading—giving you an overview of the topic—will help you see angles on the topic. You'll start to see potential audiences, purposes, and focuses. Soon you'll find yourself focusing on one approach for one particular audience. *Audience analysis* and other pre-writing techniques are particularly useful to help meet this goal as you continue to read and collect ideas.

Once you have determined your focus, audience, and purpose, you will have a good starting point for determining what information and arguments will fit into your paper (although you may refine your focus as you continue reading and writing and thus change what supporting detail you need in the paper). A preliminary focus will help you select *details* from your reading, and then you need to begin taking more *detailed notes* on your sources.

Let's look more closely at these writing techniques as they help in the process of writing from sources.

Summarizing

Most often when you read articles and editorials that argue for the writer's position, you'll feel compelled to agree or disagree. That's a natural part of the reading process. Before you start arguing your own position, however, it's best to be sure that you understand the exact arguments of the piece you've read. One way to do this is to summarize the main points of a piece. Summarizing helps you see the structure of an argument with the major points and supporting detail organized clearly.

Summarizing can also help you sort out details and main points in factual articles that don't argue for a position, so it's a skill you can use whenever you read. Once you summarize a piece, you'll have a written record of it and you needn't reread every source to remind yourself where a fact or example came from.

The best summaries aim for three features:

1. Objectivity
2. Completeness
3. Order

Objectivity. Even if you agree or disagree strongly with a piece you're summarizing, don't let your position influence your summary. Summarize what the author says, not how you feel about it. That way, when you reread your summary you can trust your writing to reflect accurately only what the author included in his or her original piece.

Completeness. A one-line summary of a five-page article won't tell you much when you come back to look at it again. Write enough to capture all the major points a piece makes. Try to include the major facts or examples used as support. If you use as a rule of thumb that a summary should be 20 to 30 percent as long as the original piece, you'll have a reasonable guideline to help you include enough detail in your summary so that it will help you later in your writing process.

Order. Start your summary with the title, author, and thesis of the article (even if the article doesn't state a thesis directly). That way, as you review your summaries, your first sentence or two will give you the focus of the piece. Then include major and minor points in the order they appear in the article. As you reread your summaries, the order of points in the summary will guide you to the appropriate place in the article for relevant quotations or supporting facts, details, and examples not included in your summary.

WRITING *Practicing the Summary*

1. Practice summarizing this article on minimum wage by the Executive Vice President of Pillsbury and Chairman of its restaurant group.

DON'T RAISE THE MINIMUM WAGE   Jeffrey Campbell/*Fortune*

A specter is haunting America. An underclass of unemployable young people, particularly minority youth, is expanding steadily, abetted by drug abuse, adolescent pregnancy, and illiteracy. This may be the single greatest threat to the competitiveness of American business. These teens need jobs, and before that, job skills. A higher minimum wage, as proposed in the well-intentioned Kennedy-Hawkins bill now before Congress, would not help them much. And it could even hurt.

The bill's laudable objective is to reduce poverty by bringing low-paid workers a higher standard of living. Unfortunately, the problem and the solution will pass like ships in the night. Virtually every economist who has studied the issue agrees that a minimum wage increase would lead to a loss of jobs. According to studies coordinated by the Minimum Wage Study Commission in 1981, each 10% increase reduces teenage employment by 0.5% to 1.5%— a loss of up to 90,000 jobs in today's job market.

The last federal minimum wage hike was a four-step, 46% increase, from $2.30 per hour in 1977 to $3.35 per hour in 1981, the current level. The Kennedy-Hawkins bill would increase the hourly wage another 39%, from $3.35 to $4.65, within 25 months. Thereafter, the minimum wage would automatically be raised to 50% of the average non-supervisory private hourly wage.

One economist estimates that the federal minimum wage linked to the Kennedy-Hawkins index could top $7 per hour in 1995. There would be an additional ripple effect as well. Employees earning more than the minimum wage would expect—and probably get—raises to maintain their historic differentials. In fact, such increases are built into some labor contracts.

Proponents of raising the minimum wage argue that it is a national disgrace for a person to work 40 hours and earn only $134 weekly, $6,968 a year. This *is* a disgrace if the wage earner is attempting to support a family solely on this income. In this context, it is extremely important to understand the makeup of today's minimum-wage work force. More than a third are teenagers, and 59% are under 25. Many are students, some of whom are technically classified in government statistics as heads of households. Two-thirds are living with a relative who also has a job. Relatively few work 40 hours weekly, all year, for the minimum wage.

A mandated raise for *everyone* is an inappropriate way to help the distinct minority whose sole livelihood is the minimum wage and public assistance. The most efficient solution would be targeted assistance for these people. The working poor can best be helped by raising the federal earned income tax credit—the negative income tax that now tops out at $851.

Another alternative to Kennedy-Hawkins deserves careful study: a training wage. The Administration has long advocated a lower minimum wage for teenagers. The training wage would be lower too, but it would apply to any new worker, regardless of age. After several months' training, the new worker's pay would be increased to a level that would reflect greater productivity. High turnover is one of the fast-food industry's big problems. The training wage would reward tenure and experience.

One big thing many young people need is what could be called general job skills—including punctuality, teamwork, initiative, personal communication, and the ability to take direction and take responsibility for one's actions. The companies in Pillsbury's restaurant group teach those things—what we call the invisible curriculum—along with making hamburgers and delivering pizza. Our restaurants are in every kind of neighborhood across the nation, from affluent suburbs to impoverished ghettos. We are in direct contact with millions of young people and employ hundreds of thousands every year. We recognize that the welfare of American youth is critical to our own future.

We have a long way to go before we will be satisfied with our job-training efforts. But we believe we can do the job more efficiently than government. If there are fewer jobs—in our restaurants and across the rest of the economy—the government will have to assume a larger and more expensive share of the burden for vocational training.

Fast-food jobs are often disparagingly described as dead ends. We do not buy that. To us they can be a very large port of entry for disadvantaged young people into the mainstream of the American economy. Our young workers can take the job skills they learn with us into any kind of work. They can also stay with us and get promoted into good jobs in a dynamic business. A lot of our managers started in hourly paid jobs. Two regional vice presidents in our Burger King division rose from jobs behind the broiler without college degrees.

We do not want to slash jobs or reduce our job-training role. But ours is a highly competitive business. If Kennedy-Hawkins passes, we would have little leeway to pass along higher wage costs in the form of higher prices. We are constantly looking for ways to increase productivity—which often means serving more customers with fewer workers. Higher wages will only accelerate that activity.

Poverty cannot be cured by higher paychecks for some citizens and unemployment for others. *Employment* should be the goal of federal policy, not raising the price of employees beyond their productivity level with resulting job loss.

a. Begin your summary with the author, title, and thesis of the article. What is Campbell's thesis?

b. Include the major points Campbell makes, *not* your interpretation of his argument.

c. Also include minor points and the most significant supporting arguments. This summary should be about 150 words.

2. Throughout the rest of this chapter, we'll be following the writing that one student did on this topic. Let's take a look at Randall's summary of Campbell's article to see how it meets our criteria of objectivity, completeness, and order.

> The country's minimum wage has come to debate. The Kennedy-Hawkins bill proposes raising the wage floors on the federal level. Jeffrey Campbell, Pillsbury's restaurant group chairman, writes about

his opposition to the bill in "Don't Raise the Minimum Wage." According to Campbell, a higher minimum wage would not help teenagers, who need jobs and job skills, or American businesses. The bill's focus centers on the reduction of poverty by bringing higher wages to low-paid workers, but the increase would actually yield a loss of jobs for teenagers. People in favor of the bill say that it is disgraceful for a full-time worker to earn only $6,968 a year. Campbell points out that these proponents fail to realize that few people work for the minimum wage full time, and it is these people that need to be helped. Instead of raising the minimum we should explore alternatives, such as a training wage or a lower minimum wage for teenagers. Pillsbury's restaurants teach job skills, according to Campbell. These skills are what teenagers need to move on to better jobs. If the minimum wage rises, Campbell says his company's role as a teacher of job skills will have to be reduced and the government will have to pick it up. Kennedy-Hawkins would result in higher prices and fewer jobs, which is a no-win situation.

   a. Does Randall include the author, title, and thesis of the article early in his summary? Underline those elements.

   b. Do you see any places where Randall's opinion overshadows Campbell's points? Mark any you find.

   c. Do you include any points in your summary that Randall does not? Bracket those in your summary and be prepared to discuss why you included ideas that Randall did not. Highlight any points Randall covers that you don't and again consider why he included those ideas.

   d. Has Randall summarized points in the appropriate order? What would you change in the order of his summary or your summary?

3. If you would like to work on a topic other than minimum wage, start now to find sources for preliminary reading. Follow the same process we have used in this chapter—first write what you already know about the topic; read a few articles and write about those in relation to what you know; summarize one or two articles; and begin a notebook for Noticing Inside Purpose.

Finding a Preliminary Focus, Audience, Purpose

Consider three additional pieces on the minimum wage. As you read, note which articles give you new information (you might star new facts or arguments in the margin) and which give you new slants on information you already know (including what you've learned from the first two readings).

LIVING AT THE EDGE   Thomas Exter/*American Demographics*

Will a higher minimum wage cut poverty? Not necessarily, according to Ralph E. Smith and Bruce Vavrichek of the Bureau of Labor Statistics. Of 52 million workers paid by the hour in 1985, 5.2 million, or 10 percent, earned the minimum wage or less. Only one in five of those minimum wage workers live in poor families. Fully 80 percent live in families with incomes above the poverty line.

Who are the minimum wage workers? One in three are teenagers, and one in four are adult men. The rest—42 percent—are adult women. Nearly 70 percent live in families with at least one other worker contributing to family income. Only 18 percent of minimum wage workers work full-time, year-round; 70 percent work part-time.

If minimum wage earners worked full-time for a year, they would earn about $7,000 each. If they live alone, their income would place them above the poverty threshold of $5,590 for a single person. However, if a minimum wage worker lives with one nonworking dependent, he or she would fall below the poverty line of $7,230 for householders under age 65. In 1981, when the minimum wage was raised to $3.35 per hour, a full-time, year-round minimum wage worker could keep a family of three above the poverty line.

More information on minimum wage workers is in the Bureau of Labor Statistics' *Monthly Labor Review,* June 1987. The review is available at the U.S. Government Printing Office, Washington, DC 20402.

JOB LOSS FROM WAGE HIKE   *Nation's Business*

Unemployment would increase significantly in every state by 1995 if Congress approves a proposed increase in the minimum wage, according to a unique study by a Clemson University economics professor. California alone would lose 220,000 jobs, Richard B. McKenzie reports in his analysis, which is the first to estimate the state-by-state impact of a specific minimum-wage hike proposal.

A total of nearly 1.9 million jobs would be lost nationwide over the next eight years, McKenzie reports.

On the state level, the biggest losers in addition to California under minimum wage legislation sponsored by Sen. Edward M. Kennedy (D-Mass) and Rep. Augustus F. Hawkins (D-Calif) would be New York (136,550 jobs), Texas (134,033) and Florida (91,492).

Under this legislation, McKenzie concludes, unemployment would increase more than 20,000 in 31 states and more than 10,000 in six others.

The Kennedy-Hawkins bills would lift the wage floor from the current $3.35 an hour to $4.65 an hour by 1990. There would be automatic increases thereafter, with the wage set at 50 percent of the average nonsupervisory private-industry wage. Under assumptions used by McKenzie, the minimum wage would be more than $7.00 an hour in 1995.

The McKenzie study was commissioned by the National Chamber Foundation, an independent, nonprofit, public-policy research organization affiliated with the U.S. Chamber of Commerce, and the Minimum Wage Coalition to Save Jobs, made up of business representatives. Findings of the study are being used by business to rebut claims that the wage floor should be increased because purchasing power of the current minimum has eroded.

STATES KNOW BEST WHAT LABOR'S WORTH
Kathy Ann Ormiston / *Wall Street Journal*

Congress soon will consider an increase in the federal minimum wage to $5.05 from $3.35 an hour. Supporters of the increase argue that a major impetus has been recent boosts in many state minimum-wage levels. Last year alone, nine states and the District of Columbia raised their minimum wage above the current federal level, and this year New York, New Jersey and Pennsylvania are considering doing the same. Yet, state and federal minimum-wage comparisons should be made with a great deal of caution.

There are many loopholes in federal minimum-wage coverage. Certain occupations, including casual babysitters and most farm workers, are excluded as well as employees of small businesses and firms not engaged in interstate commerce. State minimum-wage laws are intended to cover these workers. At the same time, if a state's minimum is higher than the federal minimum, the state minimum applies.

Moreover, the quoted minimum wage for a state is often deceptive. Some states offer what is, in reality, a menu of minimum wages rather than a single minimum. The District of Columbia, whose minimum of $4.85 is the highest in the country, actually has seven other "minimum wages," all lower than $4.85. Workers in the retail trade and laundry industry, for example, receive a minimum of only $3.50. Furthermore, the District of Columbia, like many states, has a subminimum, or "training" wage, of $3.35 for employees in some job categories who are under age 18. (Some states also have subminimums based on age, student status, approved internship programs or for new hires.) Moreover, 13 states have minimums below the federal level and nine have no minimum at all.

Another frequently overlooked point is that although 16 states have enacted minimum-wage levels above the current federal minimum of $3.35, not one has a minimum at or above $5.05. A minimum wage of $5.05 would require even the high-minimum-wage states of California and Connecticut to increase their mandated minimums by 19%.

Nonetheless, both Republican and Democrat members of Congress from high-wage states will likely find it difficult to vote against raising the federal minimum wage, since raising it would equalize wage costs among states and increase the competitiveness of labor in high-minimum-wage states. Yet the different minimum-wage levels to a large extent reflect regional variations in levels of unemployment and labor demand, as well as costs of living. Typically, states with high minimum wages have low levels of unemployment and/or high costs of living. California and Massachusetts, with unemployment rates of 5.6% and 3.8% are representative of states with high minimum wages. Compare these unemployment rates to those of Alabama and Louisiana, states that have no minimum wage. Their unemployment rates are 7.9% and 12% respectively.

The advantage of allowing state or regional differences in minimum-wage levels is that the appropriate minimum wage for Connecticut might force massive layoffs in Texas. Wyoming's minimum of $1.60 would be meaningless, even laughable, in Massachusetts, where most employers must pay well above the federal minimum wage to attract applicants for job openings. Because states are the best judges of local conditions, they are in a better position to set minimum-wage laws.

Proponents of a federal increase argue that recent state increases signal grassroots support of the current minimum-wage bill before Congress. Yet 41 states are still at or below the current federal level. As Robert Martin of the Chamber of Commerce has pointed out: "Most states recognize that what you pay someone is determined by supply and demand." This is a lesson the folks in Washington could bear learning.

Minimum Wages

Proposed federal wage (1/1/92)	**$5.05**
Wash., DC	4.85
Proposed federal wage (1/1/91)	**4.65**
Calif. (7/1/88), Conn. (10/1/88)	4.25
Minn. (1/1/90)	3.95
Alaska, Hawaii, Maine (1/1/90)	3.85
Conn., Mass. (7/1/88)	3.75
Maine, Mass., N.H. (1/1/89)	
R.I., Vt. (7/1/88)	3.65
Minn., N.H., Vt.	3.55
Current federal wage	**3.35**
Current state wages	
Calif., Del., Ill., Ken., Md., Mich., Mont., Neb., Nev., N.J., N.M., N.Y., N.C., Okla., Ore., Penn., S.D., Texas, W.V., Wisc.	3.35
Ark. (1/1/89)	3.30
Ark., Ga.	3.25
N.D.	3.10
Colo.	3.00
S.D.	2.80
Utah	2.75
Va., Iowa (7/1/88)	2.65
Idaho, Ohio, Wash.	2.30
Ind.	2.00
Kan., Wyo.	1.60
Ala., Ariz., Fla., La., Miss., Mo., S.C., Tenn.	None

Now you need to start organizing what you know and don't know but need to know. How can you determine what you need to know? First, look at your audience and purpose in writing.

Who will you write to on this topic? You might want to argue to a teenage reader that minimum wage is not "chump change." Or you might want to argue to sponsors of the minimum-wage bill that the bill is right—or wrong. Or you might write to your legislator (state or national) about your position on minimum wage. Or you might write to local business owners about paying employees minimum or so-called "subminimum" wages.

What if you don't want to argue? What other options are open to you? You might simply want to educate (Writing to Inform) teenagers about your state's laws on minimum and subminimum wages. Or you might want to propose a solution for the problem of low-income bread-winners other than raising the minimum wage. At this point, you need to make the topic your own. You need to find a purpose, a reader, and a point that will guide your further reading and writing on the topic.

Writing from Sources always implies this personal commitment to the topic. Even if you write a research paper that you think includes nothing personal, *you* write it; thus, you are involved. Consciously committing yourself to a goal for a specific reader makes research-based writing easier because you can limit what information to look for and to collect from your own experience.

As you tackle this difficult part of writing from sources, look again at prewriting techniques that will help you find a way into the topic. Track switching and chaining are especially helpful if you cannot find an angle you are interested in. Looping, clustering, and the reporter's formula may help you pull together ideas that you had with ideas from your reading. Even classical invention can show you how much you already know on the topic and help you see a workable perspective or approach. Finally, audience analysis may well be crucial to help you see why a particular reader would care about your paper and what you need to include to write clearly and convincingly.

WRITING *Finding a Focus, Audience, Purpose*

Randall felt strongly about his position on the minimum wage after reading these five pieces and considering his own job history. He knew already that he wanted to argue against Kennedy-Hawkins. But he needed to know the audience. He didn't want to write to his representatives in Congress or to the state legislature. Rather, he wanted to write to his classmates to explain and persuade them that his perspective on minimum wage was the right one. So he worked through this audience analysis.

Randall's Checklist of Questions to "See" His Reader

Just who is my reader?
I want to write my paper to my classmates, because I don't think they know much about this topic and how it might affect them.

Why is my reader reading? To be informed? Entertained? Persuaded? Other?

I'm writing mainly to persuade, but my reader will need certain information to understand the issue and my position.

How old is my reader? What sex?

My reader is probably 19 years old (most folks in my class are 19). I think I'll write to Rick.

How well does my reader know me?

We've worked together, but Rick doesn't know that much about my ideas and opinions. Or about my work background. Or about my knowledge of business issues.

Does my reader share my background (age, area of birth, upbringing, education, and so on)? Outline differences.

Like me, Rick is from Colorado, but I'm from a small town and he's from Denver. Jobs are easier to get there, even minimum-wage jobs. I'm from a *small* town, population 200! Even a minimum-wage job was hard to come by for me in the last few years.

We both are in college, and we share lots of the same interests. Rick has held part-time and summer jobs like I have, but it hasn't been as hard for him to find work and to make enough money to pay tuition.

Does my reader share my attitudes toward this topic? Outline differences.

No, I don't think he does now, but I want him to by the time he finishes reading my paper. He probably thinks that a higher minimum wage would be good for him because he would have to work fewer hours or less time in the summer to make enough money for tuition. He doesn't realize he may have a lot harder time even finding a job next summer if this legislation passes.

Does my reader have special knowledge of this topic? Outline it.
No.

If I am writing to a group, can I name one person most representative of the group? If so, can I outline that one person's characteristics that affect him or her as a reader of my paper?

I've done that. I'm writing to Rick as a representative of my class.

1. How does his audience analysis set Randall up for the writing he must do?
2. What would you include in your paper on minimum wage if you were writing to your classmates?
3. If you have begun working on a different topic, do your prewriting and audience analysis to help you work toward a preliminary focus for your paper.

Taking Detailed Notes from Your Reading

With a preliminary focus, audience, and purpose in mind, you now need to turn back to your reading to supplement the information you already have or to gather more support. Now you need specifics. The best way to collect them is to begin taking detailed notes on your reading.

Your high school teachers undoubtedly suggested that you buy note cards and carefully organize your notes on them. This advice is good, and you'll find that if you follow it you will have clear and organized notes. Basically, that note-taking system looks like this:

1. Use 4 × 6 notecards.
2. In the upper right-hand corner, write the last name of author and the name of the publication.
3. At the beginning of the note, write the page number of the source. Don't get caught in the library at midnight the day before the paper is due looking for page numbers. As soon as the page in your source changes, write the new number immediately on the notecard, even if you are in the middle of a line.
4. Number the notecard at the bottom for your own purposes. You'll probably drop the notecards a hundred times while you are doing the paper, and it takes hours to get them back in order if they aren't numbered. But number them in pencil so that you can renumber later as you reorganize them to help you write the paper.
5. When you have finished with one notecard, write a word or two at the top of the left-hand side. This is your index for the card— some words that tell you what the subject of the notecard is. This index will help you sort and reorganize cards later.

The real advantage of this system is that you have ideas captured in your own words so that your mind has already begun integrating information into your personal storehouse of facts and experiences. In addition, if you have quoted material, you have noted where the quotation begins and ends so that you know the quotation and its exact source.

Taking notes has changed for many students in recent years. As photocopying machines have become more widely available and cheaper to use, many students simply copy articles and take notes directly on those pages. Often students simply highlight text in the article; sometimes they write notes in the margins. If you use this approach, be sure that you do additional prewriting to change those facts, quotations, and other source materials into your own ideas. Simply stringing together quotations from outside sources is not an effective way to present an idea to a reader.

If you've highlighted material on photocopies, here's a procedure you might follow.

1. Jot the most pertinent notes onto a separate sheet. Be sure to note where the information came from. If you quote directly, use quotation marks.

2. Now put all the photocopies aside and work with just one or two sheets, a much more manageable set of pages.

3. Freewrite or quick draft from your notes. Try not to look back at the photocopied sheets at all. If you need more information to develop a point or if you recall some information that you would like to include, just make a note or star that point in your writing. You can look up the specific page in your photocopies later.

Remember that your notes are like any other prewriting—you'll use some of them in your drafting and not use others. Don't feel compelled to include every note in your first or final draft of the paper itself. If you find as you take notes that your perspective on the topic is changing, then be sure to step back and see where the change is taking you. If you need to revise your focus, audience, and purpose for the paper, do so, and then continue taking notes with the new focus in mind.

WRITING *Taking Detailed Notes from Reading*

As Randall worked through this topic, he first read all the preceding pieces on the minimum wage without taking any notes. He then summarized the articles he felt were most important for giving him an overview of the topic. After he determined his audience, he went back to the readings and started highlighting those ideas he thought would be most helpful in writing to his classmates. Let's look at just one of the articles as he highlighted it.

STATES KNOW BEST WHAT LABOR'S WORTH

Kathy Ann Ormiston/*Wall Street Journal*

Congress soon will consider an increase in the federal minimum wage to $5.05 from $3.35 an hour. Supporters of the increase argue that a major impetus has been recent boosts in many state minimum-wage levels. Last year alone, nine states and the District of Columbia raised their minimum wage above the current federal level,

Pennsylvania are considering doing the same.
state and federal minimum-wage comparisons should be made with a great deal of caution.

There are many loopholes in federal minimum-wage coverage. Certain occupa—casual babysitters and most farm workers, are excluded as well as employees of small businesses and firms not engaged in interstate commerce. State minimum-wage laws are intended to cover these workers. At the same time, if a state's minimum is higher than the federal minimum, the state minimum applies.

Moreover, the quoted minimum wage for a state is often deceptive. Some states offer what is, in reality a menu of minimum wages rather than a single minimum. The District of Columbia, whose minimum of $4.85 is the highest in the country, actually has seven other "minimum wages," all lower than $4.85. Workers in the retail trade and laundry industry, for example, receive a minimum of only $3.50. Furthermore, the District of Columbia, like many states, has a subminimum, or "training" wage, of $3.35 for employees in some job categories who are under age 18. (Some states also have subminimums based on age, student status, approved internship programs or for new hires.)

13 states have minimums below the federal level and nine have no minimum at all.

Another frequently overlooked point is that although 16 states have enacted minimum-wage levels above the current federal minimum of $3.35, not one has a minimum at or above $5.05. A minimum wage of $5.05 would require even the high-minimum-wage states of California and Connecticut to increase their mandated minimums by 19%.

Nonetheless, both Republican and Demo-

crat members of Congress from high-wage states will likely find it difficult to vote against raising the federal minimum wage, since raising it would equalize wage costs among states and increase the competitiveness of labor in high-minimum-wage states. Yet the different minimum-wage levels to a large extent reflect regional variations in levels of unemployment and labor demand, as well as costs of living. Typically, states with high minimum wages have low levels of unemployment and/or high costs of living. California and Massachusetts, with unemployment rates of 5.6% and 3.8% are representative of states with high minimum wages. Compare these unemployment rates to those of Alabama and Louisiana, states that have no minimum wage. Their unemployment rates are 7.9% and 12% respectively.

The advantage of allowing state or regional differences in minimum-wage levels is that the appropriate minimum wage for Connecticut might force massive layoffs in Texas. Wyoming's minimum of $1.60 would be meaningless, even laughable, in Massachusetts, where most employers must pay well above the federal minimum wage to attract applicants for job openings. Because states are the best judges of local conditions, they are in a better position to set minimum-wage laws.

Proponents of a federal increase argue that recent state increases signal grassroots support of the current minimum-wage bill before Congress. Yet 41 states are still at or below the current federal level. As Robert Martin of the Chamber of Commerce has pointed out: "Most states recognize that what you pay someone is determined by supply and demand. This is a lesson the folks in Washington could bear learning.

1. Given his audience, why might Randall have highlighted the text that he has?
2. Clearly Randall has highlighted more than he can possibly include from this article. Can you write three or four short notes that would cover the most helpful points highlighted here?

3. Practice taking notes from at least three articles you will use for your paper on your topic.

SYNTHESIZING

By this time in prewriting a paper from source material, you already have collected much raw material to work with. You have your knowledge on the topic before you started reading; the information from the sources—five different readings on minimum wage; and the connections you've drawn between the sources. In addition, you should have identified your audience and purpose in writing, and you have gathered some detailed notes that will support your preliminary focus. Now it's time to begin sifting that raw material to see what's useful for your target audience and your goal in writing.

You may feel a bit overwhelmed by this step in writing from sources, but considering your audience and purpose will help you focus on the most relevant information to include. If you know that your reader is completely unfamiliar with the topic, then you'll have to collect background information. If your reader is already familiar with the basics, you can move quickly into a more sophisticated analysis or argument.

What support will you need to flesh out your paper? Again, consider your reader. Will the reader be most likely to respond to facts, history, examples, charts and tables, analysis, or expert testimony? Look over your materials to see just what you have available in your sources and your prewriting. Sometimes quick lists will help here. You might, for instance, jot down all the basic facts about Kennedy-Hawkins.

—proposed to offset unchanged m.w. since 1981
—would raise m.w. from $3.35 to $3.85 in first year
—includes indexing feature after 1990

Then you might list who will be affected and how.

—In 1986, 5.1 to 5.2 million workers received m.w.
—one-third are teenagers; 59% under 25
—many are students
—two-thirds live with a relative who also has a job
—few work 40 hours weekly (only 18% work full-time, year-round)
—80 percent live in families with incomes above poverty line
—42 percent are adult women

Do you see how the information gathered here comes from different sources? Depending on your specific angle on the topic, your reader, and your purpose, you will need to choose information from the various sources and synthesize views. After you organize the information you have at hand, you will be able to see if you need more information or if you are ready to begin drafting.

At this point, Randall felt ready to begin pulling material together with additional prewriting, so he spent eighteen minutes cubing (three minutes on each perspective).

STUDENT EXAMPLE *Cubing on the Minimum Wage*

Describe it

The minimum-wage laws before Congressional committees are designed to raise the minimum wage from $3.35 to around $5.00 an hour. The bills are to help the poor by increasing their standard of living. The bills, however, would increase unemployment and pass on higher costs to the public. The bills are misdirected. The people who make up the minimum-wage earners are largely teens and only a few are full-time workers.

Compare it

Raising the minimum wage would be like a mandatory increase of children's allowances. If every parent was forced to raise allowances, the negative effects would far outweigh the positive. Parents would be forced to put out more money that could be better spent on food, clothing, and shelter. The only thing the children would gain is more money to spend on video games and toys, which would not enhance their lives.

Associate it

When I hear people think of raising the minimum wage I think, "don't do it." The raise would force small businesses to shovel out more money and raise their prices to cover it. But the public would not like the increase and businesses would suffer; that could lead to the businesses laying off other employees. People who work for the minimum are rarely head of the house. I see most of them are teenagers working a summer job for some extra cash.

Analyze it

The need for this bill has come from the concern about the poor and underprivileged class in America. The legislation is designed to help Americans but it will not in the end. The bill would lead to unemployment, loss of job training for young workers, and higher prices. The bill has good intentions but we need to explore alternatives.

Apply it

The bill needs to be defeated. The alternatives should be explored. Like a training wage, a lower wage for teenagers, and an increase in the earned-income tax. These alternatives could help the people who really need it. The bill would most likely hurt them by decreasing the actual take home pay. Job training for the unskilled should also be invested in.

Argue for or against

The bill must be defeated. If it passes, the local McDonald's will be forced to hire fewer people. They will look for ways to spend the same amount on employees and get the same output. The skills that McDonald's offers help teens to get experience and their next job. With a good work record at McDonald's they prove they are responsible, can show up on time, and can learn new skills. No one counts on knowing how to flip burgers.

Randall's position in the controversy became clear: he was obviously opposed to the Kennedy-Hawkins bill and any mandated raises in the minimum wage. And so he determined that he was ready to begin writing to his classmates to convince them that his position on minimum-wage legislation was the correct one. He synthesized old and new information to focus his topic for his readers and cut out much extraneous information from his reading to concentrate on the most important facts and arguments he would probably use in his paper.

DRAFTING

Perhaps even more than other kinds of writing are, writing a paper from sources is recursive. As a writer, you'll double back on the writing process several times. You'll prewrite, read, analyze, synthesize, draft, read, rewrite, prewrite, read, and so on, several times. What is sometimes most frustrating about this kind of writing is that reading and writing about source material can go on forever. The best approach is to set a deadline and write a draft.

The discovery draft is often helpful in writing a paper from sources. Give yourself a time limit, put your notes and sources in front of you, and begin writing. When you find that you cannot develop a point because you don't have enough information, leave a blank space on the page or on the computer screen and make a note about what information to check later. Don't go scurrying to the library. Instead, complete the entire draft and look over all the places you might want to supplement with more information. You may be able to rearrange or refocus rather than seek out more information. Even if you have to go look for other sources, at least you can make the next trip to the library or the next call for an interview as productive as possible for the entire paper.

Randall felt prepared at this point to draft his paper on minimum wage. He collected his prewriting, his notes, and his sources and jotted down a few points that he thought could help him through the draft.

—helps the people it needs to
—hurts small business
—hurts America's competitiveness
—raises unemployment
—the make-up of minimum wage workers
—hurts business and job training

Then he wrote this discovery draft.

STUDENT EXAMPLE *First Draft*

Poverty has finally become a concern of Congress. The Kennedy-Hawkins bill could be labeled as the solution, but it is not a good one. The bill would raise the minimum wage from the present level of $3.35 an hour to $4.65 over three years and would automatically increase the wage to 50% of the average hourly wage thereafter. The bill has good intentions but it cannot accomplish them and instead hurts the people it was designed to help, hurts small businesses, and hurts America as a whole by raising unemployment. Kennedy-Hawkins would create more harm than it would benefits.

The workers Kennedy-Hawkins was designed to help work full-time for minimum wage. Their numbers, however, make up a small percentage of the total minimum-wage employees. One-third of the minimum-wage workers are teenagers and forty-two percent are adult women. Seventy percent of minimum wage workers have another wage earner in the family. The percentage of full-time minimum-wage workers stands at only 18 percent. If the wage floor rises, many of these jobs would disappear due to the cost increase. The full-time worker receives benefits beyond his wages. As a full-time employee he or she is entitled to the company's health programs and similar benefits and in effect receives more than the wage. The cost of these programs combined with the increased wages would force companies to eliminate the positions, favoring part-time employees who are not entitled to the benefits.

Small business would be heavily burdened by any bill like Kennedy-Hawkins. The increase in the minimum wage would generate an increased operating cost that could have the potential to drive the business out of operation. The business owner's only option would be to pass the increase on to the consumer. This increase in certain markets would dramatically affect business. In Fort Collins, for example, businesses such as the restaurant, The Charco-Broiler, would suffer losses as people were forced to eat at home more often due to their inability to afford the cost increases.

This increase leads to my last point. As The Charco-Broiler suffered losses it would in turn be forced to lay off employees, thus increasing the local unemployment. The unemployment situation would be reflected throughout the nation. Richard B. McKenzie, Professor of Economics at Clemson University, estimates that 1.9 million jobs would vanish in an eight-year period. America's economic health would surely suffer from this unemployment increase.

Legislation such as Kennedy-Hawkins has good intentions but as you can see its negative aspects prevent it from being a feasible solution to the low-wage problem. The Congress might instead explore options such as increasing the earned income tax credit or redirecting tax money to more and better job-training programs. Raising the minimum wage is not the answer.

Randall has a good starting point here, but he needs to revise carefully to appeal to his target reader, connect ideas more smoothly, develop points in more detail, and identify sources for his information. Still, he may have finished the most difficult part of writing from sources—moving from the preliminary reading and writing to a draft that he can revise.

WRITING *Drafting the Paper from Sources*

1. Look back at Randall's draft to analyze what he has done up to this point in his writing process.
   a. Identify the working thesis of Randall's draft. Can he develop his points in adequate detail in a short paper? What material will he need to support these points?
   b. Has he targeted his audience successfully with the points he plans to include?
   c. Identify the weakest paragraph in Randall's draft. Does it include too many notes from sources not yet synthesized into his own language? Does it contain enough evidence to convince you that his point is valid?

  d. What suggestions would you make to Randall to help him revise this draft for a more successful paper?
2. Collect all your preliminary writing and draft your paper from sources.

FINDING ADDITIONAL SOURCES

Finding additional materials through the library has gotten considerably easier in recent years and is likely to continue to get easier. Ten years ago, students had no choice but to learn to use several kinds of bibliographic tools. Now, however, many college and even public libraries have computer-based bibliographic tools that simplify and shorten the research process.

Computerized Bibliographic Tools

Almost all libraries will have access to computer databases in several disciplines. Working with a librarian, you determine the key words that will identify your topic. The librarian connects a local computer with a large computerized database over the telephone. Sometimes within minutes, sometimes a day later, you collect a list of sources related to your topic. Unfortunately, the list may include many entries you cannot use, so you need to be selective as you look up sources. Also, you may not have all the journals and books cited on the list in your library, so you may need to use inter-library loans to get the best sources. Finally, most libraries can provide this service only for a fee based on the database searched and the size of your printed list.

The most recent technological breakthrough in bibliographic searches, though, is often available for free. Many libraries subscribe to services that provide optical disk databases (also called CD-ROM databases), which contain titles of journal articles. The library gets the disk and loads it into a computer, and then library users have direct access to the information through terminals located in the library. Using these databases, you can enter your topic or key words and immediately scan the entries under that topic. The optical disks are usually updated monthly or quarterly, so the entries are current. Many of these services cover topics in broader fields than the dial-in databases noted above. For instance, InfoTrac, a widely available optical disk database, provided the entries shown on the following page in a search under "minimum wages."

Clearly, this list covers far more aspects of minimum wage than any one person would want to write on. But just scanning this partial list gives you an idea of how such a bibliographic source can help you get ideas about different angles on a topic. The full list of 140 entries covering February, 1985, to March, 1988, took about 20 minutes to compile and print out!

MINIMUM WAGE RESTORATION ACT OF 1987 (DRAFT)

Raising the minimum wage. Congressional Digest
v66-Aug-Sept'87 p193(1)

Should the "Minimum Wage Restoration Act of 1987"
be approved? (pro and con) by Edward M. Kennedy,
Walter Ellis Jr., Lane Kirkland, Douglas Fontaine,
Jack Sheinkman, Matthew Runci, Jay Mazur and John R.
Glennie Congressional Digest v66-Aug-Sept'87
p200(24)

Minimum-wage proposal could boost labor costs. by
Teri Merrill il Hospitals v61-June 5'87 p32(2)

MINIMUM WAGE RESTORATION ACT (DRAFT)

ACTW to Congress: set still higher minimum wage.
(Amalgamated Clothing and Textile Workers Union)
Daily News Record v17-July 24'87 p4(1)

MINIMUM WAGE COALITION TO SAVE JOBS

Minimum wage myths. (response to proposed
legislation; includes membership list of Senate and
House committees considering legislation) il
Nation's Business v75-June'87 p35(4)
39J0982   31W2419

MINIMUM WAGE COALITION TO SAVE JOBS

High marks for the 100th. (includes major actions
of the 100th Congress) by Albert G. Holzinger il
Nation's Business v76-Dec'88 p14(3)

A victory on minimum wage. by Donald C. Bacon
Nation's Business v76-Nov'88 p45(1)
47A0314   41R1048

Business group fights minimum-wage increase.
(report by the Minimum Wage Coalition to Save Jobs)
by Rick Pullen American Metal Market v96-Aug 24'88
p20(1)

Minimum wage myths. (response to proposed
legislation; includes membership list of Senate and
House committees considering legislation) il
Nation's Business v75-June'87 p35(4)
39J0982   31W2419

Bibliographic Tools on Paper

If you need to search for sources without having a computer database to help you, first ask the librarian which indexes and abstracts are most likely to help you find materials on your topic. It's OK to use the *Reader's Guide to Current Periodicals,* but don't be satisfied with it alone. The *Reader's Guide* covers mostly popular magazines rather than academic ones. Look also in indexes like the following:

Art Index

Bibliographic Index

Biological Abstracts

Business Periodicals Index

Chemistry Abstracts

Economics Index

Education Index

Engineering Index

Humanities Index

New York Times Index

Psychological Abstracts

Resources in Education

Social Science Index

At the front of each index or abstract, you'll find a list of the journals indexed and a guide on how to use the index. Get familiar with the indexes and abstracts related to your field because you'll use these tools over and over. These indexes usually have one complete listing for prior years and then either quarterly or monthly listings for the current year. Be sure to begin with the current listings and to go back as far as you need to for appropriate sources.

If this is your first intensive work in the library, get to know the reference librarians. Their job is to help you find materials, and they know more about reference and bibliographic tools than you can imagine. So ask!

CITING SOURCES

When you deal with sources, take notes or summarize in your own words. (If you use the author's words and claim them as your own, you're plagiarizing.) Your mind will connect what you've read and what you know much better if you use your own words to describe what you have read. Finally, despite the temptation to quote or paraphrase extensively, most writers find that these methods are much wordier than writing the gist of a source in their own words. So quote directly only those short passages you simply can't say better, and be sure to document each quotation.

Here is a paragraph quoted from the *Encyclopaedia Britannica* followed by a paraphrase of the information. (In a direct quote, you copy the material exactly as it appears in the original, word for word, putting quotation marks around it or setting it off in an indented paragraph. In paraphrasing, you put down the author's ideas in a coherent, readable form, but in your own words.)

Quote

"*The History of Tom Jones, a Foundling* was published on February 28, 1749. With its great comic gusto, vast gallery of characters, and contrasted scenes of high and low life in London and the provinces, it has always been the most popular of his works. The reading of this work is essential both for an understanding of 18th-century England and for its revelation of the generosity and charity of Fielding's view of humanity."

Paraphrase

Three things made Henry Fielding's novel, *The History of Tom Jones, a Foundling,* published on February 28, 1749, popular. The book is full of blustering humor, there are a large number of characters in the novel, and Fielding gives pictures of upper-class and lower-class, everyday activities in England. When you read this book, you can see Fielding's attitude toward all people, rich and poor, especially how much he understood nature.

Notice that even though this quote has been completely paraphrased, it should still be acknowledged in a note, because all the ideas came from the outside source.

Plagiarism

To plagiarize is to take someone else's words and/or ideas and put them into your writing as though they were yours. Most plagiarism in students' research papers occurs through carelessness, uncertainty, or ignorance. Some simple rules will help you know how to avoid plagiarism.

1. Always put quotation marks around any direct statement from someone else's work. Also document such a quotation.

2. Document any paraphrase of another writer's ideas or statements.

3. Document any thoughts you got from a specific source in your reading.

4. Document any material, ideas, or thoughts you got from your reading that can't be described as general knowledge.

5. Document any summary (even if in your own words) of a discussion from one of your sources.

6. Document any charts, graphs, or tables made by others or any you make with others' information.

DOCUMENTATION

Documenting a paper from sources requires detailed and meticulous work—it can also be frustrating and time-consuming. Clear documentation provides the reader with all the information he or she needs to know to pursue the subject further. It tells the reader if the source of the information is a book, an article in a book or journal, a newspaper, or a personal interview. There are two main elements required to document research papers: parenthetical documentation and a bibliography.

Parenthetical documentation consists of inserting information into the body of your paper wherever you refer to the words, facts, or ideas of someone else. The author's last name and a page reference in parentheses at the point of reference will identify the source and location of the information and inform the reader that more specific details can be found in your bibliography.

Bibliography means "description of books" and is a list of all the sources you used to compile your paper. This is where you give the reader detailed information about the parenthetical references that appear earlier in your paper. The bibliography is not limited to books, magazines, journals, and newspapers. It may also contain more information about personal interviews, recordings, films, or any other sources of information.

Different areas of study have their own styles of documentation, and each instructor will tell students what style to use. As a general rule, the humanities use the Modern Language Association (MLA) style, while the American Psychological Association (APA) style is used in psychology, education, and the social sciences.

MLA Style—Parenthetical Documentation

For a full treatment of the MLA system of documentation, consult the *MLA Handbook for Writers of Research Papers, Theses, and Dissertations,* 2nd ed. (New York: Modern Language Association, 1984).

If you refer to the entire work of an author, rather than just part of it, you should include the author's name in the text.

> Clark says that Greek and Roman societies fell because they were "exhausted."

If you decide not to use the author's name in your text, then it must be included in a parenthetical reference.

Greek and Roman societies fell because they were "exhausted" (Clark).

If, however, you are citing only a specific passage in a book or article, the page number or numbers must be given in parentheses. If the author's name appears in the text you need give page numbers only.

Gould says that dinosaurs may, in fact, be living today—as birds (217).

If not:

Dinosaurs may be living today—as birds (Gould 217).

The emphasis in parenthetical documentation, as you can see, is on the author and the page number. More detailed information is reserved for the bibliographical entries. Here are more examples to show variations in documenting sources.

Two or More Authors

Always cite all authors in a work by two or three authors, but in works with more than three authors, cite the first author followed by *et al*.

(Reid and Findlay 26)

(Raymond, Larson, and Lloyd-Jones 93)

(Emig, et al. 67)

No Author

When no author is identified, use the first few words of the title or a significant word in the title.

("Anti-Darwinism")

Multiple Citations

To cite several sources at the same point in your text, refer to the last names of the authors, in alphabetical order. Include an author's first name if you have more than one title by authors with the same last name in your bibliography.

(Bellow, Fortner, Gallahad, Frank Smith)

MLA Style—Bibliographical Documentation

The bibliography, or works cited page, is usually the last page or pages of your documented paper; it lists in alphabetical order all the sources you directly cite in your work. The page should be titled Works Cited.

Punctuation, form, and information change slightly for various kinds of materials—articles, newspaper stories, essays and so on, but the basic conventions remain the same. The following examples illustrate the proper form for the most common bibliographical entries.

Books with One Author

Travis, Dempsey J. *An Autobiography of Black Jazz*. Chicago: Urban Research Institute, 1983.

Two or Three Authors

Harris, Fred R., and Paul L. Hain. *America's Legislative Processes: Congress and the States*. Glenview: Scott, 1983.

Four or More Authors

Burns, Robert E., et al. *Episodes in American History*. Lexington, MA: Ginn, 1973.

No Author Cited

Caterpillar Tractor Company. *Caterpillar and the Balance of Payments*. Peoria, IL: Caterpillar Tractor Co., 1984.

Editors

Cosman, Carol, Joan Keefe and Kathleen Weaver, eds. *The Penguin Book of Women Poets*. New York: Penguin, 1979.

Editions

Hartnoll, Phyllis, ed. *The Oxford Companion to the Theatre*. 2nd ed. Oxford: Oxford UP, 1983.

More Than One Volume

Morison, Samuel Eliot and Henry Steele Commager. *The Growth of the American Republic*. New York: Oxford UP, 1962. 2: 211–228.

A Work in an Anthology

Nemiroff, Robert, ed. "What Use Are Flowers?" *Lorraine Hansberry: The Collected Last Plays*. New York: New American Library, 1983.

A Translation

Homer. *The Odyssey*. Trans. Robert Fitzgerald. London: Panther, 1971.

Book in a Series

Wedgwood, C. V. *The World of Rubens*. Time-Life Library of Art. New York: Time, 1967.

Article in a Reference Work

(If the article is signed give the author first; if it is unsigned, give the title first.)

> Allen, Walter E. "Fielding, Henry." *Encyclopaedia Britannica.* 1980 ed.

> "Japan." *The Random House Encyclopedia.* 1977.

Article from a Monthly Magazine

> Howard, Michael. "The Bewildered American Raj." *Harper's* Mar. 1985: 55–60.

Article from a Weekly Magazine

> Sidey, Hugh. "Measure of the Man." *Time* 25 Mar. 1985: 27.

Article from a Scholarly Journal

> Adams, David Wallace. "Illinois Soldiers and the Emancipation Proclamation." *Journal of the Illinois State Historical Society.* 67 (1974): 406–421.

Review

> Corliss, Richard. "Mozart's Greatest Hit." Rev. of Amadeus. New York: *Time* 10 Sept. 1984: 74–75.

Newspaper Article (Signed and Unsigned)

> Davis, L. J. "Rochester: An Unlikely City of Surprises." *Chicago Tribune* 17 March 1985, final ed.: 12.

> "Stronger Link to Canada." Editorial. *Herald-News* [Joliet, IL] 21 Mar. 1985: 1.

Recording

> Richie, Lionel, et al. *Can't Slow Down.* Produced by Lionel Richie and James Anthony Carmichael. Motown, 6059ML, 1983.

APA Style—Parenthetical Documentation

For a full account of the APA system for preparing manuscripts, consult the *Publication Manual of the American Psychological Association,* 3rd ed. (Washington, D.C.: American Psychological Association, 1983).

While the MLA style of parenthetical documentation emphasizes the author and the page number in its system, APA style stresses the author and the date.

Within the paper acknowledgements are made informally either in the *text* of the paper, in *parentheses,* or in *both.* The information is brief, but sufficient to key each citation to the list of works at the end of the paper and to help readers find the cited material within a work.

A citation could be handled in any of these ways.

In 1985, Hibbard discovered three startling facts
In recent research on this topic (Hibbard, 1985)
Hibbard (1985) discovered

These examples show ways to document a work by one author. Here are more examples, showing variations on this model.

Two or More Authors

For two authors, use both names each time you cite their work.

Hibbard and Johnson (1985) discovered
In recent research on this topic (Hibbard & Johnson, 1985)

For more than two authors, use all names the first time you cite their work, but use only the name of the first author with *et al.* after that.

Hibbard, Johnson, Korski, and Clark (1985) discovered
Hibbard et al. (1985) discovered

No Author

For works with no identified author, use the first few words of the title of the work.

In recent research on this topic, ("Research in Writing," 1984)

Multiple Citations

For more than one work at a single point in your text, arrange the citations chronologically.

In recent research on this topic, (Hibbard, 1984, 1985)

For works by more than one author in a single citation, arrange the names alphabetically.

In recent research on this topic, (Hibbard & Johnson, 1985; Korski, 1984)

Citation of a Part of a Source

For specific pages or chapters, add page or chapter numbers after the date. Note that page numbers *must* be given for quotations.

Hibbard (1985, pp. 3–4)
Hibbard and Johnson (1985, chap. 5)

APA Style—Bibliographical Documentation

All works cited in your paper should be included in a list, entitled "References," beginning on a separate page at the end of your paper. (Do not include works you have not cited in your paper.) This reference list provides full identifying information, enabling your reader to find these works for further use.

Books with One Author

Kingstone, Brett. (1981). *The Student Entrepreneur's Guide*. Berkeley: Ten Speed Press.

Two or More Authors

Gazvoda, Edward A., Jr., Haney, William M. III, & Greenya, John. (1983). *The Harvard Entrepreneurs Society's Guide to Making Money or the Tycoon's Handbook*. Boston: Little, Brown.

No Author Cited

The Entrepreneurial Life. (1983). New York: John Wiley & Sons.

Editors

Odell, Lee. (1985). Beyond the text: Relations between writing and the social context. In L. Odell & D. Goswami (Eds.), *Writing in Nonacademic Settings*. New York: Guilford.

Editions

Toulmin, S. E., Rieke, R., & Janik, A. (1984). *An Introduction to Reasoning*. (2nd ed.). New York: Macmillan.

More Than One Volume

Scardamalia, M. (1981). How children cope with the cognitive demands of writing. In C. H. Frederiksen & J. F. Dominic, (Eds.), *Writing* (Vol. 2, pp81–103). Hillsdale, NJ: Lawrence Erlbaum.

A Work in an Anthology

Brancato, R. (1985). The fourth of July. In D. Gallo (Ed.) *Sixteen: Short Stories by Outstanding Young Adult Authors*. New York: Dell.

A Translation

Plato (1956). Phaedrus (W. C. Helmbold & W. G. Rabinowitz, Trans.). Indianapolis, IN: Liberal Arts Press, 1956. (Original work published in the 4th Century B.C.)

Article in a Reference Work

Cochran, Thomas C. (1968). Entrepreneurship. *International Encyclopedia of Social Science.*

Article from a Monthly Magazine

Silver, A. David. (1983, November). The anatomy of an entrepreneur. *Science Digest,* p. 18.

Article from a Weekly Magazine

Drucker, Peter F., Professor, Claremont Graduate School, California. (1984, March 26). Interview. *U.S. News & World Report,* pp. 68–69.

Article from a Scholarly Journal

Our entrepreneurial economy. (1984, Jan./Feb.). *Harvard Business Review,* pp. 59–64.

THE FINAL DRAFT

The final draft of a paper from sources must go through all the revising and editing that you would do on any paper. (See Chapters 12 and 13.) But in addition you need to pay attention to another set of details—the information about sources. Let's look at Randall's final draft of the paper on minimum wage to see not only what he revised but also what sources he cited for the information included in the paper.

Raising the Minimum, Raising Concern

Helping the poor to overcome their situation has become a growing concern in America. As a nation, we have looked for programs and policies to improve their status and this has led to federal legislation such as the proposed Kennedy-Hawkins bill. If passed, Kennedy-Hawkins would raise the minimum wage from the present level of $3.35 to $4.65 an hour over three years and increase the wage automatically to 50 percent of the average hourly wage thereafter ("Anti-Darwinism"). The intentions of this bill are entirely positive; however, Kennedy-Hawkins or any other legislation of the same nature would accomplish the opposite for the people it was designed for—it would increase unemployment and hurt the country's economic situation.

Giving a worker more money appears to improve his or her financial situation, but the converse actually happens. The worker very often receives more than just a money wage. In addition to hourly compensation, many employees receive extra benefits such as health insurance, company discounts, and flexible schedules (Lee and McKenzie 55). As hourly costs rise, employers cut their total costs by reducing or eliminating benefit packages, leaving the employee no better off than before the wage increase. Workers whose compensation consisted solely of the minimum wage might find themselves unemployed because the first jobs cut are those of the least value. Rarely in history has management been laid off before labor, and the first workers to go are also the youngest. Teenagers make up one-third of the minimum-wage work force (Campbell 103). As cuts are made, the jobs they hold will be eliminated first. Without these jobs, America's young lack the opportunity to develop the job skills that would allow them to move out of minimum-wage positions.

The country as a whole would also suffer a negative impact due to the increase in unemployment. The businesses would be forced to cut jobs due to the minimum wage hike. Robert B. McKenzie, a professor of economics at Clemson University, estimates that 1.9 million jobs would vanish in the eight-year period following the wage hike ("Job Loss" 103). Areas of low unemployment could absorb the increase because they already pay wages above the federal minimum to attract people to job openings (Ormiston). However, in areas with high unemployment, like the oil producing states of Texas, Oklahoma, and Louisiana, the effect would be extremely damaging. It could possibly send their local economies from recession into depression.

Another way the country would suffer economically stems from a ripple effect created by the minimum wage elevation. When the wage floor rises, the people above it demand a pay increase too (Campbell). The reason is, of course, that they feel they must be separated from workers traditionally paid less. The rise throughout the pay scale cannot be absorbed by benefit cuts or layoffs. Businesses would be forced to increase the prices they charge for their goods and services. This effect spread throughout the nation has the potential to start an upswing in the rate of inflation. That type of dollar devaluation would be felt within the country and in our overseas buying power as the dollar slips down in value against foreign currency, placing the overall economic health of America in jeopardy.

Legislation such as Kennedy-Hawkins has good intentions, but the negative aspects prevent it from being a feasible solution to the low wage earner's problem. The Congress might instead explore options such as increasing the earned-income tax credit or redirecting funds to more and better job training programs. Raising the minimum wage is not the answer.

Works Cited

"Anti-Darwinism." The Economist 9 Jan. 1988: 24–25.

Campbell, Jeffrey. "Don't Raise the Minimum Wage." Fortune 31 Aug. 1987: 103–104.

"Job Loss from Wage Hike." Nation's Business Sept. 1987: 103.

Lee, Dwight R., and Richard B. McKenzie. "Minimum Wage: A Weaker Case Both For and Against." Challenge Sept./Oct. 1987: 55–56.

Ormiston, Kathy Ann. "States Know Best What Labor's Worth." The Wall Street Journal 10 May 1988: 34.

Randall has narrowed his focus to exclude the concern with small business; clearly that point is less likely to sway his target reader thinking of getting a job next summer. By focusing on only two points in his argument, Randall has developed each point more fully.

Moreover, Randall has integrated his source material more smoothly in this draft. The notes from sources no longer seem to be tacked together without transitional elements or a flow of logic.

Finally, with the careful documentation Randall has provided, any reader could return to Randall's sources to see just how he has drawn on those materials to support his argument about minimum wage.

WRITING FROM SOURCES—A FINAL REMINDER

Throughout this text, we've emphasized using the writer's knowledge and experience, as well as writing skills, in communicating with a reader. Writing from sources is just like all other writing in that the writer must make outside source materials part of his or her fund of knowledge to draw on as a writer. From that point on, writing from sources is basically the same as any other kind of writing. The process may be more complex and extended in time, but it follows basically the same patterns as all other writing. Only in final editing must you again concern yourself with the details of citing sources and documenting your work properly. So don't let this part of the process intimidate you. Focus on your writing rather than your documentation, and you'll find that writing from sources can be informative and especially rewarding for both you and your reader.

WRITING *Writing a Paper from Sources*

1. Use the sources presented earlier to begin work on a paper on the minimum wage. Be sure to find an angle on the topic that will interest you *and your specified audience*. Some possible perspectives you might pursue are shown on the following page.

The minimum wage has been called "chump change." Is it? Why do you feel this way?

Many employers say they have a hard time filling minimum-wage jobs. Is the problem the wage or is it the location of the jobs?

How does minimum wage affect inner-city teens compared to sub-urban teens?

Do you agree that employers should be able to pay subminimum wages? For what jobs? For how long?

What is the status of minimum wage in your state? How would state laws affect you should you decide to take a summer job to help pay tuition next year?

Does the minimum wage discriminate against women? Some proponents of raising the wage argue that at its lower rate it discriminates against black youth who constitute about one third of the minimum-wage work force. But women make up 42% of the minimum-wage work force, so how does this argument apply to them?

2. Draft and document your paper from sources on the alternate topic you've chosen.

CHAPTER 16

Writing Essay Tests

The essay test is no more difficult to master than are other forms of writing. Once you learn the conventions of writing essay exams and have a chance to practice them, you should be able to write an essay exam that does justice to the time and energy you spent preparing for it.

Instructors give essay exams to see whether you can discuss the important concepts of a course. This means you don't have to come up with a topic to write about; you just have to present the instructor with an orderly essay that shows you know the assigned topic—that shows you understand what you've heard, discussed, studied, or read in the course.

PREPARING TO WRITE AN ESSAY EXAM

Here are some ways to prepare yourself to write a good essay exam.

Tip #1: Before You Enter the Exam Room

Study, of course, but with a twist. Focus on answering those questions the instructor is likely to ask. Instead of drowning yourself in a sea of dates and details, get a sense of the major ideas discussed in class. Think about relationships among these ideas. (If you're keeping a double-entry journal for the course, look at connections you've noted among ideas. Answer any questions you've jotted down in the right-hand section of your journal where you've noted points that were not clear in your reading.) Posing questions the instructor might ask will help you organize your understanding of the material. You can prepare alone, or you might want to get together with classmates. Even if the test questions are nothing like what you've come up with, asking and answering relevant questions will assure you of understanding concepts rather than simple facts.

Tip #2: Get an Overview

Instead of jumping into the first exam question and writing about it, feverishly, for 50 out of 60 minutes, look over the entire exam carefully for these two important reasons:

- If you have several topics from which to choose, you can choose the one(s) you feel most confident about.

- By finding out what questions you will be writing about later on, you encourage your mind to start collecting and remembering material that is relevant to the later questions. (Ever try hard to remember somebody's name, only to have the name surface in your mind much later, like while doing your homework? That's how the subconscious mind works.) While you are writing about the first question, your subconscious mind can be thinking ahead to the second question. This means that if you get stuck while on the first, you can move ahead to the second (making use of the "brainstorms" you experienced while doing Tip #1).

Tip #3: Read the Questions Carefully

Unfortunately, many students get stuck right at the beginning by not reading the test questions carefully. Before you plunge into the test, ask yourself, "What does this question tell me to do?" Focusing on a specific writing task can organize your thinking and writing. A secret of successful exam-taking is: *don't write until you know what you're being asked to write about*.

How do you figure out what you're being asked? The wording of the question itself will tell you. Are you being asked to explain, discuss, evaluate, summarize, analyze, classify, illustrate, or do something else? In Chapter 10, we noted that the thesis and sometimes the form for many essay tests are stated in the questions themselves. When you are asked to "explain," "illustrate," or "discuss," you know you will be Writing to Inform. Other key terms suggest *specific* forms. "Evaluate" suggests an *evaluation* essay; "argue" suggests an *assertion-with-evidence* or *persuasion* essay. Once you identify the kind of writing required by underlining or highlighting those key words in the question, you will be able to use the writing skills you already have.

GETTING STARTED

By now, you probably think about the creating stage and ways to find something to say when you approach a writing assignment. Well, this assignment is different: you don't have to come up with a topic because the instructor's question does that for you. In this case, creating means recollecting—recalling the information you have studied. No amount of cubing or looping and the like will give you material for an answer that you haven't already stored in your mind.

But let's assume that you have studied—what can you do next? Many of the Prewriting tools we discussed in Chapters 3 and 4 will serve you well.

- *Listing*. Probably the best thing to do is take a piece of paper and write down the main points that come to mind immediately. This is a time when a quick outline or a list will probably be most effective. Your aim is to draw out or remember what you have studied and apply it to the topic presented.

- *Brainstorming*. This lets you get all sorts of thoughts about your topic down on paper, even "dumb" or "irrelevant" ones. Once you see them displayed on paper, you can separate the useful ideas from the useless ones.

- *The Reporter's Formula*. All five questions that make up the Reporter's Formula might not be pertinent to the test question, but asking them will often help you remember points that you can use in your response.

- *Clustering*. Choose a key term from the test question and use it as the center idea in a cluster. You can collect details quickly and organize them efficiently later.

- *Branching*. As you would do for clustering, start with a key term from the test question. Subdivide it to help you see a possible organization for your paper. This technique is especially helpful when you are asked to analyze parts of something or to compare/contrast.

Once you have come up with a list of points or a group of ideas from the other prewriting techniques, put the ones you want to include in the margin of your paper so that you can see them from time to time as you write the answer. (Also, your instructor will be able to see the list if you run out of time and see where you had planned to go with the answer.)

FROM CREATING TO DRAFTING

Drafting is a critical step in writing an essay-test response because you won't have time for much substantial revising. In most responses, the first draft will be the final draft.

Audience as Shaper: Instructor as Audience

Your instructor is the audience for your essay-test response because he or she is the one who will evaluate it. There are two important things to keep in mind about your audience that will help you to shape your draft.

1. The instructor will have many similar tests to read and will probably get tired of reading them.

2. The instructor already knows the answer to the question and is just trying to determine if you know the answer and have included everything that should be included in a good response.

Writing essay-test answers is a limited communication process. Instead of trying to get the reader's attention, you can count on having it. Instructors are, after all, paid to read the tests, and they are usually conscientious about doing that. You can't count, however, on the instructor's not getting tired, bored, or confused, or being persuaded that you don't know a thing (any of which may affect your grade). Drafting a clear response is extremely important because it allows you to show exactly what you know and lets the instructor get right to the point in reading the test. You should have these objectives:

1. Prove immediately that you know the material.

2. Be as organized as possible.

3. Be as specific as possible.

What the instructor wants to know from your test answers is not the information itself—she or he already knows this—but rather whether *you* know the information.

Start with a Thesis

In drafting essay-test responses, begin immediately with a sentence that tells the instructor what you are going to discuss. This will be the topic sentence or thesis sentence of your answer. (In fact, your entire answer will probably be one long topic sentence paragraph or a series of topic sentence paragraphs.) Many exam questions state a thesis or at least narrow the field, telling you what *not* to write about. In either case, you must be sure to begin your response with a thesis. The best time to develop one is before you begin writing—not after. Otherwise you (and your instructor) will wander in a maze of random thoughts.

You need not begin the answer with the same kind of lead-in, attention-getting opening you use in essays when you have to attract your reader's attention. Instead, get right to the point. What is paramount here is the subject matter. The instructor is interested in knowing that you know the material, so you must immediately make it clear that you *do* know the material.

Follow Through with Specifics

The next thing you must do in the essay answer is present the information. If you can put it in a series of three to five points, give these swiftly and clearly. Then for each point give an example or two. Your instructor wants to know whether you know the material and whether you understand it. Be specific. Quote as many relevant facts, and give as many relevant examples, as you can in the time allowed.

Don't Pad. It's always a temptation to simply fill up the paper with words, any words. Avoid this temptation. An instructor who has read between 15 and 50 exams on the same subject gets tired quickly of excess baggage in an answer.

Don't Show Off. You likewise may be tempted to insert material that isn't called for, just because you know it. But most instructors aren't impressed by extraneous information—they tend to see it as a smokescreen. You're better off focusing clearly on what you *do* know and keeping to the thesis.

Decide on Form

The answer to the dilemma of what form to use lies in the question. If you are asked to "compare and contrast" A and B (that is, how are they the same and how are they different?), you would first describe A in terms of characteristics 1, 2, and 3, and then describe B in terms of the same characteristics—1, 2, and 3. That takes care of how they are the same. Then you would discuss how they are different.

If you are asked to "Trace the development of X," you would use a time order: *first this happened, then that happened, then the next thing happened,* all the way up to the conclusion.

If you are asked to "Show how U resulted in V" (or "Show how V was the result of U"), you would use a cause-and-effect form: *this cause led to that effect,* or *this effect was due to these causes.*

And so it goes. You can rely on your experience writing full-fledged essays to get you through this part.

What to Do If You Think of a New Point While Writing

As you know, writing itself often generates new ideas, retrieves information you had forgotten, and stirs up your thinking. If this happens while you are writing an essay-test answer, put a quick note to yourself in the margin (you can scratch it out later) and after you've finished the point you're making, look for a minute at your list and think where your new point might fit best. The important thing is not to run off with the new thought in the middle of what you are writing. Instructors are no different from other human beings—they like order. They, like the readers of any other essay, need to be able to see where you are going. Rambling answers will confuse and perhaps even annoy your instructor. Having a definite order to your answer, where you clearly go from one point to another, helps convince your instructor that you know the material.

You can always add your afterthoughts by inserting them above the line, using a caret (^) to indicate where they go. You can also add the new material at the end of your answer, draw a neat box around it, and make a note at the appropriate place in the essay to tell the instructor to turn to the boxed paragraph(s) on page X.

REVISING AND POLISHING

Obviously, you won't have the leisure to revise and edit extensively, but it pays to save the last 20 percent of your allotted time to re-read and edit.

Questions to Guide Your Revisions

Be sure to make it easy for your instructor to follow your thoughts. Ask yourself these questions.

1. *Have I stuck to my thesis?* Wandering off the topic is confusing to both writer and reader. It's better to present a shorter, more coherent essay than a longer, aimless one. If you get confused re-reading your answer, you can be sure the instructor will, too. Cross out any stray or extra thoughts, and keep only what relates to your thesis.

2. *Have I used topic sentences and topic sentence paragraphs?* When you write an essay exam, you need to emphasize the topic sentences; like the thesis, they tell the reader what you are writing about. In a regular essay, you would use both topic sentence paragraphs and function paragraphs; in a test essay, you use primarily topic sentence paragraphs because you must pack a lot of information into a relatively short space.

3. *Have I made sensible transitions from one paragraph to the next?* Although you won't use function paragraphs for drama or flow, don't dispense with transitions altogether. As the writer, your job is to guide the reader. One way is to insert signal words that direct your reader's attention, such as "however," "although," "consequently," "similarly," and so on. Another way is to use parallelism where appropriate—for example, "*The initial step is. . . . The second step is. . . . The final step is. . . .*" The easier you make it for the reader to follow your train of thought, the better off you (and your instructor) will be.

4. *Are my answers complete enough?* Have you presented enough evidence to let the reader agree with your thesis, or at least see how you arrived at it? Merely writing a sketchy, "that's the way it is because I say so" response won't convince the instructor that you understand the material. You need to give explanatory details—the facts and figures you have studied—to guide the reader toward your conclusion. In addition, some exams ask you to offer your own experiences, for example: *Discuss Erik*

Erikson's stages of identity, and apply these stages to your own life. In this case, your experience constitutes a legitimate illustration that the instructor wants to see to gauge your understanding of the concepts.

5. *Are the examples and illustrations I've chosen relevant?* Be selective about which illustrations and examples you offer. If the question causes five examples to spring to mind, use the two or three that are most likely to back up your thesis. Don't confuse quantity with quality. Go for quality.

What to Do If You Don't Know the Answer

Never leave a question blank. Even if you don't know specifics for an answer, write something. Two things can serve as sources of answers: (1) looping on class discussions, and (2) points you know about other things that might be applicable to the question.

If you cannot remember a single thing from what you've studied on the subject, looping may provide you with something to say. Decide how much time you have to spend on the question and divide that by thirds. Plan to loop for the first third and use the other two thirds to write the answer. Loop on class discussions.

I remember the professor saying . . .

I remember being in class and . . .

When you've finished the looping, look it over and spot as many points as you can that were made in class that you might somehow relate to the question. You may not be able to fully develop these points with textual material, but you can give *examples* that you make up. The important thing to remember is not to panic. Stir up your thinking by writing, pick out some points from class discussions that you can apply, and organize them well.

What to Do If You Run Out of Time

The best thing to do, of course, is not to run out of time. Watch the clock like a hawk. Divide the number of questions into the number of minutes and be precise about sticking to the allotted number of minutes per question. (Another way to divide the time if the questions are differing point values is to do the heavily weighted questions first and give them the most time.) Give up the illusion that you will always get to tell *everything* you know about a subject. Present the most important points first and move on when you run out of time.

If you *do* run out of time, however, you might choose one of the three alternatives listed on the following page.

1. Pick the question (from those that are left) you know most about and can give the best answer to and concentrate on that one exclusively for the time you have left. Be content to write a brilliant answer to this question in lieu of superficially answering several of the leftover questions and making up responses that don't really say anything.

2. Write one or two sentences on all the questions you have left. Use the best facts, examples, and details that you can possibly muster. This will at least show your professor that you knew some of the material at some level.

3. Outline your answers to the leftover questions. Instead of fully developing the answers, let your professor know in an introductory sentence that you have run out of time and are going to outline the answers you would have developed fully if you had had time. This approach will let your professor know that you had some information at hand, even if you didn't get to write the answers completely.

Finally, no matter which option you choose, when you run out of time, tell your professor in a note on the exam. This courtesy cannot hurt you, and most professors appreciate your letting them know that the clock caught you.

Appearance

The way your answer looks on the paper will be important in your instructor's grading. Remember these facts of life:

The instructor has many papers to grade.

The instructor already knows the material.

The instructor likes order.

The instructor appreciates legibility and correctness.

Be realistic. If a reader has to squint because he or she can't read your writing, you're the loser. The same is true of garbled sentences and misspelled words that can annoy your instructor. Therefore, be sure to save yourself enough time to edit quickly and follow these guidelines:

1. Be neat.
2. Write legibly and use a pen.
3. Be sure you use complete sentences.
4. Read over what you've written to be sure that it makes sense. Have you left out any words? Put too many in? Did you write one word when you meant another?
5. Check spelling.

You will defeat your own purpose if you write frantically to the last minute and don't leave yourself enough time to look over the answer. Your checking the answer will do more for your test than illustrating one more point will do.

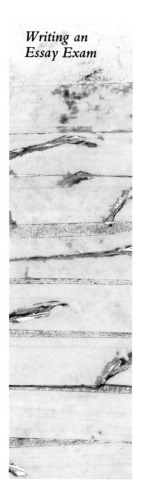

Writing an Essay Exam

Summary

1. Study with the exam in mind. Thinking ahead to what questions the instructor might ask will help you organize your thoughts, even if you are actually asked different questions.

2. Come prepared. Get a full night's sleep the night before. Bring 2-3 working pens, scratch paper—and a watch.

3. Read the questions carefully before writing. Look for clues in the wording of the question itself—look for words like *discuss, analyze, explain,* and *evaluate.*

4. Read through all the questions before writing. This lets you know what's ahead and lets your mind subconsciously prepare for the questions to come. It also lets you lead with your expertise—when you start by answering the question you know best, you feel confident and calm. Calmness is a key factor in being able to recall information.

5. Take time to prewrite before you write the answer. Even if everyone around you is writing furiously, make a quick list to help plan what you are going to say before you start writing.

6. Give complete answers. Don't just declare your thesis; explain it. Include only relevant examples, details, and illustrations.

7. Finish in time to look over the answer. You may find this difficult because of the temptation to write to the very end. But remember, the instructor doesn't want to know everything you know. If you select the most relevant information from what you know and present material clearly, you'll make a better impression on the instructor.

WRITING *Analyzing Essay-Test Responses*

1. On the following pages are two examples of essay examination answers that received *A*s from the instructor and one that did not receive an *A*. Read them and discuss why the instructor rated them as he or she did.

STUDENT EXAMPLES *Essay Question Responses*

Exam Question: *Discuss the use of the pointed arch in Gothic architecture.*

List made by student before beginning answer (appears in margin of test paper):

Pointed Arch

1. Allowed irregular spaces to be covered
   Example: a. Rhomboidal bays of ambulatory
   b. Polygonal chapels of French Chevet
   c. Polygonal chapter-houses of England

2. Made possible use of ribs
   Example: a. St. Denis Abbey Church
   b. Cathedral of Canterbury
   c. Cathedral of Salisbury

3. Made possible rectangular bays
   Example: a. Church of Sainte Chapelle
   b. Cathedral at Amiens

The answer itself:

The use of the pointed arch had a great significance to Gothic architecture. The first and most important task it accomplished was allowing an irregular area to be covered by arches and vaults. The round arch required a square vaulting bay, but the pointed arch with its extreme flexibility allowed almost any shape that was necessary. The arch allowed the steepness of the arches to vary, and this let the builders adapt the shape to whatever design might be included in the blueprint. Examples of irregular areas covered by this method are the rhomboidal bays of the ambulatory, the polygonal chapels of the French Chevet, and the polygonal chapter-houses of England.

The second achievement of the pointed arch was making possible an intricate system of vaulting ribs which served both structural and aesthetic purposes. The idea of the Gothic builder was to make a vault like a skeleton by use of the projecting ribs. Examples of the use of ribs can be seen in all Gothic cathedrals. Three such examples are the St. Denis Abbey church, the Cathedral of Canterbury, and the Cathedral of Salisbury.

Last, the pointed arch also made possible the rectangular as opposed to the square bay. This caused the total weight of the building to be distributed over twice as many points. The horizontal divisions, or bays, that were once present are then lost, causing the eye to see the church nave as one smooth continuous aisle, as seen in the Church of Sainte Chapelle in Paris or the Cathedral at Amiens.

These three uses of the pointed arch were very important because they allowed Gothic architects to achieve the structural and aesthetic qualities that Gothic architecture is noted for.

Exam Question: *How did the Peloponnesian War affect Greece?*

List made in margin of test before writing answer:

1. Ended 404 B.C.
2. Defeated Athens
3. Left Greece powerless
4. Sparta & Thebes (2nd half of 4th century B.C.)
5. States lost liberty to Philip of Macedon
6. Life structure changed
7. The individual approach to life was taught
8. Independence of city-state relationship lessened
9. Final effect of Greek civilization spreading around the world

The answer itself:

Greece was affected by the Peloponnesian War in several ways. First, Greece was left defenseless and weak after the defeat of Athens. This weakness allowed Sparta and later Thebes to control Greece. As a result, in the latter half of the fourth century B.C., Greek states lost their liberty to Philip of Macedon.

Second, with this loss of liberty, the entire structure of Greek life was changed. The original balance between the city-state and individual was destroyed. Basic simple views concerning man and the state were changed into political and social upset and turmoil. The attitudes about life changed and became more self-centered and individualistic.

Third, as a result of this individualism, the state-individual relationship soon dissolved. Greek attitude also changed, leading to the search for knowledge of the world. Through this search, the Greeks experienced a time of human discovery.

Finally, it is easy to say that the Peloponnesian War was a powerful influence on the developments in Greece. But even though the country was adversely affected, in the long run and in a roundabout way, the Peloponnesian War caused Greek civilization to spread around the known world. This was because Philip of Macedon's son was Alexander the Great, and everybody knows about his conquering the world. In this conquering, he took Greek civilization with him.

2. Here are two examination questions written by other students. Read each and write or discuss the strengths and weaknesses of the answers.

Exam Question: *Explain why the oceans are not filled in and the earth is not a slush on the surface.*

List made before answering:

1. Subduction

2. Plate tectonics

3. Deposition

4. Erosion

The answer itself:

With all the sediment from erosion flowing into the oceans, how come the oceans are not filled in and the earth surface a slush pot?

One reason is the simple idea called subduction. Subduction is a simple idea; the sheet of rock from one area is going or being forced under another. Along the west coast of South America this is evident. The Andes Mountains are a side effect of this.

Second, the way these rock plates can be explained is an idea called plate tectonics. This idea states that there are rockplates on the surface of the earth, and they are constantly colliding and something has to give. The Himalayas are a good example.

A third reason to examine is the fact that all around you are deposition of material from erosion and volcanic activity, not to mention thrust of mountains over time. Rivers are constantly flowing with large amounts of sediment. The Amazon River. The island of Hawaii is a volcanic mountain. You can see the accumulation, but the disappearance is not quite so apparent.

Fourthly, erosion is happening at an unbelievable rate. With all this erosion, the oceans should be filled in. Take the Mississippi River for instance. In the last one thousand years it has built up a seven kilometer river delta. If you multiply this by one thousand times for the whole earth and take into account the depths, the oceans should have been filled in at least twenty-five million years ago. Subduction is the best guess.

Exam Question: *List four major engineering achievements prior to the twentieth century and discuss their importance.*

Student's Answer (no list made):

The first major engineering project was the irrigation system. This idea enabled the Egyptians to farm many miles of nonproductive land. Secondly, and just as important, was the building of roads. The Romans built roads mainly for communication, not transportation. Their army was constantly changing, and roads were vital to their success. The third development was the refinement of steel. This was a significant step to modern engineering, since it allowed production of machinery. The fourth design was a result of refinement of steel. It was the invention of the steam engine. This was very useful since it gave man an alternative energy source to slavery.

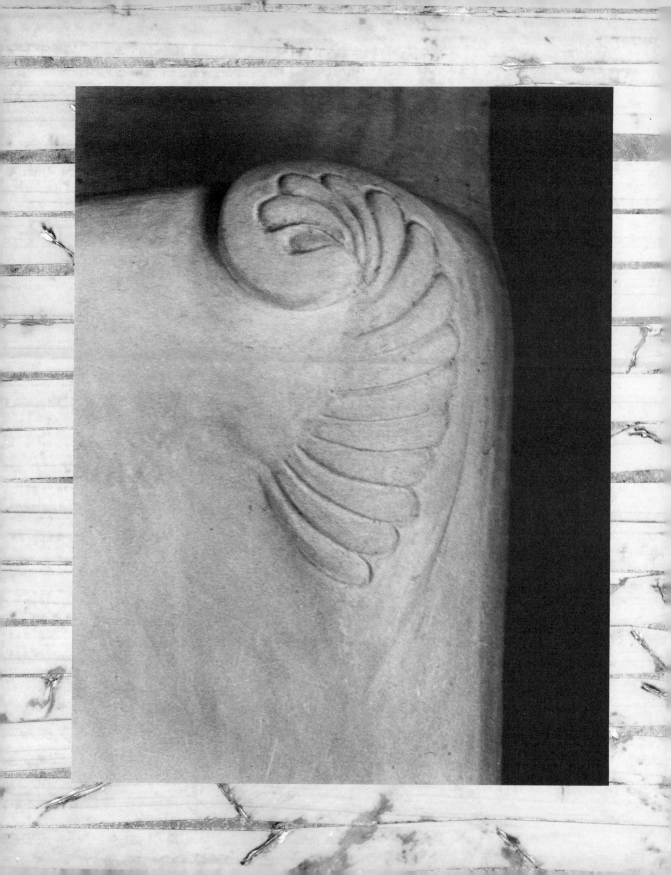

PART 5   *Special Problems in Editing*

This section will help you

■ overcome editing and proofreading problems you have encountered in polishing your writing

■ act as a quick reference guide to the most common editing problems students have

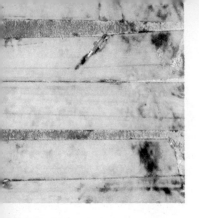

Special Problems in Editing

Readers who take the time to read your writing expect to concentrate on what you have to say rather than how you say it. Before giving a paper to a reader, you should always carefully edit to remove distracting or confusing mistakes. Careless editing of a paper can lead readers to put less value in your message—in some instances, to even ignore the message altogether.

This section includes brief summaries of some of the more troublesome areas for editing papers. The entries are arranged alphabetically so that you can find the explanation and advice you need quickly. If you need more information and practice, ask your teacher for more help. The most effective way to hone your editing skills, however, is simply to practice editing your own and your peers' papers.

AGREEMENT—*See* Subject-Verb Agreement, Pronoun Reference and Agreement, *or* Consistent Tense

APOSTROPHES—*See* Mechanics

CAPITALIZATION—*See* Punctuation

COMMA—*See* Punctuation

COMMA SPLICE

Punctuation is a system for marking sentences so that the reader can follow the writer's thought, stopping and pausing in the appropriate places.

When these marks are missing or when they are misused, readers can lose the meaning of your sentences.

A common sentence punctuation error is the comma splice. A comma splice occurs when you join two independent clauses with nothing but a comma.

> As a child, the alcoholic did not learn the things a child needs to learn, thus his life was destined to go bad.

Remember that an independent clause demands a punctuation mark that signals completion, so independent clauses should always end in a period, a colon, a semicolon, or a comma *and* a coordinating conjunction. (*See also* Coordination)

You can rewrite a comma splice in one of the following ways.

1. Rewrite the sentence as two independent sentences.

> As a child, the alcoholic did not learn the things a child needs to learn. Thus, his life was destined to go bad.

2. If the ideas of the sentences are closely related, replace the comma with a semicolon.

> As a child, the alcoholic did not learn the things a child needs to learn; thus, his life was destined to go bad.

3. Join the independent clauses with the appropriate coordinating conjunction.

> As a child, the alcoholic did not learn the things a child needs to learn, and his life was destined to go bad.

4. Make one sentence dependent on the other through subordination.

> Because the alcoholic did not learn as a child the things children need to know, his life was destined to go bad.

A comma splice is a serious punctuation error for three reasons.

1. It suggests that you are unable to distinguish between independent clauses, which should be marked with a period or semicolon, and dependent clauses, which may be marked with a comma. (*See also* Subordination)

2. It sends the reader conflicting signals. The comma signals only a pause, but each independent clause signals completion.

3. Finally, the comma splice suggests unclear thinking. A writer who mistakes a comma for a period muddies the relationships between ideas.

EDITING SAMPLE SENTENCES

Pick out the comma splices in the following sentences and rewrite each sentence.

A. A man with a higher education has a good opinion about himself, therefore other people have a good opinion about him.

B. She has a rare talent, it is to inspire anyone with the least interest to do anything to keep on trying.

C. Knowing the basics in their chosen field gives students a head start when they enter a job, otherwise they would have a hard time getting started.

D. She is always smiling and joking, even when she is tired, she always seems to have compassion for others and a ready smile.

E. Common sense cannot be deduced, this is a trait learned through actual living experience.

F. It is often said that mankind should not live in the past, but make the most of and live in the present, this is practically impossible to accomplish.

G. It is now the time since we know what we need to do, we must begin a movement of reform before we lose our identity.

H. A university is not a place in which nonfunctioning people go in and functioning people come out, it is a place for awakening.

I. Now guess what happened to me, well, some call it sea sickness and I had it bad.

CONSISTENT TENSE

A verb tense shows when the action or state of being expressed by the verb occurred. The rule is: keep the same verb tense throughout, unless you have a good reason not to. If you begin with the present tense ("I write"), don't switch to any other tense ("I wrote," "I have written," "I had written," "I will write," or "I will have written").

Avoid: He was sure that he is ready.
Write: He was sure that he was ready.
Avoid: I tell her to think about it, and she said okay.
Write: I tell her to think about it, and she says okay.

Be especially careful to watch for verb tense shifts in long and complex sentences.

EDITING SAMPLE SENTENCES

Rewrite the following sentences so that the tenses are consistent.

A. He complained about all the homework he is getting.

B. I see you as a person who thought life is a bowl of cherries.

C. Two teaspoons of baking powder are added. Then the mixture was sifted twice.

D. As we were going to the store, an old man stops us and asks us for directions.

COORDINATION

We can link ideas through coordination when we want to show that two or more words, phrases, or clauses are equal in weight. Seven coordinating conjunctions link words equally: *but, or, yet, for, and, nor, so.* (Remember these as the BOYFANS words.)

Tom had only cheese and bread for his lunch.

Eustace picked the man's pocket and spent the money moments later.

We walked to the park, but we took the bus home.

Notice that when you coordinate or link two verbs—*picked and spent*—you don't need a comma. When you coordinate two independent clauses, as in the third example, however, you do need a comma.

FRAGMENTS

A fragment is the opposite of a fused sentence. A fused sentence occurs when two sentences are run together without punctuation; a fragment occurs when part of a sentence is punctuated as a complete sentence.

Many people look down on conformity. They see those who are always following blindly as fools who are too scared to think for themselves. Perhaps not having to think is why they conform. That and the fact that there is safety in numbers.

The last sentence is an inappropriate fragment. It probably occurred when the writer got so caught up in getting the thoughts down that he or she didn't notice the grammatical form of the sentence. You could rewrite this fragment in several ways.

1. Link it to the previous sentence using either a comma

Perhaps not having to think is why they conform, or perhaps they feel there is safety in numbers.

or a dash to connect the two.

Perhaps not having to think is why they conform—that, and the fact that there is safety in numbers.

2. Make it a complete sentence.

Perhaps not having to think is why they conform. The feeling that there is safety in numbers may also explain why people conform.

Although you should try to get rid of fragments in your writing, you should know that they are not always grammatical errors. Frequently, writers use fragments intentionally for emphasis, as an afterthought, or as a transitional device. The following passages are from an article in which a writer describes his impressions and his memories as he comes back home to care for his dying mother. Notice that the fragments are necessary to create the illusion that the writer is allowing us to look into his mind.

For his mother is, in fact, near death, though lingering, and that is why he has spent three restless weeks in her house—a thousand miles west of his own, in a suburban town on the Hudson. Waiting. A duty.

John wonders if he has somehow contrived to bring his mother there. A figment, perhaps, a tilt of the mind.

He thinks, too, of how often and how far during his stay he has stumbled into the past. The house is full of things that, as he prowled it, have brought him memories or surprises. A rag doll, his mother's childhood confidante, now worn and burst at the seams, with only one button eye left. His father's telescope, the larger lens still cracked. John's own doing. And, oddly, a medal presented by the Italian government to one Professor George Niles, in March of 1922.

Intentional fragments are fine. It is the accidental ones that disturb the reader and that you want to be sure to get rid of during editing and proofreading.

EDITING SAMPLE SENTENCES

Rewrite the fragments in the following passages.

A. The ironic tone comes from an exaggerated description of the female stereotype. Using ridiculous images of women bedecked in all sorts of jewels, tottering around on sidewalks, and girls melting with joyous gratitude over a box of cheap chocolates.

B. For those who are happy with the way things are, conformity is an asset. If people think as they do, things won't change. Their happiness is secure. Conformity can also be against those who oppose change. For instance, if a new view catches on. One by one people gradually accept it not questioning it.

C. They see in each other the security which they so desire but cannot see what the price is for that security. The price being the responsibilities and commitments of marriage.

D. Students should know about the government and what has made it last for 200 years. Because it is very easy to criticize things you know nothing about.

E. Many people are successful without being an alumnus of some college or university. The key word here being success.

F. Thinking that the camera was rolling, I executed my part with great vigor. Vigorous enough that I suffered a minor head injury when I jumped off a ten-foot cliff in pursuit of the villain.

G. What we need in a realistic sense is to provide a more meaningful challenge to life. Also to simplify our lives to the point that we can regress to elementary math and the wheel.

H. The only reason I would attend a private university would be because of the curriculum it offered. For example, if the state university did not have a degree plan that I wanted to pursue or courses I wanted to take.

FUSED SENTENCES

Fused sentences (or run-on sentences) are much like comma splices except that in this kind of error all punctuation is omitted between the independent clauses. A fused sentence misleads the reader. With no period or semicolon to mark the end of one sentence, he or she reads the attached sentence as if it were part of the first one.

> Universities are an important part of our world their teaching of our children should someday bring about a better world.

When the reader discovers the writer's mistake, he or she must reread the sentences, mentally inserting the needed punctuation.

You can correct fused sentences in several ways.

1. Rewrite the fused sentence as two separate sentences.

> Universities are an important part of our world. Their teaching of our children should someday bring about a better world.

2. Insert a semicolon between the fused sentences if the two sentences are closely related in content.

Universities are an important part of our world; their teaching of our children should someday bring about a better world.

3. Separate the sentences with a comma, if they are joined by a coordinating conjunction.

Universities are an important part of our world, for their teaching of our children should someday bring about a better world.

4. Use subordination to make one sentence dependent on the other.

Universities are an important part of our world since their teaching of our children may someday bring about a better world.

EDITING SAMPLE SENTENCES

Explain why the following sentences are fused sentences. Rewrite each.

A. The author believes that the job of a university is to teach students knowledge and philosophy he also believes that the knowledge and philosophy they learn are later mistaken for virtue and conscientiousness.

B. Don't get the wrong impression Jeff is not a troublemaker he is genuinely sorry for the trouble we have gotten into and will never make that mistake again.

C. Some days I'll start to clean to the extent of clearing a pathway to my bed I'm usually in a cleaning mood but don't really have the energy.

D. This shows what a brave dog he was two nights later he was frightened by our counselor's guitar.

JARGON

Jargon sometimes refers to the vocabulary that is characteristic of a particular professional group—for example, medical jargon, educational jargon, or legal jargon. In this sense, the word *jargon* carries no negative connotations. It merely refers to the set of words that professional or social groups use to communicate efficiently among themselves. Used in a different sense, *jargon* refers to a problem in writing. Anytime a writer relies on wordiness, pretentiousness, abstractness, or overuse of the passive voice to make trivial ideas seem important, that writer uses jargon that blocks effective communication.

The following guidelines, based on what you know about effective use of words, should help you avoid the problems that contribute to jargon.

1. Make your writing as clear and as straightforward as possible. Avoid "big" words and pretentious language simply to impress your reader. Be merciless in editing your writing. Strike out any word that adds nothing to your meaning, regardless of how impressive the meaningless phrase seems.

2. Strive to make your writing vivid. Whenever possible replace *is* and other *to be* verbs with stronger verbs. Avoid too many abstract nouns (*-tion* and *-ment* endings). Remember: these nouns can frequently be replaced by a verb to make a stronger sentence.

3. Be natural. Don't avoid a first-person pronoun simply because you fear it may make your writing too casual. Don't use the third person (*one, a person, the student*) in an attempt to sound impersonal. Don't rely on passive voice as a means of sounding impressive.

4. Identify and describe your audience. If you are writing to readers who are unfamiliar with the technical or learned aspects of your topic, you'll need to avoid using "insider" terms.

EDITING SAMPLE PARAGRAPHS

The following passage is a good example of jargon; identify the problems that characterize it as jargon and then rewrite it.

Perhaps the most significant development of the Industrial Revolution (aside, of course, from the revolution itself) was the beginning of awareness in some individuals of the less favorable ramifications of technology. This awareness, although negligible at first, eventually became the vital factor in the prevention of world self-destruction through unbridled technological advances. Fortunately, vigilance against the cerebral nature of our scientific age continues to serve as a bulwark against problems which could increase severely in magnitude (e.g., the ecological balance or nuclear weapons) as time progresses.

In addition to the material problems of a technical society, there are difficulties of wider and far more abstract scope. These difficulties are evidenced most graphically by examination of technological advance in terms of the response and development of the individual. It is to be suspected (without much doubt) that previous decades of near-obsession with technology, frequently for its own sake, have resulted in a society which is over-oriented toward a systematic approach to its problems. In fact, the primary ill of modern society could well be expressed as its continuous attempt to adopt a rigid set of formulae and apply them, in toto and without exception, to human beings. Such a denial of "human variability" is, of course, a mistake, and can, as pointed out, lead only to disaster. Yet, society continues to careen, without apparent suspicion, toward a point from which there may well be no return.

HYPHEN—*See* Mechanics

MECHANICS

Mechanics are simply conventions that standardize details such as capitalization, the use of numbers, abbreviations, and the like. Fortunately, you don't have to memorize any of these rules. You can find them quickly in this book and in most books about writing. It is important that you observe these rules, though, because readers expect you to observe conventions even on things that don't substantially affect your message.

Abbreviations and Symbols

You should use abbreviations and symbols sparingly and carefully in your writing. There are few abbreviations and symbols that are acceptable for the kind of writing you do in academic classes, and if you notice the writing around you every day—newspapers, magazines, textbooks—you will see that abbreviations and symbols are rarely used there either. In general, writers avoid abbreviations because they make writing seem casual and unpolished. That's why you should avoid abbreviations like *dept., apt., Mon., assoc.,* in your writing. Don't write: *I have an appt. with the head of the math dept. tomorrow.* In some cases, abbreviations are permissible. The following guidelines should help you use abbreviations properly.

1. Abbreviate titles when they are part of a name.

   Mrs. Emma Gay Hopkins   Lt. Col. James T. Anderson.
   Dr. James Smith

2. Organizations that are more commonly known by initials than by the full name may be abbreviated.

   AFL-CIO   NATO   NOW
   NASA   SALT

   When you are not sure whether your audience will recognize the acronym, be sure you write out the whole name the first time you refer to it; you can use the initials for subsequent references.

3. Abbreviate the names of states only when they are part of an address. If you are referring to Fresno, California, in the text of your paper, do not write Fresno, Calif.

4. Latin abbreviations such as *etc., e.g.,* and *i.e.,* are permissible in most writing.
5. Other acceptable abbreviations include the following:

    A.M.   P.M.   A.D.   rpm   mph

6. Many abbreviations have become common through everyday use: TV, CB, hi-fi, stereo, C.O.D. Use them only if they fit the tone of the particular piece you are writing.
7. Use the dollar sign ($) only for exact sums or for estimates of very large sums such as *$4.83,* or *$1.6 billion,* but write out *"about three dollars."*
8. Do not use the ampersand (&) as a substitute for *and* in your writing unless it is part of an organization's name, as in Harper & Row.
9. Spell out percent (%) and cents (¢).

> The survey shows that only 9.6 percent of all college freshmen are financially independent.
>
> The price of ground beef has gone up 50 cents a pound in one month.

Capitalization

1. Capitalize the first word of every sentence.
2. Capitalize proper nouns.

Names of Persons

James Frank Harper	Jesus Christ
Herman Melville	Shirley MacLaine

Names of Museums, Buildings

the Smithsonian Institute	the Lincoln Memorial
the Library of Congress	American Buddhist Academy

Names of Places

Washington, D.C.   Luxembourg

Names of Vessels

The U.S.S. Constitution   Old Ironsides
Apollo 8

Events and Periods

the Civil War   the Stone Age   the Renaissance

3. Capitalize names of deities.

    Jehovah   Krishna   Jupiter

4. Capitalize titles before and after names.

Dr. William Muse	Professor Barbara Walker
Mrs. Jack McHenry	the Rev. Bill Baker
Ms. Carol Roberts	Rita King, Ph.D.
Capt. John Slith	Queen Elizabeth II

5. Capitalize the first word and all other words except short prepositions, conjunctions, and articles in the titles of literary works, movies, and works of art. Capitalize prepositions over five letters long.

For Whom the Bell Tolls	*Star Wars*
the *Mona Lisa*	*Romeo and Juliet*
The Color Purple	"Ode to a Nightingale"

6. Capitalize names of recognized groups and organizations.

Republicans	Christian Science
Democrats	Daughters of the American Revolution
Jaycees	National Organization for Women

7. Capitalize specific course names.

Math 130   Psychology 441

8. Capitalize North, South, East, and West when they refer to specific geographical areas.

Gone With the Wind is set in the South.

She's from West Texas.

9. Avoid unnecessary capitalization:

I am taking a history course this semester.

Dallas is northwest of Houston.

They consider themselves members of the upper class.

Robbie will be a senior next year.

Hyphen

The hyphen has two main uses: it indicates compounds and word division. Make sure you do not use a hyphen when you mean to use a dash. (On a keyboard, a dash is indicated by striking the hyphen key twice.)

1. Use a hyphen between parts of compound words.

all-night	*attorney-general*
quasi-governmental	*son-in-law.*

Compound adjectives are usually hyphenated.

fire-breathing dragon   *blood-thirsty beast*
hard-hearted professor

If you are not sure whether a compound should be hyphenated, check the dictionary.

2. Use a hyphen with certain prefixes.

Hyphenate words formed from a prefix and a proper noun.

all-American   *anti-Soviet*

Hyphenate to avoid two identical vowels next to each other.

re-entry   *anti-intellectual*

Hyphenate prefixed words to distinguish them from words spelled the same but without the hyphen.

re-create/recreate   *re-dress/redress*   *re-cover/recover*

3. Hyphenate to indicate word division at the end of a line, but observe these guidelines.
   a. Do not divide words of one syllable like *forced, though,* or *calmed.*
   b. Do not separate a suffix or syllable of less than three letters (*-ed, -le*) or a one-letter prefix or syllable (*a-, e-, o-*).
   c. Separate hyphenated words (*sister-in-law, well-known, semi-retired*) only at the hyphen.
   d. Do not divide a word on the last line of a page or paragraph.

Italics

Indicate italics in handwritten and typed work by underlining. Use italics in the following instances.

1. to indicate foreign words

   writ of habeas corpus, in absentia.

2. to indicate emphasis

   What do you mean *he* saw it?
   It was *Tom,* not Bob, who wrote the winning essay.

3. to refer to words as words

   Penultimate is one of my favorite words, but I hardly ever get to use it.

4. to indicate titles of literary works, works of art, movies, ships

   The Queen Mary   *The Agony and the Ecstasy*   *Starry Night*

Numbers

Figures used in the text of your writing should be spelled out most of the time. Follow these guidelines for using numerals clearly.

1. Spell out numbers from one to ten. In very formal writing, spell out all two-digit numbers.

    We have to read five books this semester; we may choose from a list of 25 novels.

2. Use figures to indicate exact sums, time, large figures, and dates.

2:30 A.M.	203,431	500 B.C.
$8.65	1961	

3. Avoid beginning a sentence with a figure. If you can't rewrite the sentence so the figure is not at the beginning, then spell out the number.

    Avoid: 1963 marked the beginning of an important era in American life.
    Write: In 1963, Americans began an important era in politics.

4. Numbers from 21 to 99 are hyphenated when spelled out: thirty-five, ninety-seven. Make sure you learn how to spell these: forty (not fourty), ninety (not ninty).

MODIFICATION

Modification, one means of varying sentence patterns, sometimes causes confusing sentences. The reader should always be clear about what sentence element a modifier refers to. As in most sentence errors, there may be no great loss of meaning when misplaced modifiers occur, but the resulting ambiguity may distract the reader or may create an unintentionally comical sentence. Most sentences with misplaced modifiers can be clarified through slight revision.

Having many heroic qualities, George Washington's life was colored by a handful of fables.

Did George Washington or his life have heroic qualities? The sentence now says that his life had heroic qualities. Revision can improve the sentence.

Revised: Having many heroic qualities, George Washington lived a life colored by a handful of fables.

The problem in the next example is that the introductory phrase doesn't seem to go with any part of the sentence. Again, slight revision can clarify the sentence.

Through the use of polls, it is evident that the majority of the American public thinks that voting makes a difference.

Revised: By asking their opinions in polls, we have learned that the majority of the American public thinks that voting makes a difference.

In this next sentence, the reader is led to expect examples of what it is that *most of us will never do.*

We have, for example, people who have done something that most of us will never do, such as astronauts, Arctic explorers, mountain climbers.

Instead, the "such as" phrase modifies "people" which occurs much earlier in the sentence. To avoid this confusion, the sentence should be rewritten.

Revised: We have people such as the astronauts, Arctic explorers, mountain climbers, who have done something that most of us will never do.

or

Revised: We have people who have done something that most of us will never do, such as journey to outer space, explore the Arctic, or climb mountains.

To avoid errors in modification, always place the modifier as close as possible to the word it modifies. You should always make sure that there is a word to be modified. Your goal in effective modification, as in all parts of writing, should be to make your meaning and intention clear to the reader. Don't force your readers to decipher your meaning or to mentally revise the sentences they are reading.

EDITING SAMPLE SENTENCES

Rewrite the following sentences to revise faulty modification.

A. Deeply upset, Ann's overwrought condition caused her to achieve a low score on the college entrance exam.

B. Among the examples used by the author, he remarked that although many of his teachers were Democrats, he didn't turn out to be a Democrat.

C. While taking the lab test, an assistant grader approached one of my friends and attempted to take up her paper.

D. Being computer tests, the student does not receive his answer sheet or a copy of the questions.

E. Coming from an all-girl high school, the adjustment to a co-educational college has been a very big one.

PARALLELISM

Parallel structure arranges your sentences so that related words or phrases have the same pattern. Problems in parallelism can usually be traced to faulty links between the elements that are supposed to be parallel. Remember, coordination and parallelism link grammatically equivalent sentence elements. When the coordinated parts are not grammatically equal, the sentence stumbles.

He admired Mary's arrangement of yellow roses and daisies on the piano and how she had brightened the room with smaller arrangements.

Here, the writer has coordinated *arrangement* and *how she had brightened the room*. The sentence should be revised so that the elements match in form.

Revised: He admired the arrangement of yellow roses and daisies on the piano and the smaller arrangements that brightened the room.

or

Revised: He admired how Mary had arranged the yellow roses and daisies on the piano and how she had brightened the room with smaller arrangements.

Another thing to watch out for is incomplete parallel structure. This means that if you are setting up a series of parallels—"this, then that, then that"—you need to carry it through the paragraph consistently.

Avoid: The men were strong, the men were willing, able.
Write: The men were strong, the men were willing, the men were able.

EDITING SAMPLE SENTENCES

Rewrite the following sentences to revise faulty parallelism.

A. There are many deep considerations to be made, like your new-found responsibilities, your goals and aims, and how your partner is

going to fit into them, and making sure that the real reason for marriage is not to be an escape.

B. Egoistic suicide occurs in a society where interpersonal relationships are few, unsubstantial, and tend to be utilitarian.

C. I have seen individuals who respect their rights and the rights of
others misused, slandered, their room vandalized, and labeled as
two-percenters.

D. The essay is intended to make known to the female why conditions exist between men and women and possible ways that these
conditions could be improved.

E. I would like to explain in more detail the two types of hunters,
the pleasures of hunting, and how some of the laws are set.

F. Most of these students have their own ideas of what they want to
be and can stand on their own two feet.

G. I am going to college for three reasons: the first being that it
seems like the thing to do, the second being that my parents wanted
me to go and the third because of the chance of being wealthy and
having a comfortable life.

H. Universities are places where people should know how to function in life and deal with the real world.

I. A university should be a place where students receive a degree
only through years of hard studying and because they deserve it.

J. The problem is that most teachers don't remember what it's like to
be new, to be away from home, young.

PASSIVE VOICE

Passive voice provides the writer an alternative to the usual sentence pattern. The passive voice changes the order of the sentence parts. Thus, an
active sentence

A speeding car struck a student on his way to school this morning.

becomes

A student on his way to school was struck by a speeding car this
morning.

Notice, however, that it isn't just word order that has changed. Although
the message of the sentence remains the same, the focus is different in
each. In the active sentence, the speeding car is the focus; in the passive
sentence, the student becomes the focus. This capacity for varying focus
makes passive voice a resource to writers.

Passive voice also involves changing an active subject—*speeding car*—into a prepositional phrase of agency—*by a speeding car*. Sometimes, though, the agent can be omitted to create an impersonal tone.

Students are asked to proceed to the gym immediately after lunch.

Who does the asking? Presumably, the principal, but the statement seems far less authoritative if the agent is retained.

Students are asked by the principal to proceed to the gym immediately after lunch.

In this next sentence, the passive voice is used without the phrase of agency.

It is believed that some parts of the world will suffer massive food shortages this century.

Here, the passive voice might have been used for one of the following reasons:

1. The writer is the one who believes that we will suffer food shortages, but to create an aura of authority and to sound impressive, he avoids a personal reference in an active sentence.

   I believe that some parts of the world will suffer massive food shortages this century.

2. It could be that demographers or farmers are the ones who have predicted the shortage, but by leaving out the agent—it is believed by demographers or by farmers—the information in the sentence seems absolute and factual rather than speculative.

When it is used consciously to create a desired effect as in the sentences above, the passive voice is a valuable resource in writing. However, the passive voice is frequently used carelessly and indiscriminately, contributing to wordiness and reducing vividness.

Active: The president asked Congress to carefully consider the results of the bill before overriding his veto. (16 words)

Passive: Congress was asked by the president to consider carefully the results of the bill before overriding his veto. (18 words)

Certainly two additional words will not make your writing excessively wordy, but when sentence after sentence is passive, the extra words add up.

Passive voice also reduces vividness. Remember that the verb is the heart of the sentence. Passive verbs combine a form of *to be* with the past participle—*was asked, is expected, will be hired*—and *to be* is a colorless, empty verb. It merely links; it shows no action. So, unless you have a specific reason to use passive voice, strive to make your writing vigorous and direct by preferring active verbs.

As you edit your papers, question the appropriateness of every passive verb. Can the information in that sentence be conveyed more directly and more naturally in the active voice? If it can be, then revise the sentence.

EDITING SAMPLE SENTENCES

Explain how the use of passive voice makes these sentences wordy or unclear. Rewrite each.

A. By this definition, it can be seen that heroes are very influential in American society today.

B. Technology is pointed out by the author as being one of the basic causes of the schizoid condition.

C. The topic is taken very seriously by the writer, and the persona that she uses (which is both serious and full of resentment) expresses her seriousness.

D. But a stand was taken by him, and whether he is right or wrong, this fact cannot be ignored.

E. Through the activities of Sir Thomas More, it is seen that in order to live in society a person has to give up part of himself.

PERIOD—*See* Punctuation

PREDICATION

Faculty predication occurs when the beginning of the sentence doesn't connect logically to the end of the sentence. Even though something seems to be wrong with the sentence when you read it, the meaning may come across anyway. In the following sentences, you can understand what the writer means, but the sentence relationships are illogical in each.

Any person absent on the final day of classes would have meant that the end-of-school picnic could not be held.

Here, the beginning of the sentence—*person*—is connected to the second part of the sentence—*would have meant*. The connection simply doesn't work logically. The sentence should be rewritten:

Revised: Any person's absence would have meant that the end-of-school picnic could not be held.

In the following sentence, a superfluous *about* causes faulty predication.

The subject of his talk was about employment after graduation.

You can say *The subject of his talk was employment* or *His talk was about employment,* but not both, as the original sentence does.

Sometimes the subject-verb relationship is simply illogical.

When air fares are reduced, there will no longer be so many cars driving people to vacation spots.

The actual subject is *cars* and the verb is *will be driving.* The verb needs a human subject rather than an inanimate one.

Revised: There will no longer be so many people driving cars to vacation spots.

or

Revised: There will no longer be so many cars driven to vacation spots.

EDITING SAMPLE SENTENCES

Correct faulty predication in the following sentences.

A. The oil produced by Middle East countries has developed to be the heartbeat of the United States industrial machine.

B. To charge someone with the title of hero is a very daring and challenging label.

C. The best part of the wave is usually when you take off and make your initial drop.

D. Life for me, as compared to life before I came to college, has really made me a more responsible person.

E. It was because of the way the pipes looked last night that caused the fire marshall to declare the cause of the fire to be due to a buildup of a natural gas leak.

F. Another way most students change when coming to a college or university is culturally.

G. The only method for determining the heroes of today's society is by viewing the acts that possibly contain vitality on a scale of their future impact.

PRONOUN REFERENCE AND AGREEMENT

Remember that a pronoun is a noun substitute. Usually, the sentence contains a noun to which the pronoun refers, and the pronoun must repeat the same information as the noun. If the noun is plural, the pronoun must be plural; if the noun is feminine, the pronoun must be feminine. This repetition is called pronoun agreement. Most of the time, pronoun agreement presents no problems, but some sentence constructions make pronoun agreement difficult to achieve. As in subject-verb agreement, indefinite pronouns cause problems here too.

> Everybody finished their themes in 50 minutes.
> Someone left their backpack here.
> Does everyone want their coffee with cream and sugar?

You hear constructions like this all the time. There is really no problem in communicating meaning; the problem is grammatical. Indefinite pronouns like *everybody, anyone, anybody, someone, no one, one, each* are always singular, so they must be matched by singular pronouns. Since speech is much less rigid than writing, pronoun agreement is not distracting in our conversations. However, in writing, communication is much more formalized, and lack of pronoun agreement may distract the reader. To achieve agreement in each of these sentences, *their* should be replaced with *his or her*.

Pronouns cause problems in sentences for one other reason. Sometimes, the antecedent of the pronoun is not clear. Remember: a pronoun must refer to a specific noun.

> The Swiss have not been at war for many years. It is a neutral country.

It clearly refers to Switzerland, but notice that the only possible antecedent is *Swiss*. To refer clearly to Switzerland, you would rewrite the sentence as follows:

> *Revised:* Switzerland has not been at war for many years. It is a neutral country.

In the next sentence, notice how the writer easily loses track of the pronoun referent.

> Wayne was opposed to gun control because he felt every citizen should have one for self-defense.

Any reader would know that *one* is a substitute for *gun,* but the antecedent is *gun control.* Again, revision is necessary to clarify the sentence.

> *Revised:* Wayne was opposed to gun control because he felt every citizen should be allowed to own firearms for self-defense.

EDITING SAMPLE SENTENCES

Rewrite the following sentences so that there is agreement between each pronoun and its antecedent.

A. This is possibly where a college could say they help round us out emotionally. They try to provide human activities that touch us deeply.

B. Very soon, people are either going to have to change their views on what colleges are for or colleges will change it for them.

C. In Newman's *Idea of a University,* he is first stating how a gentleman is an object of the university.

D. In Cuba today, Castro is the dominating factor in the Cuban way of life and their politics.

E. A person who would take it upon himself to deprive someone of life and happiness should get what they deserve: imprisonment.

F. Even if anyone had read it, they would not have been able to relate to it.

G. It depends on who has power and how they choose to manipulate the public.

H. A person would be very dull if they knew only facts and figures without having a personality formed from personal experiences.

I. If a criminal knew that he would receive punishment for committing murder, they might think twice before committing such an act.

J. Because of its widespread use, man has formed theories pertaining to alcoholics.

PUNCTUATION

Using clear punctuation can be one of the most difficult and frustrating parts of editing. But despite sometimes seeming arbitrary, punctuation marks help indicate the writer's purpose. We can't deny that there are rules to tell us where commas should go and when colons should be used, but punctuation is more than the mechanical application of those rules. Commas, periods, semicolons, dashes, parentheses, underlining, and other marks of punctuation help the reader follow your train of thought. Punctuation is primarily for the reader. The more you write, the more you will discover that punctuation marks can work for you in directing your reader how to read.

ELEMENTS OF PUNCTUATION

Element	Function	Examples
Apostrophe **,**	Use the apostrophe to show possession, to mark the place where the letters are omitted, and to indicate the plural of numbers and letters.	
	Possession:	
	An apostrophe is used with an *s* to form the possessive case of some nouns.	Barbara's lifestyle
	With compound nouns, the last noun takes the possessive to show that they both own something.	Bert and Ernie's capers
	When each noun possesses something (individually), then both nouns are possessive.	Jack's and Jill's pails
	With singular nouns that end in *s,* you can form the possessive by adding only an apostrophe or by adding an apostrophe and an *s.*	a waitress' job, an actress' costume a waitress's job, an actress's costume
	Use only an apostrophe for plural nouns that end in *s.*	a secretaries' meeting, students' reports
	Add only an apostrophe to nouns that end in multiple consecutive *s* sounds.	Charlies' tricks, Jesus' parables
	Don't use an apostrophe with possessive pronouns.	yours, its, his, ours, whose, theirs
	Omission:	
	An apostrophe marks where letters or numbers have been left out of a word or date.	I'm, I'll, can't, back in '43
	Plurals:	
	Apostrophes indicate the plural of numbers.	6's, 70's, seven 1,000's
	An apostrophe with an *s* shows the plural of a word as a word.	You had seventeen *you's* in that paragraph.

Element	Function	Examples
	If a term is all capital letters or ends in a capital letter, you don't need an apostrophe for the plural.	I'll have six B.A.s before it's all over. Eight ADDs are enough for that computer program.
Bracket [ ]	Brackets are used to set off material that is your own inside quotation marks which surround someone else's words.	"The trio [Kingston Trio] will appear at the Bottom Mark Sunday, November 12," read the announcement in the paper.
Colon :	A colon is a punctuation mark of anticipation that halts the reader, then connects the first statement to the following one.	
	A colon can connect a series or list to the sentence.	I have four classes: math, biology, English, and history.
	A colon can link one statement to another to develop, illustrate, explain, or amplify it. When used in this way, the colon can even link two sentences.	Any large cafeteria can have two related problems: it must fix enough food but not too much, and it must keep the food from spoiling.
	A colon can introduce a stacked list.	The following courses will be offered in the fall: Math 103 Math 209 Math 308 Math 104 Math 210 Math 309
	A colon adds emphasis to a phrase that completes a sentence.	There's only one thing I want for Christmas: a new camera.
	Colons can separate chapters and verses as well as hours and minutes.	Genesis 1:1 9:30 A.M.
	In proportions, colons mean ratios.	$8:4 = 12:x$
	A colon can follow salutations in letters.	Dear Sir: Dear Aunt Blanche: Dear Ms. Geoffry:
	When using colons with quotations, capitalize the first letter of the first word of the quotation if the quote originally began with a capital letter.	The sign stated: "No shoes, no shirt, no service."
	A colon always goes outside quotation marks.	These are qualities he calls "good": wine, women, and song.

Element	Function	Examples
	If you quote a statement that ends with a colon, drop the colon and add ellipses.	"Any large cafeteria can have two related problems . . . ," an author contends.
Comma **,**	A comma can link, enclose, separate, and show omissions.	
	To link: Place a comma before a coordinating conjunction (*and, but, or, nor, for, so, yet*) when it combines two sentences (independent clauses).	The food was good, and the company was even better.
	(Some handbooks suggest that the comma can be omitted if the sentences are short, if there is no complicated punctuation in them, and if the sentences won't be misread. You will always be safe, however, if you insert the comma. This will obviate your having to make an individual decision each time.)	
	To separate: Commas separate introductory elements from the rest of the sentence.	During the first game of the series, we had four runs, six hits, and no errors. Finally, I'm finished. Yes, I know I'm excited.
	The comma may be omitted if the introductory clause or phrase is short and does not cause confusion without the mark of punctuation. It will never be wrong, however, to insert the comma.	When you go I will go.
	Commas separate items in a series.	Fresh air helps your body, my body, and everybody's body. I ate the big, juicy, wormless, delicious red apple.
	The comma before the final item in a series is optional.	We had stories to tell of Indian pueblos, spicy food and hot summer nights.

Element	Function	Examples
	No comma is needed if all items in a series are joined by *and*.	We saw Porsches and Jaguars and Broncos on the lot.
	A comma joins two coordinate modifiers. (To identify coordinate modifiers, see if they can be switched and the meaning stays the same.)	Her romantic, optimistic view of life encouraged us.
	A comma separates a nonrestrictive element that comes at the end of the sentence.	They all like to watch old movies, especially if they can eat popcorn.
Dash ———	When typing, use two hyphens (--) to indicate a dash.	
	A dash can indicate a sharp turn in thought.	That marks the end of that class— unless I failed the last test.
	A dash can add emphasis to a pause.	I'll get the job done—after I take another break.
	Dashes can set off an explanatory series or an appositive series.	Two of the applicants—Scott and Jan—will be offered jobs.
	Dashes can add emphasis to a parenthetical element (an item inserted in the sentence that isn't essential to meaning).	Only one person—you—can control what you say.
Ellipses . . .	Ellipses are a punctuation mark to show you've left out some words.	
	When you quote only part of a statement, insert ellipses to show where you've left the information out.	
	Use three dots to indicate a break in a continuing sentence.	"Work . . . is the privilege of all citizens," the politician explained.
	Use four dots to indicate the end of a sentence.	"It's best not to tell. . . . I certainly never would," she said.
	Remember: it's not fair to leave any important information out of a quotation or to pull words from a quotation and change the meaning.	

Element	Function	Examples
Exclamation Point **!**	Exclamation points are used at the end of sentences to show surprise, anger, or emphasis.	She's married! Hell, no, I'm not giving in! I'll never do that again!
Parentheses **( )**	Parenthetical information is played-down and de-emphasized: it may not be essential to a sentence, but it may be interesting or helpful to the reader.	Many American presidents (for example, Dwight Eisenhower) were military leaders. CUNY (City University of New York) offers a variety of programs.
	Punctuation: Parenthetical material does not affect the punctuation of a sentence. If a parenthetical clause comes at the end of a sentence, for example, the period to end the sentence would go outside the parentheses.	I like some history courses (American), but hate others (ancient Greek).
	When numbering a series of items in a sentence, use parentheses around the number.	I'll eat (1) potatoes, (2) meat, (3) carrots, and (4) gravy.
Period **.**	A period indicates a full stop at the end of a sentence.	Bubble gum is still a good buy.
	A period is used with an indirect question.	She asked if I liked the opera.
	A period is used after an *acceptable* sentence fragment.	Did you enjoy the festival? Very much.
	A period always goes inside the quotation marks.	"Daffodils often grow on hills." That was the statement made by the horticulturist.
	Use periods after initials in names.	John F. Kennedy, Dr. E. K. Hambrick
	Use periods between dollars and cents.	$54.98
	Use periods with abbreviations.	Inc., Ms., M.D., Ph.D.

	Use periods following the numbers or letters in lists or outlines.	I.
		  A.
		  B.

Element	Function	Examples
Question Mark ?	Use a question mark at the end of a sentence that asks a question.	What do you think you're doing?
	With quotations, when the writer who is doing the quoting is asking the question, the question mark goes outside of the quotation marks.	Did he say, "I know exactly what I'm doing"?
	When the quotation is a question, the question mark goes inside the quotation marks.	She asked, "What do you think you're doing?"
Quotation Marks " "	Quotation marks enclose direct repetition of words.	
	When you quote anything word for word from another source, enclose those words in quotation marks.	The report said, "Too many high school graduates are going to college."
	If a quotation is longer than five lines, indent all of the lines of the quotation five spaces from the left margin, single-spaced. Don't use quotation marks with indented quotations.	
	If a quotation is more than one paragraph (and it is not indented because it's not more than five lines), put quotation marks at the beginning of every paragraph but at the end of only the last paragraph.	"I can't pay the rent; I can't pay the rent. "My kids are hungry. "My house is cold. "My husband left me. "I can't pay the rent."
	If you have a quotation within a quotation, use single quotation marks (the apostrophe key on a typewriter) on the inside quote.	She asked, "Did I hear him say 'Get Lost'?"
	Use quotation marks to indicate titles of short stories, magazine and newspaper articles, songs, and television programs.	"The Catbird Seat" "Sesame Street"

Element	Function	Examples
	Always put periods and commas inside closing quotation marks.	He said, "I'll go."
	Always put colons and semicolons outside closing quotation marks.	The hero said, "I'll pay the rent"; that surprised me. These are my favorite "classes": lunchtime, study hall, and rest period.
	For all other punctuation: if the punctuation is a part of the quotation, place it inside the quotation marks; if the punctuation is not a part of the quotation, place it outside.	
	See *question marks*.	
	Words used in a special way or words to which the writer wants to draw attention for some reason are put in quotation marks.	"Teasing" your hair is bad for it.
Semicolon **;**	A semicolon can join two sentences that are close in meaning. It indicates a greater pause than a comma but not as great a pause as a period. Semicolons can also add clarity to involved sentences.	
	Place a semicolon to join closely related sentences.	I want to go; he doesn't.
	Use a semicolon to join closely related sentences combined with a conjunctive adverb.	I want to go; however, he doesn't.
	Use the semicolon to divide series in sentences that have several series.	Please make these changes in the brochure copy: "communications" to "communication"; "phone" to "call"; "promises" to "results."
	Use a semicolon to separate sentences joined by a coordinating conjunction if the sentences already have commas.	In most cases, I would order steak, baked potato, and salad; but today I think I'll order fish.

Element	Function	Examples
Virgule/Slash /	A virgule or slash is used to separate two things which belong together as choices or to separate lines of poetry that have been run together.	Do you know the either/or rule? Roses are red / Violets are blue / Sugar is sweet / And so are you.

EDITING SAMPLE SENTENCES

1. The sentences below need several kinds of punctuation. Choose appropriate punctuation marks. Be able to explain your reason for each choice. In some sentences, several marks may be used to perform the same function.

   A. A university is one of the most important institutions in the world today with universities we all have a chance to succeed.

   B. The appeal of the editorial is essentially apolitical it is not a cry for socialism but a cry for charity.

   C. The doctor is forced to leave his town and everyone he knows but he cannot be stripped of his most valuable possession his courage.

   D. The motivation must come from within if a person is depending on someone else for her motivation the chances are very good that her motivation will never come.

   E. The bare facts are pitiable enough his ragged clothes, his poor health, and the freezing weather.

   F. He must be able to justify all of his own actions since he will be practically if not totally alone in his convictions.

   G. A university education fuels the one fire that is common in all of those who are successful the burning desire to learn.

   H. Self-motivation is most evident in someone doing something she enjoys doing therefore it is important to choose a field of study that one finds interesting.

   I. People enjoy receiving gifts education is one of the best gifts a person can give him- or herself.

   J. If we do not do something apathy will surely destroy us all if not physically then spiritually.

2. Decide how you might best punctuate the following sentences.

   A. My brother who just graduated from law school has gotten a job.

B. Time and again I've seen people many of whom I would never see again become very involved with me in what I was doing.

C. The park which I have often sat in really needs a renovation.

D. If they her mother and father knew what was happening they would be thrilled.

E. Do you think as you look back on it that the decision you made was a good one?

F. The men and boys who had just arrived found the camp very much to their liking.

G. The face of the clock which was brown with white numbers was beautiful.

H. The dish to be prepared correctly requires a particular kind of herb.

3. Edit these sentences for apostrophe use.

A. Its true that that persons hat is the funniest Ive ever seen.

B. The childrens playroom is painted orange and yellow.

C. Their parents reactions were not surprising.

D. Give everything its due.

E. Wherever you go, its not going to be home.

F. Her friends summer plans are still up in the air.

G. Tommies chickens are laying eight to twelve eggs a day.

H. Thats amazing.

I. That is Malcolms or Freds motorbike.

J. Her mother-in-laws plane arrived right on time.

4. Punctuate the following sentences:

A. Wherever you go whatever you do remember me.

B. In the dim twilight of the evening stars peeked out and we said hello.

C. Youll feel like giving them a good shake and sending them to bed without supper.

D. Sadly they put the flag at half mast.

E. Here are your color choices blue white pink purple and red.

F. My choice is for the tall glass her choice is for the short one.

G. When you see them and they see you what will you do?

H. Whatever else happens I will be at the party on time I really want to see everybody arrive.

I. Stop and see the caves whatever you do George and Nell urged.

J. The rocks of the desert refers to an arid place where plants must accommodate themselves and take on the colors of the sky the sand the plants and the animals.

K. When they go I will go.

L. What can I do asked the young woman who had joined the group.

M. Three fourths of all people on the ship had never seen the May 14 1985 edition of the paper.

N. China Syndrome is a movie that reminds people of Three Mile Island.

QUOTATION MARKS—*See* Punctuation

SENTENCE PUNCTUATION—*See* Comma Splice, Fused Sentence, Fragment

SUBJECT-VERB AGREEMENT

Subject-verb agreement simply means that a singular subject must have a singular verb. Usually, agreement occurs automatically when you speak and write. For example, when you say, "John likes to have muffins for breakfast," you know that since *John* is a singular noun, the verb must be singular too. If you had said, "My roommate and I like to have muffins for breakfast," you would have used a plural verb, *like,* to match the plural subject, *my roommate and I.*

Problems in agreement between subject and verb occur when it's not clear whether the subject is plural or singular. Notice how subtle agreement errors can be.

The tossed salad and the soup looks good.

At first, the sentence sounds clear. The sentence communicates your message, but in writing, it's hard to overlook that plural subject—*tossed salad and soup.* The verb should be plural—*look*—to agree with the plural subject.

The tossed salad and the soup look good.

Compound subjects joined by *or* and *nor* often cause agreement problems.

Neither John nor my brother are going to camp this summer.

The sentence sounds acceptable, but the conjunctions *nor* and *or* suggest singularity: not both, but one or the other is going. The verb, therefore, must be singular.

Neither John nor my brother is going to camp this summer.

Indefinite pronouns—*each, every, any, anybody, one*—cause similar agreement problems, especially when there is a prepositional phrase between the subject and verb.

Each of the boys want to try out for the team.

Only one of the flowers are wilting.

In these sentences the main word in the "of" phrase has influenced the verb choice. *Boys* and *flowers* are so close to the verb that they seem to be plural subjects. To avoid this error, simply remember that *each, none, any,* and other indefinite pronouns are singular.

Each of the boys wants to try out for the team.

Prepositional phrases affect other kinds of subjects as well.

The decreasing number of college students have been attributed to the declining birth rate over the past twenty years.

If you take out that prepositional phrase, "of college students," you notice that the subject—*decreasing number*—is singular, so the verb should be *has been attributed.*

Finally, notice that the subject follows the verb when you use "there is" or "there are" to begin a sentence. The verb must agree with the subject that follows.

There is a wonderful place to vacation just around the corner from your hometown.

There are wonderful vacation spots just down the street from where you live.

EDITING SAMPLE SENTENCES

Rewrite the following sentences so that each subject agrees with each verb.

A. I knew there was many jobs available, and I was thoroughly convinced that I would get the best one.

B. I think knowledge and good sense does not have to be obtained from a university.

C. Virtue and conscience is totally up to the individuals themselves.

D. A person's pride in achievement and his desire to live to enjoy these achievements is a good reason for capital punishment to be instituted.

E. In this atomic age, the lives of millions rests in the hands of a very small minority.

F. The huge size and appetite of the eagle also causes many people to feel threatened by these birds.

SUBORDINATION

When we want to show that two ideas are related, but that one idea is less important than the other, we use subordination. The connecting words that indicate subordination include

although	because	since
if	when	whether
as	where	whereas
until	so that	how

Subordination allows writers to show explicitly the logical connections between sentence parts. If you want to show that two ideas are related by a time sequence, you choose a subordinator that shows time—*until* or *when,* for example. If you want to show a causal connection, you choose *because.* If you want to show a hypothetical connection, you choose *if.* With these explicit markers in sentences, readers have a much easier time seeing how writers have connected ideas.

If you use the subordinating conjunction at the beginning of the sentence, be sure to follow it with a comma and an independent clause. If you use the subordinating conjunction and the subordinate idea at the end of the sentence, you don't need a comma.

When she told the story of the injured bird, all the students cried.

All the students cried when she told the story of the injured bird.

USAGE

Usage is the way ordinary people actually talk and use the language. If people throughout the country use *ain't* to mean *are/am not,* grammar books and dictionaries must recognize its occurrence; but recognizing the occurrence of a certain linguistic form is quite different from accepting it as appropriate in *all* contexts.

Learning to determine when a particular form is appropriate and when it is not is the reason we study usage in school. Formal study of our language makes us sensitive to appropriateness and context. Usage covers varieties of the language—slang, colloquialisms, and casual, formal, and informal styles. Almost any variety of English is acceptable in the appropriate context, and studying those contexts helps writers choose appropriate forms and styles.

A second concern of usage is to explain why certain words are frequently misused. Similarities in spelling and meaning often lead to confusion of words like *affect* and *effect, allusion* and *illusion.* Usage also covers stubborn grammatical problems like the appropriate use of *who* and *whom*. Below you will find a list of words that present usage problems with explanations on how to use those words appropriately.

Glossary of Usage

accept, except: easily confused because of similar spelling and pronunciation. *Accept* is a verb meaning to receive.

> She was delighted to accept the award on her sister's behalf.

Except is a preposition meaning "with the exclusion of" (*Except* can also be a verb meaning to leave out.)

> Everyone wants dessert except me.

adapt, adopt: two distinct, different verbs. *Adapt* means to change something to fit a new purpose.

> He adapted his beliefs about reincarnation to her religious beliefs.

Adopt means to accept something as one's own without change.

> He adopted Mary's beliefs about life after death.

advice, advise: both refer to helping someone with a difficult decision or a problem. *Advice* is a noun.

> His advice was to take the course now.

Advise is a verb.

> He advised me to take the course now.

affect, effect: frequently confused because of similar spelling and meaning. *Affect* is a verb meaning to influence.

> I'm not sure how this drug will affect you.

Effect is usually a noun meaning a result.

> The most common effect is dizziness.

Effect can also be a verb meaning *to accomplish.*

> The new mayor was unable to effect a change in local politics.

affective, effective: easily confused. *Affective* is a technical, psychological term for *emotional.*

> Educators claim that the affective domain influences a student's learning process.

Effective means producing the intended result.

> The drug was effective in getting rid of Pat's cold.

ain't: controversial. Often used by educated speakers in casual speech. Inappropriate in formal writing and in classroom writing, unless it is deliberately used to create a particular stylistic effect.

all ready, already: *all ready* is an adjective phrase meaning everything is ready.

> I was all ready to go on the trip when I discovered it was snowing.

Already is an adverb meaning by this time or prior to some designated time.

> Have you done your assignment already?

all right, alright: should be two words. The one-word form is incorrect.

allusion, illusion: frequently confused and misused. An *allusion* is a reference:

> It is frustrating to read something filled with allusions that I don't recognize.

Illusion is a deceptive impression.

> He had the illusion that no studying was required.

alot: should be two words—a lot. Colloquial; should be avoided in formal writing.

among, between: *among* refers to at least three items.

> The new teacher had expected to find more than ten enthusiastic writers among all five of her classes.

Between refers to two items.

> She couldn't decide between her new red dress and her favorite blue dress.

amount, number: amount refers to a total quantity not considered in units.

> The amount of homework I have each night is increasing.

Number is used with enumerated, countable items.

> The number of assignments in my English class is more than I expected.

as, like: *as* is a conjunction, so it should introduce a clause.

> She didn't clean up her room as I asked her to.

Like is a preposition.

> I want a pair of jeans like Ernestine's.

bad, badly: frequently misused. Bad is an adjective, badly an adverb.

> *Avoid:* I feel badly about forgetting to call you.
> *Write:* I feel bad about forgetting to call you.
> *Write:* He performed badly in his recital.

Using the adjective form with verbs of sense as in, *I feel bad* for I feel sick, is accepted by most experts.

being as, being that: colloquial expressions; use *because* or *since* instead.

> *Avoid:* Being as I may be late. . . .
> *Write:* Since I may be late. . . .

beside, besides: both are prepositions. *Beside* means at the side of.

> He sat down beside her.

Besides means in addition.

> He doesn't have much to do tonight besides his homework.

but that, but what: colloquial expressions that should be avoided in writing. They are redundant; use *that* alone.

> *Avoid:* There is no question but that he'll go.
> *Write:* There is no question that he'll go.

can, may: *can* expresses ability or power.

> They can finish tonight if they hurry.

May refers to permission, opportunity, or willingness.

> They may not be able to finish that tonight.

can't help but: colloquial expression acceptable in speech but not in writing.

> *Avoid:* I can't help but worry about him.
> *Write:* I can't help worrying about him.

cite, sight, site: easy to confuse in meaning and spelling. *Cite* means to quote as an authority or example.

> She cited Professor Green's book as the source of her ideas.

Site refers to a building or a piece of land.

> Construction sites usually detract from the attractiveness of the surrounding area.

Sight refers to landmarks or things to see.

> Did you see all the sights in London?

continual, continuous: *Continual* means recurring at intervals.

We've been unable to have our picnic because of the continual rain this summer.

Continuous means uninterrupted.

This afternoon it rained continuously for two hours.

convince, persuade: *convince* means to win agreement.

I convinced John that the movie was worth watching.

Persuade means to move to action.

I persuaded John to go see the movie with me.

could of: incorrect form. Always write *could have:*

Avoid: Sheryl could of called last night if she had known you were here.
Write: Sheryl could have called last night if she had known you were here.

device, devise: *device* is a noun.

The device is supposed to cut down the phone bill.

Devise is a verb.

I must devise a way of getting out of here by midnight.

different from, different than: the correct grammatical form is *different from,* but *different than* is appropriate in some cases.

These jeans are different from the ones I ordered.

It tasted different than I had expected.

enthuse, enthused: widely used, but many grammarians and English teachers still consider it colloquial and thus too informal for classroom writing.

farther, further: *farther* is an adverb referring to literal distance.

We hadn't driven to the cabin in years. Today it seemed farther out of town than it did when I was a child.

Further refers to distance only figuratively.

They had discussed the problem in two four-hour meetings. Further discussion was postponed to give the committee a chance to rest.

fewer, less: *fewer* is used in comparing quantities that can be counted separately.

I have fewer clothes than she has.

Less is used in comparisons involving amounts or quantities that aren't enumerated.

The Joneses make less money than we do.

good, well: ordinarily, *good* is an adjective,

The pie tastes good.

And *well* is an adverb,

He did the work well.

but the words are interchangeable when they refer to the state of one's health.

Aren't you feeling good?

Aren't you feeling well?

hopefully: a sentence adverb used much the same way *fortunately* is used.

Fortunately, the war ended before too much destruction occurred.

Hopefully, the war will end before many lives are lost.

However, many object that *hopefully* means "I hope that" or "It is hoped that," and they argue that those phrases should be used instead of the adverb. Its use is widespread, although it should probably be restricted to speech and informal writing.

imply, infer: confused frequently because both deal with judgments about what others say. *Imply* refers to what a statement means.

Your criticism implies that the book is not worth reading.

Infer means to take an implication; it refers to a judgment made by a speaker or a listener.

From your criticism, I infer that it would be a waste of time to read that book.

irregardless: common in speech, but a nonstandard variant of regardless. Logically, the two negative affixes—ir- and -less—should not occur in one word.

its, it's: *its,* the possessive pronoun, requires no apostrophe. *It's,* a contraction for *it is,* requires an apostrophe.

lend, loan: purists and traditionalists frown on using loan as a verb, but it is used frequently in speech.

Would you loan me a quarter?

In writing, use *lend*.

Would you lend me a quarter?

lie, lay: verbs related in meaning; frequently confused because of an overlap in their principal parts: *Lie* means to recline; *lay* means to place or set down. They share the same form for the past principal part of lie and the present of lay.

Present	Past	Perfect
lie	lay	lain
lay	laid	lain

Use them in the following senses.

I want to lie down when I get home. Yesterday, I lay in bed until 9 o'clock. I haven't lain in bed that late for a long time.

Please lay the book on the table carefully. Yesterday, you laid it on the edge and it fell off. I should have laid it down myself.

loose, lose: these two words are often confused because of their similar spelling. *Loose* is an adjective meaning unrestrained or a verb meaning to unfasten.

My bicycle chain is loose.

Lose is a verb meaning to misplace.

If I don't tighten it, I'll probably lose it.

lots, lots of: colloquial expression that should be avoided in formal writing.

may be, maybe: *may be* is a verb form: an auxiliary + verb *be*.

We may be going to New York soon.

Maybe is an adverb.

Maybe he's going sooner than he thinks.

myself: should be used only as a reflexive pronoun.

Write: I finished that job all by myself.

Write: I quickly washed myself in the basin of freezing water.

Never use *myself* as a substitute for *I* or *me*.

> *Avoid:* If you want a ride, call either Gabriel or myself.
> *Write:* If you want a ride, call either Gabriel or me.

prejudice, prejudiced: use these words carefully. If you use *prejudiced* as a participle, make sure the *d* appears.

> The defendant feared the jury would be prejudiced against him.

principal, principle: homophones that frequently are confused. As a noun, *principal* means a leader or chief or head.

> His principal was pleased with the drama coach's choice.

As an adjective, it means main.

> My brother, Frank, will play the principal character in the school play.

Principle is a noun that means theory, concept, or rule.

> The law of diminishing utility is one of the principles you study in an economics class.

proved, proven: commonly used interchangeably as the past participle and perfect forms of *prove*.

> After working five hours, he has finally proved his algebra problem.

Proven may be used as an adjective (past participle) but not as the perfect form. The correct perfect form is *proved*.

> My grandmother claims this is a proven remedy for colds. (Proved would be inappropriate here.)

raise, rise: *raise* is a transitive verb meaning to lift up.

> He raised the box above his head.

Rise is intransitive and means to get or go up.

> I saw it rise above his head.

real, really: common in colloquial speech, but should be avoided in writing when used as intensifiers. *Real* may be used in formal writing to mean *actual*.

sensual, sensuous: frequently confused. *Sensual* means carnal, or having to do with sex or gratification of the senses, as in *sensual thrill*.

> Sensual feelings appear without our permission.

Sensuous refers to the senses.

> The baby, Sarah, was delighted by sensuous impressions.

set, sit: verbs that are sometimes confused. *Set* is transitive and means to put something down.

Set the book on the table.

Sit is intransitive and means to occupy a place by sitting.

He invited me to sit by him.

shall, will: many people still claim that *shall* is the only correct form to use with the first-person pronoun.

I shall go to town tomorrow.

However, *shall* sounds formal and bears connotations of commands or prophecy.

Thou shalt not steal.

I shall return.

Will is appropriate in most contexts. However, in questions, *shall* can be used without too much formality.

Shall I join you?

should of: incorrect form. The correct form is *should have*.

unique: means *one of a kind* but is frequently used in the sense of *unusual* or *rare*.

Going to Europe was a unique experience.

The objection to the use of *unique* is that its "original" meaning has been lost or obscured through overuse.

used to: be sure the *d* is there. Since *d* and *t* merge when you use the phrase in speech, it's easy to forget that *used* is a past participle or a past form and must end in *d*.

He used to run four miles every day.

He is not used to getting up so early.

who, which, that: *which* and *that* should refer to inanimate or animate, nonhuman objects; *who* should be used when referring to persons.

who, whom: relative pronouns frequently used interchangeably. *Who* should be used when the relative pronoun is the subject of the clause, *whom* when it is the object.

the young man who will marry my sister

the young man whom my sister will marry

would of: incorrect form. The correct form is *would have*.

References

Acknowledgments

LITERARY

Chapter 2

Pages 16–18 "The Great Bicycle Wars" by Lance Morrow in *Time*, November 24, 1980. Copyright © 1980 by Time Inc. Reprinted by permission.

Page 18 From entry "Bicycle" in *Encyclopaedia Britannica*, 15th edition. Copyright © 1985 by Encyclopaedia Britannica. Reprinted by permission.

Pages 18–20 "Scaring the Public to Death" by Frank Trippett in *Time*, October 5, 1987. Copyright © 1987 by Time Inc. Reprinted by permission.

Pages 23-25 "Overdoing It" by Marj Charlier in *The Wall Street Journal*, October 1, 1987. Copyright © 1987 by Dow Jones & Company, Inc. Reprinted by permission of The Wall Street Journal. All rights reserved worldwide.

Chapter 3

Page 34 "Future Stars Aren't Ready "by Karen Devenuta in *The Wall Street Journal*, February 26, 1988. Copyright © 1988 by Dow, Jones & Company, Inc. Reprinted by permission of the Wall Street Journal. All rights reserved worldwide.

Chapter 10

Page 167 From "A Red Light for Scofflaws" by Frank Trippett in *Time*, January 24, 1983. Copyright © 1983 by Time Inc. Reprinted by permission.

Page 172 Excerpt from *Stalin, A Political Biography* by Isaac Deutscher, page 593. Copyright © by Oxford University Press.

Chapter 11

Pages 183–84 Reprinted from *Anasazi* by Donald G. Pike and David Muench. Copyright © 1974 by American West Publishing Company. Used by permission of Crown Publishers, Inc.

Pages 189–90 Excerpt from pp. 241–242 in *Four Arguments for the Elimination of Television* by Jerry Mander. Copyright © 1977, 1978 by Jerry Mander. By permission of William Morrow & Company.

Page 190 Excerpt from "Some Remarks on Humor" from *Essays of E. B. White*. Copyright 1941, 1969 by E. B. White. Reprinted by permission of Harper & Row, Publishers, Inc.

Page 195 From *A Lady's Life in The Rocky Mountains* by Isabella L. Bird. New edition copyright © 1960 by the University of Oklahoma Press. Reprinted by permission.

Pages 195–96 From *The Shirley Letters* by "Dame Shirley," (Louise Clappe). Copyright © 1983 by Peregrine Press, a division of Gibbs M. Smith, Inc. Reprinted by permission.

Pages 196–97 From "The Ten Best Cars in the World, 1971," *Road & Track*, August 1971. Reprinted with permission of Road & Track magazine.

Pages 198–99 From "Rain and the Rhinoceros" in *Raids on the Unspeakable* by Thomas Merton. Copyright © 1965 by the Abbey of Gethsemani, Inc. Reprinted by permission of New Directions Publishing Corporation.

Chapter 12

Page 215 From *A Lady's Life in the Rocky Mountains* by Isabella L. Bird. New edition copyright © 1960 by the University of Oklahoma Press. Reprinted by permission.

Pages 218–19 Reprinted with permission of Macmillan Publishing Company from *Moving Mountains* by Henry M. Boettinger. Copyright © 1969 by Henry M. Boettinger.

Page 221 From *The New Money Dynamics* by Venita Van Caspel. Copyright © 1978 Reston Publishing Company, Inc. Reprinted by permission of Simon & Schuster, Inc.

Page 221 "What is my goal in Life? . . ." is excerpted from *On Becoming a Person* by Carl R. Rogers. Copyright © 1961 by Carl R. Rogers. Reprinted with the permission of Houghton Mifflin Company.

Chapter 13

Page 242 George Stanley Odiorne, MBO II: *A System of Managerial Leadership for the 1980s*. Belmont, California: Fearon-Pitman Publishers, 1979.

Pages 242–43 Excerpt from "Death of a Pig" from *Essays of E. B. White*. Copyright 1947, 1975 by E. B. White. Reprinted by permission of Harper & Row, Publishers, Inc.

Chapter 15

Pages 263–64 "Anti-Darwinism" from *The Economist*, January 9, 1988. Copyright © 1988 by The Economist Newspaper Limited. Reprinted by permission.

Pages 267–68 "Don't Raise the Minimum Wage" by Jeffrey Campbell in *Fortune*, August 31, 1987.

Copyright © 1987 by Time Inc. Reprinted by permission.

Page 270 "Living at the Edge" by Thomas Exter in *American Demographics*, November 1987. Copyright © 1987 by American Demographics. Reprinted by permission.

Pages 270–71 "Job Loss from Wage Hike" from *Nation's Business*, September 1987. Copyright © 1987 by

U.S. Chamber of Commerce. Reprinted by permission.

Pages 271–72, 276–77 "States Know Best What Labor's Worth" by Kathy Ann Ormiston in *The Wall Street Journal*, May 10, 1988. Copyright © 1988 by Dow Jones & Company, Inc. Reprinted with permission of The Wall Street Journal. All rights reserved.

PHOTOS

Cover: Nancy Campbell, *Cremorne Lights*, 1980. Mount Holyoke College Art Museum, South Hadley, Massachusetts.

Page xvi © Gail Russell
Page 76 © Jerry Jacka
Page 206 © Jerry Jacka
Page 258 © Gail Russell
Page 310 © Gail Russell

Index